Fodor's 3rd Edition

Prague and Budapest

The Guide for All Budgets

Completely Updated

Where to Stay, Eat, and Explore

On and Off the Beaten Path

When to Go, What to Pack

Maps, Travel Tips, and Web Sites

Excerpted from *Fodor's Eastern and Central Europe*

Fodor's Travel Publications • New York, Toronto, London, Sydney, Auckland
www.fodors.com

II

Fodor's Prague and Budapest

EDITOR: Douglas Stallings

Editorial Contributors: Satu Hummasti, Raymond Johnston, Tomáš Kleisner, Scott Alexander Young
Editorial Production: Ira-Neil Dittersdorf
Maps: David Lindroth, *cartographer*; Rebecca Baer and Robert Blake, *map editors*
Design: Fabrizio La Rocca, *creative director*; Guido Caroti, *art director*; Jolie Novak, *senior picture editor*; Melanie Marin, *photo editor*
Cover Design: Pentagram
Production/Manufacturing: Colleen Ziemba
Cover Photo: Sylvain Grandadam/Stone/Getty Images

Copyright

Third Edition

ISBN 1–4000–1117–5

ISSN 1530–5384

Important Tip

Although all prices, opening times, and other details in this book are based on information supplied to us at press time, changes occur all the time in the travel world, and Fodor's cannot accept responsibility for facts that become outdated or for inadvertent errors or omissions. So **always confirm information when it matters,** especially if you're making a detour to visit a specific place.

Special Sales

This book is available for special discounts for bulk purchases for sales promotions or premiums. Special editions, including personalized covers, excerpts of existing books, and corporate imprints, can be created in large quantities for special needs. For more information, write to Special Markets/Premium Sales, 1745 Broadway, MD 6–2, New York, NY, 10019 or e-mail specialmarkets@randomhouse.com.

PRINTED IN THE UNITED STATES OF AMERICA

10 9 8 7 6 5 4 3 2

CONTENTS

ON THE ROAD WITH FODOR'S

A trip takes you out of yourself. Concerns of life at home completely disappear, driven away by more immediate thoughts—about, say, what marvels will beguile the next day, or where you'll have dinner. That's where Fodor's comes in. We make sure that you know all your options, so that you don't miss something that's around the next bend just because you didn't know it was there. Mindful that the best memories of your trip might have nothing to do with what you came to Prague and Budapest to see, we guide you to sights large and small all over the region. You might set out to see Prague Castle but back at home you find yourself unable to forget the sunset over Lake Balaton or that beautiful church in the Tabán district of Budapest. With Fodor's at your side, serendipitous discoveries are never far away.

Born and raised in New York City, **Raymond Johnston**, our updater for the Czech Republic, worked for online publications in the early days of the Internet before moving to Prague in 1996. After a stint teaching English, he returned to journalism and has written about Czech culture, film production, and travel for numerous publications including *The Prague Post,* where he is the editor of the entertainment section. His hobby of visiting castles and ruins has taken him all over Central Europe.

Tomáš Kleisner was born in Prague when it was still under Communist control. He studied art history at Charles University and now works in the National Museum in Prague. He has contributed to other travel guides on his native city and updated Smart Travel Tips for this book.

Hungary updater **Scott Alexander Young** is now back in the U.K. after quite a few years all over Central and Eastern Europe, where he lived in Budapest and Kraków. Though originally he took the attitude that writing assignments in Central and Eastern Europe would lead to "better things," he is in the process of reinventing his life in the West.

You can rest assured that you're in good hands—and that no property mentioned in the book has paid to be included. Each has been selected strictly on its merits, as the best of its type in its price range.

How to Use This Book

Up front is **Smart Travel Tips A to Z,** arranged alphabetically by topic and loaded with tips, Web sites, and contact information. **Destination: Prague and Budapest** helps get you in the mood for your trip. Both city chapters begin with exploring information, with a section for each neighborhood (each recommending a good tour and listing sights alphabetically). All regional sections are divided geographically; within each area, towns are covered in logical geographical order, and attractive stretches of road between them are indicated by the designation **En Route.** To help you decide what you'll have time to visit, both chapters begin with our writers' favorite itineraries. (Mix itineraries from the two chapters, and you can put together a really exceptional trip.) The **A to Z** sections that end the Prague and Budapest chapters list additional resources. At the end of the book you'll find some suggestions for **Further Reading,** followed by **Vocabularies** for all the languages spoken in the region.

Icons and Symbols

★   Our special recommendations
✕   Restaurant
🏠   Lodging establishment
✕🏠   Lodging establishment whose restaurant warrants a special trip
⚠   Campgrounds
🦆   Good for kids (rubber duck)
☞   Sends you to another section of the guide for more information
✉   Address
☎   Telephone number
🕑   Opening and closing times
💷   Admission prices (those we give apply to adults; substantially reduced fees are almost always available for children, students, and senior citizens)

Numbers in white and black circles ③ ❸ that appear on the maps, in the margins, and within the tours correspond to one another.

For hotels, you can assume that all rooms have private baths, phones, TVs, and air-conditioning unless otherwise noted and that all hotels operate on the European Plan (with no meals) if we don't specify another meal plan. We always list a property's facilities but not whether you'll be charged extra to use them, so when pricing accommodations, do ask what's included. For restaurants, it's always a good idea to book ahead; we mention reservations only when they're essential or are not accepted. All restaurants we list are open daily for lunch and dinner unless stated otherwise; dress is mentioned only when men are required to wear a jacket or a jacket and tie. Look for an overview of local dining-out habits in **Smart Travel Tips A to Z** and in the **Pleasures and Pastimes** section that follows each chapter introduction.

Don't Forget to Write

Your experiences—positive and negative—matter to us. If we have missed or misstated something, we want to hear about it. We follow up on all suggestions. Contact the Prague and Budapest editor at editors@fodors.com or c/o Fodor's at 1745 Broadway, New York, NY 10019. And have a fabulous trip!

Karen Cure

Karen Cure
Editorial Director

Eastern and Central Europe

Czech Republic (Česká Republika)

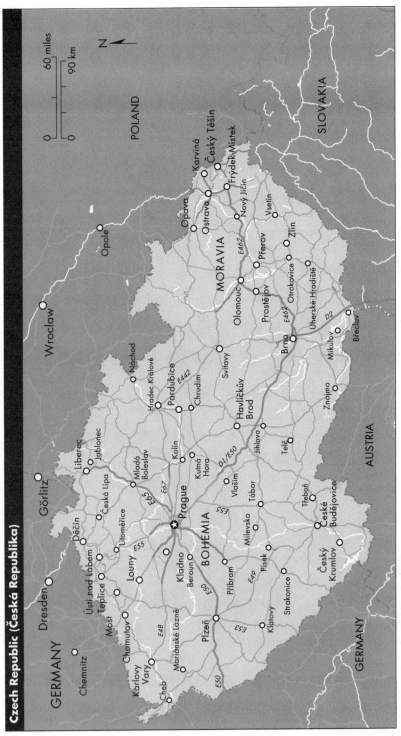

IX

Hungary (Magyarország)

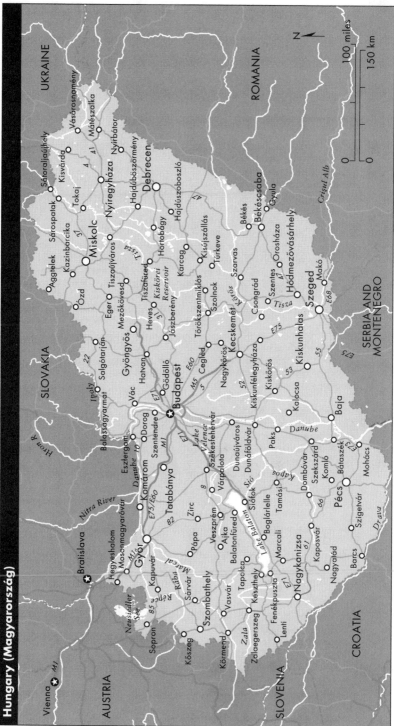

ESSENTIAL INFORMATION

AIR TRAVEL

BOOKING

When you book **look for nonstop flights** and **remember that "direct" flights stop at least once.** Try to avoid connecting flights, which require a change of plane. Two airlines may operate a connecting flight jointly, so ask if your airline operates every segment of the trip; you may find that the carrier you prefer flies you only part of the way. To find more booking tips and to check prices and make on-line flight reservations, log on to www.fodors.com.

CARRIERS

Many U.S. airlines have a European co-carrier that provides connecting service to Eastern and Central Europe from a gateway in Europe. The major European airlines listed here offer service from North America. Both Czech Airlines and Malév offer nonstop service from the U.S. to Prague and Budapest, respectively. It's also possible to connect in Europe for the short hop over to one or the other city.

➤ MAJOR U.S. AND EUROPEAN AIRLINES: **Air France** (☎ 800/237–2747 in the U.S.; 0845/084–5111 in the U.K.; WEB www.airfrance.com). **Alitalia** (☎ 800/223–5730 in the U.S.; 0870/544–8259 in the U.K.; WEB www.alitaliausa. com in the U.S.; www.alitalia.co.uk in the U.K.). **American** (☎ 800/433–7300 in the U.S.; 0845/778–9789 in the U.K.; WEB www.aa.com). **Austrian Airlines** (☎ 800/843–0002 in the U.S.; 0845/601–0948 in the U.K.; WEB www. austrianair.com in the U.S.; www. austrianairlines.co.uk in the U.K.). **British Airways** (☎ 800/247–9297 in the U.S.; 0845/733–3777 in the U.K.; WEB www.britishairways.com). **Continental** (☎ 800/231–0856 in the U.S.; 0800/776–464 in the U.K.; WEB www. continental.com). **Delta** (☎ 800/241–4141 in the U.S.; 0800/414–767 in the U.K.; WEB www.delta.com). **Finnair** (☎ 800/950–5000 in the U.S.; 0870/241–4411 in the U.K.; WEB www.finnair. com). **KLM Royal Dutch Airlines** (☎ 800/225–2525 in the U.S.; 0870/507–4074 in the U.K.; WEB www.klm. com). **Lufthansa** (☎ 800/645–3880 in the U.S.; 0845/773–7747 in the U.K.; WEB www.lufthansa.com). **Northwest** (☎ 800/447–4747 in the U.S.; 0870/507–4074 in the U.K.; WEB www.nwa. com). **SAS Scandinavian Airlines** (☎ 800/221–2350 in the U.S.; 0845/6072–7727 in the U.K.; WEB www. scandinavian.net). **Swiss International Airlines** (☎ 877/359–7947 in the U.S.; 0845/601–0956 in the U.K.; WEB www. swiss.com). **United** (☎ 800/538–2929 in the U.S.; 0845/844–4777 in the U.K.; WEB www.ual.com).

➤ NATIONAL AIRLINES WITH SERVICE FROM BOTH THE U.S. AND EUROPE: Czech Republic: **Czech Airlines** (CSA; ☎ 212/765–6022 in the U.S.; 020/7255–1898 in the U.K.; WEB www.csa. cz). Hungary: **Malév Hungarian Airlines** (☎ 212/757–6480 or 800/223–6884 in the U.S.; 020/7439–0577 in the U.K.; WEB www.malev.hu).

CHECK-IN AND BOARDING

Always **ask your carrier about its check-in policy.** Plan to arrive at the airport about 2 hours before your scheduled departure time for domestic flights and 2½ to 3 hours before international flights.

Assuming that not everyone with a ticket will show up, airlines routinely overbook planes. When everyone does, airlines ask for volunteers to give up their seats. In return, these volunteers usually get a certificate for a free flight and are rebooked on the next flight out. If there are not enough volunteers, the airline must choose who will be denied boarding. The first to get bumped are passengers who checked in late and those flying on discounted tickets, so **get to the gate and check in as early as possible,** especially during peak periods.

Always **bring a government-issued photo ID to the airport;** even when it's not required, a passport is best.

CUTTING COSTS

The least expensive airfares to Eastern and Central Europe are priced for round-trip travel and must usually be purchased in advance. Airlines generally allow you to change your return date for a fee; most low-fare tickets, however, are nonrefundable. It's smart to **call a number of airlines and check the Internet;** when you are quoted a good price, **book it on the spot**—the same fare may not be available the next day. Always **check different routings** and look into using alternate airports. Also, price off-peak flights, which may be significantly less expensive than others. Travel agents, especially low-fare specialists (☞ Discounts and Deals), are helpful.

Consolidators are another good source. They buy tickets for scheduled international flights at reduced rates from the airlines, then sell them at prices that beat the best fare available directly from the airlines. Sometimes you can even get your money back if you need to return the ticket. Carefully read the fine print detailing penalties for changes and cancellations, purchase the ticket with a credit card, and **confirm your consolidator reservation with the airline.**

➤ CONSOLIDATORS: **Cheap Tickets** (☎ 800/377–1000 or 888/922–8849, WEB www.cheaptickets.com). **Discount Airline Ticket Service** (☎ 800/576–1600). **Unitravel** (☎ 800/325–2222, WEB www.unitravel.com). **Up & Away Travel** (☎ 212/889–2345, WEB www.upandaway.com). **World Travel Network** (☎ 800/409–6753).

ENJOYING THE FLIGHT

State your seat preference when purchasing your ticket, and then repeat it when you confirm and when you check in. For more legroom, you can request one of the few emergency-aisle seats at check-in, if you are capable of lifting at least 50 pounds—a Federal Aviation Administration requirement of passengers in these seats. Seats behind a bulkhead also offer more legroom, but they don't have under-seat storage. Don't sit in the row in front of the emergency aisle or in front of a bulkhead, where seats may not recline.

Ask the airline whether a snack or meal is served on the flight. If you have dietary concerns, **request special meals when booking.** These can be vegetarian, low-cholesterol, or kosher, for example. It's a good idea to pack some healthy snacks and a small (plastic) bottle of water in your carry-on bag. On long flights, try to maintain a normal routine, to help fight jet lag. At night, **get some sleep.** By day, **eat light meals, drink water** (not alcohol), and **move around the cabin** to stretch your legs. For additional jet-lag tips consult *Fodor's FYI: Travel Fit & Healthy* (available at bookstores everywhere).

Smoking policies vary from carrier to carrier. Many airlines prohibit smoking on all of their international flights; others allow smoking only on certain routes or certain departures. Ask your carrier about its policy.

FLYING TIMES

Travel time to Central Europe can vary greatly depending on whether or not you can get a nonstop flight. A nonstop flight from NYC to Prague takes 8 hours; a nonstop from NYC to Budapest is 9 hours. Most trips from the U.S. require a change at Frankfurt, London, Paris, Prague, Zurich, Amsterdam, or Vienna and can take up to 15 hours. Direct flights from London to Prague or Budapest take between 2 and 3½ hours. From Sydney you will have to fly first of all to London or Amsterdam (23 hours).

HOW TO COMPLAIN

If your baggage goes astray or your flight goes awry, complain right away. Most carriers require that you **file a claim immediately.** The Aviation Consumer Protection Division of the Department of Transportation publishes *Fly-Rights,* which discusses airlines and consumer issues and is available on-line. At PassengerRights. com, a Web site, you can compose a letter of complaint and distribute it electronically.

➤ AIRLINE COMPLAINTS: **Aviation Consumer Protection Division** (✉ U.S. Department of Transportation, Room 4107, C-75, Washington,

DC 20590, ☎ 202/366–2220, WEB www.dot.gov/airconsumer). **Federal Aviation Administration Consumer Hotline** (☎ 800/322–7873).

RECONFIRMING

Check the status of your flight before you leave for the airport. You can do this on your carrier's Web site, by linking to a flight-status checker (many Web booking services offer these), or by calling your carrier or travel agent. Always confirm international flights at least 72 hours ahead of the scheduled departure time.

AIRPORTS

For more in-depth airport information, and for the best way to get between the airport and your destination, see Airports in the A to Z section for the city you are flying into.

➤ CZECH REPUBLIC: Prague's **Ruzyně Airport** (☎ 02/2011–1111). **Brno Airport** (☎ 05/455–21111). **Karlovy Vary Airport** (☎ 017/333–1102).

➤ HUNGARY: Budapest's **Ferihegy Repülőtér** (☎ 1/296–9696 same-day flight information; 1/296–8000 arrivals; 1/296–7000 departures; 1/296–8108 lost and found).

BIKE TRAVEL

The prevalence of bicycles varies greatly from country to country within Eastern and Central Europe. For example, bike touring and mountain biking are gaining popularity in the Czech Republic. Both Prague and Budapest have some sort of bike rental available, and in less populated areas it's sometimes possible to arrange rentals through informal sources; your hotel is often a good resource for finding rentals. For more information, see Pleasures and Pastimes and Outdoor Activities and Sports in individual chapters.

BIKES IN FLIGHT

Most airlines accommodate bikes as luggage, provided they are dismantled and boxed; check with individual airlines about packing requirements. Airlines sell bike boxes, often free at bike shops, for about $15 (bike bags start at $100). International travelers often can substitute a bike for a piece of checked luggage at no charge; otherwise, the cost is about $100.

BOAT AND FERRY TRAVEL

Ferries offer a pleasant and cheap mode of transportation to Eastern and Central Europe, although you have to be fairly close to your destination already to hop a Europe-bound ferry or hydrofoil. Flying into the appropriate hub, however, is an option. A hydrofoil shuttles visitors from Vienna to Budapest. Ferries also operate on Lake Balaton in Hungary. For further country-specific information, see Boat and Ferry Travel in the A to Z section for Budapest.

➤ FERRY LINES: Hungary: **MAHART Tours** (✉ District V, Belgrád rakpart, Budapest, ☎ 1/484–4025; 1/484–4010 information).

BUS TRAVEL

In some countries, especially where trains are largely local (and stop seemingly every 100 ft), buses are actually speedier than rail travel. Comfort and fares vary drastically by nation. See Bus Travel in the A to Z section at the end of the Prague and Budapest chapters.

Unless you latch on to a real deal on airfare, a bus ticket from London's Victoria Terminal on Eurolines is probably the cheapest transit from the United Kingdom to Eastern and Central Europe, with regularly scheduled service to both Budapest and Prague.

FROM THE U.K.

Eurolines (☎ 01582/404–511 in the U.K., WEB www.eurolines.com).

CAMERAS AND PHOTOGRAPHY

In general, people are pleased to be photographed, but ask first. Never photograph Gypsies, however colorful their attire, without explicit permission and payment clearly agreed upon. Photographing anything military, assuming you'd want to, is usually prohibited. The *Kodak Guide to Shooting Great Travel Pictures* (available at bookstores everywhere) is loaded with tips.

➤ PHOTO HELP: **Kodak Information Center** (☎ 800/242–2424, WEB www.kodak.com).

EQUIPMENT PRECAUTIONS

Don't pack film and equipment in checked luggage, where it is much more susceptible to damage. X-ray machines used to view checked luggage are becoming much more powerful and therefore are much more likely to ruin your film. Try to **ask for hand inspection of film,** which becomes clouded after repeated exposure to airport X-ray machines, and **keep videotapes and computer disks away from metal detectors.** Always **keep film, tape, and computer disks out of the sun.** Carry an extra supply of batteries, and **be prepared to turn on your camera, camcorder, or laptop** to prove to airport security personnel that the device is real.

FILM AND DEVELOPING

Major brands of film are available in both Prague and Budapest, and 24-hour developing is the rule rather than the exception in large and medium-size cities. The variable is cost—prices fluctuate widely from place to place.

VIDEOS

Due to differing television systems, VHS tapes bought in Central and Eastern Europe (which use the SECAM standard) are not compatible with U.S. machines (which use the NTSC standard).

CAR RENTAL

Major rental agencies are represented throughout the region, but **don't overlook local firms;** they can offer bargains, but watch for hidden insurance conditions. It can sometimes be impossible to get an automatic transmission in the region. Rates and regulations vary widely from country to country. For more information, *see* the A to Z sections *in* the Prague and Budapest chapters.

➤ MAJOR AGENCIES: **Alamo** (☎ 800/522–9696; WEB www.alamo.com). **Avis** (☎ 800/331–1084; 800/879–2847 in Canada; 0870/606–0100 in the U.K.; 02/9353–9000 in Australia; 09/526–2847 in New Zealand; WEB www.avis.com). **Budget** (☎ 800/527–0700; 0870/156–5656 in the U.K.; WEB www.budget.com). **Dollar** (☎ 800/800–6000; 0124/622–0111 in the U.K., where it's affiliated with Sixt; 02/9223–1444 in Australia; WEB www.dollar.com). **Hertz** (☎ 800/654–3001; 800/263–0600 in Canada; 020/8897–2072 in the U.K.; 02/9669–2444 in Australia; 09/256–8690 in New Zealand; WEB www.hertz.com). **National Car Rental** (☎ 800/227–7368; 020/8680–4800 in the U.K.; WEB www.nationalcar.com).

CUTTING COSTS

For a good deal, **book through a travel agent who will shop around.** Do **look into wholesalers,** companies that do not own fleets but rent in bulk from those that do and often offer better rates than traditional car-rental operations. Prices are best during off-peak periods. Rentals booked through wholesalers often must be paid for before you leave home.

➤ WHOLESALERS: **Auto Europe** (☎ 888/223–5555, FAX 207/842–2222, WEB www.autoeurope.com). **Destination Europe Resources** (DER; ✉ 9501 W. Devon Ave., Rosemont, IL 60018, ☎ 800/782–2424, WEB www.der.com). **Europe by Car** (☎ 212/581–3040 or 800/223–1516, FAX 212/246–1458, WEB www.europebycar.com). **Kemwel** (☎ 800/678–0678 or 800/576–1590, FAX 207/842–2124, WEB www.kemwel.com).

INSURANCE

When driving a rented car you are generally responsible for any damage to or loss of the vehicle. Collision policies that car-rental companies sell for European rentals typically do not cover stolen vehicles. Before you rent—and purchase collision or theft coverage—see what coverage you already have under the terms of your personal auto-insurance policy and credit cards. Collision-damage waivers must be purchased in all countries in Central and Eastern Europe, so car rentals are liable to be more expensive than in the West. It is advised to check that any advertised prices apply to visitors and not only locals. Most countries require that you will have held your driver's license for at least a year before you can rent a car.

REQUIREMENTS AND RESTRICTIONS

In most Eastern and Central European countries, visitors need an International Driver's Permit; U.S.

and Canadian citizens can obtain one from the American or Canadian Automobile Association, respectively. In some countries, such as Hungary, many car rental agencies will accept an international license, but the formal permit is technically required. If you intend to drive across a border, ask about **restrictions on driving into other countries.** The minimum age required for renting is usually 21 or older, and some companies also have maximum ages; be sure to inquire when making your arrangements.

SURCHARGES

Before you pick up a car in one city and leave it in another, **ask about drop-off charges or one-way service fees,** which can be substantial. Note, too, that some rental agencies charge extra if you return the car before the time specified in your contract. To avoid a hefty refueling fee, **fill the tank just before you turn in the car,** but be aware that gas stations near the rental outlet may overcharge. It's almost never a deal to buy the tank of gas in the car when you rent it; the understanding is that you'll return it empty, but some fuel usually remains.

CAR TRAVEL

The positive side of driving is an itinerary free from the constraints of bus and train schedules and lots of trunk room for extra baggage. The negatives are many, however, not the least of which are shabbily maintained secondary roads, the risk of theft and vandalism, and difficulty finding gas. Crowded roads and fast and/or careless drivers add to the danger element. However, car travel does make it much easier to get to out-of-the-way monasteries and other sights not easily accessible by public transportation. Good road maps are usually available.

A word of caution: if you have drunk any alcohol whatsoever, do not drive. Penalties are substantial, and the blood-alcohol limit is practically zero. (In the Czech Republic and Hungary, it *is* zero.)

AUTO CLUBS

➤ IN EASTERN AND CENTRAL EUROPE: Czech Republic: **Autoturist** (✉ 4, Na Strži 9, Prague, ☎ 02/6110–4333, WEB www.autoturist.cz). Hungary:

Hungarian Automobile Club (✉ District II, Rómer Flóris u. 4/A, Budapest, ☎ 1/345–1800, WEB www. autoklub.hu).

EMERGENCY SERVICES

In case of a breakdown, your best friend is the telephone. Try contacting your **rental agency** or the appropriate national breakdown service.

➤ CONTACTS: Czech Republic: **ABA** (☎ 124; 0124 in rural areas). Hungary: **Hungarian Automobile Club** (☎ 1/345–1755).

GASOLINE

Gas stations are easy to come by on major thoroughfares and near large cities. Many are open around the clock, particularly in the Czech Republic and Hungary. At least two grades of gasoline are sold in Eastern and Central European countries, usually 90–93 octane (regular) and 94–98 octane (super). Lead-free gasoline is now available in most gas stations.

ROAD CONDITIONS

Eastern and Central Europe's main roads are built to a fairly high standard. There are now quite substantial stretches of highway on main routes, and a lot of rebuilding is being done.

ROAD MAPS

In the Czech Republic, the ubiquitous 24-hour gas stations often sell road maps, or try a bookstore, such as Jan Kanzelsberger bookshop, which has a good selection of hiking maps and auto atlases.

In Hungary, good maps are sold at most large gas stations. In Budapest, the Globe Térképbolt has an excellent supply of domestic and foreign maps.

➤ CONTACTS: **Globe Térképbolt** (Globe Map Store; ✉ District VI, Bajcsy-Zsilinszky út 37, Budapest, Hungary, ☎ 1/312–6001). **Jan Kanzelsberger bookshop** (✉ Václavské nám. 42, Prague, Czech Republic, ☎ 02/2421–7335).

RULES OF THE ROAD

Throughout Eastern and Central Europe, driving is on the right and the same basic rules of the road practiced in the United States and the rest of Europe apply. For further information *see* Car Travel *in* the A to Z section at the end of the Prague and Budapest chapters.

CHILDREN IN EASTERN AND CENTRAL EUROPE

Be sure to plan ahead and **involve your youngsters** as you outline your trip. When packing, include things to keep them busy en route. On sightseeing days try to schedule activities of special interest to your children. If you are renting a car, don't forget to **arrange for a car seat** when you reserve. For general advice about traveling with children, consult *Fodor's FYI: Travel with Your Baby* (available in bookstores everywhere).

FLYING

If your children are two or older, **ask about children's airfares.** As a general rule, infants under two not occupying a seat fly at greatly reduced fares or even for free. When booking, **confirm carry-on allowances** if you're traveling with infants. In general, for babies charged 10% of the adult fare you are allowed one carry-on bag and a collapsible stroller; if the flight is full, the stroller may have to be checked or you may be limited to less.

Experts agree that it's a good idea to use safety seats aloft for children weighing less than 40 pounds. Airlines set their own policies: U.S. carriers usually require that the child be ticketed, even if he or she is young enough to ride free, since the seats must be strapped into regular seats. Do **check your airline's policy about using safety seats during takeoff and landing.** Safety seats are not allowed everywhere on the plane, so get your seat assignments as early as possible.

When reserving, **request children's meals or a freestanding bassinet** (not available at all airlines) if you need them. But note that bulkhead seats, where you must sit to use the bassinet, may lack an overhead bin or storage space on the floor.

LODGING

Most hotels in Eastern and Central Europe allow children under a certain age to stay in their parents' room at no extra charge, but others charge for them as extra adults; be sure to **find out the cutoff age for children's discounts.** Some spa hotels don't allow children under 12.

The Accor group, which owns the Novotel, Mercure, Ibis, and Sofitel chains, has hotels in both Prague and Budapest and allows up to two children under 12 to stay free in their parents' room. The Budapest Hilton has an unusual policy allowing children of any age—even middle-aged adults—to stay for free in their parents' room.

Young visitors to the Czech Republic will enjoy staying at one of Prague's picturesque floating "botels." For further information contact the Czech Tourist Authority. Prague's luxurious Palace and Savoy hotels, managed by Vienna International, allow children under 12 to stay free in their parents' room.

➤ BEST CHOICES: **Accor Hotels** (WEB www.accorhotels.com). **Budapest Hilton** (☎ 1/488–6600 in Budapest, WEB www.hilton.com).

SIGHTS AND ATTRACTIONS

Places that are especially appealing to children are indicated by a rubber duckie icon (🦆) in the margins throughout the book.

COMPUTERS ON THE ROAD

Bring an adapter for your laptop plug. Adapters are inexpensive, and some models have several plugs suitable for different systems throughout the world. Some hotels lend adapters to guests for use during their stay.

At the airport, **be prepared to turn on your laptop** to prove to security personnel that the device is real. Security X-ray machines can be damaging to a laptop, and **keep computer disks away from metal detectors.**

CONSUMER PROTECTION

Whenever buying travel services for a trip to Eastern and Central Europe, **pay with a major credit card** when you can, so you can cancel payment or get reimbursed if there's a problem. But be aware that credit cards are not as widely accepted in the region as they are in Western Europe and the United States—many hotels and restaurants operate on a cash-only basis. If you're doing business with a travel-services company for the first time, **contact your local Better Business Bureau and the attorney general's offices** in your own state and the company's home state, as well. Have any complaints been filed? Finally, if you're buying a package or tour, always **consider travel insurance** that includes default coverage (☞ Insurance).

➤ BBBs: **Council of Better Business Bureaus** (✉ 4200 Wilson Blvd., Suite 800, Arlington, VA 22203, ☎ 703/276–0100, ℻ 703/525–8277, 🕸 www.bbb.org).

CUSTOMS AND DUTIES

When shopping abroad, **keep receipts** for all purchases. Upon reentering the country, **be ready to show customs officials what you've bought.** If you feel a duty is incorrect, appeal the assessment. If you object to the way your clearance was handled, note the inspector's badge number. In either case, first ask to see a supervisor. If the problem isn't resolved, write to the appropriate authorities, beginning with the port director at your point of entry.

IN AUSTRALIA

Australian residents who are 18 or older may bring home A$400 worth of souvenirs and gifts (including jewelry), 250 cigarettes or 250 grams of tobacco, and 1,125 ml of alcohol (including wine, beer, and spirits). Residents under 18 may bring back A$200 worth of goods. Prohibited items include meat products. Seeds, plants, and fruits need to be declared upon arrival.

➤ INFORMATION: **Australian Customs Service** (Regional Director, ✉ Box 8, Sydney, NSW 2001; ☎ 02/9213–2000 or 1300/363263; 1800/020504 quarantine-inquiry line; ℻ 02/9213–4043; 🕸 www.customs.gov.au).

IN CANADA

Canadian residents who have been out of Canada for at least seven days may bring in C$750 worth of goods duty-free. If you've been away fewer than seven days but more than 48 hours, the duty-free allowance drops to C$200. If your trip lasts 24 to 48 hours, the allowance is C$50. You may not pool allowances with family members. Goods claimed under the C$750 exemption may follow you by mail; those claimed under the lesser exemptions must accompany you. Alcohol and tobacco products may be included in the seven-day and 48-hour exemptions but not in the 24-hour exemption. If you meet the age requirements of the province or territory through which you reenter Canada, you may bring in, duty-free, 1.5 liters of wine *or* 1.14 liters (40 imperial ounces) of liquor *or* 24 12-ounce cans or bottles of beer or ale. If you are 19 or older you may bring in, duty-free, 200 cigarettes and 50 cigars. Check ahead of time with the Canada Customs and Revenue Agency or the Department of Agriculture for policies regarding meat products, seeds, plants, and fruits.

You may send an unlimited number of gifts (only one gift per recipient, however) worth up to C$60 each duty-free to Canada. Label the package UNSOLICITED GIFT—VALUE UNDER $60. Alcohol and tobacco are excluded.

➤ INFORMATION: **Canada Customs and Revenue Agency** (✉ 2265 St. Laurent Blvd. S, Ottawa, Ontario K1G 4K3, ☎ 204/983–3500, 506/636–5064, 800/461–9999, 🕸 www.ccra-adrc.gc.ca/).

IN EASTERN AND CENTRAL EUROPE

You may import duty-free into Hungary 250 cigarettes or the equivalent in tobacco, 1 liter of spirits, and 2 liters of wine. In addition to the above, you are permitted to import into Hungary gifts valued up to 30,500 Ft. You may import duty-free into the Czech Republic tobacco products equivalent to 200 cigarettes, 100 cigarillos, 250 grams of tobacco, or 50 cigars; 1 liter of spirits, 2 liters of wine, and personal medicines, as well as gifts and personal items valued at up to 6,000 Kč (3,000 Kč for visitors under 15) (about $170/$85).

If you are bringing into either of these countries any valuables or foreign-made equipment from home, such as cameras, it's wise to carry the original receipts with you or register the items with U.S. Customs before you leave (Form 4457). Otherwise you could end up paying duty upon your return. When traveling to Bulgaria, you should declare video cameras, personal computers, and expensive jewelry upon arrival. Be aware that leaving the country without expensive items declared upon entering can present a huge hassle with airport police.

IN NEW ZEALAND

All homeward-bound residents may bring back NZ$700 worth of souvenirs and gifts; passengers may not pool their allowances, and children can claim only the concession on goods intended for their own use. For those 17 or older, the duty-free allowance also includes 4.5 liters of wine or beer; one 1,125-ml bottle of spirits; and either 200 cigarettes, 250 grams of tobacco, 50 cigars, *or* a combination of the three up to 250 grams. Meat products, seeds, plants, and fruits must be declared upon arrival to the Agricultural Services Department.

➤ INFORMATION: **New Zealand Customs** (Head office: ✉ The Customhouse, 17–21 Whitmore St. [Box 2218, Wellington], ☎ 09/300–5399 or 0800/428–786, 𝗪𝗘𝗕 www.customs. govt.nz).

IN THE U.K.

From countries outside the European Union, including those in Eastern and Central Europe, you may bring home, duty-free, 200 cigarettes or 50 cigars; 1 liter of spirits or 2 liters of fortified or sparkling wine or liqueurs; 2 liters of still table wine; 60 ml of perfume; 250 ml of toilet water; plus £145 worth of other goods, including gifts and souvenirs. Prohibited items include meat products, seeds, plants, and fruits.

➤ INFORMATION: **HM Customs and Excise** (✉ Portcullis House, 21 Cowbridge Rd. E, Cardiff CF11 9SS, ☎ 029/2038–6423 or 0845/010–9000, 𝗪𝗘𝗕 www.hmce.gov.uk).

IN THE U.S.

U.S. residents who have been out of the country for at least 48 hours may bring home, for personal use, $800 worth of foreign goods duty-free, as long as they haven't used the $800 allowance or any part of it in the past 30 days. This exemption may include 1 liter of alcohol (for travelers 21 and older), 200 cigarettes, and 100 non-Cuban cigars. Family members from

the same household who are traveling together may pool their $800 personal exemptions. For fewer than 48 hours, the duty-free allowance drops to $200, which may include 50 cigarettes, 10 non-Cuban cigars, and 150 ml of alcohol (or perfume containing alcohol). The $200 allowance cannot be combined with other individuals' exemptions, and if you exceed it, the full value of all the goods will be taxed. Antiques, which the U.S. Customs Service defines as objects more than 100 years old, enter duty-free, as do original works of art done entirely by hand, including paintings, drawings, and sculptures.

You may also send packages home duty-free, with a limit of one parcel per addressee per day (except alcohol or tobacco products or perfume worth more than $5). You can mail up to $200 worth of goods for personal use; label the package PERSONAL USE and attach a list of its contents and their retail value. If the package contains your used personal belongings, mark it PERSONAL GOODS RETURNED to avoid paying duties. You may send up to $100 worth of goods as a gift; mark the package UNSOLICITED GIFT. Mailed items do not affect your duty-free allowance on your return.

➤ INFORMATION: **U.S. Customs Service** (for inquiries, ✉ 1300 Pennsylvania Ave. NW, Washington, DC 20229, ☎ 202/354–1000, 𝗪𝗘𝗕 www. customs.gov; for complaints, ✉ Customer Satisfaction Unit, 1300 Pennsylvania Ave. NW, Room 5.5A, Washington, DC 20229; for registration of equipment, ✉ Office of Passenger Programs, 1300 Pennsylvania Ave. NW, Room 5.4D, Washington, DC 20229, ☎ 202/927–0530).

DINING

For city-specific dining information, *see* Dining *in* Pleasures and Pastimes at the beginning of the Prague and Budapest chapters. Additional city-specific dining information may also be found at the start of a city's dining listings. The restaurants we list are the cream of the crop in each price category.

MEALTIMES

Unless otherwise noted, the restaurants listed in this guide are open daily for lunch and dinner.

RESERVATIONS AND DRESS

Reservations are always a good idea; we mention them only when they're essential or not accepted. Book as far ahead as you can, and reconfirm as soon as you arrive. (Large parties should always call ahead to check the reservations policy.) We mention dress only when men are required to wear a jacket or a jacket and tie.

DISABILITIES AND ACCESSIBILITY

Provisions for travelers with disabilities in Eastern and Central Europe are extremely limited; probably the best solution is to travel with a companion who can help you. While many hotels, especially large American or international chains, offer some wheelchair-accessible rooms, special facilities at museums and restaurants and on public transportation are difficult to find.

➤ LOCAL RESOURCES: Czech Republic: **Sdružení zdravotné postižených** (Association of Disabled Persons; ✉ Karlínské nám. 12, Prague 8, ☎ 02/2481–5914, WEB www.czechia.com/szdp). Hungary: **Mozgáskorlátozottak Egyesületeinek Országos Szövetsége** (National Association of People with Mobility Impairments, or MEOSZ; ✉ San Marco u. 76, Budapest 1032, ☎ 1/388–5529, WEB www.meoszinfo.hu).

LODGING

Most hotels take few or no measures to accommodate travelers with disabilities. Your best bets are newer hotels and international chains.

RESERVATIONS

When discussing accessibility with an operator or reservations agent, **ask hard questions.** Are there any stairs, inside *or* out? Are there grab bars next to the toilet *and* in the shower/tub? How wide is the doorway to the room? To the bathroom? For the most extensive facilities meeting the latest legal specifications, **opt for newer accommodations.** If you reserve through a toll-free number, consider also calling the hotel's local number to confirm the information from the central reservations office. Get confirmation in writing when you can.

SIGHTS AND ATTRACTIONS

Most tourist attractions in the region pose significant problems. Many are historic structures without ramps or other means to improve accessibility. Streets are often cobblestone, and potholes are common.

TRANSPORTATION

A few Czech trains are equipped with carriages for travelers using wheelchairs. Some stations on the Prague metro have elevators, and there are two lines of accessible buses, but the system is light-years from being barrier-free. Elsewhere in the region, public transportation is difficult, if not impossible, for many travelers with disabilities.

TRAVEL AGENCIES

In the United States, the Americans with Disabilities Act requires that travel firms serve the needs of all travelers. Some agencies specialize in working with people with disabilities.

➤ TRAVELERS WITH MOBILITY PROBLEMS: **Access Adventures** (✉ 206 Chestnut Ridge Rd., Scottsville, NY 14624, ☎ 716/889–9096, dltravel@prodigy.net), run by a former physical-rehabilitation counselor. **Flying Wheels Travel** (✉ 143 W. Bridge St. [Box 382, Owatonna, MN 55060], ☎ 507/451–5005, FAX 507/451–1685, WEB www.flyingwheelstravel.com).

DISCOUNTS AND DEALS

Be a smart shopper and **compare all your options** before making decisions. A plane ticket bought with a promotional coupon from travel clubs, coupon books, and direct-mail offers or purchased on the Internet may not be cheaper than the least expensive fare from a discount ticket agency. And always keep in mind that what you get is just as important as what you save.

In Budapest, the Budapest Card entitles holders to unlimited travel on public transportation; free admission to many museums and sights; and discounts on various services from participating businesses. The cost (at this writing) is 2,800 Ft. for two days, 3,400 Ft. for three days; one card is valid for an adult plus one child under 14. It is available at many tourist offices along with a similar pass called the Hungary Card, which gives discounts to museums, sights, and service in the entire country.

DISCOUNT RESERVATIONS

To save money, **look into discount reservations services** with Web sites and toll-free numbers, which use their buying power to get a better price on hotels, airline tickets, even car rentals. When booking a room, always **call the hotel's local toll-free number** (if one is available) rather than the central reservations number—you'll often get a better price. Always ask about special packages or corporate rates.

When shopping for the best deal on hotels and car rentals, **look for guaranteed exchange rates,** which protect you against a falling dollar. With your rate locked in, you won't pay more, even if the price goes up in the local currency.

➤ AIRLINE TICKETS: ☎ **800/FLY–ASAP.**

➤ HOTEL ROOMS: **Hotel Reservations Network** (☎ 800/964–6835, WEB www.hoteldiscount.com). **International Marketing & Travel Concepts** (☎ 800/790–4682, WEB www .imtc-travel.com). **Steigenberger Reservation Service** (☎ 800/223–5652, WEB www.srs-worldhotels.com). **Travel Interlink** (☎ 800/888–5898, WEB www.travelinterlink.com). **Turbotrip.com** (☎ 800/473–7829, WEB www.turbotrip.com).

PACKAGE DEALS

Don't confuse packages and guided tours. When you buy a package, you travel on your own, just as though you had planned the trip yourself. Fly-drive packages, which combine airfare and car rental, are often a good deal. If you **buy a rail-drive pass,** you may save on train tickets and car rentals. All Eurail- and Europass holders get a discount on Eurostar fares through the Channel Tunnel.

ELECTRICITY

To use electric-powered equipment purchased in the U.S. or Canada, **bring a converter and adapter.** The electrical current in Eastern and Central Europe is 220 volts, 50 cycles alternating current (AC); wall outlets generally take plugs with two round prongs.

If your appliances are dual-voltage, you'll need only an adapter. Don't use 110-volt outlets marked FOR SHAVERS ONLY for high-wattage appliances such as blow-dryers. Most laptops operate equally well on 110 and 220 volts and so require only an adapter.

ENGLISH-LANGUAGE MEDIA

Prague in particular is remarkably rich in English-language publishing of all kinds, from general-interest newspapers to poetry chapbooks, reflecting the city's large, relatively stable community of English-speaking expatriates. *In Your Pocket* guides are available in many cities in Eastern and Central Europe.

In the broadcast media, BBC World Service and CNN are widely available.

GAY AND LESBIAN TRAVEL

Throughout Eastern and Central Europe, gay and lesbian resources are generally thin on the ground, if not underground. While the level of tolerance varies, the region is generally conservative; strongly Catholic countries are the least accepting.

The Czech Republic is one of the most liberal countries in the region, and Prague in particular fosters a growing gay and lesbian scene. You could try visiting one of the gathering places, such as Gejzeer Club.

Hungary is relatively open-minded, though even in Budapest, the gay population keeps a fairly low profile. Some of Budapest's thermal baths are popular meeting places, as are the city's several gay bars and clubs, which you can find listed in English-language newspapers and the monthly magazine *Mások,* which is available only in Hungarian.

➤ RESOURCES AND ORGANIZATIONS: **Czech Republic** (WEB www.gayguide. net/europe/czech/prague). **Hungary** (WEB www.gayguide. net/europe/hungary/budapest).

➤ GAY- AND LESBIAN-FRIENDLY TRAVEL AGENCIES: **Different Roads Travel** (✉ 8383 Wilshire Blvd., Suite 902, Beverly Hills, CA 90211, ☎ 323/651–5557 or 800/429–8747, FAX 323/651–3678, lgernert@tzell.com). **Kennedy Travel** (✉ 314 Jericho Turnpike, Floral Park, NY 11001, ☎ 516/352–

4888 or 800/237–7433, FAX 516/354–8849, WEB www.kennedytravel.com).
Now, Voyager (✉ 4406 18th St., San Francisco, CA 94114, ☎ 415/626–1169 or 800/255–6951, FAX 415/626–8626, WEB www.nowvoyager.com).
Skylink Travel and Tour (✉ 1006 Mendocino Ave., Santa Rosa, CA 95401, ☎ 707/546–9888 or 800/225–5759, FAX 707/546–9891, WEB www.skylinktravel.com), serving lesbian travelers.

HEALTH

You may gain weight, but there are few other serious health hazards for the traveler in Eastern and Central Europe. Tap water may taste bad but is generally drinkable (though see the precautions below); when it runs rusty out of the tap or the aroma of chlorine is overpowering, it might help to have some iodine tablets or bottled water handy. Buy bottled water, particularly if staying in an older home or a hotel.

No vaccinations are required for entry into either the Czech Republic or Hungary, but selective vaccinations are recommended. Those traveling in forested areas of most Eastern and Central European countries should consider vaccinating themselves against Central European, or tick-borne, encephalitis. Tick-borne Lyme disease is also a risk in the Czech Republic. Schedule vaccinations well in advance of departure because some require several doses, and others may cause uncomfortable side effects.

To avoid problems clearing customs, diabetic travelers carrying needles and syringes should have on hand a letter from their physician confirming their need for insulin injections.

OVER-THE-COUNTER REMEDIES

Pharmacies in both Prague and Budapest carry a variety of nonprescription as well as prescription drugs. For recommended pharmacies, *see* the A to Z sections *in* each chapter.

INSURANCE

The most useful travel-insurance plan is a comprehensive policy that includes coverage for trip cancellation and interruption, default, trip delay, and medical expenses (with a waiver for preexisting conditions).

Without insurance you will lose all or most of your money if you cancel your trip, regardless of the reason. Default insurance covers you if your tour operator, airline, or cruise line goes out of business. Trip-delay covers expenses that arise because of bad weather or mechanical delays. Study the fine print when comparing policies.

If you're traveling internationally, a key component of travel insurance is coverage for medical bills incurred if you get sick on the road. Such expenses are not generally covered by Medicare or private policies. U.K. residents can buy a travel-insurance policy valid for most vacations taken during the year in which it's purchased (but check preexisting-condition coverage).British and Australian citizens need extra medical coverage when traveling overseas.

Always **buy travel policies directly from the insurance company**; if you buy them from a cruise line, airline, or tour operator that goes out of business you probably will not be covered for the agency or operator's default, a major risk. Before making any purchase, **review your existing health and home-owner's policies** to find what they cover away from home.

➤ TRAVEL INSURERS: In the U.S.:
Access America (✉ 6600 W. Broad St., Richmond, VA 23230, ☎ 800/284–8300, FAX 804/673–1491 or 800/346–9265, WEB www.accessamerica.com). **Travel Guard International** (✉ 1145 Clark St., Stevens Point, WI 54481, ☎ 715/345–0505 or 800/826–1300, FAX 800/955–8785, WEB www.travelguard.com).

➤ INSURANCE INFORMATION: In the U.K.: **Association of British Insurers** (✉ 51 Gresham St., London EC2V 7HQ, ☎ 020/7600–3333, FAX 020/7696–8999, WEB www.abi.org.uk).
In Canada: **RBC Travel Insurance** (✉ 6880 Financial Dr., Mississauga, Ontario L5N 7Y5, ☎ 905/791–8700 or 800/668–4342, FAX 905/813–4704, WEB www.rbcinsurance.com). In Australia: **Insurance Council of Australia** (✉ Level 3, 56 Pitt St., Sydney,

NSW 2000, ☎ 02/9253–5100, FAX 02/9253–5111, WEB www.ica.com.au). In New Zealand: **Insurance Council of New Zealand** (✉ Level 7, 111–115 Customhouse Quay, [Box 474, Wellington], ☎ 04/472–5230, FAX 04/473–3011, WEB www.icnz.org.nz).

LODGING

If your experience of Eastern and Central European hotels is limited to capital cities such as Prague and Budapest, you may be pleasantly surprised. There are baroque mansions turned guest houses and elegant high-rise resorts, not to mention bed-and-breakfast inns presided over by matronly babushkas. Many facilities throughout the region are being upgraded.

Outside major cities, hotels and inns are more rustic than elegant. Standards of service generally do not suffer, but in most rural areas the definition of "luxury" includes little more than a television and a private bathroom. In some instances, you may have no choice but to stay in one of the cement high-rise hotels that scar skylines from Poland to the Czech Republic. Huge, impersonal concrete hotels are part of the Communist legacy, and it may take a few more years to exorcise or "beautify" these ubiquitous monsters.

In rural Eastern and Central Europe, you may have difficulty parting with more than $25–$30 per night for lodgings. Reservations are vital if you plan to visit Prague or Budapest during the summer season. Reservations are a good idea but aren't imperative if you plan to strike out into the countryside.

The lodgings we list are the cream of the crop in each price category. We always list the facilities that are available, but we don't specify whether they cost extra; when pricing accommodations, always ask what's included and what costs extra. Properties are assigned price categories based on the range from their least-expensive standard double room at high season (excluding holidays) to the most expensive. Properties marked ✕⊡ are lodging establishments whose restaurants warrant a special trip.

Assume that hotels operate on the **European Plan** (EP, with no meals) unless we specify that they use the **Breakfast Plan** (BP, with a full breakfast), **Modified American Plan** (MAP, with breakfast and dinner), or the **Full American Plan** (FAP, with all meals).

APARTMENT AND VILLA RENTALS

If you want a home base that's roomy enough for a family and comes with cooking facilities, **consider a furnished rental.** These can save you money, especially if you're traveling with a group. Home-exchange directories sometimes list rentals as well as exchanges.

If you are looking for a private room in Prague, try APT-Rent. Rental apartments are common in Hungary. In Budapest, the best bet is to go through an agency; in the rest of the country, either check with a local tourist information office or, especially in smaller cities, simply walk around until you see a sign outside a house reading APARTMAN.

➤ INTERNATIONAL AGENTS: **Hideaways International** (✉ 767 Islington St., Portsmouth, NH 03801, ☎ 603/430–4433 or 800/843–4433, FAX 603/430–4444, WEB www.hideaways.com; membership $129). **Interhome** (✉ 1990 N.E. 163rd St., Suite 110, North Miami Beach, FL 33162, ☎ 305/940–2299 or 800/882–6864, FAX 305/940–2911, WEB www.interhome.com). **Villas International** (✉ 4340 Redwood Hwy., Suite D309, San Rafael, CA 94903, ☎ 415/499–9490 or 800/221–2260, FAX 415/499–9491, WEB www.villasintl.com).

➤ LOCAL AGENTS: Hungary: In Budapest, **Amadeus Apartments** (✉ District IX, Üllői út 197, H-1091, ☎ 06/309–422–893, WEB www.amadeus.hu). **TRIBUS Welcome Hotel Service** (✉ District V, Apáczai Csere János u. 1, ☎ 1/318–5776, WEB www.tribus.hu); Czech Republic: In Prague, **APT-Rent** (✉ Ostrovni 7, ☎ 02/2499–0900, WEB www.apartments.cz).

HOSTELS

No matter what your age, you can **save on lodging costs by staying at hostels.** In some 4,500 locations in more than 70 countries around the world, Hostelling International (HI), the umbrella group for a number of national youth-hostel associations, offers single-sex, dorm-style beds and, at many hostels, rooms for couples and family accommodations. Membership in any HI national hostel association, open to travelers of all ages, allows you to stay in HI-affiliated hostels at member rates; one-year membership is about $25 for adults (C$35 for a two-year minimum membership in Canada, £13 in the U.K., A$52 in Australia, and NZ$40 in New Zealand); hostels run about $10–$30 per night. Members have priority if the hostel is full; they're also eligible for discounts around the world, even on rail and bus travel in some countries.

In Hungary, most hostels are geared toward the college crowd. Among several good ones in Budapest are the friendly, Internet-equipped Back Pack Guesthouse, where rates range from 1,300 Ft. (8- to 10-bed rooms) to 1,900 Ft. (2-bed rooms), and the Sirály Youth Hostel, situated in the relative peace, quiet, and clean air of an island-park on the Danube, where the per-person rate in 12-bed rooms is 1,400 Ft. For further information, consult the free annual accommodations directory published by Tourinform or the listings in *Budapest in Your Pocket,* available at newsstands, or visit the Web site Backpackers.hu.

All but one or two Czech hostels are located in two towns: Prague and Český Krumlov. They tend to be either backpacker-happy, party-all-night places or affiliated with sports clubs or colleges. Most accommodation services in Prague book hostel rooms. The Prague representative of Hostelling International is KMC Travel Service. A relatively well-run Prague hostel, with six local sites and affiliates in Český Krumlov, Budapest, and Berlin, is Travellers' Hostel.

➤ LOCAL CONTACTS: **Back Pack Guesthouse** (✉ District XI, Takács Menyhért u. 33, Budapest, ☎ 1/385–8946, WEB www.backpackbudapest. hu). **Backpackers.hu** (WEB www. backpackers.hu). **KMC Travel Service** (✉ Karolíny Světlé 30, Prague, ☎ 02/2222–1328). **Sirály Youth Hostel** (✉ District XIII, Margit-sziget [Margaret Island], Budapest, ☎ 1/329–3952). **Travellers' Hostel** (✉ Dlouhá 33, Český Krumlov, ☎ 02/2482–6662, WEB www.travellers.cz).

➤ ORGANIZATIONS: **Hostelling International—American Youth Hostels** (✉ 733 15th St. NW, Suite 840, Washington, DC 20005, ☎ 202/783–6161, FAX 202/783–6171, WEB www. hiayh.org). **Hostelling International—Canada** (✉ 400–205 Catherine St., Ottawa, Ontario K2P 1C3, ☎ 613/237–7884 or 800/663–5777, FAX 613/237–7868, WEB www.hihostels.ca). **Youth Hostel Association of England and Wales** (✉ Trevelyan House, Dimple Rd., Matlock, Derbyshire DE4 3YH, U.K., ☎ 0870/870–8808, FAX 0169/592–702, WEB www.yha.org. uk). **Youth Hostel Association Australia** (✉ 10 Mallett St., Camperdown, NSW 2050, ☎ 02/9565–1699, FAX 02/9565–1325, WEB www.yha.com. au). **Youth Hostels Association of New Zealand** (✉ Level 3, 193 Cashel St. [Box 436, Christchurch], ☎ 03/379–9970, FAX 03/365–4476, WEB www.yha.org.nz).

HOTELS

Throughout the past decade the quality of hotels in Eastern and Central Europe has improved notably. Many formerly state-run hotels were privatized, much to their benefit—a transition process that is still ongoing in some countries. International hotel chains have established a strong presence in the region; while they may not be strong on local character, they do provide a reliably high standard of quality.

Hotels listed throughout the book have private bath unless otherwise noted.

➤ TOLL-FREE NUMBERS: **Best Western** (☎ 800/528–1234, WEB www. bestwestern.com). **Choice** (☎ 800/424–6423, WEB www.choicehotels. com). **Days Inn** (☎ 800/325–2525, WEB www.daysinn.com). **Four Seasons** (☎ 800/332–3442, WEB www. fourseasons.com). **Hilton** (☎ 800/445–8667, WEB www.hilton.com). **Holiday Inn** (☎ 800/465–4329, WEB www.sixcontinentshotels.com). **Hyatt Hotels & Resorts** (☎ 800/233–1234, WEB www.hyatt.com). **Inter-Continental** (☎ 800/327–0200, WEB www.

intercontinental.com). **Marriott**
(☎ 888/236–2427, WEB www.
marriott.com). **Le Meridien** (☎ 800/
543–4300, WEB www.lemeridien-
hotels.com). **Radisson** (☎ 800/333–
3333, WEB www.radisson.com).
Renaissance Hotels & Resorts
(☎ 888/236–2427, WEB www.
marriott.com). **Sheraton** (☎ 800/
325–3535, WEB www.starwood.
com/sheraton).

MONEY MATTERS

For country-specific money informa-
tion, *see* Money and Expenses *in* the
A to Z section at the end of the
Prague and Budapest chapters.

Prices throughout this guide are given
for adults. Substantially reduced fees
are almost always available for children, students, and senior citizens.
For information on taxes, *see* Taxes.

ATMS

ATMs are common in both Prague
and Budapest and more often than
not are part of the Cirrus and Plus
networks; outside of urban areas,
machines are scarce and you should
plan to carry enough cash to meet
your needs.

CREDIT CARDS

Credit cards are accepted in places
that cater regularly to foreign tourists
and business travelers: hotels, restaurants, and shops, particularly in
major urban centers. When you leave
the beaten path, be prepared to pay
cash. Always inquire about credit
card policies when booking hotel
rooms. Visa and EuroCard/Master-
Card are the most commonly accepted credit cards in the region.

It's smart to **write down (and keep
separate) the number of each credit
card you're carrying** along with the
international service phone number
that usually appears on the back of
the card.

Throughout this guide, the following
abbreviations are used: **AE**, American
Express; **DC**, Diners Club; **MC**,
MasterCard; and **V**, Visa.

CURRENCY EXCHANGE

For the most favorable rates, **change
money through banks.** Although
ATM transaction fees may be higher

abroad than at home, ATM rates are
excellent because they are based on
wholesale rates offered only by major
banks. You won't do as well at exchange booths in airports or rail and
bus stations, in hotels, in restaurants,
or in stores. To avoid lines at airport
exchange booths, **get a bit of local
currency before you leave home.**

➤ EXCHANGE SERVICES: **International
Currency Express** (☎ 888/278–6628
orders). **Thomas Cook Currency
Services** (☎ 800/287–7362 orders
and retail locations, WEB www.us.
thomascook.com).

TRAVELER'S CHECKS

Do you need traveler's checks? It
depends on where you're headed. In
rural areas and small towns, go with
cash; traveler's checks are best used if
you are staying in Prague or Budapest. Lost or stolen checks can usually
be replaced within 24 hours. To
ensure a speedy refund, buy your own
traveler's checks—don't let someone
else pay for them: irregularities like
this can cause delays. The person who
bought the checks should make the
call to request a refund.

PACKING

Don't worry about packing lots of
formal clothing. Fashion was all but
nonexistent under 40 years of Communist rule, although residents of
Budapest and Prague—catching up
with their counterparts in other
European capitals—are considerably
more fashionably dressed than even a
few years ago. Still, Western dress of
virtually any kind is considered
stylish: a sports jacket for men and a
dress or pants for women are appropriate for an evening out. Everywhere
else, you'll feel comfortable in casual
pants or jeans.

Eastern and Central Europe enjoy all
the extremes of an inland climate, so
plan accordingly. In the higher eleva-
tions winter can last until April, and
even in summer the evenings will be
on the cool side.

Many areas are best seen on foot, so
take a pair of sturdy walking shoes
and be prepared to use them. High
heels will present considerable problems on the cobblestone streets of
Prague and towns in Hungary.

Some items that you take for granted at home are occasionally unavailable or of questionable quality in Eastern and Central Europe, though the situation has been steadily improving. Toiletries and personal-hygiene products have become relatively easy to find, but it's always a good idea to bring necessities when traveling in rural areas.

In your carry-on luggage, **pack an extra pair of eyeglasses or contact lenses and enough of any medication** you take to last a few days longer than the entire trip. You may also ask your doctor to write a spare prescription using the drug's generic name, since brand names may vary from country to country. In luggage to be checked, **never pack prescription drugs or valuables.** And don't forget to carry with you the addresses of offices that handle refunds of lost traveler's checks. Check *Fodor's How to Pack* (available in bookstores everywhere) for more tips.

To avoid customs and security delays, carry medications in their original packaging. Don't pack any sharp objects in your carry-on luggage, including knives of any size or material, scissors, manicure tools, and corkscrews, or anything else that might arouse suspicion.

CHECKING LUGGAGE

You are allowed one carry-on bag and one personal article, such as a purse or a laptop computer. Make sure that everything you carry aboard will fit under your seat or in the overhead bin. Get to the gate early, so you can board as soon as possible, before the overhead bins fill up.

If you are flying internationally, note that baggage allowances may be determined not by piece but by weight—generally 88 pounds (40 kilograms) in first class, 66 pounds (30 kilograms) in business class, and 44 pounds (20 kilograms) in economy.

Airline liability for baggage is limited to $2,500 per person on flights within the United States. On international flights it amounts to $9.07 per pound or $20 per kilogram for checked baggage (roughly $640 per 70-pound bag) and $400 per passenger for unchecked baggage. You can buy additional coverage at check-in for about $10 per $1,000 of coverage, but it excludes a rather extensive list of items, shown on your airline ticket.

Before departure, **itemize your bags' contents** and their worth, and label the bags with your name, address, and phone number. (If you use your home address, cover it so potential thieves can't see it readily.) Inside each bag, **pack a copy of your itinerary.** At check-in, **make sure that each bag is correctly tagged** with the destination airport's three-letter code. If your bags arrive damaged or fail to arrive at all, file a written report with the airline before leaving the airport.

PASSPORTS AND VISAS

When traveling internationally, **carry your passport** even if you don't need one (it's always the best form of ID) and **make two photocopies of the data page** (one for someone at home and another for you, carried separately from your passport). If you lose your passport, promptly call the nearest embassy or consulate and the local police.

U.S. passport applications for children under age 14 require consent from both parents or legal guardians; both parents must appear together to sign the application. If only one parent appears, he or she must submit a written statement from the other parent authorizing passport issuance for the child. A parent with sole authority must present evidence of it when applying; acceptable documentation includes the child's certified birth certificate listing only the applying parent, a court order specifically permitting this parent's travel with the child, or a death certificate for the nonapplying parent. Application forms and instructions are available on the Web site of the U.S. State Department's Bureau of Consular Affairs (www.travel.state.gov).

ENTERING EASTERN AND CENTRAL EUROPE

See the A to Z section at the end of the Prague and Budapest chapters for specific entrance requirements.

PASSPORT OFFICES

The best time to apply for a passport or to renew is in fall and winter. Before any trip, check your passport's expiration date, and, if necessary, renew it as soon as possible.

➤ AUSTRALIAN CITIZENS: **Australian State Passport Office** (☎ 131–232, WEB www.passports.gov.au).

➤ CANADIAN CITIZENS: **Passport Office** (to mail in applications: ✉ Department of Foreign Affairs and International Trade, Ottawa, Ontario K1A 0G3; ☎ 800/567–6868 in Canada; 819/994–3500; WEB www.dfait-maeci.gc.ca/passport).

➤ NEW ZEALAND CITIZENS: **New Zealand Passport Office** (☎ 0800/22–5050 or 04/474–8100, WEB www.passports.govt.nz).

➤ U.K. CITIZENS: **London Passport Office** (☎ 0870/521–0410, WEB www.passport.gov.uk).

➤ U.S. CITIZENS: **National Passport Information Center** (☎ 900/225–5674, 35¢ per minute for automated service or $1.05 per minute for operator service, WEB www.travel.state.gov).

REST ROOMS

Public rest rooms are more common, and cleaner, than they used to be in the Czech Republic. You nearly always have to pay 2 Kč–10 Kč to the attendant. Restaurant and bar toilets are generally for customers only, but, as prices are low, this isn't a significant burden.

While the rest rooms at Budapest's Ferihegy Airport may sparkle and smell of soap, don't expect the same of those at Hungarian train and bus stations—which, by the way, usually have attendants on hand who collect a fee of about 40 Ft. Especially outside Budapest, public rest rooms are often run-down and sometimes rank. Pay the attendant on the way in; you will receive toilet tissue in exchange.

SAFETY

Crime rates are still relatively low in Eastern and Central Europe, but travelers should beware of pickpockets in crowded areas, especially on public transportation, at railway stations, and in big hotels. In general, always keep your valuables with you—in open bars and restaurants, purses hung on or placed next to chairs are easy targets. Make sure your wallet is safe in a buttoned pocket, or watch your handbag.

In the Czech Republic, except for widely scattered attacks against people of color, violent crime against tourists is extremely rare. Pickpocketing and bill-padding are the most common complaints.

In Hungary, pickpocketing and car theft are the main concerns. While a typical rental car is less likely to be stolen, expensive German makes such as Audi, BMW, and Mercedes are hot targets for car thieves.

LOCAL SCAMS

To avoid potential trouble in the Czech Republic: ask taxi drivers what the approximate fare will be before getting in, and ask for a receipt (*paragon*); carefully look over restaurant bills; be extremely wary of handing your passport to anyone who accosts you with a demand for ID; and never exchange money on the street.

WOMEN IN EASTERN AND CENTRAL EUROPE

Don't wear a money belt or a waist pack, both of which peg you as a tourist. If you carry a purse, choose one with a zipper and a thick strap that you can drape across your body; adjust the length so that the purse sits in front of you at or above hip level. Store only enough money in the purse to cover casual spending. Distribute the rest of your cash and any valuables (including credit cards and your passport) between a deep front pocket, an inside jacket or vest pocket, and a hidden money pouch. Do not reach for the money pouch once in public. It isn't wise for a woman to go alone to a bar or nightclub or to wander the streets late at night. When traveling by train at night, seek out compartments that are well populated.

SENIOR-CITIZEN TRAVEL

To qualify for age-related discounts, **mention your senior-citizen status up front** when booking hotel reservations (not when checking out) and before you're seated in restaurants (not when paying the bill). Be sure to have identification on hand. When renting a car, ask about promotional car-rental discounts, which can be cheaper than senior-citizen rates.

➤ EDUCATIONAL PROGRAMS: **Elderhostel** (✉ 11 Ave. de Lafayette, Boston, MA 02111-1746, ☎ 877/426–8056, FAX 877/426–2166, WEB www.elderhostel.org). **Interhostel** (✉ University of New Hampshire, 6 Garrison Ave., Durham, NH 03824, ☎ 603/862–1147 or 800/733–9753, FAX 603/862–1113, WEB www.learn.unh.edu).

STUDENTS IN EASTERN AND CENTRAL EUROPE

➤ IDS AND SERVICES: **STA Travel** (☎ 212/627–3111 or 800/781–4040, FAX 212/627–3387, WEB www.sta.com). **Travel Cuts** (✉ 187 College St., Toronto, Ontario M5T 1P7, ☎ 416/979–2406 or 888/838–2887, FAX 416/979–8167, WEB www.travelcuts.com).

TAXES

Most Eastern and Central European countries have some form of value-added tax (VAT); rebate rules vary by country and seem to be in an ongoing state of evolution. Check with tourism offices (☞ Visitor Information) for current regulations. One thing you can depend on—you'll need to present your receipts on departure.

TELEPHONES

For additional country-specific telephone information, *see* Telephones *in* the A to Z section at the end of the Prague and Budapest chapters.

AREA AND COUNTRY CODES

The country code for the Czech Republic is 420; the city code for Prague is 2. The country code for Hungary is 36; the city code for Budapest is 1.

When dialing an Eastern or Central European number from abroad, drop the initial 0 from the local area code. The country code for the United States and Canada is 1, 61 for Australia, 64 for New Zealand, and 44 for the U.K.

LONG-DISTANCE SERVICES

AT&T, MCI, and Sprint access codes make calling long distance relatively convenient, but you may find the local access number blocked in many hotel rooms. First ask the hotel operator to connect you. If the hotel operator balks, ask for an international operator, or dial the international operator yourself. One way to improve your odds of getting connected to your long-distance carrier is to travel with more than one company's calling card (a hotel may block Sprint, for example, but not MCI). If all else fails, call from a pay phone.

➤ ACCESS CODES: **AT&T Direct** (☎ 042000101 in the Czech Republic; 0080001111 in Hungary). **MCI WorldPhone** (☎ 0042000112 in the Czech Republic; 0680001411 in Hungary). **Sprint International Access** (☎ 0042087187 in the Czech Republic; 0680001877 in Hungary).

TIME

The Czech Republic and Hungary are on Central European Time (CET), one hour ahead of Greenwich Mean Time and six hours ahead of the Eastern time zone of the United States.

TOURS AND PACKAGES

Because everything is prearranged on a prepackaged tour or independent vacation, you'll spend less time planning—and often get it all at a good price.

BOOKING WITH AN AGENT

Travel agents are excellent resources. But it's a good idea to collect brochures from several agencies, as some agents' suggestions may be influenced by relationships with tour and package firms that reward them for volume sales. If you have a special interest, **find an agent with expertise in that area**; the American Society of Travel Agents (ASTA; ☞ Travel Agencies) has a database of specialists worldwide.

Make sure your travel agent knows the accommodations and other services of the place being recommended. Ask about the hotel's location, room size, beds, and whether it has a pool, room service, or programs for children, if you care about these. Has your agent been there in person or sent others whom you can contact?

Do some homework on your own, too: local tourism boards can provide information about lesser-known and small-niche operators, some of which may sell only direct.

Each year consumers are stranded or lose their money when tour operators—even large ones with excellent reputations—go out of business. So **check out the operator.** Ask several travel agents about its reputation, and try to **book with a company that has a consumer-protection program.** (Look for information in the company's brochure.) In the United States, members of the National Tour Association and the United States Tour Operators Association are required to set aside funds to cover your payments and travel arrangements in the event that the company defaults. It's also a good idea to choose a company that participates in the American Society of Travel Agents' Tour Operator Program (TOP); ASTA will act as mediator in any disputes between you and your tour operator.

Remember that the more your package or tour includes the better you can predict the ultimate cost of your vacation. Make sure you know exactly what is covered, and **beware of hidden costs.** Are taxes, tips, and transfers included? Entertainment and excursions? These can add up.

➤ TOUR-OPERATOR RECOMMENDATIONS: **American Society of Travel Agents** (☞ Travel Agencies). **National Tour Association** (NTA; ⊠ 546 E. Main St., Lexington, KY 40508, ☎ 859/226–4444 or 800/682–8886, WEB www.ntaonline.com). **United States Tour Operators Association** (USTOA; ⊠ 275 Madison Ave., Suite 2014, New York, NY 10016, ☎ 212/599–6599 or 800/468–7862, FAX 212/599–6744, WEB www.ustoa.com).

TRAIN TRAVEL

Although standards have improved, on the whole they are far short of what is acceptable in the West. Trains are very busy, and it is rare to find one running less than full or almost so. Both the Czech Republic and Hungary operate their own dining, buffet, and refreshment services. Always crowded, they tend to open and close at the whim of the staff. In Hungary, couchette cars are second-class only and can be little more than a hard bunk without springs and adequate

bed linen. First-class couchettes are available on Czech trains, and there are two types of second-class couchettes. The cheaper have six hard beds per compartment; the slightly more expensive have three beds and a sink and are sex-segregated. Some of the most comfortable trains are the express trains in the Czech Republic and Hungary—they're normally less crowded and more comfortable. (You should make a reservation.)

Although trains in Eastern and Central Europe can mean hours of sitting on a hard seat in a smoky car, traveling by rail is very inexpensive. Rail networks in all the Eastern and Central European countries are very extensive, though trains can be infuriatingly slow. You'll invariably enjoy interesting and friendly traveling company, however; most Eastern and Central Europeans are eager to hear about the West and to discuss the enormous changes in their own countries.

For information about fares and schedules and other country-specific train information, *see* Train Travel *in* the A to Z section at the end of the Prague and Budapest chapters.

CUTTING COSTS

To save money, **look into rail passes.** But be aware that if you don't plan to cover many miles you may come out ahead by buying individual tickets.

You can use the European East Pass on the national rail networks of the Czech Republic, and Hungary. The pass covers five days of unlimited first-class travel within a one-month period for $199. Additional travel days may be purchased.

You can also combine the East Pass with a national rail pass. A pass for the Czech Republic costs $69 for 5 days of train travel within a 15-day period—far more than you'd spend on individual tickets. The Hungarian Flexipass costs $64 for five days of unlimited first-class train travel within a 15-day period or $80 for 10 days within a one-month period.

Hungary—but not the Czech Republic—is one of 17 countries in which you can **use Eurailpasses,** which provide unlimited first-class rail travel in all of the participating countries for the duration of the pass. If you plan to rack up the miles, get a standard pass. These are available for 15 days ($554), 21 days ($718), one month ($890), two months ($1,260), and three months ($1,558).

In addition to standard Eurailpasses, **ask about special rail-pass plans.** Among these are the Eurail Youthpass (for those under age 26), the Eurail Saverpass (which gives a discount for two or more people traveling together), a Eurail Flexipass (which allows a certain number of travel days within a set period), the Euraildrive Pass and the Europass Drive (which combines travel by train and rental car). Whichever pass you choose, remember that you must **purchase your pass before you leave** for Europe.

Many travelers assume that rail passes guarantee them seats on the trains they wish to ride. Not so. You need to **book seats ahead even if you are using a rail pass**; seat reservations are required on some European trains, particularly high-speed trains, and are a good idea on trains that may be crowded—particularly in summer on popular routes. You will also need a reservation if you purchase sleeping accommodations.

➤ INFORMATION AND PASSES: **Rail Europe** (✉ 500 Mamaroneck Ave., Harrison, NY 10528, ☎ 914/682–5172 or 800/438–7245, FAX 800/432–1329; ✉ 2087 Dundas E, Suite 106, Mississauga, Ontario L4X 1M2, ☎ 800/361–7245, FAX 905/602–4198, WEB www.raileurope.com). **DER Travel Services** (✉ 9501 W. Devon Ave., Rosemont, IL 60018, ☎ 800/782–2424, FAX 800/282–7474 information; 800/860–9944 brochures; WEB www.dertravel.com). **CIT Tours Corp** (✉ 15 W. 44th St., 10th floor, New York, NY 10036, ☎ 212/730–2400; 800/248–7245 in the U.S.; 800/387–0711; 800/361–7799 in Canada; WEB www.cit-tours.com).

TRAVEL AGENCIES

A good travel agent puts your needs first. Look for an agency that has been in business at least five years, emphasizes customer service, and has someone on staff who specializes in your destination. In addition, **make sure the agency belongs to a professional trade organization.** The American Society of Travel Agents (ASTA)—the largest and most influential in the field, with more than 24,000 members in some 140 countries—maintains and enforces a strict code of ethics and will step in to help mediate any agent-client disputes involving ASTA members if necessary. ASTA (whose motto is "Without a travel agent, you're on your own") also maintains a Web site that includes a directory of agents. (If a travel agency is also acting as your tour operator, *see* Buyer Beware *in* Tours and Packages.)

➤ LOCAL AGENT REFERRALS: **American Society of Travel Agents** (ASTA; ✉ 1101 King St., Suite 200, Alexandria, VA 22314, ☎ 800/965–2782 24-hr hot line, FAX 703/739–3268, WEB www.astanet.com). **Association of British Travel Agents** (✉ 68–71 Newman St., London W1T 3AH, ☎ 020/7637–2444, FAX 020/7637–0713, WEB www.abtanet.com). **Association of Canadian Travel Agents** (✉ 130 Albert St., Suite 1705, Ottawa, Ontario K1P 5G4, ☎ 613/237–3657, FAX 613/237–7052, WEB www.acta.ca). **Australian Federation of Travel Agents** (✉ Level 3, 309 Pitt St., Sydney, NSW 2000, ☎ 02/9264–3299, FAX 02/9264–1085, WEB www.afta.com.au). **Travel Agents' Association of New Zealand** (✉ Level 5, Tourism and Travel House, 79 Boulcott St. [Box 1888, Wellington 6001], ☎ 04/499–0104, FAX 04/499–0827, WEB www.taanz.org.nz).

VISITOR INFORMATION

➤ CZECH REPUBLIC: **Czech Tourist Authority** (in the U.S.: ✉ 1109–1111 Madison Ave., New York, NY 10028, ☎ 212/288–0830, FAX 212/288–0971, www.czechcenter.com; in Canada: ✉ Czech Airlines office, Simpson Tower, 401 Bay St., Suite 1510, Toronto, Ontario M5H 2YA, ☎ 416/363–3174, FAX 416/363–0239; in the U.K.: ✉ 95 Great Portland St., London W1N 5RA, ☎ 020/7291–9925, FAX 020/7436–8300, WEB www.czechcentre.org.uk).

➤ HUNGARY: In the U.S. and Canada: **Hungarian National Tourist Office** (✉ 150 E. 58th St., New York, NY 10155, ☎ 212/355–0240, FAX 212/

207–4103, WEB www.gotohungary. com). In Canada: **Hungarian Consulate General Office** (⊠ 121 Bloor St. E, Suite 1115, Toronto M4W3M5, Ontario, ☎ 416/923–8981, FAX 416/ 923–2732). In the U.K.: **Hungarian National Tourist Board** (⊠ c/o Embassy of the Republic of Hungary, Commercial Section, 46 Eaton Pl., London, SW1X 8AL, ☎ 020/7823–1032 or 020/7823–1055, FAX 020/ 7823–1459, htlondon@hungary-tourism.hu).

➤ U.S. GOVERNMENT ADVISORIES: **U.S. Department of State** (⊠ Overseas Citizens Services Office, Room 4811, 2201 C St. NW, Washington, DC 20520, ☎ 202/647–5225 interactive hot line; 888/407–4747; WEB www. travel.state.gov); enclose a business-size SASE.

WEB SITES

Do check out the World Wide Web when planning your trip. You'll find everything from weather forecasts to virtual tours of famous cities. Be sure to **visit Fodors.com** (www.fodors. com), a complete travel-planning site. You can research prices and book plane tickets, hotel rooms, rental cars, vacation packages, and more. In addition, you can post your pressing questions in the "Travel Talk" section. Other planning tools include a currency converter and weather reports, and there are loads of links to travel resources.

➤ SUGGESTED WEB SITES: Czech Republic: **Czech Tourist Authority** (WEB www.visitczechia.cz). Hungary: **Live Budapest** (www.livebudapest.com).

WHEN TO GO

The tourist season generally runs from April or May through October; spring and fall combine good weather with a more bearable level of tourism. The ski season lasts from mid-December through March. Outside the mountain resorts you will encounter few other visitors; you'll have the opportunity to see the region covered in snow, but many of the sights are closed, and it can get very, very cold. Bear in mind that many attractions are closed from November through March.

Prague and Budapest are beautiful year-round, but avoid midsummer (especially July and August) and the Christmas and Easter holidays, when the two cities are choked with visitors. Lake Balaton in Hungary becomes a mob scene in July and August.

For additional country-specific information, *see* When to Tour following the Great Itineraries at the beginning of the Prague and Budapest chapters.

CLIMATE

The following are the average daily maximum and minimum temperatures for Prague and Budapest.

➤ FORECASTS: **Weather Channel Connection** (☎ 900/932–8437), 95¢ per minute from a Touch-Tone phone.

BUDAPEST

Jan.	34F	1C	May	72F	22C	Sept.	73F	23C
	25	– 4		52	11		54	12
Feb.	39F	4C	June	79F	26C	Oct.	61F	16C
	28	– 2		59	15		45	7
Mar.	50F	10C	July	82F	28C	Nov.	46F	8C
	36	2		61	16		37	3
Apr.	63F	17C	Aug.	81F	27C	Dec.	39F	4C
	25	– 4		61	16		30	– 1

PRAGUE

Jan.	36F	2C	May	66F	19C	Sept.	68F	20C
	25	– 4		46	8		50	10
Feb.	37F	3C	June	72F	22C	Oct.	55F	13C
	27	– 3		52	11		41	5
Mar.	46F	8C	July	75F	24C	Nov.	46F	8C
	32	0		55	13		36	2
Apr.	58F	14C	Aug.	73F	23C	Dec.	37F	3C
	39	4		55	13		28	– 2

FESTIVALS AND SEASONAL EVENTS

Czech Republic

➤ DEC.: **Christmas Fairs and Programs** take place in most towns and cities; among those particularly worth catching are **Christmas in Valašsko,** in Rožnov pod Radhoštěm, and the **Arrival of Lady Winter Festival,** in Prachatice.

➤ JAN.: Prague hosts the **FebioFest International Film, Television and Video Festival.**

➤ MAR.: Prague holds **St. Matthew's Fair,** an annual children's fair at the Výstaviště exhibition grounds. Prague is also the site of **Days of European Film.**

➤ APR.: Eastertime brings two festivals of sacred music to Prague, **Musica Ecumenica** and **Musica Sacra Praga.** Brno puts on an **Easter Spiritual Music Festival.** English-language and world authors appear at the **Prague Writers' Festival.**

➤ MAY: There are events both athletic and artistic in Prague; there's the **Prague Spring International Music Festival** as well as the **Prague Marathon.**

➤ JUNE: The international dance festival **Tanec Praha** hits the capital.

➤ AUG.: Prague's **Verdi Festival** is staged at the State Opera.

➤ SEPT.: Prague holds several arts festivals, preeminently the **Prague Autumn International Music Festival.**

➤ OCT.: The capital continues its run of cultural events, including an **International Jazz Festival** and the **Dance Theater Festival.**

➤ NOV.: Prague stokes the cultural fires against the approach of winter with the **Czech Press Photo Exhibition** and **Musica Iudaica,** a festival of Jewish music.

Hungary

For contact information about most of these festivals, inquire at the Budapest Tourinform office or the local visitor information center.

➤ MID-MAR.–EARLY APR.: The season's first and biggest arts festival, the **Budapest Spring Festival,** showcases Hungary's best opera, music, theater, fine arts, and dance, as well as visiting foreign artists. Other towns—including Kecskemét, Szentendre, and Pécs—also participate.

➤ MAY: The **Balaton Festival** in Keszthely features high-caliber classical concerts and other festivities held in venues around town and outdoors on Kossuth Lajos utca.

➤ LATE JUNE–EARLY JULY: The **World Music Festival** in Budapest, held in early July, has several days of world music concerts by local and international artists. The **International Puppet Festival** draws puppeteers from Hungary and abroad to Sárospatak, July 1–4 every two years, in even-numbered years.

➤ JULY: Late in the month, Balatonfüred's **Anna Ball** is a traditional ball and beauty contest.

➤ AUG.: Toward mid-month, Budapest hosts a **Formula 1** car race, while the weeklong **BudaFest** opera and ballet festival takes place mid-month at the opera house after the opera season ends. **St. Stephen's Day** (August 20) is a major national holiday. A highlight is the **fireworks** in Budapest. The weeklong **Jewish Summer Festival,** held in late August and early September, features cantors, classical concerts, a kosher cabaret, films, and theater and dance performances, in Budapest and sometimes elsewhere.

➤ MID-OCT.–EARLY NOV.: Fans of contemporary art forms may be interested in the **Budapest Autumn Festival,** which offers dance and theater performances, film, and photographic exhibitions.

➤ DEC.: During the month of December, Christmas Fairs are held all over Budapest, including a large fair at Vörösmarty tér (Vörösmarty Square). There are cultural programs, and folk art is for sale.

1 DESTINATION: PRAGUE AND BUDAPEST

Under the Spell

What's Where

Fodor's Choice

UNDER THE SPELL

DESPITE OUR MOST lyrical fantasies, traveling through Europe has an inescapable element of the predictable. Streams of familiar landmarks and famed artworks are broken by the seemingly endless searches for comfortable hotels, public restrooms, and espressos that cost less than $7. Over a century's worth of tourism industry experience lies behind the glossy brochures and prepackaged souvenirs, and the beaten paths are now beyond well-worn. As the legs tire and the senses numb, the cities themselves begin to take on the look and feel of museums—handsome and well-organized monuments to events that happened long ago.

Then there are Prague and Budapest.

Travelers to these lively, enchanting capitals will be forgiven for wanting to throttle their brothers' friends for steering them toward Vienna or Brussels. Unlike much of Western Europe, Prague and Budapest can easily satiate the castle-and-church set while at the same time inviting adventurous spirits into a whimsical café-and-club party that seems to have been raging since 1878. All this, of course, at prices that still make Germans blush.

Prague and Budapest's intoxicating mixes of beautiful settings, dynamic times, and—not least—cheap and tasty local drink, have convinced thousands of visitors since 1989 to stay just one more week, which became one more month, which turned into years. Prague's over-documented expatriates tend toward goatees and tattoos, bookstores and rock bands, while Budapest's lower-profile expats are more likely to work for an ad agency and belong to a wine society. Both communities have produced useful little touches of home, such as vegetarian restaurants and decent newspapers. The two cities are competing, as they have for a thousand years, for the mantle of Capital of Central Europe, and the cosmopolitanism that goes with it. Since both capitals also compete directly for tourist dollars, locals have become accustomed to (and a bit cynical of) loud foreigners asking for directions or occupying the next barstool. Luckily for hospitality's sake, Czechs and Hungarians love to hunker down over beer and brandy shots with strangers, so if you go out for a polite night on the town you can easily wind up, 36 hours later, with a dozen new friends, a smoking habit, and skeleton keys to a downtown apartment.

It has not always been thus. Prague, during the Communist "normalization" period of the 1970s and '80s, was a miserable place. People lived in legitimate fear of imprisonment for listening to bootleg Velvet Underground tapes, and the nameless, soot-stained shops had few edible goods. Hungary, whose "Goulash communism" was a much less repressive strain, nonetheless suffered from the same lack of funds to maintain buildings or modernize foul factories and automobiles. The once-flourishing 19th-century cafés on Budapest's ring boulevard Nagykörút were shuttered in favor of joyless stand-up coffee shacks.

Both nations briefly and gloriously shook off the shackles during the Soviet era, only to be crushed once again by Warsaw Pact tanks—Hungary in 1956 and Czechoslovakia in 1968. After 51 consecutive years of living under failed 20th-century political systems, Czechs and Hungarians threw long and sweet coming-out parties in 1989–90. When the confetti was finally swept away, the two countries took turns playing poster child for post-communist reform, taking great pains to remind visitors with short memories that the nations were taking their rightful, historic place back in the Western family.

Twelve years into the process, the cities and people have changed seismically. In Prague, the smothering blanket of gray has given way to birthday-cake pastels. Scaffolding and corrugated tin are being rapidly shed from downtown streets and squares, giving an exhilarating sense of rediscovery and renewal to residents and visitors alike. The radio dial is jammed with good stations, although the excellent Radio One, long an independent-minded mix of international and local music, is having its personality sanded away under its new American ownership. Budapest has a rash of modern office buildings and spruced-up promenades. Signs of conspicuous wealth are everywhere, from the new mansions atop the Buda hills to the shiny Mercedes zipping through the crowded streets and the purring of cell phones—in fact, Hungary has more cellular phones per capita than the United States.

For all the cosmetic improvements, Czechs and Hungarians have suffered more this decade than most of us have in a lifetime. Meager pensions have lagged behind the mostly double-digit inflation, factory towns in the countryside have been decimated by unemployment, and the rules and certainties of a half-century of communism have been overturned. Because they enjoyed relative prosperity in the 1980s, Hungarians have had a particularly hard time adjusting; many people find it hard to understand why they need to suffer through the latest austerity program. The pension problem is a bitter example; Hungarian men, on average, die before qualifying for a pension, leaving their widows to struggle with only their own devalued portion. Often these women are reduced to selling bunches of flowers or odd bits of clothing in metro stations.

Crime, too, has gone from nearly nonexistent to pervasive, with Russian thugs setting off pipe bombs in Budapest, and corrupt Czech fund managers embezzling investor money from Prague banks to offshore accounts. Ruling parties in both countries were rocked by political corruption scandals before being tossed out in 1998 elections. These issues loom large, but most travelers need not worry about safety beyond keeping their wallets safe from pickpockets and avoiding restaurants that charge foreigners $100 for a drink.

The dramatic pace of change contributes to a sense of action and possibility too often missing in Western capitals, breathing contemporary life to the centuries of drama written on every meandering downtown street. It is here, mere steps off the beaten tourist paths, where the hidden spirits that seem to govern Prague and Budapest reveal themselves, transcending and even laughing at the political and social shifts of the moment.

Prague's spirit is clever and romantic, with a decidedly dark sense of humor. The easily walkable Malá Strana (Lesser Quarter), Staré Město (Old Town), and Nové Město (New Town) are all haunted alleyways and curves, some leading to hidden 13th-century churches, some coming to abrupt stops, others emptying into exuberant squares or regal gardens. Gaiety and paranoia forge an uneasy truce, neither keeping the upper hand for long. Czechs themselves are just as likely to snarl at you (especially if you set foot inside a restaurant or neighborhood shop), as invite you to their countryside cottage for a week of picking mushrooms and drinking three-day-old wine, called *burčak*.

This duality is crammed side-by-side into ever-smaller living quarters. Just off Wenceslas Square you can find the world's most frivolous Cubist lamp standing next to the solemn Gothic heights of the 14th-century Church of Our Lady of the Snows—and to complete the absurd picture, there's a Japanese bonsai garden in the church's backyard. The spooky St. Vitus Cathedral is a wonderful testament to architectural potluck, with one of its dark 13th-century spires topped by a goofy 18th-century onion dome, while snarling Gothic gargoyles glower above Art Nouveau stained glass.

Because the city has miraculously avoided war damage over the centuries, the streets themselves are a vivid history lesson. Walk through the sad but reemergent Jewish Quarter, and imagine how Hitler planned on "preserving" this neighborhood as a monument to the "decadent" Jewish culture he was busy annihilating. See the terrific statue of Protestant revolutionary Jan Hus on Old Town Square, imagine how his followers were executed in that very space for insisting that the laity be allowed to take Communion with the same wine reserved for the priests, and then visit any Hussite cathedral and notice the symbolic wine goblet carved above the front door. Go to a performance of *The Bartered Bride* inside the lush, gilded National Theater, and imagine how Bedřich Smetana's opera must have been received here at the height of the 19th-century National Revival, when Czechs flouted their German masters by constructing the theater entirely from private donations. (Note too, the ridiculous juxtaposition of the Communist New Theater monstrosity right next door.)

Visits to the National Gallery, the stunningly restored Art Nouveau Municipal House, and the cavernous new Museum of Modern Art will tell you much of what you need to know about Czech history and art, from the empire years of King Charles IV to the mad alchemy of Rudolf II to the exuberant but unsteady days of the interwar First Republic. You can get a feel for Prague's artistic magnetism—past and present—by catching a film, a reading, or a live band. The city is weird, inhabited by ghosts, tangled with mysterious, narrow streets—a legendary source of inspiration. But for true immersion, nothing beats stepping into any one of a thousand neighborhood pubs, drinking the best beer in the world for 50 cents a pint, watching as the dour locals suddenly spring to life when someone breaks out a guitar, and then stumbling back out into the world to watch the sun rise over a mercifully empty Charles Bridge.

Budapest, unlike Prague, is haunted by memories of more recent grandeur, specifically the Austro-Hungarian empire era of 1867–1918. The major streets are grand and broad, suitable for victory marches, and the city's dividing river is the wide, impressive Danube, a stronger presence than Prague's winsome Vltava. The city itself is almost twice as large as Prague, and shares none of the Czech capital's cloying, pastel-frosting cutesiness. Some buildings are still pockmarked with bullet holes from the 1956 uprising and the extensive battles that ripped the city apart in World War II.

The historical wounds seem fresher, more immediate here than in Prague. Besides the tragedy of 1956, residents still invoke the 1918 Treaty of Trianon, which lopped off two-thirds of prewar Hungary's territory. There is an oft-remarked melancholia in the Hungarian people, which pop psychologists attribute to being on the wrong side of seven consecutive wars, or speaking a language everyone else on earth finds incomprehensible.

But visitors expecting a mopey lot grumbling over 19th-century maps are in for a shocker. Hungarians are a hyper-smart, multilingual, and deeply sensual people who enjoy the finer things in life, from Turkish baths to good red wine to coffee cakes drenched in chocolate. Hospitality knows no limits (though one must be careful about scam artists), and people seem to have an uncanny knack for knowing exactly what foreigners want. There is a whiff of decadence and chaos in the air,

a happy remnant from the hated 1541–1686 Ottoman occupation. Hungarians seem to have picked up only the nicer of the Balkan habits, such as promenading each evening down the riverside *korzó* and other pedestrian zones.

Indeed, the country truly serves as a European crossroads between East and West, North and South. On the streets, it is common to hear Russian, Arabic, Serbo-Croatian, English, and German. Roman ruins lie next to Turkish mosques across the river from the largest synagogue in Europe. There are excellent French, Greek, Italian, Turkish, Mexican, Irish, and Japanese restaurants, and of course the blood-red Hungarian eateries with Gypsy violinists wearing folk vests. But unlike that of Prague, Budapest's arts and culture scene is still a bit hesitant, trying to weigh the past while incorporating a flood of imported entertainment.

Elegant monuments to Hungary's romanticized failures can be found throughout the city, from the new, understated statue of 1956 leader Imre Nagy looking toward the Parliament building to the riverside memorial to 1848 hero Sándor Petőfi, a young poet who accurately prophesied his own revolutionary death. Many buildings tell long, complicated stories of their own, such as the unheralded Mai Manó Photo Gallery at 20 Nagymező utca, a street known as the once and future "Hungarian Broadway." This Art Nouveau structure was commissioned in 1894 by court photographer Manó Mai, who used it as a studio for his portrait sittings of luminaries such as Franz Joseph I and composer Béla Bartók. After Mai's death, the building became a decadent cabaret called the Arizona, complete with revolving hydraulic stages and naked girls on chandeliers. The club was a favorite of international royalty and government officials, but during World War II its Jewish owners were murdered by occupying German soldiers. During Communism the building fell into disrepair, but now a small photography gallery has taken root, and the managers have ambitious plans to revamp the entire space, adding a café, exhibition rooms, and a library. The building is taking center stage in the projected rejuvenation of the theaters along the rundown avenue, which itself is a cornerstone of the city's dramatic overhaul.

As post-communism rolls toward its second decade, Prague and Budapest have emerged as the political and cultural epicenters of the former Eastern bloc. Prague has reawakened in its role as capital of Bohemia, becoming the favored European tour date for inventive rock and pop acts (including repeat performers such as Sonic Youth, Bob Dylan, and the Rolling Stones) and inspiring untold thousands of wild young souls to pursue their artistic and entrepreneurial dreams. Budapest attracts multinational companies with equal success, even luring some European headquarters away from nearby Vienna. Hungary is blazing most trails in Central European economic reform, and Budapest's activist mayor is more than halfway through an ambitious renewal plan aiming to restore the city's salon culture to its pre–World War I splendor.

Hungary and the Czech Republic are quickly distancing themselves from their Communist past; soon they will have their own stars on the European Union flag, and the best Hungarian wines and Czech beers will be sold for prices depressingly familiar to travelers from the West. Before the window closes, though, Prague and Budapest will continue to seduce, infuriate, and even ensnare those daring enough to visit.

—Matt Welch

WHAT'S WHERE

Prague and Environs

Planted firmly in the heart of Central Europe—Prague is some 320 kilometers (200 miles) north*west* of Vienna—the Czech Republic is culturally and historically more closely linked to Western, particularly Germanic, culture than any of its former East-bloc brethren. The capital city of **Prague** sits on the Vltava (Moldau) River, roughly in the middle of Bohemian territory. A stunning city of human dimensions, Prague offers the traveler a lesson in almost all the major architectural styles of Western European history; relatively unscathed by major wars, most of Prague's buildings are remarkably well preserved. The five main historic districts echo what were once five separate towns: Hradčany (Castle Area), Malá Strana (Lesser Quarter), Staré Město (Old Town), Nové Město (New Town), and Josefov (the Jewish Quarter). The stunning Karlův Most (Charles Bridge) links the Old Town and Lesser Quarter, while the Pražský Hrad (Prague Castle) overlooks the city from its hilltop west of the river.

Prague is planted in the heart of **Bohemia,** an area where the history of internal conflict, invasions, and religious revolts is almost palpable. Southern Bohemia is dotted with several stunning walled towns retaining much of their medieval appearance, many of which played important roles in the Hussite religious wars of the 15th century. The two most notable towns are Tábor and Český Krumlov. Western Bohemia, especially the far western hills near the German border, remains justly famous for its mineral springs and **spa towns,** in particular Karlovy Vary, Mariánské Lázně, and Františkový Lázně. These elegant towns are just a couple of hours away from the capital.

Budapest and Environs

Sandwiched between Slovakia and Romania, Hungary was the Austro-Hungarian Empire's eastern frontier, the geographical link between the Slavic regions of Central Europe and the Black Sea region's amalgam of Orthodox and Islamic cultures. The capital, **Budapest,** crouches on the Danube, just an hour from Bratislava in Slovakia and two-and-a-half hours from Vienna. Like Prague, Budapest is an amalgam of once-separate towns—Óbuda, Buda, and Pest were joined in the 19th century. Buda, on the Danube's western bank, is quite hilly; most of its major sights are clustered on the Várhegy (Castle Hill). Pest, on the eastern side of the river, is flat and laced with wide avenues and circular *körúts* (ring roads).

Just north of Budapest, the Danube River forms a gentle, heart-shape curve along which lie the romantic and historic towns of the region called the Danube Bend. Southwest of Budapest are the vineyards, historic villages, and popular, developed summer resorts around **Lake Balaton,** the largest lake in Central Europe. The towns along the northern shore of the lake are often less developed and thus, more attractive—these include the spa town of Balatonfüred and the abbey-crowned village of Tihany.

FODOR'S CHOICE

are loaded with excellent Hungarian home cooking. $–$$

Dining

Prague

V Zátiší. In one of the city's oldest and calmest squares—the restaurant's name means "still life"—this refined dining room offers tantalizing international specialties and wonderful service. $$–$$$$

Café Savoy. Homemade ravioli and fresh seafood are served in surprising taste combinations in this very grand café that was reborn in 2001. $$–$$$$

Zahrada v opeře. The subdued lighting makes for a romantic setting, and reasonable prices for any of a dozen superb pastas doesn't hurt either. $$–$$$

Break Café and Bar. Escape bustling Wenceslas Square for a reasonably priced, eclectic array of salads or sandwiches at lunch, or something a bit more elaborate at dinner. $

Kavárna Slavia. To lap up some of the artistic scene, come to this art deco café; the views of the Prague Castle and the National Theater aren't too shabby, either. $

Budapest

Gundel. Established at the turn of the 20th century, Budapest's most famous restaurant continues its legacy of old-world grandeur and elegant cuisine. $$$–$$$$

Empire. You'll feel transported back to 19th-century Hapsburg Budapest as you dine on some of the city's best game dishes in this quiet, traditional restaurant on Kossuth Lajos. $$–$$$

Kisbuda Gyöngye. This intimate setting is the place to look for a *liba lakodalmas* (goose wedding feast)—a roast goose leg, goose liver, and goose cracklings. $–$$$

Baraka. A welcome addition to the serious dining scene and a bargain to boot, this gleaming restaurant is on a quiet side street near all the action downtown. $–$$

Náncsi Néni. It's a bit out of the way, but that hasn't deterred the crowds from this warm restaurant—garlic and paprika hang from the ceiling and jars of home-pickled vegetables line the walls. These will hopefully sharpen your appetite, as the plates

---

Lodging

Prague

Palace. The soft pinks and greens of the room decor, the classic Continental restaurant, and the location near Wenceslas Square make this a great combination of elegance and convenience. $$$$

Savoy. From the Jugendstil facade to the afternoon tea in the library, this small hotel is all about luxury. $$$$

Dům U Červeného Lva. Just five minutes from Prague Castle's front gates, this immaculate hotel has striking details, such as the painted-beam ceilings. $$$

Romantik Hotel U Raka. There are just six rooms in this 18th-century building, so plan way ahead to snare a spot. It's just behind the Loreto Church, so you'll have a wonderful base for exploring the city. $$$

Pension Louda. While this pension is a good 20 minutes away from the city center, the south-facing rooms have stunning views of Prague. $

Budapest

Kempinski Hotel Corvinus Budapest. Sleek, modern, and luxurious, this hotel oozes solicitousness. The large, sparkling bathrooms are the city's best. $$$$

Le Méridien Budapest. The French Empire rooms are plush and luxurious, and those on higher floors have balconies. Enjoy afternoon tea in the hotel's restaurant. $$$$

Danubius Hotel Gellért. This grand 1918 Art Nouveau hotel on the Danube at the foot of Gellért Hill is the pride of Budapest. Housing an extensive, elegant complex of marble bathing facilities fed by ancient curative springs, it is also one of Europe's most famous old-world spas. $$$–$$$$

Kulturinov. Set on one of historic Castle Hill's most famous cobblestone squares, this neo-baroque castle provides budget accommodations in a priceless location. $

Museums and Religious Buildings

Prague

Chrám svatého Mikuláše (St. Nicholas Church). With its dynamic curves, dramatic statues, and remarkable dome, this church embodies the height of high Baroque.

Chrám svatého Víta (St. Vitus Cathedral). Soaring above the castle walls and dominating the city at its feet, St. Vitus Cathedral is among the most beautiful sights in Europe. Its stained-glass windows are particularly brilliant.

Kostel Panny Marie před Týnem (Týn Church). The exterior of this 15th-century cathedral, with its twin gold-tipped, jet-black spires, is a sterling example of Prague Gothic.

Národní galérie (National Gallery). Spread among a half-dozen branches around the city, the National Gallery's collections span most major periods of European art, from medieval and Baroque masters to a vast constructivist gallery of 20th-century Czech and European works.

Strahovský klášter (Strahov Monastery). Now a museum of national literature, this monastery is known for its collection of early Czech manuscripts and the striking fresco on the ceiling of its Philosophical Hall.

Židovské muzeum v Praze (Prague Jewish Museum). Actually a collection of several must-see sights and exhibits, the Jewish Museum includes the Old Jewish Cemetery, crowded with tombstones, and several historic synagogues.

Budapest

Mátyás Templom (Matthias Church). Castle Hill's soaring Gothic church is colorfully ornate inside with lavishly frescoed Byzantine pillars.

Nagy Zsinagóga (Great Synagogue). This giant Byzantine-Moorish beauty (Europe's largest synagogue) underwent a massive restoration four decades after being ravaged by Hungarian and German Nazis during World War II.

Néprajzi Múzeum (Museum of Ethnography). A majestic 1890s structure across from the Parliament building—the lavish marble entrance hall alone is worth a visit—houses an impressive exhibit on Hungary's historic folk traditions.

Szent István Bazilika (St. Stephen's Basilica). Inside this massive neo-Renaissance beauty, the capital's biggest church, is a rich collection of mosaics and statuary, as well as the mummified right hand of Hungary's first king and patron saint, St. Stephen.

Szépművészeti Múzeum (Museum of Fine Arts). Hungary's best collection of fine art includes esteemed works by Dutch and Spanish old masters, as well as exhibits of major Hungarian artists.

2 PRAGUE

The "hundred-spired" capital city of
Prague—one of the world's best-preserved
architectural cityscapes—offers world-class
cultural performances and increasingly
distinctive dining and shopping. In the
countryside beyond, medieval castles perch
quietly near lost-in-time Baroque and
Renaissance villages.

A VICTIM OF ENFORCED OBSCURITY throughout much of the 20th century, the Czech Republic, encompassing the provinces of Bohemia and Moravia, is once again in the spotlight. In 1989, in a world where revolution was synonymous with violence and in a country where truth was quashed by the tanks of Eastern-bloc socialism, Václav Havel's sonorous voice proclaimed the victory of the "Velvet Revolution" to enthusiastic crowds on Wenceslas Square and preached the value of "living in truth." Recording the dramatic events of the time, television cameras panned across Prague's glorious skyline and fired the world's imagination with the image of political renewal superimposed on somber Gothic and voluptuous baroque.

By Mark Baker

Updated by
Raymond
Johnston

Travelers have rediscovered the country, and Bohemians and Moravians have rediscovered the world. The stagnant "normalization" of the last two decades under Communist rule gave way in the 1990s to a new dynamism and international outlook. You now encounter enthusiasm and such conveniences as English-language newspapers and attentive service. Not that the Czech Republic has joined the ranks of "Western" countries—it remains the poor relation compared with its Central European neighbors Germany and Austria, with the average Czech worker's wage standing at around $400 a month. This makes the signs of modernity even more remarkable. Nowadays there are cybercafés and cell phones to help you stay in touch with the outer world. It's all happening fastest in Prague, but the pace of change is accelerating everywhere. In the small towns and villages where so many Czechs still live, however, you may struggle with a creeping sensation of melancholy and neglect—or, putting a positive spin on it, you may enjoy the slower, more relaxed tempo.

The experience of visiting the Czech Republic still involves stepping back in time. Even in Prague, now deluged by tourists two-thirds of the year, the sense of history—stretching back through centuries of wars, empires, and monuments to everyday life—remains uncluttered by the trappings of modernity. The peculiar melancholy of Central Europe still lurks in narrow streets and forgotten corners. Crumbling facades, dilapidated palaces, and treacherous cobbled streets both shock and enchant the visitor used to a world where what remains of history has been spruced up for tourist eyes.

The arrival of designer boutiques, chain restaurants, and shopping malls does mean that the country has lost some of the "feel" it had just a few years ago. Although the dark side of freedom—rising unemployment and corruption—began to hit home in the late 1990s, the Czechs continued to move toward harmonization with Western ways. The country joined the NATO alliance in 1999 and will become a European Union member state, perhaps as early as 2004. Yet the process goes slowly. Economic and social integration into the "common European home," which in the postrevolutionary euphoria seemed possible within a few years, must now be measured in decades.

The strange, old-world, and at times frustratingly bureaucratic atmosphere of the Czech Republic is not all a product of the Communist era. Many of the everyday rituals are actually remnants of the Hapsburg Empire and are also to be found, perhaps to a lesser degree, in Vienna and Budapest. The *šatna* (coat room), for example, plays a vivid role in any visit to a restaurant or theater at any time of year other than summer. Coats must be given with a few coins to the attendant, usually an old lady with a sharp eye for ignorant or disobedient tourists.

The key to enjoying Prague is to relax. There is no point in demanding high levels of service or quality. And for the budget-conscious traveler, this is Central Europe at its most beautiful, at prices that are several times lower than those of Austria and Germany.

It's been more than a decade since November 17, 1989, when Prague's students took to the streets to help bring down the 40-year-old Communist regime, and in that time the city has enjoyed an exhilarating cultural renaissance. Amid Prague's cobblestone streets and gold-tipped spires, new galleries, cafés, and clubs teem with young Czechs (the middle-aged are generally too busy trying to make a living) and members of the city's colony of "expatriates." New shops and, perhaps most noticeably, scads of new restaurants have opened, expanding the city's culinary reach far beyond the traditional roast pork and dumplings. Many have something to learn in the way of presentation and service, but Praguers still marvel at a variety that was unthinkable not so many years ago.

The arts and theater are also thriving in the "new" Prague. Young playwrights, some writing in English, regularly stage their own works. Weekly poetry readings are standing room only. Classical music maintains its famous standards, while rock, jazz, and dance clubs are jammed nightly. The arts of the new era—nonverbal theater, "installation" art, world music—are as trendy in Prague as in any European capital but possess a distinctive Czech flavor.

All of this frenetic activity plays well against a stunning backdrop of towering churches and centuries-old bridges and alleyways. Prague achieved much of its present glory in the 14th century, during the long reign of Charles IV, king of Bohemia and Moravia and Holy Roman Emperor. It was Charles who established a university in the city and laid out the New Town, charting Prague's growth.

During the 15th century, the city's development was hampered by the Hussite Wars, a series of crusades launched by the Holy Roman Empire to subdue the fiercely independent Czech noblemen. The Czechs were eventually defeated in 1620 at the Battle of White Mountain (Bílá Hora) near Prague and were ruled by the Hapsburg family for the next 300 years. Under the Hapsburgs, Prague became a German-speaking city and an important administrative center, but it was forced to play second fiddle to the monarchy's capital, Vienna. Much of the Lesser Quarter, on the left bank of the Vltava, was built up at this time, and there you could find the Austrian nobility and its baroque tastes.

Prague regained its status as a national capital in 1918, with the creation of the modern Czechoslovak state, and quickly asserted itself in the interwar period as a vital cultural center. Although the city escaped World War II essentially intact, Czechoslovakia fell under the political and cultural domination of the Soviet Union until the 1989 popular uprisings. The election of dissident playwright Václav Havel to the post of national president set the stage for the city's renaissance, which has since proceeded at a dizzying, quite Bohemian rate. Although Prague was beset by massive floods in 2002, most of the tourism infrastructure was only temporarily affected, and things are back to normal now.

Pleasures and Pastimes

Boating and Sailing

The country's main boating area is the enormous series of dams and reservoirs along the Vltava south of Prague. The most popular reservoir is Slapy, an hour's drive due south of the capital, where it is possible to rent small paddleboats or relax and swim on a hot day. Rowboats are available for rent along Prague's Vltava in summertime.

Dining

The quality of restaurant cuisine and service in the Czech Republic remains uneven. The exception is found in the capital, where dozens of restaurants compete for an increasingly discriminating clientele. The traditional dishes—roast pork or duck with dumplings, or broiled meat with sauce—can be light and tasty when well prepared. Grilled pond trout appears on most menus and is often the best item available. An annoying "cover charge" (20 Kč–50 Kč in expensive places) usually makes its way onto restaurant bills, seemingly to subsidize the salt and pepper shakers. You should discreetly check the bill, since a few unscrupulous proprietors still overcharge foreigners.

Restaurants generally fall into three categories. A *pivnice* or *hospoda* (beer hall) usually offers a simple, inexpensive menu of goulash or pork with dumplings. The atmosphere tends to be friendly and casual, and you can expect to share a table. More attractive, and more expensive, are the *vinárna* (wine cellar) and the *restaurace* (restaurant), which serve a full menu. Wine cellars, some occupying Romanesque basements, can be a real treat.

Ignoring the familiar fast-food outlets that are now a common sight, the quickest and cheapest dining option is the *lahůdky* (snack bar or deli). In larger towns, the *kavárna* (café) and *čajovna* (tea house) are ever more popular—and welcome—additions to the dining scene.

Lunch, usually eaten between noon and 2, is the main meal for Czechs and the best deal. Many restaurants put out a special luncheon menu (*denní lístek*), with more appetizing selections at better prices. If you don't see it, ask your waiter. Dinner is usually served from 5 until 9 or 10, but don't wait too long to eat. Most Czechs eat only a light meal in the evening. Also, restaurant cooks frequently knock off early on slow nights, and the later you arrive, the more likely it is that the kitchen will be closed. In general, dinner menus do not differ substantially from lunch offerings, except the prices are higher.

CATEGORY	PRAGUE*	OTHER AREAS*
$$$$	over 500 Kč	over 400 Kč
$$$	350–500 Kč	250–400 Kč
$$	150–350 Kč	100–250 Kč
$	under 150 Kč	under 100 Kč

per person for a main course at dinner

Lodging

The number of hotels and pensions has increased dramatically throughout the Czech Republic, in step with the influx of tourists. Finding a suitable room should pose no problem, although it is highly recommended that you book ahead during the peak tourist season (nationwide, July and August; in Prague, April through October and the Christmas, New Year, and Easter holidays). Hotel prices, in general, remain high. This is especially true in Prague and in the spa towns of western Bohemia. Some Prague hotels reduce rates slightly in July and August, when many European travelers prefer to head for the beaches. Better value can often be found at private pensions and with individual home owners offering rooms to let. In the outlying towns, the best strategy is to inquire at the local tourist information office or simply fan out around the town and look for room-for-rent signs on houses (usually in German: ZIMMER FREI or PRIVATZIMMER).

Most of the old-fashioned hotels away from the major tourist centers, invariably situated on a town's main square, have been modernized and now provide private bathrooms in most or all rooms and a higher comfort level throughout. Newer hotels, often impersonal concrete boxes, tend to be found on the outskirts of towns; charming, older buildings in the center of town, newly transformed into hotels and pensions, are often the best choice. Bare-bones hostels are a popular means of circumventing Prague's summer lodging crunch; many now stay open all year. In the mountains you can often find little *chaty* (chalets), where pleasant surroundings compensate for a lack of basic amenities. *Autokempink* parks (campsites) generally have a few bungalows.

Czech hotels set their own star ratings, which more or less match the international star system. Often you can book rooms—both at hotels and in private homes—through visitor bureaus. Otherwise, try contacting the hotel directly. Keep in mind that in many hotels, except at the deluxe level, a "double" bed means two singles that can be pushed together. (Single-mattress double beds are generally not available.)

At certain times, such as Easter and during festivals, prices can jump 15%–25%. As a rule, always ask the price before taking a room. Your best bet for lodging in the $ price range will usually be a private room. Unless otherwise noted, breakfast is included in the rate.

As for camping, there are hundreds of sites for tents and trailers throughout the country, but most are open only in summer (May–mid-September), although a number of campsites in and around Prague have year-round operation. You can get a map from the Prague Information Service of all the sites, with addresses, opening times, and facilities. Camping outside official sites is prohibited. Campgrounds generally have hot water and toilets.

CATEGORY	PRAGUE*	OTHER AREAS*
$$$$	over 7,000 Kč	over 3,500 Kč
$$$	5,000–7,000 Kč	2,500–3,500 Kč
$$	2,500–5,000 Kč	1,000–2,500 Kč
$	under 2,500 Kč	under 1,000 Kč

All prices are for a standard double room during peak season, including breakfast.

Shopping

In Prague, Karlovy Vary, and elsewhere in Bohemia, look for elegant and unusual crystal and porcelain. Bohemia is also renowned for the quality and deep-red color of its garnets; keep an eye out for beautiful garnet rings and brooches. You can also find excellent ceramics, especially in Moravia, as well as other folk artifacts, such as printed textiles, lace, hand-knit sweaters, and painted eggs. There are attractive crafts stores throughout the Czech Republic. In Karlovy Vary buy the strange pipelike drinking mugs used in the spas; vases left to petrify in the mineral-laden water; and Becherovka, a tasty herbal aperitif that makes a nice gift to take home.

Wine and Beer

Czechs are reputed to drink more beer per capita than any other people on Earth; small wonder, as many connoisseurs rank Bohemian lager-style beer as the best in the world. This cool, crisp brew was invented in Plzeň in 1842, although Czech beer had already been brewed for centuries prior to that time. Aside from the world-famous Plzeňský Prazdroj (Pilsner Urquell) and milder Budvar (the original Budweiser) brands, some typical beers are the slightly bitter Krušovice; fruity Radegast; and the sweeter, Prague-brewed Staropramen. *Světlé pivo*, or golden beer, is most common, although many pubs also serve *černé* (dark), which is often slightly sweeter than the light variety.

Czechs also produce quite drinkable wines: peppy, fruity whites and mild, versatile reds. Southern Moravia, with comparatively warm summers and rich soil, grows the bulk of the wine harvest. Look for the Mikulov and Znojmo regional designations. Favorite white varietals are Müller-Thurgau, with a fine muscat bouquet and light flavor, and Neuburské, yellow-green in color and with a dry, smoky bouquet. Rulandské bílé, a semidry burgundy-like white, has a flowery bouquet and full-bodied flavor. Belying the notion that northerly climes are more auspicious for white than red grapes, northern Bohemia's scant few hundred acres of vineyards produce reliable reds and the occasional jewel. Frankovka is fiery red and slightly acidic, while the cherry-red Rulandské červené is an excellent, drier choice. Vavřinecké is dark and slightly sweet.

EXPLORING PRAGUE

The spine of the city is the River Vltava (also known by its German name, Moldau), which runs through the city from south to north with a single sharp curve to the east. Prague originally comprised five independent towns, represented today by its main historic districts: Hradčany (Castle Area), Malá Strana (Lesser Quarter), Staré Město (Old Town), Nové Město (New Town), and Josefov (the Jewish Quarter).

Hradčany, the seat of Czech royalty for hundreds of years, has as its center the Pražský hrad (Prague Castle), which overlooks the city from its hilltop west of the Vltava. Steps lead down from Hradčany to the Lesser Quarter, an area dense with ornate mansions built by 17th- and 18th-century nobility.

Karlův most (Charles Bridge) connects the Lesser Quarter with the Old Town. Just a few blocks east of the bridge is the district's focal point, Staroměstské náměstí (Old Town Square). The Old Town is bounded by the curving Vltava and three large commercial avenues: Revoluční to the east, Na Příkopě to the southeast, and Národní třída to the south. North of Old Town Square, the diminutive Jewish Quarter fans out around the wide avenue called Pařížská.

Beyond the Old Town to the south is the New Town, a highly commercial area that includes the city's largest square, Karlovo náměstí (Charles Square). Roughly 1 km (½ mi) farther south is Vyšehrad, an ancient castle high above the river.

On a promontory to the east of Václavské náměstí (Wenceslas Square) stretches Vinohrady, once the favored neighborhood of well-to-do Czechs. Bordering Vinohrady are the crumbling neighborhoods of Žižkov to the north and Nusle to the south. On the west bank of the Vltava lie many older residential neighborhoods and several sprawling parks. About 3 km (2 mi) from the center in every direction, Communist-era housing projects begin their unsightly sprawl.

Great Itineraries

IF YOU HAVE ONE OR TWO DAYS

Even during such a short stay, you can get a strong taste of Prague's historical richness and buzzing energy. Start at the top with the hilltop Pražský hrad (Prague Castle), visiting the soaring, Gothic Chrám svatého Víta (St. Vitus's Cathedral) and the Královský palác (Royal Palace) and drinking in views of the city. To get to or from the castle, walk along Nerudova ulice, a steep street lined with burgher's homes—and little restaurants if you need a break. Cross over the river to the Staré Město (Old Town) and the very center of historic Prague: Staroměstské náměstí (Old Town Square). Try to time your visit to coincide with the hourly performance of the astronomical clock on the Staroměstská radnice (Old Town Hall); you can also visit the Gothic-on-the-outside, Baroque-on-the-inside Kostel Panny Marie před Týnem

14

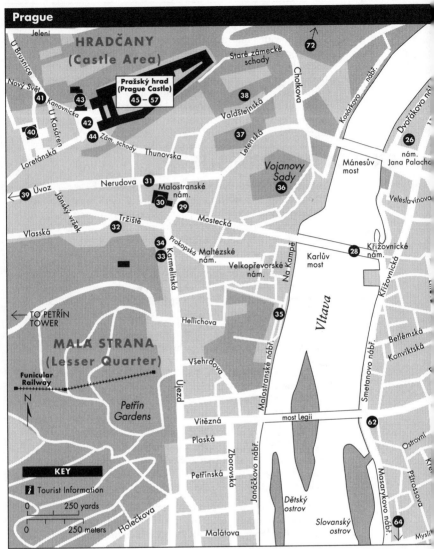

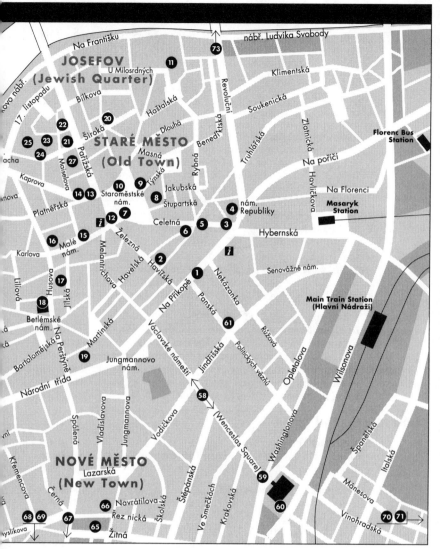

JOSEFOV
(Jewish Quarter)

STARÉ MĚSTO
(Old Town)

Florenc Bus
Station

Masaryk
Station

Main Train Station
(Hlavní Nádraží)

NOVÉ MĚSTO
(New Town)

(Týn Church). Stretching southeast of the Old Town is Václavské náměstí (Wenceslas Square), actually a long avenue humming with activity—be sure to duck into some of the arcades that branch off the boulevard. In the evening, go back toward the river for the unforgettable view from the statue-lined Karlův most (Charles Bridge). If you have another morning here, head to the Josefov (Jewish quarter) early, before the crowds of tourists pack its tiny streets. You can also dip into the Malá Strana (Lesser Quarter) to see the voluptuous Baroque curves of Chrám svatého Mikuláše (St. Nicholas Church).

IF YOU HAVE THREE TO FIVE DAYS

With a few extra days, you can devote more time to the historic quarters, spending most of a day taking in the castle and later visiting the Strahovský klášter (Strahov Monastery) and Národní galerie (National Gallery) in the castle district. You could also duck into one of the city's beautiful gardens, such as the Vrtbovská zahrada (Vrtba Garden), or take a ride on one of the many sightseeing boats that ply the Vltava River. If you're interested in modern architecture, head to the Nové Město (New Town), where you can see the "Fred and Ginger" building by Frank Gehry and Vlado Milunić as well as several Cubist buildings. For indoor modern art, head to either the Galerie hl. města Prahy (Prague City Gallery) or the Galerie Rudolfinum, both in the Old Town, or check out the Veletržní palác (Trade Fair Palace) gallery.

IF YOU HAVE FIVE TO SEVEN DAYS

Besides the explorations described above, take a quick trip out to the spa towns in Western Bohemia. The rich, famous, and curious flocked here in the 19th century, and you can walk through the colonnades and sip the waters that drew everyone from Chopin to Mark Twain to Karl Marx. The classic resort hotels in Karlovy Vary or Mariánské Lázně are tempting places to overnight.

Staré Město (Old Town)

A Good Walk

Numbers in the text correspond to numbers in the margin and on the Prague map.

Ever-hopping Wenceslas Square, convenient to hotels and transportation, is an excellent place to begin a tour of the Old Town, although it actually lies within the New Town. To begin the approach to the Old Town proper, start at the lower end of the square, walk past the tall art deco Koruna complex, and turn right onto the handsome pedestrian zone of **Na Příkopě** ①. Turn left onto Havířská ulice and follow this small alley to the glittering green-and-cream splendor of the 18th-century theater called the **Stavovské divadlo** ②.

Return to Na Příkopě, turn left, and continue to the end of the street. On weekdays between 8 AM and 5 PM, it's well worth taking a peek at the stunning interior of the Živnostenská banka (Merchant's Bank), at No. 20.

Na Příkopě ends abruptly at náměstí Republiky (Republic Square), an important New Town transportation hub (with a metro stop). The severe Depression-era facade of the Česká Národní banka (at Na Příkopě 30) makes the building look more like a fortress than the nation's central bank. Close by stands a stately tower, the **Prašná brána** ③, its festive Gothic spires looming above the square. Adjacent to this dignified building, the **Obecní dům** ④ concert hall looks decidedly decadent.

Walk through the arch at the base of the Prašná brána and down the formal **Celetná ulice** ⑤, the first leg of the so-called Royal Way. Monarchs favored this route primarily because the houses along Celetná were among the city's finest, providing a suitable backdrop to the coronation procession. Baroque influence is even visible in the Cubist department store **Dům U černé Matky Boží** ⑥, now a museum.

Staroměstské náměstí ⑦, at the end of Celetná, is dazzling, thanks partly to the double-spired **Kostel Panny Marie před Týnem** ⑧, which rises over the square from behind a row of patrician houses. To the immediate left of this church, at No. 13, is Dům U Kamenného zvonu (House at the Stone Bell), a baroque town house that has been stripped down to its original Gothic elements.

Next door stands the gorgeous pink-and-ocher **Palác Kinských** ⑨. At this end of the square, you can't help noticing the expressive **Jan Hus monument** ⑩. At this point, you may wish to take a detour to see the National Gallery's Gothic art collection at **Klášter svaté Anežky České** ⑪. Go northeast from the square up Dlouha Street, and then straight along Kozi Street all the way until it ends at U Milosrdných.

Return to Staroměstské náměstí, and just beyond the Jan Hus monument is the Gothic **Staroměstská radnice** ⑫, which, with its impressive 200-ft tower, gives the square its sense of importance. As the hour approaches, join the crowds milling below the tower's 15th-century astronomical clock for a brief but spooky spectacle taken straight from the Middle Ages, every hour on the hour. The square's second church, the baroque **Kostel svatého Mikuláše** ⑬, is not to be confused with the Lesser Quarter's Chrám svatého Mikuláše on the other side of the river.

You'll find the **Franz Kafka Exposition** ⑭ adjoining Kostel svatého Mikuláše on náměstí Franze Kafky, a little square that used to be part of U Radnice Street. Continue along U Radnice proper just a few yards until you come to **Malé náměstí** ⑮, a mini-square with arcades on one side. Look for tiny Karlova ulice, which begins in the southwest corner of the square, and take another quick right to stay on it (watch the signs—this medieval street seems designed to confound the visitor). At the České muzeum výtvarných umění (Czech Museum of Fine Arts), pause and inspect the exotic **Clam-Gallas palác** ⑯, behind you at Husova 20. You'll recognize it easily: look for the Titans in the doorway holding up what must be a very heavy baroque facade. Head the other way down Husova for a glimpse of ecstatic baroque stuffed inside somber Gothic at the **Kostel svatého Jiljí** ⑰, at No. 8.

Continue walking along Husova to Na Perštýně and turn right at tiny Betlémská ulice. The alley opens up onto a quiet square, Betlémské náměstí, and upon the most revered of all Hussite churches in Prague, the **Betlémská kaple** ⑱.

Return to Na Perštýně and continue walking to the right. As you near the back of the buildings of the busy Národní třída (National Boulevard), turn left at Martinská ulice. At the end of the street, the forlorn but majestic church **Kostel svatého Martina ve zdi** ⑲ looks as if it got lost. Walk around the church to the left and through a little archway of apartments onto the bustling Národní třída. To the left, a five-minute walk away, lies Wenceslas Square and the starting point of this walk.

TIMING

Wenceslas Square and Old Town Square are busy with activity around-the-clock almost all year round. If you're in search of a little peace and quiet, you will find the streets at their most subdued on early weekend mornings or right after a sudden downpour. The streets in this walking tour are reasonably close together and can be covered in a half-day.

Remember to be in the Old Town Square just before the hour if you want to see the astronomical clock in action.

Sights to See

® **Betlémská kaple** (Bethlehem Chapel). The original church was built at the end of the 14th century, and the Czech religious reformer Jan Hus was a regular preacher here from 1402 until his exile in 1412. After the Thirty Years' War the church fell into the hands of the Jesuits and was finally demolished in 1786. Excavations carried out after World War I uncovered the original portal and three windows, and the entire church was reconstructed during the 1950s. Although little remains of the first church, some remnants of Hus's teachings can still be read on the inside walls. ⊠ *Betlémské nám. 5, Staré Město.* 🖭 *30 Kč.* ☉ *Daily 10–5.*

❺ **Celetná ulice.** Most of this street's facades indicate the buildings are from the 17th or 18th century, but appearances are deceiving: many of the houses in fact have parts that date back to the 12th century. Be sure to look above the street-level storefronts to see the fine examples of baroque detail.

⑯ **Clam-Gallas palác** (Clam-Gallas Palace). The beige-and-brown palace, the work of Johann Bernhard Fischer von Erlach, the famed Viennese architectural virtuoso of the day, was begun in 1713 and finally finished in 1729. Enter the building for a glimpse of the finely carved staircase, the work of the master himself, and of the Italian frescoes featuring Apollo that surround it. The building now houses the municipal archives and is rarely open to visitors (so walk in as if you have business there). Classical music concerts are sometimes held in the Great Hall in the evening, which is one way to peek inside. ⊠ *Husova 20, Staré Město,* ⓦ *www.ahmp.cz/eng.* ☉ *Weekdays 8–4.*

❻ **Dům U černé Matky Boží** (House of the Black Madonna). In the second decade of the 20th century, young Czech architects boldly applied Cubism's radical reworking of visual space to structures. Adding a decided jolt to the architectural styles along Celetná, this Cubist building, designed by Josef Gočár, is unflinchingly modern yet topped with an almost baroque tile roof. The museum interior was renovated in 2002 to better suit the permanent collection of Cubist art. A café in the basement reopened as well. ⊠ *Celetná 34, Staré Město,* ☎ *224–211–732,* ⓦ *www.ngprague.cz.* 🖭 *100 Kč.* ☉ *Tues.–Sun. 10–6.*

⑭ **Franz Kafka Exposition.** Kafka came into the world on July 3, 1883, in a house next to the Kostel svatého Mikuláše (Church of St. Nicholas). For years the writer was only grudgingly acknowledged by the Communist cultural bureaucrats, reflecting the traditionally ambiguous attitude of the Czech government toward his work. As a German and a Jew, moreover, Kafka could easily be dismissed as standing outside the mainstream of Czech literature. Following the 1989 revolution, however, Kafka's popularity soared, and his works are now widely available in Czech. Though only the portal of the original house remains, inside the building is a fascinating little exhibit (mostly photographs) on Kafka's life, with commentary in English. ⊠ *Nám. Franze Kafky 3, Staré Město.* 🖭 *50 Kč.* ☉ *Tues.–Fri. 10–6, Sat. 10–5.*

❿ **Jan Hus monument.** Few memorials have elicited as much controversy as this one, which was dedicated in July 1915, exactly 500 years after Hus was burned at the stake in Constance, Germany. Some maintain that the monument's Secessionist style (the inscription seems to come right from turn-of-the-20th-century Vienna) clashes with the Gothic and baroque of the square. Others dispute the romantic depiction of Hus, who appears here in flowing garb as tall and bearded. The real

Hus, historians maintain, was short and had a baby face. Still, no one can take issue with the influence of this fiery preacher, whose ability to transform doctrinal disputes, both literally and metaphorically, into the language of the common man made him into a religious and national symbol for the Czechs. ⊠ *Staroměstské nám., Staré Město.*

⑪ Klášter svaté Anežky České (St. Agnes's Convent). Situated near the river between Pařížská and Revoluční streets, this peaceful complex has Prague's first buildings in the Gothic style, built between the 1230s and the 1280s. The convent now provides a fitting home for the National Gallery's marvelous collection of Czech Gothic art, including altarpieces, portraits, and statues. ⊠ *U Milosrdných 17, Staré Město,* ☎ 224–810–628, WEB *www.ngprague.cz.* ⌁ *100 Kč.* ☾ *Tues.–Sun. 10–6.*

★ ⑧ Kostel Panny Marie před Týnem (Church of the Virgin Mary Before Týn). The exterior of the church is one of the best examples of Prague Gothic and is in part the work of Peter Parler, architect of the Charles Bridge and Chrám svatého Víta (St. Vitus's Cathedral). Construction of its twin black-spire towers was begun later, by King Jiří of Poděbrad in 1461, during the heyday of the Hussites. Jiří had a gilded chalice, the symbol of the Hussites, proudly displayed on the front gable between the two towers. Following the defeat of the Czech Protestants by the Catholic Hapsburgs, the chalice was removed and eventually replaced by a Madonna. As a final blow, the chalice was melted down and made into the Madonna's glimmering halo (you still can see it by walking into the center of the square and looking up between the spires). The entrance to the church is through the arcades on Old Town Square, under the house at No. 604.

Much of the interior, including the tall nave, was rebuilt in the baroque style in the 17th century. Some Gothic pieces remain, however: look to the left of the main altar for a beautifully preserved set of early Gothic carvings. The main altar itself was painted by Karel Škréta, a luminary of the Czech baroque. Before leaving the church, look for the grave marker (tucked away to the right of the main altar) of the great Danish astronomer Tycho Brahe, who came to Prague as "Imperial Mathematicus" in 1599 under Rudolf II. As a scientist, Tycho had a place in history that is assured: Johannes Kepler (another resident of the Prague court) used Tycho's observations to formulate his laws of planetary motion. But it is myth that has endeared Tycho to the hearts of Prague residents. The robust Dane, who was apparently fond of duels, lost part of his nose in one (take a closer look at the marker). He quickly had a wax nose fashioned for everyday use but preferred to parade around on holidays and festive occasions sporting a bright silver one. ⊠ *Staroměstské nám, between Celetná and Týnská, Staré Město.*

⑰ Kostel svatého Jiljí (Church of St. Giles). This church was an important outpost of Czech Protestantism in the 16th century. The exterior is a powerful example of Gothic architecture, including the buttresses and a characteristic portal. The interior, as in many important Czech churches, is baroque, with a design by Johann Bernhard Fischer von Erlach and sweeping frescoes by Václav Reiner. The interior can be viewed during the day from the vestibule or at the evening concerts held several times a week. ⊠ *Husova 8, Staré Město.*

⑲ Kostel svatého Martina ve zdi (Church of St. Martin-in-the-Wall). It was here in 1414 that Holy Communion was first given to the Bohemian laity in the form of both bread and wine, in defiance of the Catholic custom of the time, which dictated that only bread was to be offered to the masses, with wine reserved for the priests and clergy. From then on, the chalice came to symbolize the Hussite movement. The church is open for evening concerts, held several times each week. ⊠ *Martinská ul., Staré Město.*

⓭ Kostel svatého Mikuláše (Church of St. Nicholas). Designed in the 18th century by Prague's own master of late baroque, Kilian Ignaz Dientzenhofer, this church is probably less successful in capturing the style's lyric exuberance than its namesake across town, the Chrám svatého Mikuláše. Still, Dientzenhofer utilized the limited space to create a well-balanced structure. The interior is compact, with a beautiful but small chandelier and an enormous black organ that seems to overwhelm the rear of the church. The church hosts almost continuous afternoon and evening tourist concerts. ⊠ *Staroměstské nám., Staré Město.* ☉ *Apr.–Oct., Mon. noon–4, Tues.–Sat. 10–4, Sun. noon–3; Nov.–Mar., Tues., Fri., and Sun. 10–noon; Wed. 10–4.*

⓯ Malé náměstí (Small Square). Note the iron fountain dating from around 1560 in the center of the square. The colorfully painted house at No. 3, originally a hardware store, is not as old as it looks, but here and there you can find authentic Gothic portals and Renaissance sgraffiti that betray the square's true age.

❶ Na Příkopě. The name means "At the Moat" and harks back to the time when the street was indeed a moat separating the Old Town from the New Town. Today the pedestrian zone Na Příkopě is prime shopping territory. At No. 19 an oversize new building, one of the worst excesses of the 1990s in Prague, houses a Marks & Spencer store. Have a look at the chic, hard-edged black-and-white Černá Růže (Black Rose) arcade at No. 12. A little ways farther at No. 22, the late-18th-century neoclassical facade of Slovanský dům hides a modern mall filled with stores, restaurants, and a cinema multiplex.

❹ Obecní dům (Municipal House). The city's Art Nouveau showpiece still fills the role it had when it was completed in 1911: it's a center for concerts, rotating art exhibits, and café society. The mature Art Nouveau style recalls the lengths the Czech middle classes went to at the turn of the 20th century to imitate Paris, then the epitome of style and glamour. Much of the interior bears the work of Art Nouveau master Alfons Mucha, Max Švabinský, and other leading Czech artists. Mucha decorated the Hall of the Lord Mayor upstairs with impressive, magical frescoes depicting Czech history; unfortunately it's not open to the public. The beautiful **Smetanova síň** (Smetana Hall), which hosts concerts by the Prague Symphony Orchestra as well as international players, is on the second floor. The ground-floor café is touristy but lovely with its glimmering chandeliers and exquisite woodwork. There's also a beer hall in the cellar with passable beer, mediocre food, and superbly executed ceramic murals on the walls. ⊠ *Nám. Republiky 5, Staré Město,* ☎ *222–002–100,* W̅E̅B̅ *www.obecnidum.cz.* ☉ *Information center and box office daily 10–6.*

NEED A BREAK? If you prefer subtle elegance, head around the corner from the Obecní dům to the café at the **Hotel Paříž** (⊠ U Obecního domu 1, Staré Město, ☎ 224–222–151), a Jugendstil jewel tucked away on a relatively quiet street.

---

❾ Palác Kinských (Kinský Palace). This exuberant building, built in 1765 from Kilian Ignaz Dientzenhofer's design, is considered one of Prague's finest late-baroque structures. With its exaggerated pink overlay and numerous statues, the facade looks extreme when contrasted with the more staid baroque elements of other nearby buildings. (The interior, however, was "modernized" under Communism.) The palace once housed a German school—where Franz Kafka was a student for nine misery-laden years—and presently contains the National Gallery's graphics collection. It was from this building that Communist leader Klement Gottwald, flanked by his Slovak comrade Vladimír Clementis, first addressed the crowds after seizing power in February 1948—an event recounted in the first chapter of Milan Kundera's novel *The Book of Laughter and Forgetting.* ⊠ *Staroměstské nám. 12, Staré Město,* ☎ *224–210–758,* WEB *www.ngprague.cz.* 🔊 *100 Kč.* ⊘ *Tues.–Sun. 10–6.*

❸ Prašná brána (Powder Tower). Construction of the tower, which replaced one of the city's 13 original gates, was begun by King Vladislav II of Jagiello in 1475. At the time, the kings of Bohemia maintained their royal residence next door, on the site of the current Obecní dům, and the tower was intended to be the grandest gate of all. But Vladislav was Polish and thus heartily disliked by the rebellious Czech citizens of Prague. Nine years after he assumed power, fearing for his life, he moved the royal court across the river to Prague Castle. Work on the tower was abandoned, and the half-finished structure was used for storing gunpowder—hence its odd name—until the end of the 17th century. The oldest part of the tower is the base. The golden spires were not added until the end of the 19th century. Climb to the top for a striking view of the Old Town and Prague Castle in the distance. ⊠ *Nám. Republiky, Staré Město.* 🔊 *30 Kč.* ⊘ *Apr.–Oct., daily 9–6.*

★ ⑫ Staroměstská radnice (Old Town Hall). This is one of Prague's magnets: hundreds of people gravitate to it to see the hour struck by the mechanical figures of the **astronomical clock.** Just before the hour, look to the upper part of the clock, where a skeleton begins by tolling a death knell and turning an hourglass upside down. The Twelve Apostles parade momentarily, and then a cockerel flaps its wings and crows, piercing the air as the hour finally strikes. To the right of the skeleton, the dreaded Turk nods his head, seemingly hinting at another invasion like those of the 16th and 17th centuries. This small spectacle doesn't clue viewers in to the way this 15th-century marvel indicates the time—by the season, the zodiac sign, and the positions of the sun and moon. The calendar under the clock dates from the mid-19th century.

The Old Town Hall served as the center of administration for the Old Town beginning in 1338, when King John of Luxembourg first granted the city council the right to a permanent location. The impressive 200-ft **Town Hall Tower,** where the clock is mounted, was first built in the 14th century and given its current late-Gothic appearance around 1500 by the master Matyáš Rejsek. For a rare view of the Old Town and its maze of crooked streets and alleyways, climb the ramp or ride the elevator to the top of the tower.

If you walk around the hall to the left, you'll see it's actually a series of houses jutting into the square; they were purchased over the years and successively added to the complex. On the other side, jagged stonework reveals where a large, neo-Gothic wing once adjoined the tower until it was destroyed during fighting between townspeople and Nazi troops in May 1945.

Guided tours (most guides speak English, and English texts are on hand) of the Old Town Hall depart from the main desk inside. Previously unseen parts of the tower were opened to the public in 2002, and you can now see the inside of the famous clock. ⊠ *Staroměstské nám., Staré Město.* ⊘ *May–Sept., Tues.–Sun. 9–6, Mon. 11–6; Oct.–Apr., Tues.–Sun. 9–5, Mon. 11–5.* 🔊 *Tower 30 Kč, tours 40 Kč.*

★ ❼ Staroměstské náměstí (Old Town Square). There are places that, on first glimpse, stop you dead in your tracks in sheer wonder. Old Town Square is one such place. Long the heart of the Old Town, the square grew to its present proportions when the city's original marketplace was moved away from the river in the 12th century. Its shape and appearance have changed little over the years. During the day the square is festive, as musicians vie for the favor of onlookers and artists display renditions of Prague street scenes. At night, the gaudily lit towers of the Church of the Virgin Mary Before Týn rise ominously over the glowing baroque facades. The crowds thin out, and the ghosts of the square's stormy past return.

During the 15th century the square was the focal point of conflict between Czech Hussites and German Catholics. In 1422 the radical Hussite preacher Jan Želivský was executed here for his part in storming the New Town's town hall three years earlier. In the 1419 uprising, three Catholic consuls and seven German citizens were thrown out the window—the first of Prague's many famous defenestrations. Within a few years, the Hussites had taken over the town, expelled the Germans, and set up their own administration.

Twenty-seven white crosses set flat in the paving stones in the square, at the Old Town Hall's base, mark the spot where 27 Bohemian noblemen were killed by the Hapsburgs in 1621 during the dark days following the defeat of the Czechs at the Battle of White Mountain. The grotesque spectacle, designed to quash any further national or religious opposition, took some five hours to complete, as the men were put to the sword or hanged one by one.

One of the most interesting houses on the Old Town Square juts out into the small extension leading into Malé náměstí. The house, called **U Minuty** (⊠ 3 Staroměstské nám., Staré Město), with its 16th-century Renaissance sgraffiti of biblical and classical motifs, was the home of the young Franz Kafka in the 1890s.

❷ **Stavovské divadlo** (Estates Theater). Built in the 1780s in the classical style, this handsome theater was for many years a beacon of Czech-language culture in a city long dominated by the German variety. It is probably best known as the site of the world premiere of Mozart's opera *Don Giovanni* in October 1787, with the composer himself conducting. Prague audiences were quick to acknowledge Mozart's genius: the opera was an instant hit here, though it flopped nearly everywhere else in Europe. Mozart wrote most of the opera's second act in Prague at the Villa Bertramka, where he was a frequent guest. You must attend a performance here to see inside. ⊠ *Ovocný tř. 1, Staré Město,* ☎ *224–215–001 box office,* WEB *www.narodni-divadlo.cz.*

Josefov (Jewish Quarter)

Prague's Jews survived centuries of discrimination, but two unrelated events of modern times have left their historic ghetto little more than a collection of museums. Around 1900, city officials decided for hygienic purposes to raze the minuscule neighborhood—it had ceased to be a true ghetto with the political reforms of 1848–49, and by this time the majority of its residents were poor Gentiles—and pave over its crooked streets. Only some of the synagogues, the town hall, and the cemetery survived this early attempt at urban renewal. The second event was the Holocaust. Under Nazi occupation, a staggering percentage of the city's Jews were deported or murdered in concentration camps. Of the 35,000 Jews living in Prague before World War II, only about 1,200 returned to resettle the city after the war. The community is still tiny. Only a scant few Jews, mostly elderly, live in the "ghetto" today.

Treasures and artifacts of the ghetto are now the property of the **Židovské muzeum v Praze** (Prague Jewish Museum), which includes the

Old Jewish Cemetery and collections installed in four surviving syna-gogues and the Ceremony Hall. (The Staronová synagóga, or Old-New Synagogue, a functioning house of worship, technically does not belong to the museum, but the Prague Jewish Community oversees both.) The museum was founded in 1906 but traces the vast majority of its hold-ings to the Nazis' destruction of 150 Jewish communities in Bohemia and Moravia. Dedicated museum workers, nearly all of whom were to die at Nazi hands, gathered and cataloged the stolen artifacts under Ger-man supervision. Exhibitions were even held during the war. A ticket good for all museum sites may be purchased at any of the synagogues but the Old-New Synagogue; single-site tickets apply only at the Old-New Synagogue and during occasional exhibits at the Spanish Syna-gogue. All museum sites are closed Saturday and Jewish holidays.

Numbers in the text correspond to numbers in the margin and on the Prague map.

A Good Walk

To reach the Jewish Quarter, leave Old Town Square via handsome Pařížská ulice, centerpiece of the urban renewal effort, and head north toward the river. The festive atmosphere changes suddenly as you enter the area of the ghetto. The buildings are lower here; the mood is hushed. Take a right on Široká and stroll two blocks down to the recently restored **Španělská synagóga** ⑳. Head back the other way, past Pařížská, turn right on Maiselova, and you'll come to the **Židovská radnice** ㉑, which is now the Jewish Community Center. Adjoining it on Červená is the 16th-century High Synagogue. Across the street, at Červená 2, you see the **Staronová synagóga** ㉒, the oldest surviving synagogue in Prague.

Go west on the little street U starého hřbitova. The main museum ticket office is at the **Klausová synagóga** ㉓ at No. 3A. Separated from the synagogue by the exit gate of the Old Jewish Cemetery is the former building of the Jewish Burial Society, Obřadní síň, which exhibits tra-ditional Jewish funeral objects.

Return to Maiselova and follow it to Široká. Turn right to find the **Pinkasova synagóga** ㉔, a handsome Gothic structure. Here also is the entrance to the Jewish ghetto's most astonishing sight, the **Starý židovský hřbitov** ㉕.

For a small detour, head down Široká street to the **Rudolfinum** ㉖ con-cert hall and gallery; across the street is the Uměleckoprůmyslové muzeum (Museum of Decorative Arts). Both are notable neo-Renais-sance buildings.

Return to Maiselova once more and turn right in the direction of the Old Town. Look in at the displays of Czech Jewish history in the **Maiselova synagóga** ㉗.

TIMING

The Jewish Quarter is one of the most popular areas in Prague, espe-cially in the height of summer, when its tiny streets are jammed to burst-ing with tourists almost all the time. The best time for a quieter visit is early morning when the museums and cemetery first open. The area itself is very compact, and a fairly thorough tour should only take half a day, but don't go on the Sabbath (Saturday), when all the museums are closed.

Sights to See

❷❸ **Klausová synagóga** (Klausen Synagogue). This baroque former syn-agogue was built at the end of the 17th century in the place of three small buildings (a synagogue, school, and ritual bath) that were destroyed in a fire that devastated the ghetto in 1689. Inside, displays of Czech Jewish traditions emphasize celebrations and daily life. In the neo-Romanesque **Obřadní síň** (Ceremony Hall), which adjoins the Klausen Synagogue, the focus is on rather grim subjects: Jewish funeral paraphernalia, old gravestones, and medical instruments. Special attention is paid to the activities of the Jewish Burial Society through many fine objects and paintings. ⊠ *U starého hřbitova 3A, Josefov,* ☎ *224–819–456,* WEB *www.jewishmuseum.cz.* ◻ *Combined ticket to museum sites and Old-New Synagogue 500 Kč; museum sites only, 300 Kč.* ☉ *Apr.–Oct., Sun.–Fri. 9–6; Nov.–Mar., Sun.–Fri. 9–4:30.*

㉗ Maiselova synagóga (Maisel Synagogue). Here, the history of Czech Jews from the 10th to the 18th century is illustrated with the aid of some of the Prague Jewish Museum's most precious objects, including silver Torah shields and pointers, spice boxes, and candelabra; historic tombstones; and fine ceremonial textiles, including some donated by Mordechai Maisel to the synagogue he founded. The richest items come from the late 16th and early 17th century—a prosperous era for Prague's Jews. ⊠ *Maiselova 10, Josefov,* ☎ *224–819–456,* WEB *www.jewishmuseum.cz.* ◻ *Combined ticket to museum sites and Old-New Synagogue 500 Kč; museum sites only, 300 Kč.* ☉ *Apr.–Oct., Sun.–Fri. 9–6; Nov.–Mar., Sun.–Fri. 9–4:30.*

㉔ Pinkasova synagóga (Pinkas Synagogue). This synagogue has two particularly moving testimonies to the appalling crimes perpetrated against the Jews during World War II. One tribute astounds by sheer numbers: the inside walls are covered with nearly 80,000 names of Bohemian and Moravian Jews murdered by the Nazis. Among them are the names of the paternal grandparents of former U.S. Secretary of State Madeleine Albright, who learned of their fate only in 1997. There is also an exhibition of drawings made by children at the Nazi concentration camp Terezín. The Nazis used the camp for propaganda purposes to demonstrate their "humanity" toward the Jews, and prisoners were given relative freedom to lead "normal" lives. However, transports to death camps in Poland began in earnest in 1944, and many thousands of Terezín prisoners, including many of these children, eventually perished. The entrance to the old Jewish cemetery is through this synagogue. ⊠ *Enter from Široká 3, Josefov,* ☎ *224–819–456,* WEB *www.jewishmuseum.cz.* ◻ *Combined ticket to museum sites and Old-New Synagogue 500 Kč; museum sites only, 300 Kč.* ☉ *Apr.–Oct., Sun.–Fri. 9–6; Nov.–Mar., Sun.–Fri. 9–4:30.*

㉖ Rudolfinum. Thanks to a thorough makeover and exterior sandblasting, this neo-Renaissance monument designed by Josef Zítek and Josef Schulz presents the cleanest, brightest stonework in the city. Completed in 1884 and named for then–Hapsburg Crown Prince Rudolf, the rather low-slung sandstone building was meant to be a combination concert hall and exhibition gallery. After 1918 it was converted into the parliament of the newly independent Czechoslovakia until German invaders reinstated the concert hall in 1939. Czech writer Jiří Weil's novel *Mendelssohn Is on the Roof* tells of the cruel farce that ensued when officials ordered the removal of the Jewish composer's statue from the roof balustrade. Now the Czech Philharmonic has its home base here. The 1,200-seat **Dvořákova síň** (Dvořák Hall) has superb acoustics (the box office faces 17 listopadu). To see the hall, you must attend a concert.

Behind Dvořák Hall is a set of large exhibition rooms, the **Galerie Rudolfinum** (WEB www.galerierudolfinum.cz), an innovative, state-supported gallery for rotating shows of contemporary art. Four or five large shows are mounted here annually, showcasing excellent Czech work along with international artists such as photographer Cindy Sherman. The gallery is open Tuesday–Sunday 10–6; admission is 100 Kč. ⊠ *Nám. Jana Palacha, Josefov,* ☎ *224–893–111 box office; 224–893–205 gallery,* WEB *www.czechphilharmonic.cz.*

★ ㉔ **Španělská synagóga** (Spanish Synagogue). A domed Moorish-style synagogue was built in 1868 on the site of the Altschul, the city's oldest synagogue. Here, the historical exposition that begins in the Maisel Synagogue continues, taking the story up to the post–World War II period. The displays are not that compelling, but the building's painstakingly restored interior definitely is. ⊠ *Vězeňská 1, Josefov,* ☎ *224–819–456.* 🎫 *Combined ticket to museum sites and Old-New Synagogue 500 Kč; museum sites only, 300 Kč,* ☎ *224–819–456,* WEB *www.jewishmuseum. cz.* ☾ *Apr.–Oct., Sun.–Fri. 9–6; Nov.–Mar., Sun.–Fri. 9–4:30.*

★ ㉒ **Staronová synagóga** (Old-New Synagogue, or Altneuschul). Dating from the mid-13th century, this is one of the most important works of early Gothic in Prague. The odd name recalls the legend that the synagogue was built on the site of an ancient Jewish temple and that stones from the temple were used to build the present structure. The oldest part of the synagogue is the entrance, with its vault supported by two pillars. The synagogue has not only survived fires and the razing of the ghetto at the end of the last century but also emerged from the Nazi occupation intact; it is still in active use. As the oldest synagogue in Europe that still serves its original function, it is a living storehouse of Bohemian Jewish life. Note that men are required to cover their heads inside and that during services men and women sit apart. ⊠ *Červená 2, Josefov,* ☎ *224–819–456,* WEB *www.jewishmuseum.cz.* 🎫 *Combined ticket to Old-New Synagogue and museum sites 500 Kč; Old-New Synagogue only, 200 Kč.* ☾ *Apr.–Oct., Sun.–Thurs. 9–6; Nov.–Mar., Sun.– Thurs. 9–4:30; closes 2–3 hrs early on Fri.*

★ ㉕ **Starý židovský hřbitov** (Old Jewish Cemetery). This unforgettably melancholy sight not far from the busy city was, from the 15th century to 1787, the final resting place for all Jews living in Prague. The confined space forced graves to be piled one on top of the other. Tilted at crazy angles, the 12,000 visible tombstones are but a fraction of countless thousands more buried below. Walk the path amid the gravestones; the relief symbols you see represent the names and professions of the deceased. The oldest marked grave belongs to the poet Avigdor Kara, who died in 1439; the grave is not accessible from the pathway, but the original tombstone can be seen in the Maisel Synagogue. The best-known marker is that of Jehuda ben Bezalel, the famed Rabbi Loew (died 1609), a chief rabbi of Prague and profound scholar who is credited with creating the mythical Golem. Even today, small scraps of paper bearing wishes are stuffed into the cracks of the rabbi's tomb in the hope he will grant them. Loew's grave lies near the exit. ⊠ *Široká 3, Josefov (enter through Pinkasova synagóga),* ☎ *224–819–456,* WEB *www. jewishmuseum.cz.* 🎫 *Combined ticket to museum sites and Old-New Synagogue 500 Kč; museum sites only, 300 Kč.* ☾ *Apr.–Oct., Sun.– Fri. 9–6; Nov.–Mar., Sun.–Fri. 9–4:30.*

㉑ **Židovská radnice** (Jewish Town Hall). The hall was the creation of Mordechai Maisel, an influential Jewish leader at the end of the 16th century. It was restored in the 18th century and given its clock and bell tower at that time. A second clock, with Hebrew numbers, keeps time counterclockwise. Now the Jewish Community Center, the building also houses a kosher restaurant, Shalom. ⊠ *Maiselova 18, Josefov,* ☎ *222– 319–012.*

Karlův most (Charles Bridge) and
Malá Strana (Lesser Quarter)

One of Prague's most exquisite neighborhoods, the Lesser Quarter (or Little Town) was established in 1257 and for years was where the merchants and craftsmen who served the royal court lived. The Lesser Quarter is not for the methodical traveler. Its charm lies in the tiny lanes, the sudden blasts of bombastic architecture, and the soul-stirring views that emerge for a second before disappearing behind the sloping roofs.

Numbers in the text correspond to numbers in the margin and on the Prague map.

A Good Walk

Begin your tour on the Old Town side of **Karlův most** ㉘, which you can reach by foot in about 10 minutes from the Old Town Square. Rising above it is the majestic Staroměstská mostecká věž. The climb of 138 steps is worth the effort for the view you get of the Old Town and, across the river, of the Lesser Quarter and Prague Castle.

It's worth pausing to take a closer look at some of the statues as you walk across Karlův most toward the Lesser Quarter. You'll see Kampa Island below you, separated from the mainland by an arm of the Vltava known as Čertovka (Devil's Stream).

By now you are almost at the end of the bridge. In front of you is the striking conjunction of the two Malá Strana bridge towers, one Gothic, the other Romanesque. Together they frame the baroque flamboyance of Chrám svatého Mikuláše in the distance. At night this is an absolutely wondrous sight.

Walk under the gateway of the towers into the little uphill street called Mostecká. You have now entered the Lesser Quarter. Return to Mostecká and follow it up to the rectangular **Malostranské náměstí** ㉙, now the district's traffic hub rather than its heart. In the middle of the square stands **Chrám svatého Mikuláše** ㉚.

Nerudova ulice ㉛ runs up from the square toward Prague Castle. Lined with gorgeous houses (and in recent years an ever-larger number of places to spend money), it's sometimes burdened with the moniker "Prague's most beautiful street." A tiny passageway at No. 13, on the left-hand side as you go up, leads to Tržiště ulice and the **Schönbornský palác** ㉜, once Franz Kafka's home, now the embassy of the United States. Tržiště winds down to the quarter's traffic-plagued main street, Karmelitská, where the famous Infant Jesus of Prague resides in the **Kostel Panny Marie vítězné** ㉝. A few doors away, closer to Tržiště, is a quiet oasis, the **Vrtbovská zahrada** ㉞. Tiny Prokopská ulice leads off of Karmelitská, past the former Church of St. Procopius (now converted, oddly, into an apartment block), and into Maltézské náměstí (Maltese Square), a characteristically noble compound.

A tiny bridge at the cramped square's lower end takes you across the creeklike Čertovka to the island of **Kampa** ㉟ and its broad lawns, cafés, and river views. Winding your way underneath Karlův most and along the street U lužického semináře brings you to a quiet walled garden, **Vojanovy sady** ㊱. To the northwest, hiding off busy Letenská ulice near the Malostranská metro station, is **Zahrada Valdštejnského paláce** ㊲, a more formal garden with an unbeatable view of Prague Castle looming above. A bit farther north is another garden, the baroque **Ledeburská zahrada** ㊳.

TIMING

The area is at its best in the evening, when the softer light brings you into a world of glimmering beauty. The basic walk described here could take as little as half a day—longer if you'd like to explore the area's lovely nooks and crannies.

Sights To See

★ ③⓪ **Chrám svatého Mikuláše** (Church of St. Nicholas). With its dynamic curves, this church is one of the purest and most ambitious examples of high baroque. The celebrated architect Christoph Dientzenhofer began the Jesuit church in 1704 on the site of one of the more active Hussite churches of 15th-century Prague. Work on the building was taken over by his son Kilian Ignaz Dientzenhofer, who built the dome and presbytery. Anselmo Lurago completed the whole in 1755 by adding the bell tower. The juxtaposition of the broad, full-bodied dome with the slender bell tower is one of the many striking architectural contrasts that mark the Prague skyline. Inside, the vast pink-and-green space is impossible to take in with a single glance. Every corner bristles with movement, guiding the eye first to the dramatic statues, then to the hectic frescoes, and on to the shining faux-marble pillars. Many of the statues are the work of Ignaz Platzer, and in fact they constitute his last blaze of success. Platzer's workshop was forced to declare bankruptcy when the centralizing and secularizing reforms of Joseph II toward the end of the 18th century brought an end to the flamboyant baroque era. The tower, with an entrance on the side of the church, is open in summer. ✉ *Malostranské nám., Malá Strana.* ▭ *30 Kč.* ☽ *Daily 9–4.*

③⑤ **Kampa.** Prague's largest island is cut off from the "mainland" by the narrow Čertovka streamlet. The name Čertovka, or Devil's Stream, reputedly refers to a cranky old lady who once lived on Maltese Square (given the river's present filthy state, the name is certainly appropriate). The unusually well-kept lawns of the **Kampa Gardens** that occupy much of the island are one of the few places in Prague where sitting on the grass is openly tolerated. At night this stretch along the river is especially romantic. The spotlit jewel on Kampa Island is **Museum Kampa,** a remodeled mill house that now displays a private collection of paintings by Czech artist František Kupka and other artists, which opened in 2002. Kampa was heavily damaged during the floods of 2002, but at this writing the Museum Kampa was scheduled to reopen in January 2003. ✉ *U Sovových mlýnů 2, Malá Strana,* ☎ *257–786–147.* ▭ *100 Kč.* ☽ *Tues.–Sun. 10–5.*

★ ②⑧ **Karlův most** (Charles Bridge). The view from the foot of the bridge on the Old Town side is nothing short of breathtaking, encompassing the towers and domes of the Lesser Quarter and the soaring spires of St. Vitus's Cathedral to the northwest. This heavenly vision changes subtly in perspective as you walk across the bridge, attended by the host of baroque saints that decorate the bridge's peaceful Gothic stones. At night its drama is spellbinding: St. Vitus's Cathedral lit in a ghostly green, the castle in monumental yellow, and the Church of St. Nicholas in a voluptuous pink, all viewed through the menacing silhouettes of the bowed statues and the Gothic towers. If you do nothing else in Prague, you must visit the Charles Bridge at night. During the day the pedestrian bridge buzzes with activity. Street musicians vie with artisans hawking jewelry, paintings, and glass for the hearts and wallets of the passing multitude. At night the crowds thin out a little, the musicians multiply, and the bridge becomes a long block party—nearly everyone brings a bottle.

When the Přemyslid princes set up residence in Prague in the 10th century, there was a ford across the Vltava at this point—a vital link along one of Europe's major trading routes. After several wooden bridges and the first stone bridge had washed away in floods, Charles IV appointed the 27-year-old German Peter Parler, the architect of St. Vitus's Cathedral, to build a new structure in 1357. After 1620, following the defeat of Czech Protestants by Catholic Hapsburgs at the Battle of White Mountain, the bridge became a symbol of the Counter-Reformation's vigorous re-Catholicization efforts. The many baroque statues that began to appear in the late 17th century, commissioned by Catholics, eventually came to symbolize the totality of the Austrian (hence Catholic) triumph. The Czech writer Milan Kundera sees the statues from this perspective: "The thousands of saints looking out from all sides, threatening you, following you, hypnotizing you, are the raging hordes of occupiers who invaded Bohemia 350 years ago to tear the people's faith and language from their hearts."

The religious conflict is less obvious nowadays, leaving only the artistic tension between baroque and Gothic that gives the bridge its allure. It's worth pausing to take a closer look at some of the statues as you walk toward the Lesser Quarter. The third on the right, a bronze crucifix from the mid-17th century, is the oldest of all. It is mounted on the location of a wooden cross destroyed in a battle with the Swedes (the golden Hebrew inscription was reputedly financed by a Jew accused of defiling the cross). Eighth on the right, the statue of St. John of Nepomuk, designed by Johann Brokoff in 1683, begins the baroque lineup of saints. On the left-hand side, sticking out from the bridge between the 9th and 10th statues (the latter has a wonderfully expressive vanquished Satan), stands a Roland (Bruncvík) statue. This knightly figure, bearing the coat of arms of the Old Town, was once a reminder that this part of the bridge belonged to the Old Town before Prague became a unified city in 1784.

In the eyes of most art historians, the most valuable statue is the 12th on the left, near the Lesser Quarter end. Mathias Braun's statue of St. Luitgarde depicts the blind saint kissing Christ's wounds. The most compelling grouping, however, is the second from the end on the left, a work of Ferdinand Maxmilian Brokoff (son of Johann) from 1714. Here the saints are incidental; the main attraction is the Turk, his face expressing extreme boredom at guarding the Christians imprisoned in the cage at his side. When the statue was erected, just 31 years after the second Turkish siege of Vienna, it scandalized the Prague public, who smeared it with mud. A half-dozen of the 30 bridge sculptures are 19th-century replacements for originals damaged in wars or sunk in a 1784 flood. All but a couple of the bridge's surviving baroque statues, including St. Luitgarde and the Turk, have been replaced by modern copies. The 17th- and 18th-century originals are in safer quarters, protected from Prague's acidic air. Several, including St. Luitgarde, can be viewed in the Lapidarium museum at the Výstaviště exhibition grounds in Prague 7; a few more occupy a man-made cavern at Vyšehrad.

Staroměstská mostecká věž (Old Town Bridge Tower), at the bridge entrance on the Old Town side, is where Peter Parler, the architect of the Charles Bridge, began his bridge building. The carved facades he designed for the sides of the tower were destroyed by Swedish soldiers in 1648, at the end of the Thirty Years' War. The sculptures facing the Old Town, however, are still intact (although some are recent copies); they depict an old and gout-ridden Charles IV with his son, who later became Wenceslas IV. Above them are two of Bohemia's patron saints, Adalbert of Prague and Sigismund. The top of the tower offers a spectacular view of the city for 30 Kč; it's open daily 10–5 (until 7 in the summer).

㉝ Kostel Panny Marie vítězné (Church of Our Lady Victorious). This comfortably ramshackle church on the Lesser Quarter's main street is the unlikely home of one of Prague's best-known religious artifacts, the *Pražské Jezulátko* (Infant Jesus of Prague). Originally brought to Prague from Spain in the 16th century, this tiny wax doll is renowned worldwide for showering miracles on anyone willing to kneel before it and pray. Nuns from a nearby convent arrive at dawn each day to change the infant's clothes; pieces of the doll's extensive wardrobe have been sent by believers from around the world. A museum in the church tower displays many of the outfits and a jewel-studded crown. ⊠ *Karmelitská 9A, Malá Strana.* ⛲ *Free.* ⊙ *Mon.–Sat. 10–5:30, Sun. 1–5.*

㊳ Ledeburská zahrada (Ledeburg Garden). Rows of steeply banked baroque gardens rise behind the palaces of Valdštejnská ulice. This one makes a pleasant spot for a rest amid shady arbors and niches. The garden, with its frescoes and statuary, was restored with support from a fund headed by Czech president Václav Havel and Charles, Prince of Wales. You can also enter directly from the south gardens of Prague Castle in the summer. ⊠ *Valdštejnské nám. 3, Malá Strana.* ⛲ *40 Kč.* ⊙ *Daily 10–6.*

㉙ Malostranské náměstí (Lesser Quarter Square). The arcaded houses on the east and south sides of the square, dating from the 16th and 17th centuries, exhibit a mix of baroque and Renaissance elements. The Czech Parliament resides partly in the gaudy yellow-and-green palace on the square's north side, partly in the street behind the palace, Sněmovní. The huge bulk of the Church of St. Nicholas divides the lower, busier section—buzzing with restaurants, street vendors, clubs, and shops—from the quieter, upper part.

㉛ Nerudova ulice. This steep little street used to be the last leg of the Royal Way walked by the king before his coronation, and it is still the best way to get to Prague Castle. It was named for the 19th-century Czech journalist and poet Jan Neruda (after whom Chilean poet Pablo Neruda renamed himself). Until Joseph II's administrative reforms in the late 18th century, house numbering was unknown in Prague. Each house bore a name, depicted on the facade, and these are particularly prominent on Nerudova ulice. House No. 6, **U červeného orla** (At the Red Eagle), proudly displays a faded painting of a red eagle. No. 12 is known as **U tří housliček** (At the Three Fiddles). In the early 18th century, three generations of the Edlinger violin-making family lived here. Joseph II's scheme numbered each house according to its position in its "town" (here the Lesser Quarter) rather than its sequence on the street. The red plates record the original house numbers; the blue ones are the numbers used in addresses today. To confuse the tourist, many architectural guides refer to the old, red-number plates.

Two palaces break the unity of the burghers' houses on Nerudova ulice. Both were designed by the adventurous baroque architect Giovanni Santini, one of the Italian builders most in demand by wealthy nobles of the early 18th century. The **Morzin Palace,** on the left at No. 5, is now the Romanian Embassy. The fascinating facade, with an allegory of night and day, was created in 1713 and is the work of Ferdinand Brokoff of Charles Bridge statue fame. Across the street at No. 20 is the **Thun-Hohenstein Palace,** now the Italian Embassy. The gateway with two enormous eagles (the emblem of the Kolovrat family, who owned the building at the time) is the work of the other great Charles Bridge statue sculptor, Mathias Braun. Santini himself lived at No. 14, the **Valkoun House.**

The archway at Nerudova 13 hides one of the many winding passageways that give the Lesser Quarter its enchantingly ghostly character at night. Higher up the street at No. 33 is the **Bretfeld Palace,** a rococo house on the corner of Jánský vršek. The relief of St. Nicholas on the facade is the work of Ignaz Platzer, a sculptor known for his classic and rococo work, but the building is valued more for its historical associations than for its architecture: this is where Mozart, his lyricist partner Lorenzo da Ponte, and the aging but still infamous philanderer and music lover Casanova stayed at the time of the world premiere of *Don Giovanni* in 1787.

NEED A
BREAK?
Nerudova ulice is filled with little restaurants and snack bars and offers something for everyone. **U zeleného čaje** (⊠ Nerudova 19) is a fragrant little tearoom offering herbal and fruit teas as well as light salads and sweets. **U Kocoura** (⊠ Nerudova 2) is a popular local pub.

㉜ Schönbornský palác (Schönborn Palace). Franz Kafka had an apartment in this massive baroque building at the top of Tržiště ulice in mid-1917, after moving from Zlatá ulička, or Golden Lane. The heavily guarded U.S. Embassy now occupies this prime location. If you look through the gates, you can see the beautiful formal gardens rising up to the Petřín hill. They are unfortunately not open to the public but can be glimpsed from the neighboring garden, Vrtbovská zahrada. ⊠ *Tržiště at Vlašská, Malá Strana.*

㊱ Vojanovy sady (Vojan Park). Once the gardens of the Monastery of the Discalced Carmelites, later taken over by the Order of the English Virgins, and now part of the Ministry of Finance, this walled garden, with its weeping willows, fruit trees, and benches, makes another peaceful haven in summer. Exhibitions of modern sculptures are often held here, contrasting sharply with the two baroque chapels and the graceful Ignaz Platzer statue of John of Nepomuk standing on a fish at the entrance. The park is surrounded by the high walls of the old monastery and new Ministry of Finance buildings, with only an occasional glimpse of a tower or spire to remind you that you're in Prague. ⊠ *U lužického semináře, between Letenská ul. and Míšeňská ul., Malá Strana.* ☺ *Nov.–Mar., daily 8–5; Apr.–Oct., daily 8–7.*

★ **㉞ Vrtbovská zahrada** (Vrtba Garden). An unobtrusive door on noisy Karmelitská hides the entranceway to a fascinating oasis that also has one of the best views over the Lesser Quarter. The street door opens onto the intimate courtyard of the Vrtbovský palác (Vrtba Palace), which is now private housing. Two Renaissance wings flank the courtyard; the left one was built in 1575, the right one in 1591. The owner of the latter house was one of the 27 Bohemian nobles executed by the Hapsburgs in 1621 before the Old Town Hall. The house was given as confiscated property to Count Sezima of Vrtba, who bought the neighboring property and turned the buildings into a late-Renaissance palace. The Vrtba Garden, created a century later, reopened in summer 1998 after an excruciatingly long renovation. This is the most elegant of the Lesser Quarter's public gardens, built in five levels rising behind the courtyard in a wave of statuary-bedecked staircases and formal terraces to reach a seashell-decorated pavilion at the top. (The fenced-off garden immediately behind and above belongs to the U.S. Embassy.) The powerful stone figure of Atlas that caps the entranceway in the courtyard and most of the other classically derived statues are from the workshop of Mathias Braun, perhaps the best of the Czech baroque sculptors. ⊠ *Karmelitská 25, Malá Strana.* ☐ *20 Kč.* ☺ *Apr.–Oct., daily 10–6.*

OFF THE
BEATEN PATH
VILLA BERTRAMKA – Mozart fans won't want to pass up a visit to this villa, where the great composer lived during a couple of his visits to Prague. The small, well-organized W. A. Mozart Museum is packed

with memorabilia, including a flyer for a performance of *Don Giovanni* in 1788, only months after the opera's world premiere at the Estates Theater. Also on hand is one of the master's pianos. Take Tram No. 12 from Karmelitská south (or ride metro Line B) to the Anděl metro station; then transfer to Tram No. 4, 7, 9, or 10 and ride to the first stop (Bertramka). A 10-minute walk, following the signs, brings you to the villa. ⊠ *Mozartova ul. 169, Smíchov,* ☎ *257–327–732,* WEB *www. bertramka.cz.* ☞ *90 Kč.* ☉ *Apr.–Oct., daily 9:30–6; Nov.–Mar., daily 9:30–5.*

★ ❸❼ **Zahrada Valdštejnského paláce** (Wallenstein Palace Gardens). Albrecht von Wallenstein, onetime owner of the house and gardens, began a meteoric military career in 1622 when the Austrian emperor Ferdinand II retained him to save the empire from the Swedes and Protestants during the Thirty Years' War. Wallenstein, wealthy by marriage, offered to raise 20,000 men at his own cost and lead them personally. Ferdinand II accepted and showered Wallenstein with confiscated land and titles. Wallenstein's first acquisition was this enormous area. Having knocked down 23 houses, a brick factory, and three gardens, in 1623 he began to build his magnificent palace with its idiosyncratic high-walled gardens and superb, vaulted Renaissance *sala terrena* (room opening onto a garden). Walking around the formal paths, you'll come across numerous statues, an unusual fountain with a woman spouting water from her breasts, and a lava-stone grotto along the wall. Most of the palace itself now serves the Czech Senate as meeting chamber and offices. The palace's cavernous former *Jízdárna,* or riding school, now hosts occasional art exhibitions. ⊠ *Letenská 10, Malá Strana.* ☞ *Free.* ☉ *May–Sept., daily 9–7; mid-Mar.–Apr. and Oct., daily 10–6.*

Hradčany (Castle Area)

To the west of Prague Castle is the residential Hradčany (Castle Area), the town that during the early 14th century emerged out of a collection of monasteries and churches. The concentration of history packed into Prague Castle and Hradčany challenges those not versed in the ups and downs of Bohemian kings, religious uprisings, wars, and oppression. The picturesque area surrounding Prague Castle, with its breathtaking vistas of the Old Town and the Lesser Quarter, is ideal for just wandering. But the castle itself, with its convoluted history and architecture, is difficult to appreciate fully without investing a little more time.

Numbers in the text correspond to numbers in the margin and on the Prague map.

A Good Walk

Begin on Nerudova ulice, which runs east–west a few hundred yards south of Prague Castle. At the western (upper) end of the street, look for a flight of stone steps guarded by two saintly statues. Take the stairs up to Loretánská ulice, and enjoy panoramic views of the Church of St. Nicholas and the Lesser Quarter. At the top of the steps, turn left and walk a couple hundred yards until you come to a dusty, elongated square named Pohořelec (Scene of Fire), which suffered tragic fires in 1420, 1541, and 1741. Go through the inconspicuous gateway at No. 8 and up the steps, and you'll find yourself in the courtyard of one of the city's richest monasteries, the **Strahovský klášter** ㊴.

Retrace your steps to Loretánské náměstí, the square at the head of Loretánská ulice that is flanked by the feminine curves of the baroque church **Loreta** ㊵. Across the road, the 29 half pillars of the Černínský palác (Černín Palace) now mask the Czech Ministry of Foreign Affairs.

At the bottom of Loretánské náměstí, a little lane trails to the left into the area known as **Nový Svět** ㊶; the name means "New World," though the district is as old-world as they come. Turn right onto the street Nový Svět. Around the corner you get a tantalizing view of the cathedral through the trees. Walk down the winding Kanovnická ulice past the Austrian Embassy and the dignified but melancholy Kostel svatého Jana Nepomuckého (Church of St. John of Nepomuk). At the top of the street on the left, the rounded, Renaissance corner house, Martinický palác, catches the eye with its detailed sgraffiti decorations. Martinický palác opens onto **Hradčanské náměstí** ㊷, with its grandiose gathering of Renaissance and baroque palaces. To the left of the bright yellow Arcibiskupský palác (Archbishop's Palace) on the square is an alleyway leading down to the **Národní galerie** ㊸ and its collections of European art. Across the square, the handsome sgraffito sweep of **Schwarzenberský palác** ㊹ beckons; this is the building you saw from the back side at the beginning of the tour.

TIMING

To do justice to the subtle charms of Hradčany, allow at least an hour just for ambling and admiring the passing buildings and views of the city. The Strahovský klášter halls need about a half-hour to take in, more if you tour the small picture gallery there, and the Loreta and its treasures need at least that length of time. The Národní galerie in the Šternberský palác deserves at least a couple of hours. Keep in mind that several places are not open on Monday.

Sights to See

㊷ **Hradčanské náměstí** (Hradčany Square). With its fabulous mixture of baroque and Renaissance housing, topped by the castle itself, the square had a prominent role (disguised, ironically, as Vienna) in the film *Amadeus*, directed by the then-exiled Czech director Miloš Forman. The house at No. 7 was the set for Mozart's residence, where the composer was haunted by the masked figure he thought was his father. Forman used the flamboyant rococo Arcibiskupský palác (Archbishop's Palace), on the left as you face the castle, as the Viennese archbishop's palace. The plush interior, shown off in the film, is open to the public only on Maundy Thursday. No. 11 was home for a brief time after World War II to a little girl named Marie Jana Korbelová, who would grow up to be Madeleine Albright.

㊶ **Loreta** (Loreto Church). The church's seductive lines were a conscious move on the part of Counter-Reformation Jesuits in the 17th century who wanted to build up the cult of Mary and attract the largely Protestant Bohemians back to the church. According to legend, angels had carried Mary's house from Nazareth and dropped it in a patch of laurel trees in Ancona, Italy. Known as *Loreto* (from the Latin for laurel), it immediately became a center of pilgrimage. The Prague Loreto was one of many symbolic reenactments of this scene across Europe, and it worked: pilgrims came in droves. The graceful facade, with its voluptuous tower, was built in 1720 by Kilian Ignaz Dientzenhofer, the architect of the two St. Nicholas churches in Prague. Most spectacular of all is a small exhibition upstairs displaying the religious treasures presented to Mary in thanks for various services, including a monstrance studded with 6,500 diamonds. ✉ *Loretánské nám. 7, Hradčany.* ☎ *80 Kč.* ☉ *Tues.–Sun. 9–12:15 and 1–4:30.*

★ ㊸ **Národní galerie** (National Gallery). Housed in the 18th-century Šternberský palác (Sternberg Palace), this collection, though impressive, is limited compared to German and Austrian holdings. During the time when Berlin, Dresden, and Vienna were building up superlative old-master galleries, Prague languished, neglected by her Viennese rulers—

one reason why the city's museums lag behind. Part of the museum reopened in 2002 after a long renovation, but some floors are still closed. Works by Rubens and Rembrandt are already back on display, while some other key pieces in the collection are still waiting in the wings. Other branches of the National Gallery are scattered around town. ⊠ *Hradčanské nám. 15, Hradčany,* ☎ *220–514–634,* WEB *www.ngprague. cz.* ▣ *60 Kč.* ⊙ *Tues.–Sun. 10–6.*

㊶ Nový Svět. This picturesque, winding little alley, with facades from the 17th and 18th centuries, once housed Prague's poorest residents; now many of the homes are used as artists' studios. The last house on the street, No. 1, was the home of the Danish-born astronomer Tycho Brahe. Living so close to the Loreto, so the story goes, Tycho was constantly disturbed during his nightly stargazing by the church bells. He ended up complaining to his patron, Emperor Rudolf II, who instructed the Capuchin monks to finish their services before the first star appeared in the sky.

㊹ Schwarzenberský palác (Schwarzenberg Palace). This boxy palace with its extravagant sgraffito facade is the **Vojenské historické muzeum** (Military History Museum), one of the largest of its kind in Europe. The beautifully decorated exterior is all that is on display while the interior undergoes a long-term renovation. ⊠ *Hradčanské nám. 2, Hradčany.*

★ **㊴ Strahovský klášter** (Strahov Monastery). Founded by the Premonstratensian order in 1140, the monastery remained in its hands until 1952, when the Communists suppressed all religious orders and turned the entire complex into the **Památník národního písemnictví** (Museum of National Literature). The major building of interest is the **Strahov Library,** with its collection of early Czech manuscripts, the 10th-century Strahov New Testament, and the collected works of famed Danish astronomer Tycho Brahe. Also of note is the late-18th-century **Philosophical Hall.** Engulfing its ceilings is a startling sky-blue fresco that depicts an unusual cast of characters, including Socrates' nagging wife, Xanthippe; Greek astronomer Thales, with his trusty telescope; and a collection of Greek philosophers mingling with Descartes, Diderot, and Voltaire. Also on the premises is the order's small art gallery, highlighted by late-Gothic altars and paintings from Rudolf II's time. The library and gallery are accessible only on a guided tour; you can arrange for a tour in English with several days' advance notice. ⊠ *Strahovské nádvoří 1/132, Hradčany,* ☎ *220–516–671 to arrange tours.* ▣ *Library tour 50 Kč, gallery tour 30 Kč.* ⊙ *Gallery Tues.–Sun. 9– noon and 12:30–5; library daily 9–noon and 1–5.*

OFF THE
BEATEN PATH

PETŘÍN – For a superb view of the city—from a mostly undiscovered, tourist-free perch—stroll over from the Strahov Monastery along the paths toward Prague's own miniature version of the Eiffel Tower, which was restored in 2002. You'll find yourself in a hilltop park, laced with footpaths, with several buildings clustered together near the tower—just keep going gradually upward until you reach the tower's base. The tower and its breathtaking view, the mirror maze (*bludiště*) in a small structure near the tower's base, and the seemingly abandoned svatý Vavřinec (St. Lawrence) church are beautifully peaceful and well worth an afternoon's wandering. You can also walk up from Karmelitská ulice or Újezd down in the Lesser Quarter or ride the funicular railway from U lanové dráhy ulice, off Újezd. Regular public-transportation tickets are valid. For the descent, take the funicular or meander on foot down through the stations of the cross on the pathways leading back to the Lesser Quarter.

Pražský Hrad (Prague Castle)

Numbers in the text correspond to numbers in the margin and on the Prague Castle (Pražský hrad) map.

Despite its monolithic presence, the Prague Castle is not a single structure but rather a collection of buildings dating from the 10th to the 20th century, all linked by internal courtyards. The most important structures are **Chrám svatého Víta** ⑤⓪, clearly visible soaring above the castle walls, and the **Královský palác** ⑤①, the official residence of kings and presidents and still the center of political power in the Czech Republic. The castle is compact and easy to navigate. Be forewarned: in summer, the castle, especially Chrám svatého Víta, is hugely popular. **Zlatá ulička** ⑤⑤ became so crowded that in 2002 a separate admission fee was imposed for it.

TIMING
The castle is at its mysterious best in early morning and late evening, and it is incomparable when it snows. The cathedral deserves an hour, as does the Královský palác, while you can easily spend an entire day taking in the museums, the views of the city, and the hidden nooks of the castle. Remember that some sights, such as the Lobkovický palác and the National Gallery branch at Klášter svatého Jiří, are not open on Monday.

Sights to See

⑤③ **Bazilika svatého Jiří** (St. George's Basilica). This church was originally built in the 10th century by Prince Vratislav I, the father of Prince (and St.) Wenceslas. It was dedicated to St. George (of dragon fame), who it was believed would be more agreeable to the still largely pagan people. The outside was remodeled during early baroque times, although the striking rusty-red color is in keeping with the look of the Romanesque edifice. The interior looks more or less as it did in the 12th century and is the best-preserved Romanesque relic in the country. The effect is at once barnlike and peaceful, the warm golden yellow of the stone walls and the small arched windows exuding a sense of enduring harmony. The house-shape painted tomb at the front of the church holds the remains of the founder, Vratislav I. Up the steps, in a chapel to the right, is the tomb Peter Parler designed for St. Ludmila, the grandmother of St. Wenceslas. ✉ *Nám. U sv. Jiří, Hradčany,* ☎ *224–373–368 castle information,* WEB *www.hrad.cz.* ✆ *Requires 1-day castle ticket (180 Kč).* ☉ *Apr.–Oct., daily 9–5; Nov.–Mar., daily 9–4.*

★ ⑤⓪ **Chrám svatého Víta** (St. Vitus's Cathedral). With its graceful, soaring towers, this Gothic cathedral—among the most beautiful in Europe—is the spiritual heart not only of Prague Castle but of the entire country. It has a long and complicated history, beginning in the 10th century and continuing to its completion in 1929. If you want to hear its history in depth, English-speaking guided tours of the cathedral and the Královský palác can be arranged at the information office across from the cathedral entrance.

Once you enter the cathedral, pause to take in the vast but delicate beauty of the Gothic and neo-Gothic interior glowing in the colorful light that filters through the startlingly brilliant stained-glass windows. This western third of the structure, including the facade and the two towers you can see from outside, was not completed until 1929, following the initiative of the Union for the Completion of the Cathedral, set up in the last days of the 19th century. Don't let the neo-Gothic illusion keep you from examining this new section. The six stained-glass windows to your left and right and the large rose window behind are modern masterpieces. Take a good look at the third window up on the

Prague Castle (Pražský hrad)

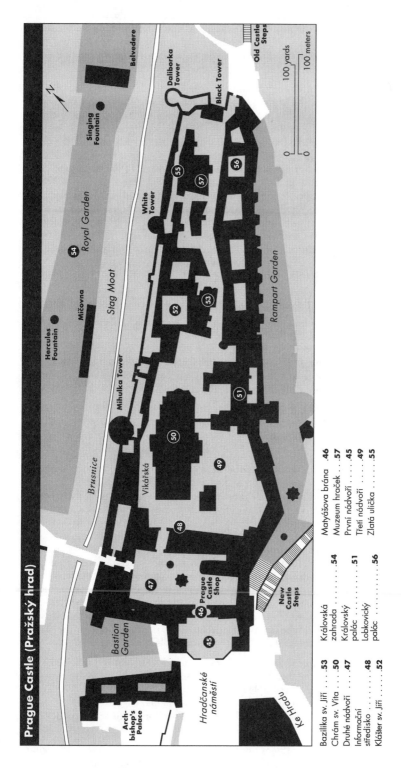

Arch-bishop's Palace

Hradčanské náměstí

Ke Hradu

Bastion Garden

Brusnice

Hercules Fountain

Míčovna

Royal Garden

Stag Moat

Singing Fountain

Belvedere

N

Mihulka Tower

White Tower

Daliborka Tower

Black Tower

Vikářská

54

52

53

55

57

56

50

49

51

48

47

46

45

Prague Castle Shop

New Castle Steps

Rampart Garden

Old Castle Steps

0   100 yards
0   100 meters

Bazilika sv. Jiří **53**
Chrám sv. Víta **50**
Druhé nádvoří **47**
Informační
středisko **48**
Klášter sv. Jiří **52**

Královská
zahrada **54**
Královský
palác **51**
Lobkovický
palác **56**

Matyášova brána . . **46**
Muzeum hraček . . . **57**
První nádvoří **45**
Třetí nádvoří **49**
Zlatá ulička **55**

left. The familiar Art Nouveau flamboyance, depicting the blessing of Sts. Cyril and Methodius (9th-century missionaries to the Slavs), is the work of the Czech father of the style, Alfons Mucha. He achieved the subtle coloring by painting rather than staining the glass.

If you walk halfway up the right-hand aisle, you will find the **Svatováclavská kaple** (Chapel of St. Wenceslas). With a tomb holding the saint's remains, walls covered in semi-precious stones, and paintings depicting the life of Wenceslas, this square chapel is the ancient heart of the cathedral. Stylistically, it represents a high point of the dense, richly decorated though rather gloomy Gothic favored by Charles IV and his successors. Wenceslas (the "good king" of Christmas-carol fame) was a determined Christian in an era of widespread paganism. Around 925, as prince of Bohemia, he founded a rotunda church dedicated to St. Vitus on this site. But the prince's brother, Boleslav, was impatient to take power, and he ambushed Wenceslas in 929 (or 935 according to some experts) near a church at Stará Boleslav, northeast of Prague. Wenceslas was originally buried in that church, but his grave produced so many miracles that he rapidly became a symbol of piety for the common people, something that greatly irritated the new Prince Boleslav. Boleslav was finally forced to honor his brother by reburying the body in the St. Vitus Rotunda. Shortly afterward, Wenceslas was canonized.

The rotunda was replaced by a Romanesque basilica in the late 11th century. Work was begun on the existing building in 1344. For the first few years the chief architect was the Frenchman Mathias d'Arras, but after his death in 1352 the work was continued by the 22-year-old German architect Peter Parler, who went on to build the Charles Bridge and many other Prague treasures.

The small door in the back of the chapel leads to the **Korunní komora** (Crown Chamber), the repository of the Bohemian crown jewels. It remains locked with seven keys held by seven important people (including the president) and is definitely not open to the public.

A little beyond the Chapel of St. Wenceslas on the same side, stairs lead down to the underground **royal crypt**, interesting primarily for the information it provides about the cathedral's history. As you descend the stairs, you'll see parts of the old Romanesque basilica and portions of the foundations of the rotunda. Moving around into the second room, you'll find a rather eclectic group of royal remains ensconced in new sarcophagi dating from the 1930s. In the center is Charles IV, who died in 1378. Rudolf II, patron of Renaissance Prague, is entombed at the rear in the original tin coffin. To his right is Maria Amalia, the only child of Empress Maria Theresa to reside in Prague. Ascending the wooden steps back into the cathedral, you'll come to the white-marble **Kralovské mausoleum** (Royal Mausoleum), atop which lie stone statues of the first two Hapsburg kings to rule in Bohemia, Ferdinand I and Maximilian II, and of Ferdinand's consort, Anne Jagiello.

The cathedral's **Kralovské oratorium** (Royal Oratory) was used by the kings and their families when attending mass. Built in 1493, the work is a perfect example of late Gothic, laced on the outside with a stone network of gnarled branches very similar in pattern to the ceiling vaulting in the Královský palác. The oratory is connected to the palace by an elevated covered walkway, which you can see from outside.

A few more steps toward the east end, you can't fail to catch sight of the ornate silver **sarcophagus of St. John of Nepomuk.** According to legend, when Nepomuk's body was exhumed in 1721 to be reinterred, the tongue was found to be still intact and pumping with blood. This strange tale served a highly political purpose. The Catholic Church and the Hapsburgs were seeking a new folk hero to replace the Protestant forerunner Jan Hus, whom they despised. The 14th-century priest Nepomuk, killed during a power struggle with King Václav IV, was sainted and reburied a few years later with great ceremony in the 3,700-pound silver tomb, replete with angels and cherubim; the tongue was enshrined in its own reliquary.

The eight chapels around the back of the cathedral are the work of the original architect, Mathias d'Arras. A number of old tombstones, including some badly worn grave markers of medieval royalty, can be seen within, amid furnishings from later periods. Opposite the wooden relief, depicting the looting of the cathedral by Protestants in 1619, is the **Valdštejnská kaple** (Wallenstein Chapel). Since the 19th century, the chapel has housed the Gothic tombstones of its two architects, d'Arras and Peter Parler, who died in 1352 and 1399, respectively. If you look up to the balcony, you can just make out the busts of these two men, designed by Parler's workshop. The other busts around the triforium depict royalty and other VIPs of the time.

The Hussite wars in the 15th century put an end to the first phase of the cathedral's construction. During the short era of illusory peace before the Thirty Years' War, the massive south tower was completed, but lack of money quashed any idea of finishing the building, and the cathedral was closed by a wall built across from the Chapel of St. Wenceslas. Not until the 20th century was the western side of the cathedral, with its two towers, completed in the spirit of Parler's conception.

A key element of the cathedral's teeming, rich exterior decoration is the **Last Judgment mosaic** above the ceremonial entrance, called the Golden Portal, on the south side. The use of mosaic is quite rare in countries north of the Alps; this work, dating from the 1370s, is made of 1 million glass and stone chunks. The once-clouded glass now sparkles again thanks to many years of restoration funded by the Getty Conservation Institute, which was finished in 2001. The central field shows Christ in glory, adored by Charles IV and his consort, Elizabeth of Pomerania, as well as several saints; the risen dead and attendant angels are on the left; and on the right the flames of Hell lick around the figure of Satan. ⊠ *St. Vitus's Cathedral, Hradčany,* ☎ *224–373–368 Castle Information,* WEB *www.hrad.cz.* ⊠ *Western section free; chapels, crypt, and tower require 1-day castle ticket (180 Kč).* ☉ *Apr.–Oct., daily 9–5; Nov.–Mar., daily 9–4.*

❹❼ Druhé nádvoří (Second Courtyard). Empress Maria Theresa's court architect, Nicolò Pacassi, received the imperial approval to remake the castle in the 1760s, as it was badly damaged by Prussian shelling during the Seven Years' War in 1757. The Second Courtyard was the main victim of Pacassi's attempts at imparting classical grandeur to what had been a picturesque collection of Gothic and Renaissance styles. Except for the view of the spires of St. Vitus's Cathedral, the exterior courtyard offers little for the eye to feast upon. This courtyard also houses the rather gaudy **Kaple svatého Kříže** (Chapel of the Holy Cross), with decorations from the 18th and 19th centuries, which now serves as a souvenir and ticket stand.

Built in the late 16th and early 17th century, the Second Courtyard was originally part of a reconstruction program commissioned by Rudolf II, under whom Prague enjoyed a period of unparalleled cultural development. Once the Prague court was established, the emperor gathered around him some of the world's best craftsmen, artists, and scientists, including the brilliant astronomers Johannes Kepler and Tycho Brahe.

Rudolf II amassed a large and famed collection of fine and decorative art, scientific instruments, philosophic and alchemical books, natural wonders, coins, and everything else under the sun. The bulk of the collection was looted by the Swedes during the Thirty Years' War, removed to Vienna when the imperial capital returned there after Rudolf's death, or auctioned off during the 18th century. Artworks that survived the turmoil, for the most part acquired after Rudolf's time, are displayed in the **Obrazárna** (Picture Gallery), on the left side of the courtyard as you face St. Vitus's. In rooms elegantly redecorated by the official castle architect, Bořek Šípek, there are good Renaissance, mannerist, and baroque paintings that hint at the luxurious tastes of Rudolf's court. Across the passageway by the gallery entrance is the **Císařská konírna** (Imperial Stable), where temporary exhibitions are held. The passageway at the northern end of the courtyard forms the northern entrance to the castle and leads out over a luxurious ravine known as the **Jelení příkop** (Stag Moat), which can be entered (from April through October) either here or at the lower end via the metal catwalk off Chotkova ulice, when it isn't closed for sporadic renovations. ⊠ *Obrazárna: Second Courtyard, Hradčany,* ☎ *224–373–368 Castle Information,* 🕸 *www.hrad.cz.* ⊡ *Courtyard free, Picture Gallery 100 Kč.* ☉ *Picture Gallery daily 10–6.*

㊽ **Informační středisko** (Castle Information Office). This is the place to come for entrance tickets, guided tours, headphones for listening to recorded tours in English, tickets to cultural events held at the castle, and money changing. Tickets are valid for one day and allow admission to the older parts of St. Vitus's Cathedral (the 20th-century sections are free), Královský palác, St. George's Basilica (but not the adjacent National Gallery exhibition, which has an additional entry fee), and a medieval bastion called Mihulka with an exhibition on alchemy. Other castle sights—including Golden Lane—require separate tickets, and you purchase these at the door. If you just want to walk through the castle grounds, note that the gates close at midnight April–October and at 11 PM the rest of the year, while the gardens are open April–October only. ⊠ *Třetí nádvoří, across from entrance to St. Vitus's Cathedral, Hradčany,* ☎ *224–373–368,* 🕸 *www.hrad.cz.* ⊡ *1-day Castle tickets 180 Kč; Golden Lane 40 Kč; combination 1-day and Golden Lane 220 Kč; English-language guided tours 400 Kč for up to 5 people, 60 Kč per additional person (advance booking recommended); grounds and gardens free.* ☉ *Apr.–Oct., daily 9–5; Nov.–Mar., daily 9–4.*

㊾ **Klášter svatého Jiří** (St. George's Convent). The first convent in Bohemia was founded here in 973 next to the even older St. George's Basilica. The National Gallery collections of Czech mannerist and baroque art are housed here. The highlights include the voluptuous work of Rudolf II's court painters, the giant baroque religious statuary, and some fine paintings by Karel Škréta and Petr Brandl. ⊠ *Nám. U sv. Jiří, Hradčany,* ☎ *257–320–536,* 🕸 *www.ngprague.cz.* ⊡ *100 Kč.* ☉ *Tues.–Sun. 10–6.*

㊿ **Královská zahrada** (Royal Garden). This peaceful swath of greenery affords an unusually lovely view of St. Vitus's Cathedral and the castle's walls and bastions. Originally laid out in the 16th century, it endured devastation in war, neglect in times of peace, and many redesigns, reaching its present parklike form early in the 20th century. Luckily, its Renaissance treasures survive. One of these is the long, narrow **Míčovna** (Ball Game Hall), built by Bonifaz Wohlmut in 1568, its garden front completely covered by a dense tangle of allegorical sgraffiti.

The **Královský letohrádek** (Royal Summer Palace, also known as the Belvedere), at the garden's eastern end, deserves its usual description as one of the most beautiful Renaissance structures north of the Alps. Italian architects began it; Wohlmut finished it off in the 1560s with a copper roof like an upturned boat's keel riding above the graceful arcades of the ground floor. During the 18th and 19th centuries, military engineers tested artillery in the interior, which had already lost its rich furnishings to Swedish soldiers during their siege of the city in 1648. The Renaissance-style *giardinetto* (little garden) adjoining the summer palace centers on another masterwork, the Italian-designed, Czech-cast Singing Fountain, which resonates to the sound of falling water. ✉ *U Prašného mostu ul. and Mariánské hradby ul. near Chotkovy Park, Hradčany,* ☎ *224–373–368 Castle Information,* WEB *www.hrad.cz.* 🎟 *Free.* 🕑 *Apr.–Oct., daily 10–5:45.*

🔢 **Královský palác** (Royal Palace). The palace is an accumulation of the styles and add-ons of many centuries. The best way to grasp its size is from within the **Vladislavský sál** (Vladislav Hall), the largest secular Gothic interior space in Central Europe. The enormous hall was completed in 1493 by Benedikt Ried, who was to late-Bohemian Gothic what Peter Parler was to the earlier version. The room imparts a sense of space and light, softened by the sensuous lines of the vaulted ceilings and brought to a dignified close by the simple oblong form of the early Renaissance windows. In its heyday, the hall was the site of jousting tournaments, festive markets, banquets, and coronations. In more recent times, it has been used to inaugurate presidents, from the Communist Klement Gottwald in 1948 to Václav Havel in 1989, 1993, and 1998.

From the front of the hall, turn right into the rooms of the **Česká kancelář** (Bohemian Chancellery). This wing was built by the same Benedikt Ried only 10 years after the hall was completed, but it shows a much stronger Renaissance influence. Pass through the Renaissance portal into the last chamber of the chancellery. This room was the site of the second defenestration of Prague, in 1618, an event that marked the beginning of the Bohemian rebellion and, ultimately, the Thirty Years' War. This peculiarly Bohemian method of expressing protest (throwing someone out a window) had first been used in 1419 in the New Town Hall, during the lead-up to the Hussite wars. Two hundred years later the same conflict was reexpressed in terms of Hapsburg-backed Catholics versus Bohemian Protestants. Rudolf II had reached an uneasy agreement with the Bohemian nobles, allowing them religious freedom in exchange for financial support. But his next-but-one successor, Ferdinand II, was a rabid opponent of Protestantism and disregarded Rudolf's tolerant "Letter of Majesty." Enraged, the Protestant nobles stormed the castle and chancellery and threw two Catholic officials and their secretary, for good measure, out the window. Legend has it they landed on a mound of horse dung and escaped unharmed, an event the Jesuits interpreted as a miracle. The square window in question is on the left as you enter the room.

At the back of the Vladislav Hall, a staircase leads up to a gallery of the **Kaple všech svatých** (All Saints' Chapel). Little remains of Peter Parler's original work, but the church contains some fine works of art. The large room to the left of the staircase is the **Stará sněmovna** (council chamber), where the Bohemian nobles met with the king in a kind of prototype parliament. The descent from Vladislav Hall toward what remains of the **Romanský palác** (Romanesque Palace) is by way of a wide, shallow set of steps. This **Jezdecké schody** (Riders' Staircase) was the entranceway for knights who came for the jousting tournaments. ✉ *Royal Palace, Třetí nádvoří, Hradčany,* ☎ *224–373–368 Castle Information,* WEB *www.hrad.cz.* 🎟 *Requires 1-day Castle ticket (180 Kč).* 🕑 *Apr.–Oct., daily 9–5; Nov.–Mar., daily 9–4.*

56 **Lobkovický palác** (Lobkowicz Palace). From the beginning of the 17th century until the 1940s, this building was the residence of the powerful Catholic Lobkowicz family. It was supposedly to this house that the two defenestrated officials escaped after landing on the dung hill in 1618. During the 1970s the building was restored to its early baroque appearance and now houses the National Museum's permanent exhibition on Czech history. If you want to get a chronological understanding of Czech history from the beginnings of the Great Moravian Empire in the 9th century to the Czech national uprising in 1848, this is the place. Copies of the crown jewels are on display here, but it is the rich collection of illuminated Bibles, old musical instruments, coins, weapons, royal decrees, paintings, and statues that makes the museum well worth visiting. Detailed information on the exhibits is available in English. ⌂ *Jiřská ul., Hradčany,* WEB *www.nm.cz.* ⌗ *40 Kč.* ☯ *Tues.–Sun. 9–5.*

46 **Matyášova brána** (Matthias Gate). Built in 1614, the stone gate once stood alone in front of the moats and bridges that surrounded the castle. Under the Hapsburgs, the gate survived by being grafted as a relief onto the palace building. As you go through it, notice the ceremonial white-marble entrance halls on either side that lead up to President Václav Havel's reception rooms (which are only rarely open to the public).

57 **Muzeum hraček** (Toy Museum). The building that once belonged to a high royal official called the Supreme Burgrave houses a private collection of modern dolls and other toys, somewhat incongruous to the historical surroundings but fun for those who still love Barbie. Enter at the eastern entrance to the Castle. ⌂ *Jiřská ul., Hradčany.* ⌗ *40 Kč.* ☯ *Daily 9:30–5:30.*

45 **První nádvoří** (First Courtyard). The main entrance to Prague Castle from Hradčanské náměstí is a little disappointing. Going through the wrought-iron gate, guarded at ground level by Czech soldiers and from above by the ferocious *Battling Titans* (a copy of Ignaz Platzer's original 18th-century work), you'll enter this courtyard, built on the site of old moats and gates that once separated the castle from the surrounding buildings and thus protected the vulnerable western flank. The courtyard is one of the more recent additions to the castle, designed by Maria Theresa's court architect, Nicolò Pacassi, in the 1760s. Today it forms part of the presidential office complex. Pacassi's reconstruction was intended to unify the eclectic collection of buildings that made up the castle, but the effect of his work is somewhat flat.

49 **Třetí nádvoří** (Third Courtyard). The contrast between the cool, dark interior of St. Vitus's Cathedral and the brightly colored Pacassi facades of the Third Courtyard just outside is startling. The courtyard's clean lines are the work of Slovenian architect Josip Plečnik in the 1930s, but the modern look is a deception. Plečnik's paving was intended to cover an underground world of house foundations, streets, and walls dating from the 9th through 12th centuries and rediscovered when the cathedral was completed. (You can see a few archways through a grating in a wall of the cathedral.) Plečnik added a few eclectic features to catch the eye: a granite obelisk to commemorate the fallen of the First World War, a black-marble pedestal for the Gothic statue of St. George (a copy of the National Gallery's original statue), the inconspicuous entrance to his Bull Staircase leading down to the south garden, and the peculiar golden ball topping the eagle fountain near the eastern end of the courtyard.

☺ **55** **Zlatá ulička** (Golden Lane). An enchanting collection of tiny, ancient, brightly colored houses crouched under the fortification wall looks remarkably like a set for *Snow White and the Seven Dwarfs.* Legend has it that these were the lodgings of the international group of alchemists whom Rudolf II brought to the court to produce gold. The truth is a little less romantic: the houses were built during the 16th century for the castle guards, who supplemented their income by practicing various crafts. By the early 20th century, Golden Lane had become the home of poor artists and writers. Franz Kafka, who lived at No. 22 in 1916 and 1917, described the house on first sight as "so small, so dirty, impossible to live in and lacking everything necessary." But he soon came to love the place. As he wrote to his fiancée: "Life here is something special . . . to close out the world not just by shutting the door to a room or apartment but to the whole house, to step out into the snow of the silent lane." The lane now houses tiny stores selling books, music, and crafts and has become so popular that a separate admission fee is now charged.

Within the walls above Golden Lane, a timber-roof **corridor** (enter between No. 23 and No. 24) is lined with replica suits of armor and weapons (some of it for sale), mock torture chambers, and the like. A shooting range allows you to fire five bolts from a crossbow for 50 Kč. ✉ *Hradčany,* ☎ *224–373–368,* WEB *www.hrad.cz.* 💴 *40 Kč; combination 1-day and Golden Lane 220 Kč.* ⏲ *Castle and Golden Lane Apr.–Oct., daily 9–5; Nov.–Mar., daily 9–4. Golden Lane Corridor Apr.–Oct., Tues.–Sun. 10–5, Mon. 1–5; Nov.–Mar., Tues.–Sun. 10–4, Mon. 1–4.*

Nové Město (New Town) and Vyšehrad

To this day, Charles IV's building projects are tightly woven into the daily lives of Praguers. His most extensive scheme, the New Town, is still such a lively, vibrant area you may hardly realize that its streets, Gothic churches, and squares were planned as far back as 1348. With Prague fast outstripping its Old Town parameters, Charles IV extended the city's fortifications. A high wall surrounded the newly developed 2½ square km (1½ square mi) area south and east of the Old Town, tripling the walled territory on the Vltava's right bank. The wall extended south to link with the fortifications of the citadel called Vyšehrad. In the mid-19th century, new building in the New Town boomed in a welter of Romantic and neo-Renaissance styles, particularly on Wenceslas Square and avenues such as Vodičkova, Na Poříčí, and Spálená. One of the most important structures was the Národní divadlo (National Theater), meant to symbolize in stone the revival of the Czechs' history, language, and sense of national pride. Both preceding and following Czechoslovak independence in 1918, modernist architecture entered the mix, particularly on the outer fringes of the Old Town and in the New Town. One of modernism's most unexpected products was Cubist architecture, a form unique to Prague, which produced four notable examples at the foot of ancient Vyšehrad.

Numbers in the text correspond to numbers in the margin and on the Prague map.

A Good Walk

Václavské náměstí ⑤⑧ is a long, gently sloping boulevard rather than a square in the usual sense. Marked by the **Statue of St. Wenceslas** ⑤⑨, it is bounded at the "top" (actually the southern end) by the **Národní muzeum** ⑥⓪ and at the "foot" (actually the northern end) by the pedestrian shopping areas of Národní třída and Na Příkopě. Today Václavské náměstí has Prague's liveliest street scene. Don't miss the dense maze of arcades tucked away from the street in buildings that line both sides. You'll find an odd assortment of cafés, shops, ice cream parlors, and movie houses, all seemingly unfazed by the passage of time. One eye-catching building on the square is the Hotel Europa, at No. 25, a riot of Art Nouveau that recalls the glamorous world of turn-of-the-20th-century Prague. Work by the Czech artist whose name is synonymous with Art Nouveau is on show just a block off the square, via Jindřišská, at the **Mucha Museum** ⑥.

From the foot of the square, head down 28 řijna to Jungmannovo náměstí, a small square named for the linguist and patriot Josef Jung-mann (1773–1847). In the courtyard off the square at No. 18, have a look at the Kostel Panny Marie Sněžné (Church of the Virgin Mary of the Snows). Building ceased during the Hussite wars, leaving a very high, foreshortened church that never grew into the monumental struc-ture planned by Charles IV. Beyond it lies a quiet sanctuary: the walled Františkánská zahrada (Franciscan Gardens). A busy shopping street, Národní třída, extends from Jungmannovo náměstí about ¾ km (½ mi) to the river and the **Národní divadlo** ⑥. From the theater, follow the embankment, Masarykovo nábřeží, south toward Vyšehrad. Note the Art Nouveau architecture of No. 32, the amazingly eclectic design by Kamil Hilbert at No. 26, and the tile-decorated Hlahol building at No. 16. Opposite, on a narrow island, is a 19th century, yellow-and-white ballroom-restaurant, Žofín.

Straddling an arm of the river at Myslíkova ulice are the modern Ga-lerie Mánes (1928–1930) and its attendant 15th-century water tower, where, from a lookout on the sixth floor, Communist-era secret po-lice used to observe Václav Havel's apartment at Rašínovo nábřeží 78. This building, still part-owned by the president, and the adjoining **Tančící dům** ⑥ are on the far side of a square named Jiráskovo náměstí after the historical novelist Alois Jirásek. From this square, Resslova ulice leads uphill four blocks to a much larger, parklike square, **Karlovo náměstí** ⑥. On the park's northern end is the **Novoměstská radnice** ⑥ (New Town Hall).

If you have the energy to continue on toward Vyšehrad, a convenient place to rejoin the riverfront is Palackého náměstí via Na Moráni street at the southern end of Karlovo náměstí. The square has a (melo)dra-matic monument to the 19th-century historian František Palacký, "awakener of the nation," and the view from here of the Benedictine **Klášter Emauzy** ⑥ is lovely. The houses grow less attractive south of here, so you may wish to hop a tram (No. 3, 16, or 17 at the stop on Rašínovo nábřeží) and ride one stop to Výtoň, at the base of the **Vyšehrad** ⑥ citadel. Walk under the railroad bridge on Rašínovo nábřeží to find the closest of four nearby **Cubist buildings** ⑥. Another lies just a minute's walk far-ther along the embankment; two more are on Neklanova, a couple of minutes' walk "inland" on Vnislavova. To get up to the fortress, make a hard left onto Vratislavova (the street right before Neklanova), an an-cient road that runs tortuously up into the heart of Vyšehrad.

It's about 2¼ km (1½ mi) between Národní divadlo and Vyšehrad. Note that Tram No. 17 travels the length of the embankment, if you'd like to make a quicker trip between the two points.

TIMING

You might want to divide the walk into two parts, first taking in the busy New Town between Václavské náměstí and Karlovo náměstí, then doing Vyšehrad and the Cubist houses as a side trip. A leisurely stroll from the Národní divadlo to Vyšehrad may easily absorb two hours, as may an exploration of Karlovo náměstí and the Klášter Emauzy. Vyšehrad is open every day, year-round, and the views are stunning on a clear day or evening, but keep in mind that there is little shade along the river walk on hot afternoons.

Sights to See

68 Cubist buildings. Born of zealous modernism, Prague's Cubist architecture followed a great Czech tradition in that it fully embraced new ideas while adapting them to existing artistic and social contexts. Between 1912 and 1914, Josef Chochol (1880–1956) designed several of the city's dozen or so Cubist projects. His apartment house **Neklanova 30**, on the corner of Neklanova and Přemyslova, is a masterpiece in dingy concrete. The pyramidal, kaleidoscopic window mouldings and roof cornices are completely novel while making an expressive link to baroque forms; the faceted corner balcony column elegantly alludes to Gothic forerunners. On the same street, at **Neklanova 2**, is another apartment house attributed to Chochol; like the building at Neklanova 30, it uses pyramidal shapes and the suggestion of Gothic columns.

Nearby, Chochol's **villa,** on the embankment at Libušina 3, has an undulating effect created by smoothly articulated forms. The wall and gate around the back of the house use triangular moldings and metal grating to create an effect of controlled energy. The **three-family house,** about 100 yards away from the villa at Rašínovo nábřeží 6–10, was completed slightly earlier, when Chochol's Cubist style was still developing. Here, the design is touched with baroque and neoclassical influence, with a mansard roof and end gables.

64 Karlovo náměstí (Charles Square). This square began life as a cattle market, a function chosen by Charles IV when he established the New Town in 1348. The horse market (now Wenceslas Square) quickly overtook it as a livestock-trading center, and an untidy collection of shacks accumulated here until the mid-1800s, when it became a green park named for its patron. ⊠ *Bounded by Řeznická on the north, U Nemocnice on the south, Karlovo nám. on the west, and Vodičkova on the east, Nové Město.*

66 Just south of Karlovo náměstí is another of Charles IV's gifts to the city, the Benedictine **Klášter Emauzy** (Emmaus Monastery). It is often called Na Slovanech, literally "At the Slavs'," in reference to its purpose when established in 1347: the emperor invited Croatian monks here to celebrate mass in Old Slavonic and thus cultivate religion among the Slavs in a city largely controlled by Germans. A faded but substantially complete cycle of biblical scenes by Charles's court artists lines the four cloister walls. The frescoes, and especially the abbey church, suffered heavy damage from a February 14, 1945, raid by Allied bombers that may have mistaken Prague for Dresden, 121 km (75 mi) away. The church lost its spires, and the interior remains a blackened shell. Some years after the war, two curving concrete "spires" were set atop the church. ⊠ *Vyšehradská 49, Vyšehrad (cloister entrance on left at rear of church).* 🎫 *10 Kč.* ☉ *Weekdays 8–6 or earlier depending on daylight.*

61 Mucha Museum. For decades it was almost impossible to find an Alfons Mucha original in the homeland of this famous Czech artist, until, in 1998, this private museum opened with nearly 100 works from his long career. What you'd expect to see is here—the theater posters of actress Sarah Bernhardt, the magazine covers, and the luscious, sinuous Art Nouveau designs. There are also paintings, photographs taken in Mucha's studio (one shows Paul Gauguin playing the piano in his underwear), and even Czechoslovak banknotes designed by the artist. ⊠ *Panská 7, Nové Město (1 block off Wenceslas Square, across from Palace Hotel),* ☎ *221–451–335,* 🌐 *www.mucha.cz.* 🎫 *120 Kč.* ☉ *Daily 10–6.*

62 Národní divadlo (National Theater). The idea for a Czech national theater began during the revolutionary decade of the 1840s. In a telling display of national pride, donations to fund the plan poured in from all over the country, from people of every socioeconomic stratum. The cornerstone was laid in 1868, and the "National Theater generation" who built the neo-Renaissance structure became the architectural and artistic establishment for decades to come. Its designer, Josef Zítek (1832–1909), was the leading neo-Renaissance architect in Bohemia. The nearly finished interior was gutted by a fire in 1881, and Zítek's onetime student Josef Schulz (1840–1917) saw the reconstruction through to completion two years later. Statues representing Drama and Opera rise above the riverfront side entrances; two gigantic chariots flank figures of Apollo and the nine Muses above the main facade. The performance space itself is filled with gilding, voluptuous plaster figures and plush upholstery. Next door is the modern (1970s–1980s) Nová scéna (New Stage), where the popular Magic Lantern black-light shows are staged. The Národní divadlo is one of the best places to see a performance; ticket prices start as low as 30 Kč, and you'll have to buy a ticket if you want to see inside because there are no public tours. ⊠ *Národní tř. 2, Nové Město,* ☎ *224–901–448 box office,* WEB *www.narodni-divadlo.cz.*

60 **Národní muzeum** (National Museum). This imposing structure, designed by Prague architect Josef Schulz and built between 1885 and 1890, does not come into its own until it is bathed in nighttime lighting. By day the grandiose edifice seems an inappropriate venue for a musty collection of stones and bones, minerals, and coins. This museum is only for dedicated fans of the genre. ⊠ *Václavské nám. 68, Nové Město,* ☎ *224–497–111,* WEB *www.nm.cz.* ☑ *80 Kč.* ☉ *May–Sept., daily 10–6; Oct.–Apr., daily 9–5; except for first Tues. of each month, when it is closed.*

65 **Novoměstská radnice** (New Town Hall). At the northern edge of Karlovo náměstí, the New Town Hall has a late-Gothic tower similar to that of the Old Town Hall, as well as three tall Renaissance gables. The first defenestration in Prague occurred here on July 30, 1419, when a mob of townspeople, followers of the martyred religious reformer Jan Hus, hurled Catholic town councilors out the windows. Historical exhibitions and contemporary art shows are held here regularly (admission prices vary), and you can climb the tower for a view of the New Town. ⊠ *Karlovo nám. at Vodičkova, Nové Město.* ☑ *Tower 20 Kč.* ☉ *Tower May–Sept., Tues.–Sun. 10–6; gallery Tues.–Sun. 10–6.*

59 **Statue of St. Wenceslas.** Josef Václav Myslbek's huge equestrian grouping of St. Wenceslas with other Czech patron saints around him is a traditional meeting place at times of great national peril or rejoicing. In 1939, Praguers gathered to oppose Hitler's takeover of Bohemia and Moravia. It was here also, in 1969, that the student Jan Palach set himself on fire to protest the bloody invasion of his country by the Soviet Union and other Warsaw Pact countries in August of the previous year. The invasion ended the "Prague Spring," a cultural and political movement emphasizing free expression, which was supported by Alexander Dubček, the popular leader at the time. Although Dubček never intended to dismantle Communist authority completely, his political and economic reforms proved too daring for fellow comrades in the rest of Eastern Europe. In the months following the invasion, conservatives loyal to the Soviet Union were installed in all influential positions. The subsequent two decades were a period of cultural stagnation. Hundreds of thousands of Czechs and Slovaks left the country, a few became dissidents, and many more resigned themselves to lives of minimal expectations and small pleasures. ⊠ *Václavské nám., Nové Město.*

63 **Tančící dům** (Dancing House). This whimsical building was partnered into life in 1996 by architect Frank Gehry (of Guggenheim Museum in Bilbao fame) and his Croatian-Czech collaborator Vlado Milunic. A wasp-waisted glass-and-steel tower sways into the main structure as though they were a couple on the dance floor—a "Fred and Ginger" effect that gave the wacky, yet somehow appropriate, building its nickname. The French restaurant La Perle de Prague occupies the top floors, and there is a café at street level. ⊠ *Rašínovo nábř. 80, Nové Město.*

⑤⑧ Václavské náměstí (Wenceslas Square). You may recognize this spot from your television set, for it was here that some 500,000 students and citizens gathered in the heady days of November 1989 to protest the policies of the former Communist regime. The government capitulated after a week of demonstrations, without a shot fired or the loss of a single life, bringing to power the first democratic government in 40 years (under playwright-president Václav Havel). Today this peaceful transfer of power is half-ironically referred to as the "Velvet" or "Gentle" Revolution (*něžná revoluce*). It was only fitting that the 1989 revolution should take place on Wenceslas Square: throughout much of Czech history, the square has served as the focal point for popular discontent. The long "square," which is more like a broad, divided boulevard, was first laid out by Charles IV in 1348 as a horse market at the center of the New Town.

At No. 25, the **Hotel Europa** (⊠ Vaclavske nám. 25) is an Art Nouveau gem, with elegant stained glass and mosaics in the café and restaurant. The terrace is an excellent spot for people-watching. Note in particular the ornate sculpture work of two figures supporting a glass egg on top of the building and the ornate exterior mural. In 1906, when the hotel opened, this was a place for the elite; now the rooms reflect a sense of sadly faded grandeur.

🐚 **⑥⑦ Vyšehrad.** Bedřich Smetana's symphonic poem *Vyšehrad* opens with four bardic harp chords that seem to echo the legends surrounding this ancient fortress. Today, the flat-topped bluff standing over the right bank of the Vltava is a green, tree-dotted expanse showing few signs that splendid medieval monuments once made it a landmark to rival Prague Castle.

The historical father of Vyšehrad, the "High Castle," is Vratislav II (ruled 1061–92), a Přemyslid duke who became first king of Bohemia. He made the fortified hilltop his capital, but, under subsequent rulers, it fell into disuse until the 14th century, when Charles IV transformed the site into an ensemble of palaces, the Gothicized main church, battlements, and a massive gatehouse called *Špička,* whose scant remains are on V pevnosti ulice. By the 17th century, royalty had long since departed, and most of the structures they built were crumbling. Vyšehrad was turned into a fortress.

Vyšehrad's place in the modern Czech imagination is largely thanks to the National Revivalists of the 19th century, particularly writer Alois Jirásek (1851–1930), who mined medieval chronicles for legends and facts to glorify the early Czechs. In his rendition, Vyšehrad was the court of the prophetess-ruler Libuše, who had a vision of her husband-to-be, the ploughman Přemysl—father of the Přemyslid line—and of "a city whose glory shall reach the heavens" called Praha. (In truth, the Czechs first came to Vyšehrad around the beginning of the 900s, slightly later than the building of Prague Castle.)

Traces of the citadel's distant past do remain. A heavily restored **Romanesque rotunda,** built by Vratislav II, stands on the east side of the compound. Foundations and a few embossed floor tiles from the late-10th-century **Basilika svatého Vavřince** (St. Lawrence Basilica) are in a structure on Soběslavova Street (if it is locked, you can ask for the key at the refreshment stand just to the left of the basilica entrance;

admission is 5 Kč). Part of the medieval fortifications stand next to the surprisingly confined foundation mounds of a medieval palace overlooking a ruined watchtower called Libuše's Bath. A nearby plot of grass hosts a statue of Libuše and her consort Přemysl, one of four large sculpted images of couples from Czech legend by J. V. Myslbek (1848–1922), the sculptor of the St. Wenceslas monument.

The military history of the fortress and the city is covered in a small exposition inside the **Cihelná brána** (Brick Gate). The gate is also the entrance to the **casemates**—a long, dark passageway within the walls that ends at a dank hall used to store several original, pollution-scarred Charles Bridge sculptures. A guided tour into the casemates and the statue storage room starts at the military history exhibit. With its neo-Gothic spires, **Kapitulní kostel svatých Petra a Pavla** (Chapter Church of Sts. Peter and Paul; ⊠ K rotundì 10, Vyšehrad, ☎ 224–911–353) dominates the plateau as it has since the 11th century. Next to the church lies the burial ground of the nation's revered cultural figures. Most of the buildings still standing are from the 19th century, but scattered among them are a few older structures and some foundation stones of the medieval palaces. Surrounding the ruins are gargantuan, excellently preserved brick fortifications built from the 17th to the mid-19th century; their broad tops allow strollers to take in sweeping vistas up- and downriver.

A concrete result of the National Revival was the establishment of the **Hřbitov** (cemetery; Vinohradská 294/212, Vyšehrad, ☎ 224–919–815, 🌐 www.slavin.cz) in the 1860s, adjacent to the Church of Sts. Peter and Paul—it peopled the fortress with the remains of luminaries from the arts and sciences. The grave of Smetana faces the Slavín, a mausoleum for more than 50 honored men and women including Alfons Mucha, sculptor Jan Štursa, inventor František Křižík, and the opera diva Ema Destinnová. All are guarded by a winged genius who hovers above the inscription AČ ZEMŘELI, JEŠTĚ MLUVÍ ("Although they have died, they yet speak"). Antonín Dvořák (1841–1904) rests in the arcade along the north wall of the cemetery. Among the many writers buried here are Jan Neruda, Božena Němcová, Karel Čapek, and the Romantic poet Karel Hynek Mácha, whose grave was visited by students on their momentous November 17, 1989, protest march. ⊠ V Pevnosti 159/5b, Vyšehrad, ☎ 241–410–348, 🌐 www.praha-vysehrad. cz. 🎫 Casemates tour 20 Kč, military exhibit 10 Kč, cemetery free, Church of Sts. Peter and Paul 10 Kč. ☉ Grounds daily. Casemates, military history exhibit, and St. Lawrence Basilica Apr.–Oct., daily 9:30–5:30; Nov.–Mar., daily 9:30–4:30. Cemetery Apr.–Oct., daily 8–6; Nov.–Mar., daily 8–4. Church of Sts. Peter and Paul daily 9–noon and 1–5. Metro: Vyšehrad (Line C).

Vinohrady

From Riegrovy Park and its sweeping view of the city from above the National Museum, the eclectic apartment houses and villas of the elegant residential neighborhood called Vinohrady extend eastward and southward. The pastel-tint ranks of turn-of-the-20th-century apartment houses—many crumbling after years of neglect—are slowly but unstoppably being transformed into upscale flats, slick offices, eternally packed new restaurants, and all manner of shops unthinkable only a half decade ago. Much of the development lies on or near Vinohradská, the main street, which extends from the top of Wenceslas Square to a belt of enormous cemeteries about 3 km (2 mi) eastward. Yet the flavor of daily life persists: smoky old pubs still ply their trade on the quiet side streets; the stately theater, Divadlo na Vinohradech, keeps putting on excellent shows as it has for decades; and on the squares and in the parks nearly everyone still practices Prague's favorite form of outdoor exercise—walking the dog.

Numbers in the margin correspond to numbers on the Prague map.

69 **Kostel Nejsvětějšího Srdce Páně** (Church of the Most Sacred Heart). If you've had your fill of Romanesque, Gothic, and baroque, this church will give you a look at a startling art deco edifice. Designed in 1927 by Slovenian architect Josip Plečnik (the same architect commissioned to update Prague Castle), the church resembles a luxury ocean liner more than a place of worship. The effect was conscious: during the 1920s and 1930s, the avant-garde imitated mammoth objects of modern technology. Plečnik used many modern elements on the inside. Notice the hanging speakers, seemingly designed to bring the word of God directly to the ears of each worshiper. You may be able to find someone at the back entrance of the church who will let you walk up the long ramp into the fascinating glass clock tower. ⊠ *Nám. Jiřího z Poděbrad, Vinohrady.* ☑ *Free.* ☉ *Daily 10–5. Metro: Jiřího z Poděbrad (Line A).*

70 **Nový židovský hřbitov** (New Jewish Cemetery). Tens of thousands of Czechs find eternal rest in Vinohrady's cemeteries. In this, the newest of the city's half-dozen Jewish burial grounds, you'll find the modest **tombstone of Franz Kafka,** which seems grossly inadequate to Kafka's stature but oddly in proportion to his own modest ambitions. The cemetery is usually open, although guards sometimes inexplicably seal off the grounds. Men may be required to wear a yarmulke (you can buy one here). Turn right at the main cemetery gate and follow the wall for about 100 yards. Kafka's thin, white tombstone lies at the front of section 21. City maps may label the cemetery *Židovské hřbitovy.* ⊠ *Vinohradská at Jana Želivského, Vinohrady.* ☑ *Free.* ☉ *June–Aug., Sun.–Thurs. 9–5, Fri. 9–1; Sept.–May, Sun.–Thurs. 9–4, Fri. 9–1. Metro: Želivského (Line A).*

71 **Pavilon.** This gorgeous, turn-of-the-20th-century, neo-Renaissance, three-story market hall is one of the most attractive sites in Vinohrady. It used to be a major old-style market, a vast space filled with stalls selling all manner of foodstuffs plus the requisite grimy pub. After being spiffed up in the 1990s, it mutated into an upscale shopping mall. Off the tourist track, Pavilion is a good place to watch Praguers—those who can afford its shops' gleaming designer pens and Italian shoes—ostentatiously drinking in *la dolce vita,* cell phones in hand. Walk west two blocks down Vinohradská after exiting the metro. ⊠ *Vinohradská 50, Vinohrady,* ☎ *222–097–111.* ☉ *Mon.–Sat. 8:30 AM–9 PM, Sun. noon–6. Metro: Jiřího z Poděbrad (Line A).*

Letná and Holešovice

From above the Vltava's left bank, the large, grassy plateau called Letná gives you one of the classic views of the Old Town and the many bridges crossing the river. (To get to Letná from the Old Town, take Pařížská Street north, cross the Čechův Bridge, and climb the stairs.) Beer gardens, tennis, and Frisbee attract people of all ages, while amateur soccer players emulate the professionals of Prague's top team, Sparta, which plays in the stadium just across the road. A 10-minute walk from Letná, down into the residential neighborhood of Holešovice, brings you to a massive, gray-blue building whose cool exterior gives no hint of the treasures of Czech and French modern art that line its corridors. Just north along Dukelských hrdinů Street is Stromovka—a royal hunting preserve turned gracious park.

Numbers in the margin correspond to numbers on the Prague map.

72 **Letenské sady** (Letna Park). Come to this large, shady park for an unforgettable view of Prague's bridges. From the enormous cement pedestal at the center of the park, the largest statue of Stalin in Eastern Europe once beckoned to citizens on the Old Town Square far below. The statue was ripped down in the 1960s, when Stalinism was finally discredited. On sunny Sundays expatriates often meet up here to play ultimate Frisbee. Head east on Milady Horáové street after exiting the metro. ⊠ *Holešovice. Metro: Hradčanská.*

73 **Veletržní palác** (Trade Fair Palace). The National Gallery's **Sbírka moderního a soucasného umění** (Collection of Modern and Contemporary Art) has become a keystone in the city's visual-arts scene since its opening in 1995. Touring the vast spaces of this 1920s Constructivist exposition hall and its comprehensive collection of 20th-century Czech art is the best way to see how Czechs surfed the forefront of the avant-garde wave until the cultural freeze following the Communist takeover in 1948. Also on display are works by Western European—mostly French—artists from Delacroix to the present. Especially noteworthy are the early Cubist paintings by Picasso and Braque. The 19th-century Czech art collection of the National Gallery was installed in the palace in the summer of 2000. Watch the papers and posters for information on traveling shows and temporary exhibits. The collection is divided into sections, so be sure to get a ticket for exactly what you want to see. ⊠ *Dukelských hrdinů 47, Holešovice,* ☎ *224–301–111,* WEB *www.ngprague.cz.* ☒ *One floor 100 Kč, 2 floors 150 Kč, 3 floors 200 Kč, special exhibits 40 Kč.* ☉ *Tues.–Wed. and Fri.–Sun. 10–6, Thurs. 10–9. Metro: Vltavská (Line C).*

DINING

Dining choices in Prague have increased greatly in the past decade as hundreds of new places have opened to meet the soaring demand from tourists and locals alike. These days, out-and-out rip-offs have almost disappeared, but before paying up at the end of a meal it's a good idea to take a close look at the added cover charge on your bill. Also keep an eye out for a large fee tacked on to a credit card bill. In pubs and neighborhood restaurants, ask if there is a *denní lístek* (daily menu) of cheaper and often fresher selections, but note that many places provide daily menus for the midday meal only. Special local dishes worth making a beeline for include *cibulačka* (onion soup), *kulajda* (potato soup with sour cream), *svíčková* (beef sirloin in cream sauce), and *ovocné knedlíky* (fruit dumplings, often listed under "meatless dishes").

The crush of tourists has placed tremendous strain on the more popular restaurants. The upshot: reservations are an excellent idea, especially for dinner during peak tourist periods. If you don't have reservations, try arriving a little before standard meal times: 11:30 AM for lunch or 5:30 PM for dinner.

For a cheaper and quicker alternative to the sit-down establishments listed below, try a light meal at one of the city's growing number of street stands or fast-food places. Look for stands offering *párky* (hot dogs) or the fattier *klobásy* (grilled sausages served with bread and mustard). Also, chic new cafés and bakeries spring up all the time. For more exotic fare, try the very good vegetarian cooking at **Country Life** (⊠ Melantrichova 15, Staré Město, ☎ 224–213–366). **Vzpomínky na Afriku** (⊠ Rybná at Jakubská, Staré Město, near the Kotva department store) has the widest selection of gourmet coffees in town, served at the single table or to go.

Staré Město (Old Town)

$$$–$$$$ ✕ **Bellevue.** The first choice for visiting dignitaries and businesspeople blessed with expense accounts, Bellevue has creative, freshly prepared cuisine, more nouvelle than Bohemian—and the elegant location not far from Charles Bridge doesn't hurt. Look for the lamb carpaccio with fresh rosemary, garlic, and extra-virgin olive oil or the wild berries marinated in port and cognac, served with vanilla-and-walnut ice cream. Window seats have stunning views of Prague Castle. The Sunday jazz brunch is a winner, too. ⊠ *Smetanovo nábř. 18, Staré Město,* ☎ *222–221–449. AE, MC, V.*

$$–$$$$ ✕ **Allegro.** Some of the best—and most expensive—Italian food in town can be had at the restaurant in the Four Seasons Prague. Don't plan on just dropping in, though; reservations are essential and the dress code bans shorts and sneakers. Jackets are suggested for the evening. In the summer, dining on the terrace, with a spectacular view of the Charles Bridge, makes it worth the extra effort it takes to polish your shoes. The international wine list features selections from the National Wine Bank. ⊠ *Veleslavinova 21, Staré Město, 110 00 Prague 1,* ☎ *221–427–000. Reservations essential. AE, DC MC, V.*

$$–$$$$ ✕ **Jewel of India.** Although generally Asian cooking of any stripe is not Prague's forte, here is a sumptuous spot well worth seeking out for northern Indian tandooris and other moderately spiced specialties, including some delicious vegetarian dishes. ⊠ *Pařížská 20, Staré Město,* ☎ *224–811–010. AE, MC, V. Metro: Staroměstská.*

$$–$$$$ ✕ **V Zátiší.** White walls and casual grace accentuate the subtle flavors
★ of smoked salmon, plaice, beef Wellington, and other non-Czech specialties. Here, as at most of the city's better establishments, the wine list has expanded in recent years and now includes most of the great wine-producing regions, though good Moravian vintages are still kept on hand. In behavior unusual for the city, the benign waiters fairly fall over each other to serve diners. ⊠ *Liliová 1 at Betlémské nám., Staré Město,* ☎ *222–222–025. AE, MC, V.*

$$$ ✕ **Barock.** Call it chic or call it pretentious, Barock exemplifies the revolution in Prague's dining and social life since those uncool Communists decamped. Thai and Japanese dishes predominate, and there are other Asian choices and international standards. Although eating isn't the main point here—being seen is—the fish dishes and sushi won't let you down. ⊠ *Pařížská 24, Josefov,* ☎ *222–329–221. AE, DC, MC, V.*

$–$$ ✕ **Chez Marcel.** At this authentic French bistro on a quiet street you can get a little taste of that *other* riverside capital. French-owned and -operated, Chez Marcel has a smallish but reliable menu listing pâtés, salads, rabbit, and chicken, as well as some of the best steaks in Prague. The specials board usually has some tempting choices, such as salmon, beef daube, or foie gras. ⊠ *Haštalská 12, Staré Město,* ☎ *222–315– 676. No credit cards.*

$–$$ ✕ **Pizzeria Rugantino.** Bright and spacious, this buzzing pizzeria serves up thin-crust pies; big, healthy salads; and good Italian bread. It can get quite loud when full, which is most nights. ⊠ *Dušní 4, Staré Město,* ☎ *222–318–172. No credit cards. No lunch Sun.*

$ ✕ **Kavárna Slavia.** This legendary hangout for the best and brightest
★ in Czech arts—from composer Bedřich Smetana and poet Jaroslav Seifert to then-dissident Václav Havel—reopened after being held hostage in absurd real-estate wrangles for most of the 1990s. Its Art Deco interior is a perfect backdrop for people-watching, and the vistas (the river and Prague Castle on one side, the National Theater on the other) are a compelling reason to linger for hours over a coffee—although it's not the best brew in town. The Slavia is a café to its core, but you can also get a light meal, such as a small salad with Balkan

Prague Dining and Lodging

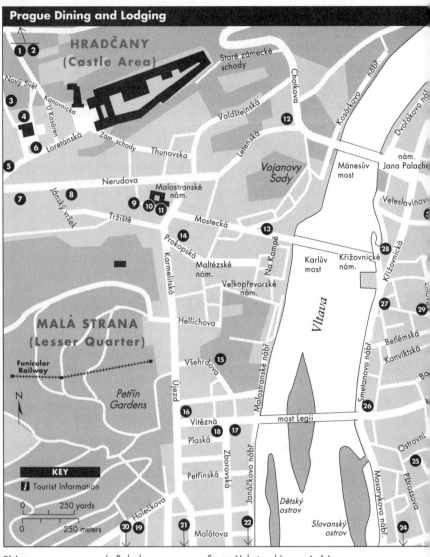

Dining

Allegro **28**
Barock **33**
Bella Napoli **55**
Bellevue **27**
Bohemia Bagel . . **16**
Break Café
and Bar **55**
Café Savoy **17**
Chez Marcel **35**
Circle Line **9**
Jewel of India . . . **32**
Kavárna Slavia . . **26**
La Crêperie **40**

La Perle de
Prague **24**
Lotos **31**
Mailsi **47**
Myslivna **62**
Novoměstský
pivovar **53**
Pasha **12**
Pizzeria
Coloseum **51**
Pizzeria
Rugantino **34**
Radost FX Café . . **58**

Square-Malostranská
Kvárna **11**
The Sushi Bar . . . **18**
U Maltézských
rytířů **14**
U Mecenáše **10**
U Počtů **39**
U Sedmi Švábů . . . **8**
U Ševce Matouše . . **6**
U Zlaté hrušky **4**
Universal **25**
V Krakovské **56**
V Zátiší **29**
Zahrada v opeře . . **33**

Lodging

Anna **59**
Apollo **37**
Arbes Mepro **21**
Astra **60**
Axa **43**
Balkan **22**
Bern **48**
City Hotel
Moran **52**
Diplomat **1**
Dům U
Červeného lva **7**

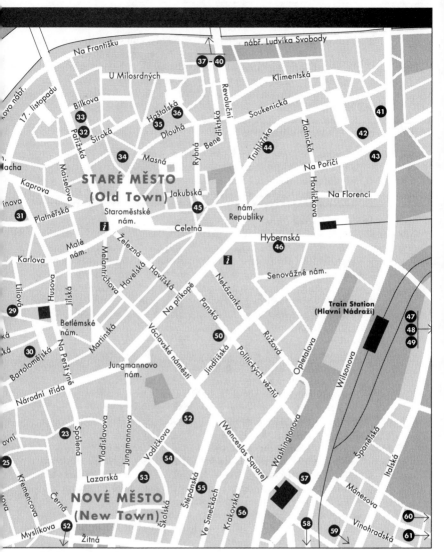

cheese, or an open-face sandwich. ⊠ *Smetanovo nábř. 1012/2, Staré Město,* ☎ *224–220–957. AE, MC, V.*

$ ✕ Lotos. Banana ragoût with polenta and broccoli strudel are two favorites at what is undoubtedly the best of the city's scant selection of all-vegetarian restaurants. Blond-wood tables and billowing tie-dyed fabric wall-hangings set an informal yet elegant atmosphere. The salads and soups are wonderful. ⊠ *Platnéřská 13, Staré Město,* ☎ *222–322–390. MC, V.*

Malá Strana (Lesser Quarter)

$$$–$$$$ ✕ Pasha. This inviting Middle Eastern spot at the foot of Prague Castle hits just the right notes of luxury and easiness. The à la carte menu includes luscious *adana kebab* (skewer of minced lamb), pilaf, and shish kebab. Baklava served with fresh mint tea makes a splendid dessert. ⊠ *U Lužického semináře 23, Malá Strana,* ☎ *257–532–439. AE, MC, V. Closed Mon.*

$$–$$$$ ✕ Café Savoy. Opened in 1887 as a grand café, the Savoy lasted only
★ a few years before the long, airy room was divided up to be made into shops. In 2001 the grand café was reborn as an upscale restaurant with bright cloth ceiling hangings and a shocking orange facade. Menu items include duck appetizers, homemade ravioli, and fresh seafood, served in a variety of surprising taste combinations and presented with an artistic, nouvelle flair. Lunch specials are a real value. ⊠ *Vítězná 5, Malá Strana,* ☎ *257–329–860. MC, V.*

$$–$$$$ ✕ Circle Line. Now moved out of the cellar into two elegant dining rooms, one done up in blue and the other in pink, Circle Line maintains its high standards with such dishes as fallow deer with spaetzle, pike perch, and yellowfin tuna carpaccio. The service can't be faulted. There are creative seasonal specials such as the warm foie gras with cherries, but be sure to save room for the chocolate plate for dessert. Brunch is served daily until 6 PM. ⊠ *Malostranské nám. 12, Malá Strana,* ☎ *257–530–022. AE, MC, V.*

$$–$$$$ ✕ Square - Malostranská kvárna. An older café on this main square has been given an upscale new look that might not please all preservationists. The food, which includes such main courses as grilled skate wing or bucatini and duck ragoût, should put smiles on the faces of those looking for something different at a central location. Outdoor seating in the summer makes this a prime spot for people-watching, but make sure to peek inside at the trendy decor. ⊠ *Malostranské nám, Malá Strana,* ☎ *257–532–109. AC, DC, MC, V.*

$$–$$$$ ✕ The Sushi Bar. This chic little joint with the wacky whale sculpture floating overhead could have been transported straight from San Francisco. Given Prague's distance from the sea, the selection of sushi and sashimi is excellent. For the same reason, call ahead to check when the fresh seafood is due (it's delivered twice a week), or stick to the broiled salmon or tempura dishes. ⊠ *Zborovská 49, Malá Strana,* ☎ *0603–244–882. DC, MC, V.*

$$–$$$ ✕ U Maltézských rytířů. The tongue-twisting name means "At the Knights of Malta," a reference to the Catholic order whose embassy is nearby. The upstairs dining room and bar are cozy, but ask for a table in the deep cellar—then ask the proprietress to regale you with yarns about this ancient house. They've dropped some old favorites from the menu but still offer good steaks, game, and fish. ⊠ *Prokopská 10, Malá Strana,* ☎ *257–533–666. AE, MC, V.*

$$ ✕ U Mecenáše. A fetching Renaissance inn from the 17th century, with dark, high-back benches in the front room and cozy, elegant sofas and chairs in back, this is a place to splurge. From the aperitifs to the specialty steaks or beef Wellington and the cognac (swirled lovingly in oversize glasses), the presentation is seamless. ⊠ *Malostranské nám. 10, Malá Strana,* ☎ *257–531–631. AE, MC, V.*

$–$$ ✕ **U Sedmi Švábů.** Medieval decorations and waitresses in peasant dresses serving beer and mead to diners seated at long wooden tables make this medieval-theme restaurant worth a stop. Unusual menu items include millet pancakes with herbs, carp on garlic, and roast pork knuckle for two. Special multicourse "knight's feasts" are also available. Chicken, steaks, and other mundane dishes are available for the less adventuresome. ⊠ *Jánský vršek 14, Malá Strana,* ☎ *257–531–645. AE, MC, V.*

$ ✕ **Bohemia Bagel.** It's not New York, but the friendly, North American–owned Bohemia Bagel still serves up a plentiful assortment of fresh bagels, from raisin-walnut to "supreme," with all kinds of toppings. The thick soups are among the best in Prague for the price, and the bottomless cups of coffee are a further draw. ⊠ *Újezd 16, Malá Strana,* ☎ *257–310–694. No credit cards.*

Hradčany

$$–$$$$ ✕ **U Zlaté hrušky.** At this fetching little rococo house perched on one of Prague's prettiest cobblestone streets, slide into one of the cozy darkwood booths and let the cheerful staff advise you on wines and specials. Among the regular offerings are a superb leg of venison with pears and millet gnocchi, and an excellent appetizer of foie gras in wine sauce. After dinner, stroll to the castle for an unforgettable panorama. ⊠ *Nový Svět 3, Hradčany,* ☎ *220–514–778. AE, MC, V.*

$–$$ ✕ **U Ševce Matouše.** Steaks are the raison d'être at this former shoemaker's shop, where a gold shoe still hangs from the ceiling of the arcade outside to guide patrons into the vaulted dining room. Appetizers are hit-and-miss; stick with the dozen or so tenderloins and filet mignons. ⊠ *Loretánské nám. 4, Hradčany,* ☎ *220–514–536. MC, V.*

Nové Město (New Town) and Vyšehrad

$$–$$$$ ✕ **Bella Napoli.** The decor may make you think you're in Las Vegas, but the food is genuine and the price-to-quality ratio hard to beat. Close your eyes to the alabaster Venus de Milos astride shopping-mall fountains and head straight for the antipasto bar, which will distract you with fresh olives, eggplant, squid, and mozzarella. For your main course, go with any of a dozen superb pasta dishes or splurge with shrimp or chicken parmigiana. ⊠ *V Jámě 8, Nové Město,* ☎ *222–232–933. No credit cards.*

$$–$$$$ ✕ **La Perle de Prague.** Delicious Parisian cooking awaits at the top of the curvaceous "Fred and Ginger" building. The interior of the main room is washed with soft tones of lilac and sea green. This room also has smallish windows—typical of architect Frank Gehry's designs—and rather cheesy nude photographs, but the semi-private dining room at the very top has a riveting view over the river. Try the red snapper Provençal, freshwater *candát* (pike perch), or tournedos of beef Béarnaise. Make reservations as early as you can. This is also a good reason to unpack your tie. ⊠ *Rašínovo nábř. 80, Nové Město,* ☎ *221–984–160. AE, DC, MC, V. Closed Sun. No lunch Mon.*

$$–$$$ ✕ **Zahrada v opeře** (Garden in the Opera). Ignore the concrete barri-
★ cades, armored personnel carriers, and machine-gun toting soldiers. They are on hand to protect the adjacent Radio Free Europe headquarters. The pebbled floor, subdued lighting, and gentle classical music of "the safest garden in the world" make for a romantic setting that contrasts sharply with the security outside. The prices for fresh seafood, steaks, and salads are quite reasonable, and the international wine list offers some surprising selections. ⊠ *Legerova 75, Nové Město,* ☎ *224–239–685. AE, MC, V.*

$–$$ ✕ **Break Café and Bar.** A reasonably priced selection of salads and sand-
★ wiches in the daytime gives way to an international menu in the evening
that includes such extremes as Scandinavian gravlax and steak tartare,
the latter according to a recipe from Maxim's. A comfortable, relaxed
atmosphere makes this a nice break from the hustle of nearby Wenceslas Square. ⊠ *Štepanská 32, Nové Město,* ☎ *222–231–065. No credit
cards.*

$–$$ ✕ **Novoměstský pivovar.** It's easy to lose your way in this crowded
microbrewery-restaurant with its maze of rooms, some painted in
mock-medieval style, others covered with murals of Prague street
scenes. *Vepřové koleno* (pork knuckle) is a favorite dish. The beer is
the cloudy, fruity "fermented" style. ⊠ *Vodičkova 20, Nové Město,*
☎ *222–231–662. AE, MC, V.*

$–$$ ✕ **Pizzeria Coloseum.** An early entry in the burgeoning pizza-and-
pasta trade, this one has kept its popularity due largely to its position
right off Wenceslas Square. Location doesn't have everything to do with
it, though; the pizzas have a wonderfully thin, crisp crust, and the pasta
with Gorgonzola sauce will have you blessing Italian cows. Steaks and
seafood are also on the menu. Long picnic tables make this an ideal
spot for an informal lunch or dinner. There's even a salad bar. ⊠
Vodičkova 32, Nové Město, ☎ *224–214–914. AE, MC, V.*

$–$$ ✕ **Radost FX Café.** Colorful and campy in design, this lively café is a
street-level adjunct to the popular Radost dance club. It's a favorite vegetarian outpost for both Czechs and expatriates. The creative specials
of a Mexican or Italian persuasion are tasty and filling enough to satisfy carnivores. If you suddenly find yourself craving a brownie, this is
the place to get a fudge fix. Another plus: it's open until around 3 AM.
⊠ *Bělehradská 120, Nové Město,* ☎ *224–254–776. No credit cards.*

$–$$ ✕ **Universal.** A pioneer in the neighborhood behind the National The-
ater that's fast becoming a trendy dining ghetto, Universal serves up
satisfying French- and Indian-influenced main courses, giant side orders of scalloped potatoes, and luscious lemon tarts or chocolate
mousse—all at ridiculously low prices. ⊠ *V Jirchářích 6, Nové Město,*
☎ *224–918–182. No credit cards.*

$ ✕ **V Krakovské.** At this clean, proper pub close to the major tourist
sights, the food is traditional and hearty. This is the place to try
svíčková na smetaně (thinly sliced sirloin beef in cream sauce) paired
with an effervescent pilsner beer. ⊠ *Krakovská 20, Nové Město,* ☎
222–210–204. No credit cards.

Vinohrady

$–$$ ✕ **Myslivna.** The name means "Hunting Lodge," and the cooks at this
neighborhood eatery certainly know their way around venison, quail,
and boar. Attentive staff can advise on wines: try Vavřinecké, a hearty
red that holds its own with any beast. The roasted pheasant with
bacon and the leg of venison with walnuts get high marks. ⊠ *Jagel-
lonská 21, Vinohrady,* ☎ *222–723–252. AE, MC, V.*

Letná and Holešovice

$–$$ ✕ **U Počtů.** This is a charmingly old-fashioned neighborhood restau-
rant with comparatively skilled service. Garlic soup and chicken livers
in wine sauce are flawlessly rendered, and the grilled trout is delicious.
⊠ *Milady Horákové 47, Letná,* ☎ *233–371–419. AE, MC, V.*

$ ✕ **La Crêperie.** Started by a Czech-French couple, this creperie near
the Veletržní palác (Trade Fair Palace) serves all manner of crepes, both
sweet and savory. (It may take at least three or four to satisfy a hearty
appetite.) Make sure to leave room for the dessert crepe with cinna-
mon-apple puree layered with lemon cream. The wine list offers both

French and Hungarian vintages. ✉ *Janovského 4, Holešovice,* ☎ 220–878–040. *No credit cards.*

Žižkov

$–$$$ ✕ **Mailsi.** Funky paintings of Arabian Nights–type scenes in a low-ceil-
★ ing cellar make this Pakistani restaurant casual and cheerful. Chicken
is done especially well here—the *murgh vindaloo* may well be the
spiciest dish in Prague, and the thin-sliced marinated chicken (*murgh
tikka*) appetizer is a favorite. Take Tram 5, 9, or 26 to the Lipanská
stop, and then walk one block uphill. ✉ *Lipanská 1, Žižkov,* ☎ 222–
717–783. *No credit cards.*

LODGING

A slow rise in lodging standards continues, but at all but the most ex-
pensive hotels standards lag behind those of Germany and Austria—
as do prices. In most of the $$$$ and $$$ hotels, you can expect to
find a restaurant and an exchange bureau on or near the premises. Dur-
ing the peak season reservations are absolutely imperative; for the re-
mainder of the year they are highly recommended. Many hotels in Prague
go by a three-season system: the lowest rates are charged from December
through February, excluding Christmas (at some hotels) and New
Year's (at all hotels), when high-season rates are charged; the middle
season includes March, November, and often July and August; and spring
and fall bring the highest rates. Easter sees higher-than-high-season rates,
and some hotels up the price for other holidays and trade fairs. It always pays to ask first. Standard room rates almost always include breakfast. Only the top-end hotels have air-conditioning.

A private room or apartment can be a cheaper and more interesting alternative to a hotel. You'll find agencies offering such accommodations
all over Prague, including at the main train station (Hlavní nádraží),
Holešovice station (Nádraží Holešovice), and at Ruzyně Airport. These
bureaus normally are staffed with people who can speak some English,
and most can book rooms in hotels and pensions as well as private accommodations. Rates for private rooms start at around $15 per person
per night and can go much higher for better-quality rooms. In general,
there is no fee, but you may need to try several bureaus to find the accommodation you want. Ask to see a photo of the room before accepting it, and be sure to pinpoint its location on a map—you don't want to
wind up in an inconveniently distant location. You may be approached
by (usually) men in the stations hawking rooms, and while these deals
aren't always rip-offs, you should be wary of them. **Prague Information
Service** arranges lodging from all of its central offices, including the branch
in the main train station, which is in the booth marked TURISTICKÉ IN-
FORMACE on the left side of the main hall as you exit the station.

The bluntly named **Prague Accommodation Service** (✉ Opato-
vická 20, Nové Město, ☎ FAX 233–376–638, WEB www.
accommodation-prague-centre.cz) can help you find a reasonably
priced apartment in the center of town for a short stay. **Stop In** (✉
V Holešovičkách 15, Libeň, ☎ FAX 284–680–115, WEB www.stopin.
cz) offers private apartments and rooms, some in the more residential areas.

Staré Město (Old Town)

$$$$ ⊡ **Four Seasons Prague.** A new central building joins together a
baroque house from 1737 and a renovated neoclassical former factory
from 1846 into a large, modern hotel with an unbeatable riverside

location. Rooms with a view of the Charles Bridge or the Castle cost more. Movie stars such as Sean Connery and Owen Wilson made this their base when they worked in Prague. Breakfast can be included for a little extra. ⊠ *Veleslavinova 21, Staré Město, 110 00 Prague 1,* ☎ *221–427–000,* FAX *221–426–977,* WEB *www.fourseasons.com/prague. 142 rooms, 20 suites. Restaurant, cable TV with movies, in-room safe, minibars, health club, massage, sauna, bar, concierge, Internet, business services, meeting rooms, parking (fee), some pets allowed (fee), no-smoking rooms. AE, DC, MC, V.*

$$$$ 🏨 **Grand Hotel Bohemia.** This beautifully refurbished Art Nouveau town palace sits across the street from Obecní dům (Municipal House), near the Prašná brána (Powder Tower). During the Communist era it was a nameless, secure hideaway for ranking foreign party members. Once it was restored to private hands, the hotel was remodeled by its new Austrian owners, who opted for a muted, modern look in the rooms but left the sumptuous Boccaccio ballroom in its faux-rococo glory. In the rooms, sweeping, long drapes frame spectacular views of the Old Town. Each has a trouser press and answering machine. ⊠ *Králodvorská 4, Staré Město, 110 00 Prague 1,* ☎ *224–804–111,* FAX *222–329–545,* WEB *www.grandhotelbohemia.cz. 73 rooms, 5 suites. Restaurant, café, in-room fax, in-room safes, minibars, cable TV, bar, meeting rooms, some pets allowed (fee); no-smoking floor. AE, DC, MC, V. BP.*

$$$ 🏨 **Maximilian.** Oversize beds, classic French cherrywood furniture, and thick drapes make for a relaxing stay in this luxurious hotel. A relatively new property (opened in 1995), it's on a peaceful square, well away from traffic, noise, and crowds, yet within easy walking distance to Old Town Square and Pařížská Street. ⊠ *Haštalská 14, Staré Město, 110 00 Prague 1,* ☎ *221–806–111,* FAX *221–806–110,* WEB *www. goldentulip.com. 72 rooms. In-room fax, in-room safes, minibars, cable TV, Internet, meeting rooms, some pets allowed (fee), parking (fee); no-smoking rooms. AE, DC, MC, V. BP.*

$ 🏨 **Pension Unitas.** The spartan rooms of this former convent, now operated by the Christian charity Unitas, used to serve as interrogation cells for the Communist secret police. (Václav Havel was once a "guest.") Today conditions are much more comfortable, though it feels much more like a hostel than a pension. There's a common (but clean) bathroom on each floor. You'll need to reserve well in advance, even in the off-season. Note that there is an adjacent three-star hotel, Cloister Inn, using the same location and phone number, so when calling, specify the pension. ⊠ *Bartolomějská 9, Staré Město, 110 00 Prague 1,* ☎ *224–211–020,* FAX *224–210–800,* WEB *www.unitas.cz. 40 rooms with shared bath. Restaurant; no a/c, no smoking. No credit cards. BP.*

Malá Strana (Lesser Quarter)

$$$$ 🏨 **U Tří Pštrosů.** The location could not be better: a romantic corner just a stone's throw from the river and within arms' reach of the Charles Bridge. The airy rooms of the centuries-old building still have their original oak-beam ceilings and antique furniture, and many have views over the river. Massive walls keep out the noise of the crowds on the bridge. An excellent in-house restaurant serves traditional Czech dishes to guests and nonguests alike. Rates drop slightly in July and August—probably because there's no air-conditioning, though the building's thick walls help keep it cool. ⊠ *Dražického nám. 12, Malá Strana, 118 00 Prague 1,* ☎ *257–532–410,* FAX *257–533–217,* WEB *www.utripstrosu.cz. 14 rooms, 4 suites. Restaurant, cable TV, minibar, Internet; no a/c. AE, DC, MC, V. BP.*

$$$ 🏨 **Dům U Červeného lva.** On the Lesser Quarter's main, historic thor-
★ oughfare, a five-minute walk from Prague Castle's front gates, the

baroque "House at the Red Lion" is an intimate, immaculately kept hotel. Guest rooms have parquet floors, 17th-century painted-beam ceilings, superb antiques, and all-white bathrooms with brass fixtures. The two top-floor rooms can double as a suite. Note that there is no elevator, and the stairs are steep. ⊠ *Nerudova 41, Malá Strana, 118 00 Prague 1,* ☎ *257–533–832,* 𝖥𝖠𝖷 *257–532–746,* 𝖶𝖤𝖡 *www.hotelredlion. com. 5 rooms, 3 suites. 2 restaurants, in-room safes, minibars, cable TV, bar, some pets allowed; no a/c. AE, DC, MC, V. BP.*

$$$ 🏨 **Kampa.** This early baroque armory turned hotel is tucked away on
★ an abundantly picturesque street at the southern end of the Lesser Quarter, just off Kampa Island. The bucolic setting and comparatively low rates make it one of the city's better bargains. Note the late-Gothic vaulting in the massive dining room. ⊠ *Všehrdova 16, Malá Strana, 118 00 Prague 1,* ☎ *257–320–508 or 257–320–404,* 𝖥𝖠𝖷 *257–320–262,* 𝖶𝖤𝖡 *www.bestwestern-ce.com/kampa. 85 rooms. Restaurant, minibars, cable TV; no a/c. AE, MC, V. BP.*

Hradčany

$$$$ 🏨 **Savoy.** A restrained yellow Jugendstil facade conceals one of the city's
★ most luxurious small hotels. Once a budget hotel, the building was gutted and lavishly refurbished in the mid-1990s. A harmonious maroon-and-mahogany color scheme carries through the public spaces and the rooms, some of which are furnished in purely modern style, while others have a rococo look. The Restaurant Hradčany is one of the city's best hotel dining rooms. The biggest disappointment: although Prague Castle is just up the road, none of the rooms have a view of it. ⊠ *Keplerova 6, Hradčany, 118 00 Prague 6,* ☎ *224–302–430,* 𝖥𝖠𝖷 *224–302–128,* 𝖶𝖤𝖡 *www.hotel-savoy.cz. 55 rooms, 6 suites. Restaurant, café, in-room safes, minibars, cable TV, sauna, gym, meeting rooms, Internet, some pets allowed (fee); no-smoking floor. AE, DC, MC, V. BP.*

$$$ 🏨 **Romantik Hotel U Raka.** This private guest house, since 1997 a
★ member of the Romantik Hotels & Restaurants organization, has a quiet location on the ancient, winding streets of Nový Svět, just behind the Loreto Church and a 10-minute walk from Prague Castle. One side of the 18th-century building presents a rare example of half-timbering, and the rooms sustain the country feel with heavy furniture reminiscent of a Czech farmhouse. There are only six rooms, but if you can get a reservation (try at least a month in advance), you will have a wonderful base for exploring Prague. ⊠ *Černínská 10/93, Hradčany, 118 00 Prague 1,* ☎ *220–511–100,* 𝖥𝖠𝖷 *220–510–511,* 𝖶𝖤𝖡 *www.romantikhotels.com. 5 rooms, 1 suite. Cable TV; no kids under 10. AE, MC, V. BP.*

Nové Město (New Town)

$$$$ 🏨 **Palace.** For the well-heeled, this is Prague's most coveted address—
★ a muted, pistachio-green Art Nouveau building perched on a busy corner only a block from Wenceslas Square. The hotel's spacious, well-appointed rooms, each with a white-marble bathroom, are dressed in velvety pinks and greens cribbed straight from an Alfons Mucha print. The hotel's restaurant is pure Continental, from the classic garnishes to the creamy sauces. Two rooms are set aside for travelers with disabilities. Children 12 and under stay for free. ⊠ *Panská 12, Nové Město, 111 21 Prague 1,* ☎ *224–093–111,* 𝖥𝖠𝖷 *224–221–240,* 𝖶𝖤𝖡 *www. hotel-palace.cz. 114 rooms, 10 suites. 2 restaurants, in-room safes, minibars, sauna; no-smoking floors. AE, DC, MC, V. BP.*

$$$ 🏨 **City Hotel Moran.** This renovated 19th-century town house has a bright, inviting lobby and equally bright and clean rooms that are modern, if slightly bland. Some upper-floor rooms have good views of Prague Castle. ⊠ *Na Moráni 15, Nové Město, 120 00 Prague 2,* ☎ *224–915–*

208, FAX *224–920–625,* WEB *www.bestwestern-ce.com/moran. 57 rooms. Restaurant, cable TV, Internet, meeting room, some pets allowed; no-smoking floor. AE, DC, MC, V. BP.*

$$$ 🏨 **Elite.** An extensive renovation preserved the 14-century Gothic facade and many interior architectural details of this building while allowing for modern comforts. Rooms are furnished with antiques, and many have decorated Renaissance-style wooden ceilings and large desks. One of the suites has a mural ceiling. The central garden, with bar service in the daytime, makes a nice refuge from busy nearby Náodní třída. ⊠ *Ostrovní 32, Nové Město, 110 00 Prague 1,* ☎ *224–932–250,* FAX *224–930–787,* WEB *www.hotelelite.cz. 77 rooms, 2 suites. Restaurant, room service, cable TV with movies, in-room safes, minibars, hair salon, bar, laundry service, business services, meeting room, some pets allowed (fee), parking (fee). AE, DC, MC, V. BP.*

$$$ 🏨 **Meteor Plaza.** This Best Western hotel offers modern conveniences in a historical building (Empress Maria Theresa's son, Joseph II, stayed here when he was passing through in the 18th century). The baroque building is only five minutes on foot from downtown. Renovations have left most of the rooms with a surprisingly modern look that masks the hotel's history. To get a sense of the hotel's age, visit the original 14th-century wine cellar. Rates drop markedly in midsummer and even more in winter. ⊠ *Hybernská 6, Nové Město, 110 00 Prague 1,* ☎ *224–192–111,* FAX *224–213–005,* WEB *www.hotel-meteor.cz. 90 rooms, 6 suites. Restaurant, minibars, cable TV with movies, gym, parking (fee). AE, DC, MC, V. BP.*

$$ 🏨 **Axa.** Funky and functional, this 1932 high-rise was once a mainstay of the budget-hotel crowd. Over the years, the rooms have certainly improved; however, the lobby and public areas are still decidedly tacky, with plastic flowers, lots of mirrors, and glaring lights. There are scores of free weights in Axa's gym, making it one of the best in Prague. ⊠ *Na Poříčí 40, Nové Město, 113 03 Prague 1,* ☎ *224–812–580,* FAX *224–214–489,* WEB *www.vol.cz/axa. 126 rooms, 6 suites. Restaurant, cable TV, indoor pool, hair salon, health club, sauna, meeting room, bar, some pets allowed; no a/c. AE, DC, MC, V. BP.*

$$ 🏨 **Harmony.** This is one of the renovated, formerly state-owned standbys. A stern 1930s facade clashes with the bright 1990s interior, but cheerful receptionists, comfortably casual rooms, and an easy 10-minute walk to the Old Town compensate for the aesthetic flaws. Ask for a room away from the bustle of one of Prague's busiest streets. ⊠ *Na Poříčí 31, Nové Město, 110 00 Prague 1,* ☎ *222–311–229,* FAX *222–310–009. 60 rooms. 2 restaurants, cable TV, meeting rooms, some pets allowed; no a/c. AE, DC, MC, V. BP.*

$$ 🏨 **Opera.** Once the lodging of choice for divas performing at the nearby Státní opera (State Theater), the Opera greatly declined under the Communists. The mid-1990s saw the grand fin-de-siècle facade rejuvenated with a perky pink-and-white exterior paint job. This exuberance is strictly on the outside, though, and the rooms are modern and easy on the eyes. ⊠ *Těšnov 13, Nové Město, 110 00 Prague 1,* ☎ *222–315–609,* FAX *222–311–477,* WEB *www.hotel-opera.cz. 64 rooms. Restaurant, minibars, cable TV, bar, meeting room, some pets allowed; no a/c. AE, DC, MC, V. BP.*

$–$$ 🏨 **Salvator.** An efficiently run establishment just outside the Old Town, this pension offers more comforts than most in its class, including satellite TV and minibars in most rooms, and a combination breakfast room and bar with a billiard table. Rooms are pristine if plain, with the standard narrow beds; those without private bath also lack TVs but are a good value nonetheless. ⊠ *Truhlářská 10, Nové Město, 110 00 Prague 1,* ☎ *222–312–234,* FAX *222–316–355,* WEB *www.salvator.cz. 28 rooms, 16 with bath; 7 suites. Restaurant, some minibars, cable TV in some* rooms, bar, some pets allowed (fee), parking (fee); no a/c, no TV in some rooms. AE, MC, V. BP.

Vinohrady

$$ ⊞ **Anna.** The bright neoclassical facade and Art Nouveau details have been lovingly restored on this 19th-century building. While the street it's on is quiet, a few minutes' walk will get you to bustling New Town. The suites on the top floors offer a nice view of the historic district. In 2002, the hotel opened an annex, the Dependance Anna, in the central courtyard of the block with 12 less expensive rooms, but you must return to the main hotel for breakfast. ⊠ *Budečská 17, Vinohrady, 120 21 Prague 2,* ☎ *222–513–111,* FAX *222–515–158,* WEB *www.hotelanna.cz. 22 rooms, 2 suites, 12 annex rooms. Cable TV, meeting room, Internet, some pets allowed (fee); no a/c. AE, MC, V. BP.*

Smíchov

The name means "mixed neighborhood" because, when the city had walls, Smíchov was on the outside, and all manner of people could live there. While it's still a colorful, working-class area, lots of new construction has made it a shopping and entertainment hub with relatively easy access, by tram, metro, or foot, to the city's historical center.

$$$ ⊞ **Kinsky Garden.** You could walk the mile or so from this hotel to Prague Castle entirely on the tree-lined paths of Petřín, the hilly park that starts across the street. Opened in 1997, the hotel takes its name from a garden established by Count Rudolf Kinsky in 1825 on the southern side of Petřín. The public spaces are not spaces, nor are some rooms, but everything is tasteful and comfortable. Try to get a room on one of the upper floors for a view of the park. The management and restaurant are Italian. ⊠ *Holečkova 7, Smíchov, 150 00 Prague 5,* ☎ *257–311–173,* FAX *257–311–184,* WEB *www.hotelkinskygarden.cz. 60 rooms. Restaurant, cable TV with movies, bar, Internet, meeting room, some pets allowed; no-smoking floor. AE, DC, MC, V. BP.*

$$ ⊞ **Arbes Mepro.** During renovations in 2001, decorators added fancier furniture and room safes to this conveniently located hotel. The Smíchov neighborhood has several good restaurants (including the U Mikuláše Dačického wine tavern, across the street from the hotel) and nice strolls along the river or up the Petřín hill. The wine cellar serves as a breakfast room and can be booked for group dinners. Trams to the historical center are just a block away, or it's a 10-minute walk to the historic center. ⊠ *Viktora Huga 3, Smíchov, 150 00 Prague 5,* ☎ *257–210–410,* FAX *257–215–263,* WEB *www.arbes-mepro.cz. 27 rooms. Cable TV, in-room safes, bar, meeting room; no a/c. AE, MC, V. BP.*

$$ ⊞ **Petr.** Set in a quiet part of Smíchov, just a few minutes' stroll from the Lesser Quarter, this is an excellent value. As a "garni" hotel, it does not have a full-service restaurant, but it does serve breakfast (included in the price). The rooms are simply but adequately furnished. It's a 10-minute walk from the closest metro stop. ⊠ *Drtinova 17, Smíchov, 150 00 Prague 5,* ☎ *257–314–068,* FAX *257–314–072,* WEB *www.hotelpetr.cz. 37 rooms, 2 suites. Restaurant, cable TV, Internet, some pets allowed (fee); no a/c. AE, MC, V. BP. Metro: Anděl (Line B).*

$ ⊞ **Balkan.** A fresh coat of bright paint on the outside helps this bare-knuckles hotel to stand out from its run-down surroundings. The spartan Balkan is on a busy street not far from the Lesser Quarter and the Národní divadlo (National Theater). Breakfast is available for an additional 85 Kč. ⊠ *Svornosti 28, Smíchov, 150 00 Prague 5,* ☎ FAX *25732–7180, 25732–2150, or 25732–5583. 30 rooms. Restaurant, cable TV, sauna, some pets allowed (fee); no a/c. AE, MC, V.*

Žižkov

It's hard to go for more than a block in this densely populated neighborhood without finding a pub or a nightclub. Several places offer live music, making it a center of nightlife. Plus, the restaurants here are generally quite good and a bit cheaper than those in the center. As in all cities, some of the nightlife has a slightly seamy side. It's best to exercise a moderate amount of caution, especially on side streets, and avoid the seedier pubs that offer gambling machines or other dubious attractions.

$$ ⊞ **Olšanka.** The main calling card of this boxy modern hotel is its outstanding 50-meter swimming pool and modern sports center, which includes a pair of tennis courts and aerobics classes. Rooms are clean and, though basic, have the most important hotel amenities. There's also a relaxing sauna with certain nights reserved for men, women, or both. Note that the sports facilities may be closed in August. The neighborhood is nondescript, but the Old Town is only 10 minutes away by direct tram. ⊠ *Táboritská 23, Žižkov, 130 87 Prague 3,* ☎ *267–092–212,* FAX *222–713–315,* WEB *www.hotelolsanka.cz. 200 rooms. Restaurant, cable TV, tennis court, pool, aerobics, health club, bar, Internet, meeting rooms, some pets allowed (fee). AE, MC, V.*

$ ⊞ **Bern.** The cream-colored Bern is a comfortable alternative to staying in the city center. Rooms are on the plain side, with fairly basic, dark-wood furniture. Bathrooms have showers only. Although rather far out, it is situated on several city bus routes into the New and Old Towns; buses run frequently even on evenings and weekends, and the trip takes 10 to 15 minutes. ⊠ *Koněvova 28, Žižkov, 130 00 Prague 3,* ☎ FAX *22258–4420. 26 rooms. Restaurant, cable TV, minibars, bar, some pets allowed. AE, DC, MC, V. BP.*

Eastern Suburbs

$ ⊞ **Apollo.** This is a standard, no-frills, square-box hotel where clean rooms come at a fair price. Its primary flaw is its location: roughly 20 minutes away by metro and tram from the city center. ⊠ *Kubišova 23, Libeň, 182 00 Prague 8,* ☎ *284–680–628. 35 rooms. Restaurant, cable TV; no a/c. MC, V. BP. Metro: Nádraží Holešovice (Line C), then Tram 5, 14, or 17 to Hercovka stop.*

$ ⊞ **Astra.** The location of this modern hotel best serves drivers coming into town from the east, although the nearby metro station makes it easy to reach from the center. The neighborhood is quiet, if ordinary, and the rooms are more comfortable than most in this price range. ⊠ *Mukařovská 1740/18, Stodůlky, 100 00 Prague 10,* ☎ *274–813–595,* FAX *274–810–765,* WEB *www.hotelastra.cz. 43 rooms, 10 suites. Restaurant, cable TV, nightclub, meeting room, some pets allowed, parking (fee); no a/c. AE, DC, MC, V. BP. Metro: Skalka (Line A), then walk south on Na padesátém about 5 minutes to Mukařovská.*

$ ⊞ **Pension Louda.** The friendly owners of this family-run guest house
★ go out of their way to make you feel welcome. The large, spotless rooms are an exceptional bargain, and although the place is in the suburbs, the hilltop site offers a stunning view of greater Prague from the south-facing rooms. ⊠ *Kubišova 10, Libeň, 182 00 Prague 8,* ☎ *284–681–491,* FAX *284–681–488. 9 rooms. Gym, sauna; no a/c. No credit cards. BP. Metro: Nádraží Holešovice (Line C), then Tram 5, 14, or 17 to Hercovka stop.*

Western Suburbs

$$–$$$$ ⊞ **Diplomat.** This sprawling complex opened in 1990 and remains popular with business travelers thanks to its location between the airport and downtown. From the hotel, you can easily reach the city center by metro. The modern rooms may not exude much character, but they are tastefully furnished and quite comfortable. You can drive a miniature racing car at the indoor track next door. ⊠ *Evropská 15, Dejvice, 160 00 Prague 6,* ☎ *296–559–111,* FAX *296–559–215,* WEB *www.diplomatpraha. cz. 369 rooms, 13 suites. 2 restaurants, café, cable TV with movies, gym, sauna, bar, nightclub, meeting room, Internet, parking (fee); no-smoking floors. AE, DC, MC, V. BP. Metro: Dejvická (Line A).*

$ 🖫 **Penzion Sprint.** Straightforward rooms, most of which have their own bathroom (however tiny), make the Sprint a fine choice. This pension is on a quiet residential street, next to a large track and soccer field in the outskirts of Prague. It's about 20 minutes from the airport. Tram 18 rumbles directly to the Old Town from the Batérie stop just two blocks away. ⊠ *Cukrovárnická 62, Střešovice, 160 00 Prague 6,* ☎ *233–343– 338,* FAX *233–344–871,* WEB *web.telecom.cz/penzionsprint. 21 rooms, 6 with bath. Restaurant, some pets allowed; no a/c. AE, MC, V. BP.*

NIGHTLIFE AND THE ARTS

The fraternal twins of the performing arts and nightlife continue to enjoy an exhilarating growth spurt in Prague, and the number of concerts, plays, musicals, and clubs keeps rising. Some venues in the city center pitch themselves to tourists, but there are dozens of places where you can join the local crowds for music, dancing, or the rituals of beer and conversation. For details of cultural and nightlife events, look for the English-language newspaper the *Prague Post* or one of the multilingual monthly guides available at hotels, tourist offices, and newsstands.

Nightlife

Cabaret

For adult stage entertainment (with some nudity) try the **Varieté Praga** (⊠ Vodičkova 30, Staré Město, ☎ 224–215–945).

Discos

Dance clubs come and go regularly. **Gejzeer Club** (⊠ Vinohradská 40, Vinorhady, ☎ 02/2251–6036, WEB www.gejzeer.com) is one of the newer gay discos to emerge on the scene in Prague. **Karlovy Lázně** (⊠ Novotného lávka, Staré Město), near the Charles Bridge, is a four-story dance palace with everything from Czech oldies to ambient chill-out sounds. A longtime favorite is **Radost FX** (⊠ Bělehradská 120, Nové Město, ☎ 222–513–144), with imported and homegrown DJs playing the latest house, hip-hop, and dance music.

Jazz Clubs

Jazz gained notoriety under the Communists as a subtle form of protest, and the city still has some great jazz clubs, featuring everything from swing to blues and modern. All listed clubs have a cover charge. **AghaRTA** (⊠ Krakovská 5, Nové Město, ☎ 222–211–275) presents jazz acts in an intimate space. Music starts around 9 PM, but come earlier to get a seat. **Jazz Club U staré paní** (⊠ Michalská 9, Staré Město, ☎ 224–228–090, WEB www.ustarepani.cz) has a rotating list of tried-and-true Czech bands. **Jazz Club Železná** (⊠ Železná 16, Staré Město, ☎ FAX 224–239–697, WEB www.jazzclub.cz) mixes its jazz acts with world music. **Reduta** (⊠ Národní 20, Nové Město, ☎ 224–912–246) has a full program of local and international musicians.

Pubs and Bars

Bars and lounges are not traditional Prague fixtures, but bars catering to a young crowd have elbowed their way in over the past few years. Still, most social life of the drinking variety takes place in pubs (*pivnice* or *hospody*), which are liberally sprinkled throughout the city's neighborhoods. Tourists are welcome to join in the evening ritual of sitting around large tables and talking, smoking, and drinking beer. Before venturing in, however, it's best to familiarize yourself with a few points of pub etiquette: always ask if a chair is free before sitting down (*Je tu volno?*). To order a beer (*pivo*), do not wave the waiter down or shout across the room; he will usually assume you want beer—most pubs serve one brand—and bring it over to you without asking. He will also bring subsequent rounds to the table without asking. To refuse, just shake your head or say no thanks (*ne, děkuju*). At the end of the evening, usually around 10:30 or 11, the waiter will come to tally the bill. There are plenty of popular pubs in the city center, all of which can get impossibly crowded.

The oldest brewpub in Europe, **U Fleků** (⊠ Křemencova 11, Nové Město, ☎ 224–930–831, WEB www.ufleku.cz) has been open since 1499 and makes a tasty, if overpriced, dark beer. **U Medvídků** (⊠ Na Perštýně 7, Staré Město, ☎ 224–211–916, WEB www.umedkidku.cz) was a brewery at least as long ago as the 15th century. Beer is no longer made on the premises; rather, they serve draft Budvar shipped from České Budějovice. **U svatého Tomáše** (⊠ Letenská 12, Malá Strana, ☎ 257–320–101) brewed beer for Augustinian monks starting in 1358. Now it serves commercially produced beer in a tourist-friendly, mock-medieval hall in the Lesser Quarter. **U Zlatého Tygra** (⊠ Husova 17, Staré Město, ☎ 222–221–111) is famed as one of the three best Prague pubs for Pilsner Urquell, the original and perhaps the greatest of the pilsners. It also used to be a hangout for such raffish types as the writer Bohumil Hrabal, who died in 1997.

The **James Joyce Pub** (⊠ Liliová 10, Staré Město, ☎ 224–248–793, WEB www.jamesjoyce.cz) is authentically Irish (it has Irish owners), with Guinness on tap and excellent food of the fish-and-chips persuasion. **U Malého Glena** (⊠ Karmelitská 23, Malá Strana, ☎ 257–531–717, WEB www.malyglen.cz) offers a popular bar and a stage for local and expat jazz, blues, and folk music.

Rock Clubs

Prague's rock, alternative, and world-music scene is thriving. The younger crowd flocks to **Lucerna Music Bar** (⊠ Vodičkova 36, Nové Město, ☎ 224–217–108, WEB www.lucerna.cz) to catch popular Czech rock and funk bands and visiting acts. **Malostranská Beseda** (⊠ Malostranské nám. 21, Malá Strana, ☎ 257–532–092) is a dependable bet for sometimes bizarre but always good musical acts from around the country. The cavernous **Palác Akropolis** (⊠ Kubelíkova 27, Žižkov, ☎ 299–330–913, WEB www.palacakropolis.cz) has top Czech acts and major international world-music performers; as the name suggests, the space has an Acropolis theme. Hard-rock enthusiasts should check out the **Rock Café** (⊠ Národní 20, Nové Město, ☎ 224–914–416, WEB www.rockcafe.cz). For dance tracks, hip locals congregate at **Roxy** (⊠ Dlouhá 33, Staré Město, ☎ 224–810–951, WEB www.roxy.cz).

The Arts

Prague's cultural flair is legendary, and performances are sometimes booked far in advance by all sorts of Praguers. The concierge at your hotel may be able to reserve tickets for you. Otherwise, for the cheapest tickets go directly to the theater box office a few days in advance or immediately before a performance. Ticket agencies may charge higher prices than box offices do. American Express offices sell tickets to many concerts. **Bohemia Ticket International** (⊠ Na Příkopě 16,

Nové Město, ☎ 224–215–031, WEB www.ticketsbti.cz; Malé nám. 13, Staré Město, ☎ 224–227–832) specializes in mostly classical music. **Ticketpro** (✉ Salvátorská 10, Staré Město, ☎ 224–814–020, WEB www.ticketpro.cz), with outlets all over town, accepts major credit cards. Tickets for some club and live music events are handled by **Ticketstream** (✉ Koubkova 8, Nové Město, ☎ 224–263–049, WEB www.ticketstream.cz), which also has outlets at some hotels and restaurants.

Classical Music

Classical concerts are held all over the city throughout the year. In addition to Prague's two major professional orchestras, classical ensembles are the most common finds, and the standard of performance ranges from adequate to superb, though the programs tend to take few risks. Serious fans of baroque music may have the opportunity to hear works of little-known Bohemian composers at these concerts. Some of the best chamber ensembles are the Martinů Ensemble, the Prague Chamber Philharmonic (also known as the Prague Philharmonia), the Wihan Quartet, the Czech Trio, and the Agon contemporary music group.

Performances are held regularly at many of the city's palaces and churches, including the Garden on the Ramparts below Prague Castle (where the music comes with a view); both Churches of St. Nicholas; the Church of Sts. Simon and Jude on Dušní in the Old Town; the Church of St. James on Malá Štupartská, near Old Town Square; the Zrcadlová kaple (Mirror Chapel) in the Klementinum on Mariánské náměstí in the Old Town; and the Lobkowicz Palace at Prague Castle. If you're an organ-music buff, you'll most likely have your pick of recitals held in Prague's historic halls and churches. Popular programs are offered at the Church of St. Nicholas in the Lesser Quarter and the Church of St. James, where the organ plays amid a complement of baroque statuary.

Dvořák Hall (✉ Rudolfinum, nám. Jana Palacha, Staré Město, ☎ 224–893–111, WEB www.czechphilharmonic.cz) is home to one of Central Europe's best orchestras, the Czech Philharmonic. Frequent guest conductor Sir Charles Mackerras is a leading proponent of modern Czech music. One of the best orchestral venues is the resplendent Art Nouveau **Smetana Hall** (✉ Obecní dům, nám. Republiky 5, Staré Město, ☎ 222–002–100, WEB www.obecnidum.cz), home of the excellent Prague Symphony Orchestra and major venue for the annual Prague Spring music festival. Concerts at the **Villa Bertramka** (✉ Mozartova 169, Smíchov, ☎ 257–318–461, WEB www.bertramka.cz) emphasize the music of Mozart and his contemporaries.

Film

If a film was made in the United States or Britain, the chances are good that it will be shown with Czech subtitles rather than dubbed. (Film titles, however, are usually translated into Czech, so your only clue to the movie's country of origin may be the poster used in advertisements.) Movies in the original language are normally indicated with the note *českými titulky* (with Czech subtitles). Prague's English-language publications carry film reviews and full timetables. Many downtown cinemas cluster near Wenceslas Square. A wave of new construction has left the city with several modern multiplexes that have giant screens and digital sound. **Slovanský dům** (✉ Na Příkopě 22, Nové Město, ☎ 257–181–212, WEB www.stercentury.cz) is the most central, but also the most expensive. Among the largest cinemas in Prague is **Blaník** (✉ Václavské nám. 56, ☎ 224–033–172). At this writing, an IMAX theater was scheduled to open by early 2003 at **Flora Plaza** (✉ Vinohradská and Jičinská, Žižkov) right above the metro Flora stop on the A line. **Lucerna** (✉ Vodičkova 36, Nové Město, ☎ 224–216–972) is a classic picture palace in the shopping arcade of the same name.

Opera

The Czech Republic has a strong operatic tradition. Unlike during the Communist period, operas are almost always sung in their original tongue, and the repertoire offers plenty of Italian favorites as well as the Czech national composers Janaček, Dvořák, and Smetana. (Czech operas are supertitled in English.) The major opera houses also often stage ballets. Appropriate attire is recommended for all venues; the National and Estates theaters instituted a "no jeans" rule in 1998. Ticket prices are still quite reasonable, at 40 Kč–900 Kč.

A great venue for a night at the opera is the plush **Národní divadlo** (National Theater; ✉ Národní tř. 2, Nové Město, ☎ 224–901–448, WEB www.narodni-divadlo.cz). Performances at the **Statní Opera Praha** (State Opera House; ✉ Wilsonova 4, Nové Město, ☎ 224–227–266, WEB www.opera.cz), near the top of Wenceslas Square, can also be excellent. The historic **Stavovské divadlo** (Estates Theater; ✉ Ovocný tř. 1, Staré Město, ☎ 224–215–001, WEB www.narodni-divadlo.cz), where Mozart's *Don Giovanni* premiered in the 18th century, plays host to a mix of operas and dramatic works.

Puppet Shows

This traditional form of Czech popular entertainment has been given new life thanks to the productions mounted at the **Národní divadlo marionet** (National Marionette Theater; ✉ Žatecká 1, Staré Město, ☎ 224–819–322; in season, shows are also performed at Celetná 13). Children and adults alike can enjoy the hilarity and pathos of famous operas adapted for nonhuman "singers." The company's bread and butter is a production of Mozart's *Don Giovanni*.

Theater

A dozen or so professional theater companies play in Prague to everpacked houses. Visiting the theater is a vital activity in Czech society, and the language barrier can't obscure the players' artistry. Nonverbal theater also abounds: not only tourist-friendly mime and "Black Light Theater"—a melding of live acting, mime, video, and stage trickery—but also serious (or incomprehensible) productions by top local and foreign troupes. Several English-language theater groups operate sporadically. For complete listings, pick up a copy of the *Prague Post.* The famous **Laterna Magika** (Magic Lantern) puts on a multimedia extravaganza in the National Theater's glass-encased modern hall (✉ Národní tř. 4, Nové Město, ☎ 224–914–129). The popular **Archa Theater** (✉ Na Poříčí 26, Nové Město, ☎ 221–716–333) offers avantgarde and experimental theater, music, and dance and has hosted world-class visiting ensembles such as the Royal Shakespeare Company.

OUTDOOR ACTIVITIES AND SPORTS

Boating

Rowboats and paddle boats can be rented on Slovanský ostrov, the island in the Vltava just south of the National Theater.

Fitness Clubs

Some luxury hotels have well-equipped fitness centers with swimming pools. The centrally located **Hilton** (✉ Pobřežní 1, Karlín, ☎ 224–841–111, WEB www.hilton.com; metro: Florenc [Line B or C]) has full fitness facilities and tennis courts. Excellent and inexpensive facilities can be found at the **Hotel Axa** (✉ Na Poříčí 40, Nové Město, ☎ 224–812–580, WEB www.vol.cz/axa).

Golf

Prague's only course is a 9-holer in the western suburbs at the **Hotel Golf** (✉ Plzeňská 215, Motol, ☎ 257–215–185). Take a taxi to the hotel or Tram 4, 7, or 9 from metro station Anděl to the Hotel Golf stop. **Praha Karlštejn Golf Club** (✉ Bělec 280, Liteň, ☎ 0/724–084–600, WEB www.karlstejn-golf.cz) offers a challenging course with a view of the famous Karlštejn Castle. It's 30 km (18 mi) southwest of Prague, just across the Berounka River from the castle.

Jogging

The best place for jogging is **Stromovka,** a large, flat park adjacent to the Výstaviště fairgrounds in Prague 7 (take Tram 5, 12, or 17 to the Výstaviště stop). Closer to the center, another popular park is **Letenské sady** (Letna Park), the park east of the Royal Garden at Prague Castle, across Chotkova Street. For safety's sake, unaccompanied women should avoid the more remote corners of this park.

Spectator Sports

The best place to find out what's going on (and where) is the weekly sports page of the *Prague Post,* or you can inquire at your hotel.

Soccer

National and international matches are played regularly at the home of Prague's Sparta team, **Stadión Spartra Praha** (Sparta Stadium; ✉ Milady Horákové, Letná, ☎ 220–571–167 box office, WEB www.sparta.cz), behind Letna Park. To reach the stadium, take Tram 1, 25, or 26 to the Sparta stop.

Swimming

The **Hilton** (✉ Pobřežní 1, Karlín, ☎ 224–841–111, WEB www.hilton.com; metro: Florenc [Line B or C]) has a pool that is open to the public. **Hotel Axa** (✉ Na Poříčí 40, Nové Město, ☎ 224–812–580, WEB www.vol.cz/axa) has a nice indoor pool. The best public swimming pool in Prague is at the **Plavecký Stadión Podolí** (Podolí Swimming Stadium; ✉ Podolská 74, Podolí, ☎ 241–433–952), which you can get to from the city center in 15 minutes or less by taking Tram 3 or 17 to the Kublov stop. The indoor pool is 50 meters long, and the complex also includes two open-air pools, a sauna, a steam bath, and a wild-ride water slide. A word of warning: Podolí, for all its attractions, is notorious as a local hot spot of petty thievery. Don't entrust any valuables to the lockers—it's best either to check them in the safe with the *vrátnice* (superintendent), or better yet, don't bring them at all.

Tennis

The **Hilton** (✉ Pobřežní 1, Karlín, ☎ 224–841–111, WEB www.hilton.com; metro: Florenc [Line B or C]) has two public indoor courts. There are public tennis courts at the **Stadión Strahov** (Strahov Stadium; ✉ Vaničkova, Břevnov, ☎ no phone), but it's not possible to reserve one in advance. Take Bus 176 from Karlovo náměstí in New Town, or Bus 143 from the Dejvická metro station (Line A), to the Stadion Strahov stop.

SHOPPING

While Prague has a long way to go before it can match such great European shopping cities as Paris and Rome, the Czech Republic capital is a great place to pick up gifts and souvenirs. Bohemian crystal and porcelain deservedly enjoy a worldwide reputation for quality, and plenty of shops offer excellent bargains. The local market for antiques and art is still relatively undeveloped, although dozens of antiquarian bookstores harbor some excellent finds, particularly German and Czech books and graphics.

Shopping Districts

The major shopping areas are **Na Příkopě,** which runs from the foot of Wenceslas Square to náměstí Republiky (Republic Square), and the area around **Old Town Square.** The Old Town **Pařižská ulice** and **Karlova ulice** are streets dotted with boutiques and antiques shops. In the Lesser Quarter, try **Nerudova ulice,** the street that runs up to Hradčany. An artistically designed modern glass shopping mall, **Anděl City** (✉ Corner of Plzeňská and Nádražní, Smíov, WEB www.angelcity. com; metro: Anděl) covers an entire city block. It partly opened in 2001 and eventually will include a multiplex cinema, a four-star hotel, and bowling alley plus clothing, perfume, electronics, and book stores. A large Carrefour supermarket and another multiplex are right across the street.

Department Stores

Prague's department stores are catching up quickly to their Western counterparts. **Bílá Labut'** (✉ Na Poříčí 23, Nové Město, ☎ 224–811–364, WEB www.bilalabut.cz) has a decent selection, but the overall shabbiness harks back to socialist times. **Kotva** (✉ Nám. Republiky 8, Nové Město, ☎ 224–801–111, WEB www.od-kotva.cz) is comparatively upscale, with a nice stationery section and a basement supermarket with wine and cheese aisles. The centrally located **Tesco** (✉ Národní tř. 26, Nové Město, ☎ 222–003–111) is generally the best place for one-stop shopping and a supermarket with peanut butter and other hard-to-find items.

Street Markets

For fruits, vegetables, and souvenirs, the best street market in central Prague is on **Havelská ulice** in the Old Town. The biggest market is the one in **Holešovice,** north of the city center; it offers food, jewelry, electronic goods, clothes, and imported liquor. Take the metro (Line C) to the Vltavská station and then catch any tram heading east (running to the left as you exit the metro station). Exit at the first stop and follow the crowds. It's better to shop during the week, as both are closed Saturday afternoon and all day on Sunday.

Specialty Stores

Antiques

For antiques connoisseurs, Prague can be a bit of a letdown. Even in comparison to other former Communist capitals such as Budapest, the choice of antiques in Prague can seem depressingly slim, as the city lacks large stores with a diverse selection of goods. The typical Prague *starožitnosti* (antiques shop) tends to be a small, one-room jumble of old glass and bric-a-brac. The good ones distinguish themselves by focusing on one particular specialty.

On the pricey end of the scale is the Prague affiliate of the Austrian auction house **Dorotheum** (✉ Ovocný tř. 2, Nové Město, ☎ 224–222–001, WEB www.dorotheum.cz), an elegant pawnshop that specializes in small things: jewelry, porcelain knickknacks, and standing clocks, as well as the odd military sword. The small **JHB Starožitnosti** (✉ Panská 1, Nové Město, ☎ 222–245–836) is the place for old clocks: everything from rococo to Empire standing clocks and Bavarian cuckoo clocks. The shop also sells antique pocket watches. **Nostalgie Antique**

(✉ Jánský Vršek 8, Malá Strana, ☏ 257–530–049) specializes in old textiles and jewelry. Most of the textiles are pre–World War II and include clothing, table linens, curtains, hats, and laces. **Papillio** (✉ Týn 1, Staré Město, ☏ 224–895–454, [WEB] www.papilio.cz), in the elaborately refurbished medieval courtyard behind the Church of the Virgin Mary Before Týn, is probably one of the best antiques shops in Prague, offering furniture, paintings, and especially museum-quality antique glass. Here you can find colorful Biedermeier goblets by Moser and wonderful Loetz vases. **Zlatnictví František Vomáčka** (✉ Náprstkova 9, Staré Město, ☏ 222–222–017) is a cluttered shop that redeems itself with its selection of old jewelry in a broad price range, including rare Art Nouveau rings and antique garnet brooches. In the shop's affiliate next door, jewelry is repaired, cleaned, and made to order.

Art Galleries

The best galleries in Prague are quirky and eclectic affairs, places to sift through artworks rather than browse at arms' length. Many are also slightly off the beaten track and away from the main tourist thoroughfares. Prague's as-yet-untouristed Nový Svět neighborhood is something of a miniature artist's quarter. **Galerie Litera** (✉ Karlinske nám. 13, Karlín, ☏ 222–317–195) is in a neighborhood where tourists rarely set foot—it's not rough but pretty seedy. (Karlín is northeast of the city center; get off the metro at Florenc and walk five minutes up Sokolovská.) Most of the gallery space is given over to temporary shows of unique, high-quality graphics. There are also some lovely ceramics as well as a refined selection of antiquarian art books. **Galerie Nový Svět** (✉ Nový Svět 5, Hradčany, ☏ 220–514–611) displays interesting paintings and drawings by somewhat obscure Czech artists, as well as ceramics, glass, and art books. At the high end is **Galerie Peithner-Lichtenfels** (✉ Michalská 12, Staré Město, ☏ 224–227–680) in the Old Town, which specializes in modern Czech art. Paintings, prints, and drawings crowd the walls and are propped against glass cases and window sills. Comb through works by Czech Cubists, currently fetching high prices at international auctions.

Books and Prints

Like its antiques shops, Prague's rare-book shops, or *antikvariáts,* were once part of a massive state-owned consortium that, since privatization, has split up and diversified. Now most shops tend to cultivate their own specialties. Some have a small English-language section with a motley blend of potboilers, academic texts, classics, and tattered paperbacks. Books in German, on the other hand, are abundant.

For new books in English, try **Anagram Books** (✉ Týn 4, Staré Město, ☏ 224–895–737). **Antikvariát Karel Křenek** (✉ Celetná 31, Staré Město, ☏ 222–322–919), near the Powder Tower, specializes in books with a humanist slant. It has a good selection of modern graphics and prides itself on its avant-garde periodicals and journals from the 1920s and 1930s. It also has a small collection of English books. There's a great selection of English-language books at **Big Ben Bookshop** (✉ Malá Štupartská 5, Staré Město, ☏ 224–826–565). If you'd just like a good read, be sure to check out the **Globe Bookstore and Coffeehouse** (✉ Pštrossova 6, Nové Město, ☏ 224–916–264), a longtime magnet for the local English-speaking community, in its new, more central site. For hiking maps and auto atlases, try the downstairs level of the **Jan Kanzelsberger bookshop** (✉ Václavské nám. 42, Nové Město, ☏ 224–217–335) on Wenceslas Square. **U Karlova Mostu** (✉ Karlova 2, Staré Město, ☏ 222–220–286) is the preeminent Prague bookstore. In a suitably bookish location opposite the Klementinum, it's the place to go if you are looking for that elusive 15th-century manuscript. In addition to housing ancient books too precious to be leafed through, the store has a good selection of books on local subjects, a small foreign-language section, and a host of prints, maps, drawings, and paintings.

Food and Wine

Cellarius (⌧ Lucerna Passage, Václavské nám., between Vodičkova and Štěpánská, Nové Město, ☎ 224–210–979, WEB www.cellarius.cz) has a wide choice of Moravian and Bohemian wines and spirits, as well as products from more recognized wine-making lands. **Fruits de France** (⌧ Jindřišská 9, Nové Město, ☎ 224–220–304; Bělehradská 94, Nové Město, ☎ 222–511–261, WEB www.fdf.cz) charges Western prices for fruits and vegetables imported directly from France.

Glass

Glass has traditionally been Bohemia's biggest export, and it was one of the few products manufactured during Communist times that managed to retain an artistically innovative spirit. Today Prague has plenty of shops selling Bohemian glass, though much of it is tourist kitsch. A good place to find modern works of art in glass is **Galerie Pyramida** (⌧ Národní 11, Nové Město, ☎ 224–213–117). **Galerie 'Z'** (⌧ U lužického semináře 7, Malá Strana, ☎ 257–535–563) sells limited-edition mold-melted and blown glass. **Moser** (⌧ Na Příkopě 12, Nové Město, ☎ 224–211–293, WEB www.moser.cz), the opulent flagship store of the world-famous Karlovy Vary glassmaker, offers the widest selection of traditional glass. Even if you're not in the market to buy, stop by the store simply to look at the elegant wood-paneled salesrooms on the second floor. The staff will gladly pack goods for traveling.

Home Design

Czech design is wonderfully rich both in quality and imagination, emphasizing old-fashioned craftsmanship while often taking an offbeat, even humorous approach. Strained relations between Czech designers and producers have reined in the potential selection, but there are nevertheless a handful of places showcasing Czech work. **Arzenal** (⌧ Valentinská 11, Josefov, ☎ 224–814–099, WEB www.arzenal.cz) is a design shop that offers Japanese and Thai food in addition to vases and chairs; it exclusively sells work by Bořek Šípek, President Havel's official designer. **Fast** (⌧ Sázavská 32, Vinohrady, ☎ 224–250–538, WEB www.fast.cz) is a little bit off the beaten track but worth the trek. Besides ultramodern furniture, there are ingenious (and more portable) pens, binders, and other office and home accoutrements. **Galerie Bydlení** (⌧ Truhlářská 20, Nové Město, ☎ 222–312–383) is a father-and-son operation focusing exclusively on Czech-made furniture.

Jewelry

Alfons Mucha is perhaps most famous for his whiplash Art Nouveau posters, but he also designed furniture, lamps, clothing, and jewelry. **Art Décoratif** (⌧ U Obecního domu, Staré Město, ☎ 222–002–350, WEB www.artdecoratif.cz), right next door to the Art Nouveau Obecní Dům, sells Mucha-inspired designs—the jewelry is especially remarkable. **Granát** (⌧ Dlouhá 28, Staré Město, ☎ 222–315–612, WEB www.granat.cz) has a comprehensive selection of garnet jewelry, plus contemporary and traditional pieces set in gold and silver. **Halada** (⌧ Karlova 25, Staré Město, ☎ 224–228–938, WEB www.halada.cz) sells sleek, Czech-designed silver jewelry; an affiliate shop at Na Příkopě 16 specializes in gold, diamonds, and pearls.

Marionettes

Marionettes have a long tradition in Bohemia, going back to the times when traveling troupes used to entertain children with morality plays on town squares. Now, although the art form survives, it has become yet another tourist lure, and you'll continually stumble across stalls selling almost identical marionettes. Secondhand and antique marionettes are surprisingly hard to find. One place to look is **Antikva Ing. Bürger** (⊠ Betlémské nám. 8, in courtyard, Nové Město, ☎ 222–221–595; Karlova 12, Staré Město, ☎ 0/602–315–729). The marionettes at **Obchod Pod lampou** (⊠ U Lužického semináře 5, Malá Strana, ☎ no phone) are the real thing. These puppets—hand-crafted knights, princesses, and pirates—are made by the same artists who supply professional puppeteers. Prices may be higher than for the usual stuff on the street, but the craftsmanship is well worth it.

Music and Musical Instruments
Capriccio (⊠ Újezd 15, Malá Strana, ☎ 257–320–165) has sheet music of all kinds. **Guitarpark** (⊠ Jungmannova nám. 17, Nové Město, ☎ 224–222–500, WEB www.guitarpark.cz) carries a comprehensive selection of quality musical instruments at reasonable prices.

Sporting Goods
For quality hiking and camping equipment, try **Hudy Sport** (⊠ Na Perštýně 14, Nové Město, ☎ 224–218–600, WEB www.hudy.cz). **Kotva** (⊠ Nám. Republiky 8, Nové Město, ☎ 224–801–111, WEB www.od-kotva.cz) has a good selection of sports gear and clothing.

Toys and Gifts for Children
Nearly every stationery store has beautiful watercolor and colored-chalk sets available at rock-bottom prices. The Czechs are also master illustrators, and the books they've made for young "pre-readers" are some of the world's loveliest. For the child with a theatrical bent, a marionette—they range from finger-size to nearly child-size—can be a wonder. For delightful and reasonably priced Czech-made wooden toys and wind-up trains, cars, and animals, look in at **Hračky** (⊠ Pohořelec 24, Hradčany, ☎ 0/603–515–745).

SIDE TRIPS TO BOHEMIAN SPA TOWNS

Until World War II, western Bohemia was the playground of Central Europe's rich and famous. Its three well-known spas, Karlovy Vary, Mariánské Lázně, and Františkovy Lázně (better known by their German names, Karlsbad, Marienbad, and Franzensbad, respectively), were the annual haunts of everybody who was anybody: Johann Wolfgang von Goethe, Ludwig van Beethoven, Karl Marx, and England's King Edward VII, to name but a few. Although strictly "proletarianized" in the Communist era, the spas still exude a nostalgic aura of a more elegant past and, unlike most of Bohemia, offer a basic tourist infrastructure that makes dining and lodging a pleasure.

Numbers in the margin correspond to numbers on the Western Bohemia map.

Karlovy Vary

★ ❶ *132 km (79 mi) due west of Prague on Rte. 6 (E48).*

Karlovy Vary, better known outside the Czech Republic by its German name, Karlsbad, is the most famous Bohemian spa. It is named for Emperor Charles IV, who allegedly happened upon the springs in 1358 while on a hunting expedition. As the story goes, the emperor's hound—chasing a harried stag—fell into a boiling spring and was scalded. Charles had the water tested and, familiar with spas in Italy, ordered baths to be established in the village of Vary. The spa reached its heyday in the 19th century, when royalty came here from all over Europe for treatment. The long list of those who "took the cure" includes Peter the Great, Goethe (no fewer than 13 times, according to a plaque on one

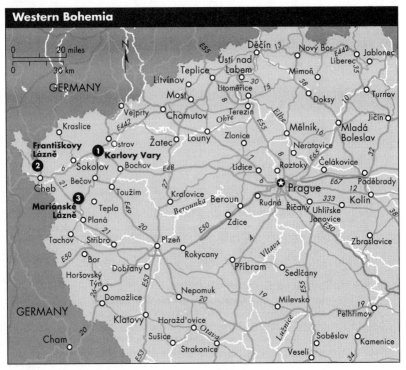

Western Bohemia

house by the main spring), Schiller, Beethoven, and Chopin. Even Karl Marx, when he wasn't decrying wealth and privilege, spent time at the resort; he wrote some of *Das Kapital* here between 1874 and 1876.

After decades of neglect under the Communists that left many buildings crumbling behind their beautiful facades, the town leaders today face the daunting task of carving out a new role for Karlovy Vary, since few Czechs can afford to set aside weeks or months at a time for a leisurely cure. To raise some quick cash, many sanatoriums have turned to offering short-term accommodations to foreign visitors (at rather expensive rates). By the week or by the hour, "classical" spa procedures, laser treatments, plastic surgery, and even acupuncture are purveyed to German clients or to large numbers of Russians who bought property in town in the late 1990s. For most visitors, though, it's enough simply to stroll the streets and parks and allow the eyes to feast awhile on the splendors of the past.

Whether you're arriving by bus, train, or car, your first view of the town on the approach from Prague will be of the ugly new section on the banks of the Ohře River. Don't despair: continue along the main road—following the signs to the Grandhotel Pupp—until you reach the lovely main street of the older spa area, situated gently astride the banks of the little Teplá ("Warm") River. (Drivers, note that driving through or parking in the main spa area is allowed only with a permit obtainable from your hotel.) The walk from the new town to the spa area is about 20 minutes.

The **Historická čtvrt** (Historic District) is still largely intact. Tall 19th-century houses, boasting decorative and often eccentric facades, line the spa's proud riverside streets. Throughout you'll see colonnades full of people sipping the spa's hot sulfuric water from odd pipe-shape drinking cups. At night the streets fill with steam escaping from cracks in the earth, giving the town a slightly macabre feel.

Karlovy Vary's jarringly modern **Vřídelní kolonáda** (Vřídlo Colonnade; ⊠ Vřídelní ul. near Kosterní nám.) is built around the spring of the same name, the town's hottest and most dramatic gusher. The Vřídlo is indeed unique, shooting its scalding water to a height of some 40 ft. Walk inside the arcade to watch the hundreds of patients here take the famed Karlsbad drinking cure. They promenade somnambulistically up and down, eyes glazed, clutching drinking glasses filled periodically at one of the five "sources." The waters are said to be especially effective against diseases of the digestive and urinary tracts. They're also good for gout (which probably explains the spa's former popularity with royals). If you want to join the crowds and take a sip, you can buy your own spouted cup from vendors within the colonnade.

To the right of the Vřídlo Colonnade are steps up to the white **Kostel Maři Magdaleny** (Church of Mary Magdalene). Designed by Kilian Ignaz Dientzenhofer (architect of the two Churches of St. Nicholas in Prague), this church is the best of the few baroque buildings still standing in Karlovy Vary. ⊠ *Moravská ul.,* ☎ *no phone.* ☉ *Daily 9–6.*

The neo-Renaissance pillared hall **Mlýnská kolonáda** (Mill Colonnade), along the river, is the spa town's centerpiece. Built from 1871 to 1881, it has four springs: Rusalka, Libussa, Prince Wenceslas, and Millpond. ⊠ *Mlýnské nábřeží.*

The very elegant **Sadová kolonáda** (Park Colonnade) is a white, wrought-iron construction. It was built in 1882 by the Viennese architectural duo Fellner and Helmer, who sprinkled the Austro-Hungarian Empire with many such edifices during the late 19th century and who also designed the town's theater, the quaint wooden Tržní kolonáda (Market Colonnade) next to the Vřídlo Colonnade, and one of the old bathhouses. ⊠ *Zahradní.*

The 20th century emerges at its most disturbing across the river from the historic district in the form of the huge, bunkerlike **Thermal Hotel**, built in the late 1960s. Although the building is a monstrosity, the view of Karlovy Vary from the rooftop pool is nothing short of spectacular. (The pool is open 8 AM–8 PM.) Even if you don't feel like a swim, it's worth taking the winding road up to the baths for the view. ⊠ *I. P. Pavlova 11.*

A five-minute walk up the steep Zámecký vrch from the Market Colonnade brings you to the redbrick Victorian **Kostel svatého Lukáše** (St. Luke's Church), once used by the local English community. ⊠ *Zámecký vrch at Petra Velikého.*

From Kostel svatého Lukáše, take a sharp right uphill on the redbrick road. Then turn left onto a footpath through the woods, following the signs to **Jelení skok** (Stag's Leap). After a while you'll see steps leading up to a bronze statue of a deer looking over the cliffs, the symbol of Karlovy Vary. From here a winding path leads up to a little red gazebo opening onto a fabulous panorama. ⊠ *Sovava trail in Petrova Výšina park.*

NEED A BREAK?   Reward yourself for making the climb to Stag's Leap with a light meal at the nearby restaurant **Jelení skok.** You may have to pay an entrance fee if there is a live band (but you'll also get the opportunity to polka). If you don't want to walk up, you can drive up a signposted road from the Victorian church.

The splendid Russian Orthodox **Kostel svatých Petra a Pavla** (Church of Sts. Peter and Paul) has five domes. It dates from the end of the 19th century and was built with help from the Russian aristocracy. ⊠ *Tř. Krále Jiřího.*

It's not necessary to walk to one of the best views of the town. Higher even than Stag's Leap is an observation tower, **rozhledna Diana,** accessible by funicular from behind the Grandhotel Pupp. There's an elevator to the top of the tower. ✉ *Výšina přátelství.* 🚠 *Funicular 25 Kč one-way, 40 Kč round-trip; tower 10 Kč.* ☉ *June–Sept., Mon.–Thurs. and Sun. 11–9, Fri.–Sat. 11–11; May and Oct., Tues.–Wed. and Sun. 11–6, Fri.–Sat. 11–7; Mar.–Apr. and Nov.–Dec., Wed.–Sun. 11–5.*

On one of the town's best shopping streets you'll find **Elefant,** one of the last of a dying breed of sophisticated coffeehouses. Happily, the café as an institution is making a real comeback in the Czech Republic. ✉ *Stará louka 30.*

Dining and Lodging

$$–$$$ ✕ **Embassy.** This cozy, sophisticated wine restaurant, conveniently near the Grandhotel Pupp, serves an innovative menu by local standards. Tagliatelle with smoked salmon in cream sauce makes an excellent main course, as does roast duck with cabbage and dumplings. The wine list features Czech varieties like the dry whites Rulandské bílé and Ryzlink Rýnský (the latter being the domestic version of the Riesling grape) and some pricey imports. ✉ *Nová louka 21,* ☎ *353–221–161. AE, DC, MC, V.*

$$–$$$ ✕ **Karel IV.** This restaurant's location atop an old castle tower not far from the Market Colonnade gives diners the best view in town. Good renditions of traditional Czech standbys—*bramborák* (potato pancake) and chicken breast with peaches—are served in small, secluded dining areas that are particularly intimate after sunset. ✉ *Zámecký vrch 2,* ☎ *353–227–255. AE, MC, V.*

$$$–$$$$ 🏨 **Grandhotel Pupp.** This enormous hotel with a 215-year history is ★ one of Central Europe's most famous resorts. Standards and service slipped under the Communists, but the highly professional management has more than made up for the decades of neglect. Some rooms are furnished in 18th-century period style. The vast public rooms exude the very best taste, circa 1913, when the present building was completed. Every July, the Pupp houses international movie stars in town for the Karlovy Vary International Film Festival. (The adjacent Parkhotel Pupp, under the same management, is a more affordable alternative.) Breakfast is 400 Kč extra. ✉ *Mírové nám. 2, 360 91,* ☎ *353–109–111,* FAX *353–109–620 or 353–224–032,* WEB *www.pupp.com. 75 rooms, 34 suites. 4 restaurants, cable TV with movies, in-room safes, minibars, health club, sauna, spa, casino, lounge, 2 nightclubs, Internet, some pets allowed (fee); no a/c in some rooms. AE, DC, MC, V.*

$$$ 🏨 **Dvořák.** Consider a splurge here if you're longing for Western stan★ dards of service and convenience. Opened in late 1990, this Austrian-owned hotel occupies three renovated town houses that are just a five-minute walk from the main spas. If possible, request a room with a bay-window view of the town. Spa treatments here run to about $750 per person per week in the high season. ✉ *Nová louka 11, 360 21,* ☎ *353–224–145,* FAX *353–222–814,* WEB *www.hotel-dvorak.cz. 76 rooms, 3 suites. Restaurant, café, cable TV with movies, pool, gym, hair salon, massage, sauna, casino, Internet, some pets allowed (fee). AE, DC, MC, V. BP.*

$$$ 🏨 **Elwa.** Renovations have successfully integrated modern comforts into this older, elegant spa resort midway between the old and new towns. Modern features include clean, comfortable rooms with contemporary furnishings, including overstuffed chairs. There's also an on-site fitness center. The spa specializes in digestive diseases. ✉ *Zahradní 29, 360 01,* ☎ *353–228–472,* FAX *353–228–473,* WEB *www.hotelelwa.com. 10 rooms, 7 suites. Restaurant, cable TV, minibars, hair salon, health club, spa, bar, some pets allowed (fee); no a/c. AE, MC, V. BP.*

$$ ☎ **Růže.** More than adequately comfortable and well priced given its location smack in the center of the spa district, this is a good choice for those who prefer a hotel to a pension or private room. ⊠ *I. P. Pavlova 1, 360 01,* ☎ FAX *353–221–846 or 353–221–853. 20 rooms. Restaurant, cable TV; no a/c. AE, V. BP.*

Nightlife and the Arts

Club Propaganda (⊠ Jaltská 7, ☎ 353–233–792) is Karlovy Vary's best venue for live rock and new music. The upscale action centers on the two nightclubs and the casino of the **Grandhotel Pupp** (⊠ Mírové nám. 2, ☎ 353–109–111). The Karlovy Vary Symphony Orchestra plays regularly at **Lázně III** (⊠ Mlýnské nábř. 5, ☎ 353–225–641).

Outdoor Activities and Sports

Karlovy Vary's warm, open-air public pool on top of the **Thermal Hotel** (⊠ I. P. Pavlova) offers the unique experience of swimming comfortably even in the coolest weather; the view over the town is outstanding. Marked **hiking trails** snake across the beech-and-pine-covered hills that surround the town on three sides. The **Karlovy Vary Golf Club** (⊠ Pražská 125, ☎ 353–331–101) is just out of town on the road to Prague.

Shopping

The town's most exclusive shopping clusters around the Grandhotel Pupp and back toward town along the river on Stará louka. A number of outlets for lesser-known, although high-quality, makers of glass and porcelain can be found along this street. If you are looking for an inexpensive but nonetheless unique gift from Karlovy Vary, consider a bottle of the ubiquitous bittersweet (and potent) Becherovka, a liqueur produced by the town's own Jan Becher distillery. Another neat gift would be one of the pipe-shaped ceramic drinking cups used to take the drinking cure at spas; you can find them at the colonnades. You can also buy boxes of tasty *oplatky* (wafers), sometimes covered with chocolate, at shops in all of the spa towns.

In western Bohemia, Karlovy Vary is best known to glass enthusiasts as the home of **Moser** (⊠ Tržiště 7, ☎ 353–235–303, WEB www.moser. cz), one of the world's leading producers of crystal and decorative glassware. For excellent buys in porcelain, try **Karlovarský porcelán** (⊠ Tržiště 27, ☎ 353–225–660, WEB www.dolphin.cz/thun).

Františkovy Lázně

➋ *6 km (4 mi) from Cheb.*

Františkovy Lázně, or Franzensbad, the smallest of the three main Bohemian spas, isn't really in the same league as the other two (Karlovy Vary and Mariánské Lázně). Built on a more modest scale at the start of the 19th century, the town's ubiquitous kaiser-yellow buildings have been spruced up after their neglect under the previous regime and now present cheerful facades, almost too bright for the few strollers. The poorly kept parks and the formal yet human-scale neoclassical architecture retain much of their former charm. This little spa town couldn't be a more distinct contrast to nearby Cheb's slightly seedy, hustling air and medieval streetscapes. Overall, a pleasing torpor reigns in Františkovy Lázně. There is no town to speak of, just **Národní ulice,** the main street, which leads down into the spa park. The waters, whose healing properties were already known in the 16th century, are used primarily for treating heart problems—and infertility, hence the large number of young women wandering the grounds.

You might enjoy walking the path, indicated with red markers, from Cheb's main square westward along the river and then north past

Komorní Hůrka. The extinct volcano is now a tree-covered hill, but excavations on one side have laid bare the rock, and one tunnel is still open. Goethe instigated and took part in the excavations, and you can still—though barely—make out a relief of the poet carved into the rock face.

The most interesting sight in town may be the small **Lázeňský muzeum** (Spa Museum), just off Národní ulice. There is a wonderful collection of spa-related antiques, including copper bathtubs and a turn-of-the-20th-century exercise bike called a Velotrab. The guest books provide an insight into the cosmopolitan world of pre–World War I Central Europe. The book for 1812 contains the entry "Ludwig van Beethoven, composer from Vienna." ⊠ *Ul. Doktora Pohoreckého 8,* ☎ *354–542–344.* 🖭 *20 Kč.* ☺ *Tues.–Fri. 10–5, weekends 10–4 (usually closed mid-Dec.–mid-Jan.).*

The main spring, **Františkův pramen,** is under a little gazebo filled with brass pipes. The colonnade to the left was decorated with a bust of Lenin that was replaced in 1990 by a memorial to the American liberation of the town in April 1945. The oval neoclassical temple just beyond the spring (amazingly, *not* painted yellow and white) is the **Glauberova dvorana** (Glauber Pavilion), where several springs bubble up into glass cases. ⊠ *Národní ul.*

Dining and Lodging
Most of the establishments in town do a big trade in spa patients, who generally stay for several weeks. Spa treatments usually require a medical check and cost substantially more than the normal room charge. Walk-in treatment can be arranged at some hotels or at the information center. Signs around town advertise massage therapy and other treatments for casual visitors.

$$ ✕🏨 **Slovan.** This gracious place is the perfect complement to this re-
★ laxed little town. The eccentricity of the original turn-of-the-20th-century design survived a thorough renovation during the 1970s. The airy rooms are clean and comfortable, and some have a balcony overlooking the main street. The main-floor restaurant serves above-average Czech dishes such as tasty *svíčková* (beef sirloin in a citrusy cream sauce) and roast duck. ⊠ *Národní 5, 351 01,* ☎ *354–542–841,* 𝖥𝖠𝖷 *354–542–843. 25 rooms, 19 with bath. Restaurant, café, refrigerators, cable TV, bar, meeting room, Internet, some pets allowed (fee). AE, MC, V.*

$$ 🏨 **Centrum.** Rooms in this barnlike building are well appointed, if a bit sterile. Still, it is among the best-run hotels in town and only a short walk from the main park and central spas. ⊠ *Anglická 392, 351 01,* ☎ *354–543–156,* 𝖥𝖠𝖷 *354–543–157. 30 rooms. Restaurant, cable TV, bar, some pets allowed. AE, MC, V. BP.*

$$ 🏨 **Tři Lilie.** Reopened in 1995 after an expensive refitting, the "Three Lilies," which once accommodated the likes of Goethe and Metternich, immediately reestablished itself as the most comfortable spa hotel in town. It is thoroughly elegant, from guest rooms to brasserie. ⊠ *Národní 3,* ☎ 𝖥𝖠𝖷 *354–542–415. 31 rooms. Restaurant, brasserie, café, cable TV, some pets allowed (fee). AE, MC, V. BP.*

Mariánské Lázně

★ ❸   *30 km (18 mi) southeast of Cheb, 47 km (29 mi) south of Karlovy Vary.*

Your expectations of what a spa resort should be may come nearest to fulfillment here. It's far larger and more active than Františkovy Lázně and greener and quieter than Karlovy Vary. This was the spa favored by Britain's Edward VII. Goethe and Chopin also repaired here frequently. Mark Twain, on a visit to the spa in 1892, labeled the town a "health factory" and couldn't get over how new everything looked. Indeed, at that time everything was new. The sanatoriums, most built during the 19th century in a confident, outrageous mixture of "neo" styles, fan out impressively around a finely groomed oblong park. Cure takers and curiosity seekers alike parade through the Empire-style Cross Spring pavilion and the long colonnade near the top of the park. Buy a spouted drinking cup (available at the colonnades) and join the rest of the sippers taking the drinking cure. Be forewarned, though: the waters from the Rudolph, Ambrose, and Caroline springs, though harmless, all have a noticeable diuretic effect. For this reason they're used extensively in treating disorders of the kidney and bladder.

A stay in Mariánské Lázně can be healthful even without special treatment. Special walking trails of all difficulty levels surround the resort in all directions. The best advice is simply to put on comfortable shoes, buy a hiking map, and head out. One of the country's few golf courses lies about 3 km (2 mi) to the east of town. Hotels can also help to arrange special activities, such as tennis and horseback riding. For the less intrepid, a simple stroll around the gardens, with a few deep breaths of the town's famous air, is enough to restore a healthy sense of perspective.

For information on spa treatments, inquire at the main **spa offices** (⊠ Masarykova 22, ☎ 354–623–061, WEB www.marienbad.cz). Walk-in treatments can be arranged at the **Nové Lázně** (New Spa; ⊠ Reitenbergerova 53, ☎ 354–644–111).

OFF THE
BEATEN PATH

CHODOVÁ PLANÁ – If you need a break from the rigorous healthiness of spa life, the Pivovarská restaurace a muzeum ve skále (Brewery Restaurant and Museum in the Rock) is just a few miles south of Mariánské Lázně in an underground complex of granite tunnels that have been used to age beer since the 1400s. Generous servings of Czech dishes including a whole roast suckling pig can be ordered to accompany the strong, fresh Chodovar beer tapped directly from granite storage vaults. Giant tanks of aging beer and brewing memorabilia can be seen through glass windows on the way in. You can tour the brewery, but at this writing, tours were conducted in German only. ⊠ *Pivovarská 107, Chodová Planá,* ☎ *374–798–122,* WEB *www.chodovar.cz.* ☞ *Museum free, tour 50 Kč.* ☉ *Daily 11–11; brewery tours daily at 2.*

Dining and Lodging
The best place to look for private lodgings is along Paleckého ulice and Hlavní třída, south of the main spa area. Private accommodations can also be found in the neighboring villages of Zádub and Závišín in the woods to the east of town.

$–$$$ ✕ **Koliba.** This combination hunting lodge and wine tavern, set in the
★ woods roughly 10 minutes on foot from the spas, is an excellent alternative to the hotel restaurants in town. Grilled meats and shish kebabs, plus tankards of Moravian wine (try the dry, cherry red Rulandské červené), are served with traditional gusto while fiddlers play rousing Moravian tunes. ⊠ *Dusíkova 592, in the direction of Karlovy Vary,* ☎ *354–625–169. V.*

$–$$ ✕ **Filip.** This bustling wine bar is where locals come to find relief from the sometimes large hordes of tourists. There's a tasty selection of traditional Czech dishes—mainly pork, grilled meats, and steaks. ⊠ *Poštovní 96,* ☎ *354–626–161. No credit cards.*

$$$$ 🏨 **Excelsior.** This lovely older hotel is on the main street and is convenient to the spas and colonnade. Rooms have traditional cherry-wood furniture and marble bathrooms, and the views over the town are

enchanting. The staff is friendly and multilingual. While the food in the restaurant is only average, the romantic setting provides adequate compensation. ⊠ *Hlavní tř. 121, 353 01,* ☎ *354–622–705,* FAX *354–625–346,* WEB *www.orea.cz/excelsior. 64 rooms. Restaurant, café, cable TV with movies, minibars, massage, sauna, some pets allowed (fee); no a/c. AE, DC, MC, V. BP.*

$$$$ 🏨 **Parkhotel Golf.** Book in advance to secure a room at this stately villa situated 3½ km (2 mi) out of town on the road to Karlovy Vary. The large, open rooms are cheery and modern. The restaurant on the main floor is excellent, but the big draw is the 18-hole golf course on the premises, one of the few in the Czech Republic. The course was opened in 1905 by King Edward VII. ⊠ *Zádub 55, 353 01,* ☎ *354–622–651 or 354–622—652,* FAX *354–622–655,* WEB *web.telecom.cz/parkhotel-golf. 25 rooms. Restaurant, minibars, cable TV, pool, 18-hole golf course, tennis court, nightclub, meeting room, Internet, some pets allowed (fee). AE, DC, MC, V. BP.*

$$$ 🏨 **Bohemia.** At this gracious, late-19th-century hotel, beautiful crys-
★   tal chandeliers in the main hall set the stage for a comfortable and el-egant stay. The crisp beige-and-white rooms let you spread out and *really* unpack; they're spacious and high ceilinged. (If you want to indulge, request one of the enormous suites overlooking the park.) The help-ful staff can arrange spa treatments and horseback riding. A renova-tion in 2001 brightened up the facade and modernized the kitchen. ⊠ *Hlavní tř. 100, 353 01,* ☎ *354–623–251,* FAX *354–622–943,* WEB *www. orea.cz/bohemia. 73 rooms, 4 suites. Restaurant, café, cable TV, lounge, some pets allowed (fee); no a/c. AE, MC, V. BP.*

Nightlife and the Arts

The West Bohemian Symphony Orchestra performs regularly in the New Spa (Nové Lázně). The town's annual Chopin festival each August brings in pianists from around Europe to perform the Polish composer's works.

Casino Lil (⊠ Anglická 336, ☎ 354–623–293) is open daily 2 PM–7 AM. For late-night drinks, try the **Parkhotel Golf** (⊠ Zádub 55, ☎ 354–622–651 or 354–622–652), which has a good nightclub with dancing in season.

Bohemian Spa Towns A to Z

BUS TRAVEL

Most major towns are easily reachable by bus service. Smaller towns, though, might only have one bus a day or even fewer. Be sure to know when the next bus comes so you won't be stranded. Frequent bus ser-vice between Prague and Karlovy Vary makes the journey only about two hours each way, but you must consider differences of both time and price in making a decision if taking the bus is worth it (☞ Bus Travel to and from Prague *in* Prague A to Z).

CAR TRAVEL

If you're driving, you can take the E48 directly from Prague to Karlovy Vary. Roads in the area tend to be in good condition, though they can sometimes be quite narrow.

TOURS

Most of Prague's tour operators offer excursions to Karlovy Vary. Čedok offers one-day and longer tours covering western Bohemia's major sights, as well as curative vacations at many Czech spas.

➤ CONTACT: Čedok (☎ 224–197–111, WEB www.cedok.cz).

TRAIN TRAVEL

Good, if slow, train service links all the major towns west of Prague. The best stretches are from Františkovy Lázně to Plzeň and from Plzeň to Prague. The Prague–Karlovy Vary run takes far longer than it should—more than three hours by the shortest route.

TRAVEL AGENCIES

The American Express representative in Karlovy Vary is Incentives CZ.
➤ CONTACT: **Incentives CZ** (✉ Vřídelní 51, Karlovy Vary, ☎ 353–226–027, WEB www.incentives.cz).

VISITOR INFORMATION

➤ CONTACTS: **Františkovy Lázně Tourist Information** (✉ Tři Lilie Travel Agency, Národní 3, Františkovy Lázně, ☎ 354–542–430, WEB www.franzensbad.cz). **Karlovy Vary Tourist Information** (Kur-Info; ✉ Vřídelní kolonáda [Vřídlo Colonnade], Karlovy Vary, ☎ 353–322–4097, WEB www.karlovyvary.cz; ✉ Nám. Dr. M. Horákové 18, Karlovy Vary [near bus station], ☎ 353–222–833). **Mariánské Lázně Tourist Information** (Cultural and Information Center; ✉ Hlavní 47, Mariánské Lázně, ☎ 354–625–892 or 354–622–474, WEB www.marianskelazne.cz).

PRAGUE A TO Z

ADDRESSES

Navigation is relatively simple once you know the basic street-sign words: *ulice* (street, abbreviated to ul., commonly dropped in printed addresses); *náměstí* (square, abbreviated to nám.); and *třída* (avenue). In most towns, each building has two numbers, a confusing practice with historic roots. In Prague, the blue tags mark the street address (usually); in Brno, ignore the blue tags and go by the white ones.

AIR TRAVEL

ČSA (Czech Airlines), the Czech national carrier, offers the only direct flights from New York (JFK) to Prague, with six flights a week most times (daily flights during the busiest season). It's also possible to connect through a major European airport and continue to Prague. The flight from New York to Prague takes about 8 hours; from the West Coast, including a stopover, 12 to 16 hours. Go Airways offers discount flights to Prague from Britain, but you must leave from Stansted or East Midlands airport; at this writing, Go had been purchased by easyJet, another discount European carrier, and plans were underway to merge the operations under the easyJet name, a process that will not be complete until sometime in 2004. Another way to save money is either changing flights in Frankfurt or catching a bus from Frankfurt to Prague.
➤ CARRIERS: **Air Canada** (☎ 224–810–181). **Air France** (☎ 224–227–164). **Alitalia** (☎ 224–194–150). **Austrian Airlines** (☎ 224–826–199). **American Airlines** (☎ 224–234–985). **British Airways** (☎ 222–114–444). **British Midland** (☎ 224–810–180). **ČSA** (☎ 220–104–310, WEB www.csa.cz). **Delta** (☎ 224–946–733). **Go** (☎ 296–333–333, WEB www.go-fly.com or www.easyjet.com). **KLM** (☎ 233–090–933). **Lufthansa** (☎ 224–811–007). **SAS** (☎ 220–114–456). **Swiss** (☎ 224–812–211).

AIRPORTS AND TRANSFERS

Ruzyně Airport is 20 km (12 mi) northwest of the downtown area. It's small but easily negotiated. A still-expanding main terminal has eased traffic flow. The trip to downtown is a straight shot down Evropská Boulevard and takes approximately 20 minutes. The road is not usually busy, but anticipate an additional 20 minutes during rush hour (7 AM–9 AM and 3 PM–6 PM).

➤ AIRPORT INFORMATION: **Ruzyně Airport** (☎ 220–111–111, WEB www. csl.cz).

TRANSFERS

The Cedaz minibus shuttle links the airport with náměstí Republiky (Republic Square, just off the Old Town). It runs hourly, more often at peak periods, between 5:30 AM and 9:30 PM daily and makes an intermediate stop at the Dejvická metro station. The one-way fare is 90 Kč. The minibus also serves many hotels for 370 Kč—650 Kč, which is sometimes less than the taxi fare. Regular municipal bus service (Bus 119) connects the airport and the Dejvická station; the fare is 12 Kč (15 Kč if purchased from the driver), and the ticket is transferrable to trams or the metro. From Dejvická you can take the metro to the city center. To reach Wenceslas Square, get off at the Můstek station.

The transportation company FIX has cars waiting at the airport, and these are your only choice if you want a taxi. Technically, though, these aren't taxis and they charge a fixed rate based on zones. The fees range from 120 Kč to 870 Kč for travel into the city. Be sure to find out how much it will cost—preferably in writing from their airport representative—before entering the car, because overcharging is a problem. The ride should cost 500 Kč–700 Kč.

You can call a taxi on your own; the rates might be a little cheaper than if you use a FIX car, but beware of dishonest taxi drivers.
➤ CONTACT: **Cedaz** (☎ 220–114–296), WEB www.aas.cz/cedaz).

BUS TRAVEL TO AND FROM PRAGUE
The Czech complex of regional bus lines known collectively as ČSAD operates its dense network from the sprawling Florenc station. For information about routes and schedules, call, consult the confusingly displayed timetables posted at the station, or visit the information window in the lower level lobby, which is open daily 6 AM–9 PM. The company's Web site will give you bus and train information in English (click on the British flag).
➤ BUS LINES: **ČSAD** (✉ Florenc station, Křižíkova, Karl'n, ☎ 12999; 224–214–990 route and schedule information, WEB www.jizdnirady.cz; metro: Florenc [Line B or C]).

BUS AND TRAM TRAVEL WITHIN PRAGUE
Prague's extensive bus and streetcar network allows for fast, efficient travel throughout the city. Tickets are the same as those used for the metro, although you validate them at machines inside the bus or tram. Tickets (*jízdenky*) can be bought at hotels, some newsstands, and from dispensing machines in the metro stations. The basic, transferrable ticket costs 12 Kč. It permits one hour's travel throughout the metro, tram, and bus network between 5 AM and 8 PM on weekdays, or 90 minutes' travel at other times. Single-ride tickets cost 8 Kč and allow one 15-minute ride on a tram or bus, without transfer, or a metro journey of up to four stations lasting less than 30 minutes (transfer between lines is allowed). You can also buy a one-day pass allowing unlimited use of the system for 70 Kč, a three-day pass for 200 Kč, a seven-day pass for 250 Kč, or a 15-day pass for 280 Kč. The passes can be purchased at the main metro stations, from ticket machines, and at some newsstands in the center. A pass is not valid until stamped in the orange machines in metro stations or aboard trams *and* the required information is entered on the back (there are instructions in English). A refurbished old tram, No. 91, travels through the Old Town and Lesser Quarter on summer weekends. The metro shuts down at midnight, but Trams 50–59 and Buses 500 and above run all night. Night trams run at 40-minute intervals, and all routes intersect at the corner of Lazarská and

Spálená streets in the New Town near the Národní třída metro station. Schedules and regulations in English are on the transportation department's official Web site.

➤ INFORMATION: **Dopravní Podnik** (WEB www.dp-praha.cz).

CAR RENTALS

Several major agencies have offices at the airport and also in the city. There are no special requirements for renting a car in the Czech Republic, but be sure to shop around, as prices can differ greatly. Major firms like Avis and Hertz offer Western makes starting at around $45 per day or $300 per week, which includes insurance, damage waiver, and VAT (value-added tax); cars equipped with automatic transmission and air-conditioning are available, but it's best to reserve your rental car before you leave home, and it may be less expensive as well. Smaller local companies, on the other hand, can rent Czech cars for significantly less, but the service and insurance coverage may be inferior. A surcharge of 5%–12% applies to rental cars picked up at Prague's Ruzyně Airport.

➤ MAJOR AGENCIES: **Alamo** (✉ Ruzyně Airport, Ruzyně, ☎ 220–114–340; ✉ Hilton, Pobřežní 1, Karlín, ☎ 224–842–407). **Avis** (✉ Ruzyně Airport, Ruzyně, ☎ 220–114–270; Klimentská 46, Nové Město, ☎ 221–851–225). **Budget** (✉ Ruzyně Airport, Ruzyně, ☎ 220–113–253; Hotel Inter-Continental, nám. Curieových 5, Staré Město, ☎ 224–889–995). **Europcar** (✉ Ruzyně Airport, Ruzyně, ☎ 235–364–531; Pařižská 28, Staré Město, ☎ 224–811–290). **Hertz** (✉ Ruzyně Airport, Ruzyně, ☎ 220–114–340; Karlovo nám. 28, Nové Město, ☎ 222–231–010; Diplomat hotel, Evropská 15, Dejvice, ☎ 224–394–175).

CAR TRAVEL

If your visit is restricted to the Czech capital, you'll do better not to rent a car. The capital is congested, and you'll save yourself a lot of hassle if you rely on public transportation. If you are planning to take excursions into the country, then a car will be useful, but don't pick it up until you are ready to depart. If you are arriving by car, you'll find that Prague is well served by major roads and highways from anywhere in the country. On arriving in the city, simply follow the signs to CENTRUM (city center).

PARKING

Parking is permitted in the center of town on a growing number of streets with parking meters or in the few small lots within walking distance of the historic center—but parking spaces are scarce. A meter with a green stripe lets you park up to six hours; an orange-stripe meter gives you two. (Use change in the meters.) A sign with a blue circle outlined in red with a diagonal red slash indicates a no-parking zone. Avoid the blue-marked spaces, which are reserved for local residents. Violators may find a "boot" immobilizing their vehicle. If your hotel offers parking, you will have to pay a daily rate.

There's an underground lot at náměstí Jana Palacha, near Old Town Square. There are also park-and-ride (P+R) lots at some suburban metro stations, including Skalka (Line A), Zličín and Černý Most (Line B), and Nádraží Holešovice and Opatov (Line C).

TRAFFIC

During the day, traffic can be stop-and-go. Pay particular attention to the trams, which have the right-of-way in every situation. Avoid, when possible, driving in the congested and labyrinthine Old Town.

CUSTOMS AND DUTIES

The export of items considered to have historical value is not allowed. To be exported, an antique or work of art must have an export certificate. Reputable shops should be willing to advise customers on how to comply with the regulations. If a shop can't provide proof of the item's suitability for export, be wary. The authorities do not look kindly on unauthorized "export" of antiques, particularly of baroque religious pieces. Under certain circumstances, the value-added tax (VAT) on purchases over 1,000 Kč can be refunded if the goods are taken out of the country within 30 days.

EMBASSIES AND CONSULATES

➤ CONTACTS: **Canadian Embassy** (✉ Mickiewiczova 6, Hradčany, ☎ 272–101–890, WEB www.dfait-maeci.gc.ca/prague). **U.K. Embassy** (✉ Thunovská 14, Malá Strana, ☎ 257–530–278, WEB www.britain.cz). **U.S. Embassy** (✉ Tržiště 15, Malá Strana, ☎ 257–530–663, WEB www. usembassy.cz).

EMERGENCIES

➤ DOCTORS AND DENTISTS: **Dentist Referrals** (✉ Palackého 5, ☎ 224–946–981 24-hr emergency service). **Lékařská služba první pomoci** (district first-aid clinic; ✉ Palackého 5, Nové Město, ☎ 224–946–982).
➤ EMERGENCY SERVICES: **Ambulance** (☎ 155). **Autoklub Bohemia Assistance** (☎ 1240, WEB www.aba.cz). **Federal Police** (☎ 158). **Prague city police** (☎ 156). **ÚAMK Emergency Roadside Assistance** (☎ 1230, WEB www.uamk.cz).
➤ HOSPITALS: **American Medical Center** (✉ Janovského 48, Holešovice, ☎ 220–807–756 24-hr service). **First Medical Clinic of Prague** (✉ Tylovo nám. 3/15, Nové Město, ☎ 224–251–319). **Na Homolce Hospital** (✉ Roentgenova 2, Prague 5, ☎ 257–272–146 weekdays [foreigners' department]; 257–211–111; 257–272–191).
➤ LATE-NIGHT PHARMACIES: **Lékárna U Anděla** (✉ Štefánikova 6, Smíchov, ☎ 257–320–918). **Lékárna** (✉ Belgická 37, Nové Město, ☎ 222–513–396).

ENGLISH-LANGUAGE MEDIA

In the city center nearly every bookstore carries a few guidebooks and paperbacks in English. Street vendors on Wenceslas Square and Na Příkopě carry leading foreign newspapers and periodicals. To find out what's on and to get the latest tips for shopping, dining, and entertainment, consult Prague's weekly English-language newspaper, the *Prague Post* (WEB www.praguepost.com). It prints comprehensive entertainment listings and can be bought at most downtown newsstands as well as in major North American and European cities.

HOLIDAYS AND LANGUAGE

HOLIDAYS

January 1; Easter Monday; May 1 (Labor Day); May 8 (Liberation Day); July 5 (Sts. Cyril and Methodius Day); July 6 (Jan Hus Day); September 28 (Day of Czech Statehood); October 28 (Czech National Day); November 17 (Day of a Struggle for Liberty and Democracy); and December 24, 25, and 26.

LANGUAGE

Czech, a Slavic language closely related to Slovak and Polish, is the official language of the Czech Republic. Learning English is popular among young people, but German is still the most useful language for tourists, especially outside Prague.

LODGING

BED-AND-BREAKFAST RESERVATION AGENCIES

Most local information offices also book rooms in hotels, pensions, and private accommodations. Do-it-yourself travelers should keep a sharp eye out for room-for-rent signs reading ZIMMER FREI, PRIVAT, or

UBYTOVÁNÍ. The Good Bed Agency specializes in Prague and Karlovy Vary. Many other B&Bs have home pages on the Web site of the IDS International Database System.

➤ CONTACTS: **The Good Bed Agency** (✉ Kříženeckého nám. 322, Prague, ☎ 267–073–456, 🕸 www.goodbed.cz). **International Database System** (🕸 www.hotel.cz).

MONEY MATTERS

The Czech Republic is still generally a bargain by Western standards. Prague remains the exception. Hotel prices in particular are often higher than the facilities would warrant, but prices at tourist resorts outside the capital are lower and, in the outlying areas and off the beaten track, very low. Unfortunately, many museums, castles, and certain clubs charge a higher entrance fee for foreigners than they charge for Czechs. A few hotels still follow this practice, too.

CREDIT CARDS

Visa, MasterCard, and American Express are widely accepted by major hotels and stores, Diners Club less so. Smaller establishments and those off the beaten track are less likely to accept a wide variety of credit cards.

➤ LOST CREDIT CARDS: **American Express** (☎ 336–393–111). **Diners Club** (☎ 267–314–485). **MasterCard** (☎ 261–354–650). **Visa** (☎ 224–125–353).

CURRENCY

The unit of currency in the Czech Republic is the koruna, or crown (Kč), which is divided into 100 haléřů, or hellers. There are (little-used) coins of 10, 20, and 50 hellers; coins of 1, 2, 5, 10, 20, and (rarely) 50 Kč; and notes of 50, 100, 200, 500, 1,000, 2,000, and 5,000 Kč. Notes of 1,000 Kč and up may not always be accepted for small purchases.

CURRENCY EXCHANGE

Try to avoid exchanging money at hotels or private exchange booths, including the ubiquitous Chequepoint and Exact Change booths. They routinely take commissions of 8%–10%. The best places to exchange are at bank counters, where the commissions average 1%–3%, or at ATMs. The koruna is fully convertible, which means it can be purchased outside the country and exchanged into other currencies. Of course, never change money with people on the street. Not only is it illegal, you will almost definitely be ripped off.

At this writing the exchange rate was around 33 Kč to the U.S. dollar, 21 Kč to the Canadian dollar, 48 Kč to the pound sterling, and 30 Kč to the euro.

PASSPORTS AND VISAS

United States and British citizens need only a valid passport to visit the Czech Republic as tourists. U.S. citizens may stay for 30 days without a visa; British citizens three or six months, depending on the type of passport. Canadian citizens require a visa, which is valid for up to 90 days and which must be obtained in advance. Long-term and work visas for all foreigners now must be obtained from outside the country. Those interested in working or living in the Czech Republic are advised to contact the Czech embassy or consulate in their home country well in advance of their trip.

SUBWAY TRAVEL

Prague's subway system, the metro, is clean and reliable; the stations are marked with an inconspicuous M sign. Trains run daily 5 AM–midnight. Validate your ticket at an orange machine before descending the escalator. Trains are patrolled often; the fine for riding without a valid

82

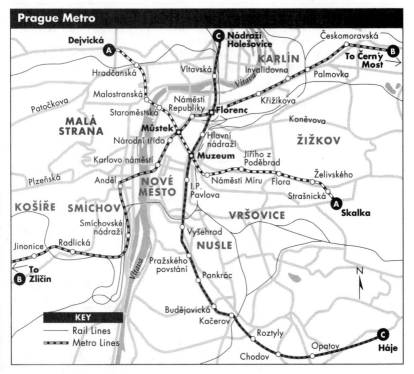

Prague Metro

KEY
— Rail Lines
▪▪▪ Metro Lines

ticket is 400 Kč. Beware of pickpockets, who often operate in large groups on crowded trams and metro cars. At this writing, parts of the metro system were still closed due to flooding in August 2002; although service has been restored to most of the central areas of the city, full service will not be in effect until sometime late in 2003.

TAXIS

Dishonest taxi drivers are the shame of the nation. Luckily you probably won't need to rely on taxis for trips within the city center (it's usually easier to walk or take the subway). Typical scams include drivers doctoring the meter or simply failing to turn the meter on and then demanding an exorbitant sum at the end of the ride. In an honest cab, the meter starts at 30 Kč and increases by 22 Kč per km (½ mi) or 4 Kč per minute at rest. Most rides within town should cost no more than 80 Kč–150 Kč. To minimize the chances of getting ripped off, avoid taxi stands in Wenceslas Square, Old Town Square, and other heavily touristed areas. The best alternative is to phone for a taxi in advance. Many radio-taxi firms have English-speaking operators.

➤ CONTACTS: **AAA Taxi** (☎ 233–113–311, WEB www.aaa.radiotaxi.cz). **Profitaxi** (☎ 261–314–151).

TELEPHONES

The country code for the Czech Republic is 420. The country dropped regional codes and adopted a nationwide nine-digit standard in late 2002. Prefixes 0/601 to 0/777 denote mobile phones (omit the "0" when calling from outside the country).

Now that most people have mobile phones, working phone booths are harder to find. If you can't find a booth, the telephone office of the main post office is the best place to try. Once inside, follow signs for TELEGRAF/TELEFAX.

INTERNATIONAL CALLS

The international dialing code is 00. For calls to the United States, Canada, or the United Kingdom, dial the international operator. Otherwise, ask the receptionist at any hotel to put a call through for you, but the surcharges and rates will be tremendously high.

With the prepaid Karta X (300 Kč–1,000 Kč), rates to the U.S. are roughly 13 Kč per minute; a call to the U.K. costs about 12 Kč per minute. The cards are available at many money-changing stands and can work with any phone once you enter a 14-digit code. You do not need to find a booth with a card slot to use the cards.

You can reach an English-speaking operator from one of the major long-distance services on a toll-free number. The operator will connect your collect or credit-card call at the carrier's standard rates. In Prague, many phone booths allow direct international dialing.
➤ LONG-DISTANCE ACCESS NUMBERS: **AT&T** (☎ 0/042–000–101). **BT Direct** (☎ 0/042–004–401). **CanadaDirect** (☎ 0/042–000–151). **MCI** (☎ 0/042–000–112). **Sprint** (☎ 0/042–087–187).
➤ OTHER CONTACTS: **International Operator** (☎ 133004). **International Directory Assistance** (☎ 1181).

LOCAL CALLS

Coin-operated pay phones are hard to find. Most newer public phones operate only with a special telephone card, available from post offices and some newsstands in denominations of 150 Kč and up. Since the boom in mobile phone use, both the cards and working pay phones are harder to find. A short call within Prague costs a minimum of 4 Kč from a coin-operated phone or the equivalent of 3.5 Kč (1 unit) from a card-operated phone. The dial tone is a series of alternating short and long buzzes.

TIPPING

Service is usually not included in restaurant bills. Round the bill up to the next multiple of 10 (if the bill comes to 83 Kč, for example, give the waiter 90 Kč); 10% is considered appropriate in all but the most expensive places. Tip porters who bring bags to your rooms 40 Kč total. For room service, a 20 Kč tip is enough. In taxis, round the bill up by 10%. Give tour guides and helpful concierges between 50 Kč and 100 Kč for services rendered.

TOURS

Čedok offers a 3½-hour "Grand City Tour," a combination bus and walking venture that covers all the major sights with commentary in English. It departs daily at 9:30 AM year-round, and also at 2 PM from April through October, from opposite the Prašná brána (Powder Tower) on Republic Square, near the main Čedok office. The price is about 750 Kč. "Historic Prague on Foot" is a slower-paced, three-hour walking tour for 400 Kč. From April through October, it departs Republic Square on Wednesday, Friday, and Sunday at 9:30 AM; in the off-season, it departs Friday at 9:30 AM. More tours are offered, especially in summer, and the schedules may well vary according to demand. You can also contact Čedok's main office to arrange a personalized walking tour. Times and itineraries are negotiable; prices start at around 500 Kč per hour.

Very similar tours by other operators also depart daily from Republic Square, Národní třída near Jungmannovo náměstí, and Wenceslas Square. Prices are generally a couple hundred crowns less than for Čedok's tours. Themed walking tours are very popular as well. You can choose medieval architecture, "Velvet Revolution walks," visits to

Communist monuments, and any number of pub crawls. Each year, four or five small operators do these tours, which generally last a couple of hours and cost 200 Kč–300 Kč. Inquire at Prague Information Service or a major ticket agency for the current season's offerings.

TRAIN TRAVEL

International trains arrive at and depart from either of two stations: the main station, Hlavní nádraží, is about 500 yards east of Wenceslas Square on Opletalova or Washingtonova street. Then there's the suburban Nádraží Holešovice, about 2 km (1 mi) north of the city center. This is an unending source of confusion—always make certain you know which station your train is using. Note also that trains arriving from the west usually stop at Smíchov station, on the west bank of the Vltava, before continuing to the main station. Prague's other central train station, Masarykovo nádraží, serves mostly local trains but has an international ticket window that is often much less crowded than those at the main station.

For train times, consult timetables in a station or get in line at the information office upstairs at the main station (for domestic trains, open daily 3 AM–11:45 PM) or downstairs near the exits under the ČD Centrum sign (open daily 6 AM–7:30 PM). The main Čedok office also provides train information and issues tickets.

Wenceslas Square is a convenient five-minute walk from the main station (best not undertaken late at night), or you can take the subway (Line C) one stop in the Háje direction to Muzeum. A taxi ride from the main station to the center should cost about 100 Kč, but the station cabbies are known for overcharging. To reach the city center from Nádraží Holešovice, take the metro (Line C) four stops to Muzeum; a taxi ride should cost roughly 200 Kč–250 Kč.

➤ CONTACT: **Čedok** (✉ Na Příkopě 18, Staré Město, ☎ 224–197–111, WEB www.cedok.cz).

➤ TRAIN STATIONS: **Hlavní nádraží** (✉ Wilsonova ul., Nové Město, ☎ 224–224–200 schedules and fares). **Masarykovo nádraží** (✉ Hybernská 13, Nové Město). **Nádraží Holešovice** (✉ Vrbenskehóo, Holešovice).

TRAVEL AGENCIES

American Express and Thomas Cook, two big international agencies, have convenient offices in Prague. For bus tickets to just about anywhere in Europe, Bohemia Tour is useful. Čedok, the ubiquitous Czech travel agency, provides general tourist information and city maps. Čedok will also exchange money, book accommodations, arrange guided tours, and book passage on airlines, buses, and trains. You can pay for Čedok services, including booking rail tickets, with any major credit card. Note limited weekend hours. The main office is open weekdays 8:30–6 and Saturday 9–1.

➤ CONTACTS: **American Express** (✉ Václavské nám. 56, Nové Město, ☎ 224–219–992; Mostecká 12, Malá Strana, ☎ 257–313–636). **Bohemia Tour** (✉ Jungmannova 4, Nové Město, ☎ 224–947–707, WEB www.bohemiatour.cz). **Čedok** (✉ Na Příkopě 18, Staré Město, ☎ 224–197–111, WEB www.cedok.cz). **Thomas Cook** (✉ Karlova 3, Staré Město, ☎ 222–221–055).

VISITOR INFORMATION

The Czech Tourist Authority office on Old Town Square can provide information on tourism outside Prague but does not sell tickets or book accommodations. The Prague Information Service has four central offices. The Town Hall branch is open weekdays 9–6, weekends 9–5. The Na Příkopě office, just a few doors down from Čedok's main office, is open weekdays 9–6 and Saturday 9–3. The Hlavní nádraží branch is open April–October, weekdays 9–7 and weekends 9–4, and November–March, weekdays 9–6 and Saturday 9–3. The Charles Bridge tower office on the Malá Strana end of Charles Bridge, is open April–October, daily 10–6.

➤ CONTACTS: **Czech Tourist Authority** (✉ Staroměstské nám. 6, Staré Město, ☎ 227–158–111). There are four central offices of the municipal **Prague Information Service,** or PIS (✉ Staroměstská radnice [Old Town Hall], Staré Město, ☎ 224–482–562, WEB www.pis.cz; Na Příkopě 20, Nové Město, ☎ no phone; Hlavní nádraží, lower hall, Staré Město, ☎ no phone; Malostranská mostecká věž, Malá Strana, ☎ no phone).

3   BUDAPEST

Revitalization continues full-swing in Hungary as the Communist legacy fades into 20th-century history. Budapest offers breathtaking Old World grandeur and thriving cultural life—a must-stop on any trip to Central Europe. Hearty meals spiced with rich red paprika, the generosity and warmth of the Magyar soul: These and more sustain visitors in this land of vital spirit and beauty.

By Alan Levy
and Julie
Tomasz

Updated
by Scott
Alexander
Young

HUNGARY SITS AT THE CROSSROADS of Central Europe, having retained its own identity by absorbing countless invasions and foreign occupations. Its industrious, resilient people have a history of brave but unfortunate uprisings: against the Turks in the 17th century, the Hapsburgs in 1848, and the Soviet Union in 1956. With the withdrawal of the last Soviet soldiers from Hungarian soil in 1991, Hungary embarked on a decade of sweeping changes. The adjustment to a free-market economy has not all been easy sailing, but Hungary at long last has regained self-determination and a chance to rebuild an economy devastated by years of Communist misrule.

A few years into the new millennium much indeed seems possible. Hungary joined NATO in 1999, and European Union (EU) membership could come as soon as 2004. In 2002, then 39-year-old Prime Minister Viktor Orbán was the subject of gentle mockery when he suggested that the Hungarian economy was like a guided missile that had taken off and which could not be shot down. At the same time, people knew what he was talking about. For international investors, too, Hungary is seen as a good bet, one of the better in this fast-developing region.

An entire generation is coming of age in Hungary for whom foreign occupation, long lines to buy bananas, coupon books, and repression of the press are an increasingly distant memory. Their parents remember every precious, incremental gain in freedom during the years of so-called "goulash socialism" of the 1960s and '70s. Their grandparents may even look back to this time of protectionist economic policies and cradle-to-the-grave social welfare with a certain nostalgia.

The stage was set then for a tightly fought electoral contest in 2002 and a battle of ideologies, between Orbán's increasingly right-wing FIDESZ party and the Hungarian Socialist Party, which narrowly won the parliamentary elections.

Because Hungary is a small, agriculturally oriented country, visitors are often surprised by its grandeur and charm, especially in the capital, Budapest, which bustles with life as never before. These days most are spared bureaucratic hassles at border crossings, and most Westerners can stay in the country for three months (out of every six) without obtaining a visa.

Situated on both banks of the Danube, Budapest unites the colorful hills of Buda and the wide, businesslike boulevards of Pest. Though it was the site of a Roman outpost during the 1st century, the city was not officially created until 1873, when the towns of Óbuda, Pest, and Buda united. Since then, Budapest has been the cultural, political, intellectual, and commercial heart of Hungary; for the 20% of the nation's population who live in the capital, anywhere else is simply *vidék* ("the country").

Budapest has suffered many ravages in the course of its long history. It was totally destroyed by the Mongols in 1241, captured by the Turks in 1541, and nearly destroyed again by Soviet troops in 1945. But this bustling industrial and cultural center survived as the capital of the People's Republic of Hungary after the war—and then, as the 1980s drew to a close, it became one of the Eastern Bloc's few thriving bastions of capitalism. Today, judging by the city's flourishing cafés and restaurants, markets and bars, the stagnation enforced by the Communists seems a thing of the very distant past.

Much of the charm of a visit to Budapest lies in unexpected glimpses into shadowy courtyards and in long vistas down sunlit cobbled streets. Although some 30,000 buildings were destroyed during World War II and in the 1956 Revolution, the past lingers on in the often crumbling architectural details of the antique structures that remain.

Hungarians are known for their hospitality and love talking to foreigners, although their unusual language can be a challenge. Today, however, everyone seems to be learning English, especially young people. But what all Hungarians share is a deep love of music, and the calendar is studded with it, from Budapest's famous opera to its annual spring music festival. And at many restaurants Gypsy violinists serenade you during your evening meal.

Pleasures and Pastimes

Dining

Through the lean postwar years the Hungarian kitchen lost none of its spice and sparkle. Meats, rich sauces, and creamy desserts predominate, but the more health-conscious will also find salads, even out of season. (Strict vegetarians should note, however, that even meatless dishes are often cooked with lard [zsír].) In addition to the ubiquitous dishes most foreigners are familiar with, such as chunky beef gulyás (goulash) and paprikás csirke (chicken paprika) served with galuska (little pinched dumplings), traditional Hungarian classics include fiery halászlé (fish soup), scarlet with hot paprika; fogas (pike perch) from Lake Balaton; and goose liver, duck, and veal specialties. Lake Balaton is the major source of fish in Hungary, particularly for süllő, a kind of perch. Hungarians are also very fond of carp (ponty), catfish (harcsa), and eel (angolna), which are often stewed in a garlic-and-tomato sauce. There's also turós csusza, which is a strange mixture of lukewarm pasta covered in curded cheese. It may not be to everyone's taste, but it is most definitely authentically Hungarian.

Portions are large, so don't plan to eat more than one main Hungarian meal a day. Desserts are lavish, and every inn seems to have its house torta (cake), though rétes (strüdels), Somlói galuska (a steamed sponge cake soaked in chocolate sauce and whipped cream), and palacsinta (stuffed crêpes) are ubiquitous. Traditional rétes fillings are mák (sugary poppy seeds), meggy (sour cherry), and túró (sweetened cottage cheese); palacsintas always come rolled with dió (sweet ground walnuts), túró, or lekvár (jam)—often sárgabarack (apricot). Finally, try the Zserbó, a delicious layered cake with apricot-jam and walnut filling.

In major cities, there is a good selection of restaurants, from the grander establishments that echo the imperial past of the Hapsburg era to trendy new international restaurants to cheap but cheerful spots favored by the working populace. In addition to trying out the standard vendéglő or étterem (restaurants), you can eat at a bisztró étel bár (sit-down snack bar), a büfé (snack counter), an eszpresszó (café), or a söröző (pub). And no matter how strict your diet, don't pass up a visit to at least one cukrászda (pastry shop). Finally, if you find yourself longing for something non-Hungarian—anything from pizza to Indian, Turkish to Korean, Greek to American-style fast food—you can find it aplenty in the larger cities.

Although prices are steadily increasing, there are plenty of good, affordable restaurants offering Hungarian and international dishes. Even in Budapest, eating out can provide you with some of the best value for the money of any European capital. In almost all restaurants, an inexpensive prix-fixe lunch called a menü is available, usually for as little as 1,000 Ft. It includes soup or salad, a main course, and a dessert. The days of charging customers for each slice of bread taken from the bread basket and of embellishing tourists' bills are, happily, fast receding. The glaring exception to this is along Váci utca, a downtown pedestrian thoroughfare in Budapest. If someone (usually a young lady) approaches you on this street and invites you to join her at a nearby café or restaurant, politely decline: unless you want to be presented later with a three-figure bill for a cup of coffee by a burly and intimidating "waiter."

Hungarians eat early—you still risk offhand service and cold food if you arrive at some traditional Hungarian restaurants after 9 PM. Lunch, the main meal for many, is served from noon to 2. At most moderately priced and inexpensive restaurants, casual but neat dress is acceptable.

CATEGORY	COST*
$$$$	over 3,500 Ft.
$$$	2,500 Ft.–3,500 Ft.
$$	1,500 Ft.–2,500 Ft.
$	under 1,500 Ft.

*per person for a main course at dinner

Folk Art

Hungary's centuries-old traditions of handmade, often regionally specific folk art are still beautifully alive. Intricately carved wooden boxes, vibrantly colorful embroidered tablecloths and shirts, matte-black pottery pitchers, delicately woven lace collars, ceramic plates splashed with painted flowers and birds, and decorative heavy leather whips are among the favorite handcrafted pieces you can purchase. You'll find them in folk-art stores around the country but can purchase them directly from the artisans at crafts fairs and from peddlers on the streets. Dolls dressed in national costume are also popular souvenirs.

Lodging

Outside Budapest there are not many expensive hotels, so you will improve your chances of having a memorable lodging experience by arranging a stay in one of the alternative options noted below. For specific recommendations or information about how to book lodging in these accommodations, see the lodging and information sections throughout the chapter.

Bought back from the government over the last several years, more and more of Hungary's magnificent, centuries-old castles and mansions are being restored and opened as country resorts; a night or two in one of these majestic old places makes for an unusual and romantic (but not always luxurious) lodging experience. Northern Hungary has some of the best.

Guest houses, also called *panziók* (pensions), provide simple accommodations—well suited to people on a budget. Like B&Bs, most are run by couples or families and offer simple breakfast facilities and usually have private bathrooms; they're generally outside the city or town center. Arrangements can be made directly with the panzió or through local tourist offices and travel agents abroad. Another good budget option is renting a room in a private home. In the provinces it is safe to accept rooms offered to you directly; they will almost always be clean and in a relatively good neighborhood, and the prospective landlord will probably not cheat you. Look for signs reading SZOBA KIADÓ (or the German ZIMMER FREI). Reservations and referrals can also be made by any tourist office, and if you go that route, you have someone to complain to if things don't work out.

Village tourism is a growing trend in Hungary, affording a chance to sink into life in tiny, typical villages around the country. The Hungarian Tourist Board produces a guide called *Village Tourism* with descriptions and color photos of many of the village homes now open to guests, either by the week or the night. Apartments in Budapest and cottages at Lake Balaton are available for short- and long-term rental and can make the most economic lodging for families—particularly for those who prefer to cook their own meals. Rates and reservations can be obtained from tourist offices in Hungary and abroad. Also consult the free annual accommodations directory published by **Tourinform**; published in five languages, it lists basic information about hotels, pensions, bungalows, and tourist hostels throughout the country. A separate brochure lists the country's campgrounds.

For single rooms with bath, count on paying about 80% of the double-room rate. During the off-season (in Budapest, September through March; at Lake Balaton, September through May), rates can drop considerably. Prices at Lake Balaton tend to be significantly higher than those in the rest of the countryside. Note that most large hotels set their rates and require payment in U.S. dollars or euros. Breakfast and VAT are usually—but not always—included in your quoted room rate. There is also a "tourist tax" of 3% in Budapest; outside the capital it varies region to region but is always less than 1,000 Ft. This tax is usually not included in the quoted rates.

CATEGORY	BUDAPEST*	OTHER AREAS*
$$$$	over 50,000 Ft.	over 19,000 Ft.
$$$	35,000 Ft.–50,000 Ft.	14,000 Ft.–19,000 Ft.
$$	25,000 Ft.–35,000 Ft.	8,100 Ft.–14,000 Ft.
$	under 25,000 Ft.	under 8,100 Ft.

*All prices are for a standard double room with bath and breakfast during peak season (June–August).

Porcelain

Among the most sought-after items in Hungary are the exquisite hand-painted Herend and Zsolnay porcelain. Unfortunately, the prices on all makes of porcelain have risen considerably in the last few years. For guaranteed authenticity, make your purchases at the specific Herend and Zsolnay stores in major cities, or at the factories themselves in Herend and Pécs, respectively.

Spas and Thermal Baths

Several thousand years ago, the first settlers of the area that is now Budapest chose their home because of its abundance of hot springs. Centuries later, the Romans and the Turks built baths and developed cultures based on medicinal bathing. Now there are more than 1,000 medicinal hot springs bubbling up around the country. Budapest alone has some 14 historic working baths, which attract ailing patients with medical prescriptions for specific water cures as well as "recreational" bathers—locals and tourists alike—wanting to soak in the relaxing waters, try some of the many massages and treatments, and experience the architectural beauty of the bathhouses themselves.

For most, a visit to a bath involves soaking in several thermal pools of varying temperatures and curative contents—perhaps throwing in a game of aquatic chess—relaxing in a steam room or sauna, and getting a brisk, if not brutal, massage (average cost: 800 Ft. for 15 minutes). Many bath facilities are single-sex or have certain days set aside for men or women only, and most people walk around nude or with miniature loincloths, provided at the door. Men should be aware that some men-only baths have a strong gay clientele.

In addition to the ancient beauties there are newer, modern baths open to the public at many spa hotels. They lack the charm and aesthetic appeal of their older peers but provide the latest treatments in sparkling facilities. For more information, look through the "Hungary: Land of Spas" brochure published by the Hungarian Tourist Board, available free from most tourist offices.

Wine, Beer, and Spirits

Hungary tempts wine connoisseurs with its important wine regions, especially Villány, near Pécs, in the south; Eger and Tokaj in the north; and the northern shore of Lake Balaton. Szürkebarát (a pinot gris varietal) and especially Olaszrizling (a milder Rhine Riesling) are common white table wines; Tokay, one of the great wines of the world, can be heavy, dark, and sweet, and its most famous variety is drunk as an aperitif or a dessert wine. Good Tokay is expensive, especially by Hungarian standards, so it's usually reserved for special occasions.

The red table wine of Hungary, Egri Bikavér (Bull's Blood of Eger, usually with *el toro* himself on the label), is the best buy and the safest bet with all foods. Villány produces superb reds and the best rosés; the most adventurous reds—with sometimes successful links to both Austrian and Californian wine making and viticulture—are from the Sopron area.

Before- and after-dinner drinks tend toward schnapps, most notably *Barack-pálinka,* an apricot brandy. A plum brandy called *Kosher szilva-pálinka,* bottled under rabbinical supervision, is the very best of the brandies available in stores. *Vilmos körte-pálinka,* a pear variety, is almost as good. Note than any bottle under 1,000 Ft. or so probably contains more ethyl alcohol than pure fruit brandy. Unicum, Hungary's national liqueur, is a dark, thick, and potent herbal bitter that could be likened to Germany's Jägermeister. Its chubby green bottle makes it a good souvenir to take home.

Major Hungarian beers are Dreher, Kőbányai, and Aranyászok, and several good foreign beers are produced in Hungary under license.

EXPLORING BUDAPEST

The principal sights of the city fall roughly into three areas, each of which can be comfortably covered on foot. The Budapest hills are best explored by public transportation. Note that, by tradition, the district number—a Roman numeral designating one of Budapest's 22 districts—precedes each address. For the sake of clarity, in this book, the word "District" precedes the number. Districts V, VI, and VII are in downtown Pest; District I includes Castle Hill, the main tourist district of Buda.

Great Itineraries

IF YOU HAVE ONE OR TWO DAYS

A whistle-stop visit should start at Várhegy (Castle Hill), where you can walk along cobblestone streets lined with Baroque, Gothic, and Renaissance houses and visit the Királyi Palota (Royal Palace). Zip down the hill for a soak or massage at one of the beautiful baths, such as those at the Gellért Hotel, and then cross to the Pest side of the river for a walk along the *korzó* (promenade) up toward the lovely Széchenyi lánchíd (Chain Bridge). If you're determined to shop, Váci utca is your best bet—the pedestrian-only street is unabashedly touristy, but there's a wealth of shops selling everything from paprika to crystal. Vörösmarty tér (Vörösmarty Square) is a good place to find a café and take a break. With extra time, you could visit Szent István Bazilika (St. Stephen's Basilica) and then walk up the grand avenue Andrássy út to

Hősök tere (Heroes' Square). If at all possible, catch a performance at the neo-Renaissance Operaház (Opera House).

IF YOU HAVE THREE TO FIVE DAYS
Take time to thoroughly explore the museums, squares, and religious buildings on Castle Hill, including Mátyás templom (Matthias Church), the Budapesti Történeti Múzeum (Budapest History Museum), and quiet, tree-lined Tóth Árpád sétány promenade. (This could easily take a full day and a half.) Spend a couple of afternoons in Budapest's other wonderful museums, such as the Magyar Nemzeti Múzeum (Hungarian National Museum), where you can see the epic Hungarian history exhibit and sundry treasures (but to see the Crown of St. Stephen, which used to be here, visit the Parliament building, where it's been kept since early 2000 (at this writing, a permanent location has not been decided); the Szépművészeti Múzeum (Museum of Fine Arts), which has Hungary's finest collection of European art, or the Néprajzi Múzeum (Museum of Ethnography) and its detailed exhibit on Hungarian folk culture. You could also visit Europe's largest synagogue, the Nagy Zsinagóga (Great Synagogue). If it's a sunny afternoon and you can't bear to be indoors, head to Margit-sziget (Margaret Island). If you enjoy classical music, try to nip in to a performance at the Liszt Ferenc Zeneakadémia (Franz Liszt Academy of Music).

IF YOU HAVE FIVE TO SEVEN DAYS
After spending a few days exploring the city as described above, take a trip to the north shore of Lake Balaton. Here you can swim, hike up the vineyard-covered slopes of Mount Badacsony, do some wine tasting, and have incredible fresh fish for dinner. Tihany is a good place to spend the night; in the morning you can wander its twisting streets and visit its hilltop abbey. Alternatively, you could spend the night in the busy spa town of Balatonfüred.

Várhegy (Castle Hill)

Most of the major sights of Buda are on Várhegy (Castle Hill), a long, narrow plateau laced with cobblestone streets, clustered with beautifully preserved baroque, Gothic, and Renaissance houses and crowned by the magnificent Royal Palace. The area is theoretically banned to private cars (except for those of neighborhood residents and Hilton hotel guests), but the streets manage to be lined bumper to bumper with Trabants and Mercedes all the same—sometimes the only visual element to verify you're not in a fairy tale. As in all of Budapest, thriving urban new has taken up residence in historic old; international corporate offices, diplomatic residences, restaurants, and boutiques occupy many of its landmark buildings. The most striking example, perhaps, is the Hilton hotel on Hess András tér, which has ingeniously incorporated remains of Castle Hill's oldest church (a tower and one wall), built by Dominican friars in the 13th century.

Numbers in the text correspond to numbers in the margin and on the Castle Hill (Várhegy) maps.

A Good Walk

Castle Hill's cobblestone streets and numerous museums are best explored on foot: plan to spend about a day here. Most of the transportation options for getting to Castle Hill deposit you on Szent György tér or Dísz tér. It's impossible not to find Castle Hill, but it is possible to be confused about how to get on top of it. If you're already on the Buda side of the river, you can take the Castle bus—*Várbusz*—from the Moszkva tér metro station, northwest of Castle Hill. If you're starting out from Pest, you can take a taxi or Bus 16 from Erzsébet tér

93

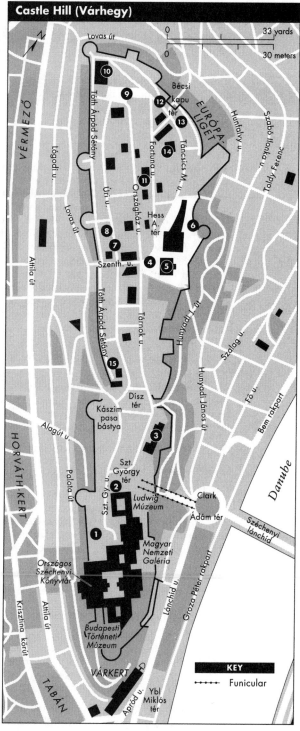

or, the most scenic alternative, cross the Széchenyi Lánchíd (Chain Bridge) on foot to Clark Ádám tér and ride the *Sikló* (funicular) up Castle Hill.

Begin your exploration by walking slightly farther south to visit the **Királyi Palota** ① at the southern end of the hill. Of the palace's wealth of museums, the Ludwig Múzeum, the Magyar Nemzeti Galéria, the Budapesti Történeti Múzeum, and Országos Széchenyi Könyvtár are all interesting. Stop to take a look at the **Statue of Prince Eugene of Savoy** ② outside the entrance to Wing C before moving on. From here, you can cover the rest of the area by walking north along its handful of cobbled streets.

From Dísz tér, you can visit the **Várszínház** ③ theater on Szinház utca, then walk up Tárnok utca, whose houses and usually open courtyards offer glimpses of how Hungarians have integrated contemporary life into Gothic, Renaissance, and baroque settings. Of particular interest are the houses at No. 16, now the Aranyhordó restaurant, and at No. 18, the 15th-century Arany Sas Patika (Golden Eagle Pharmacy Museum), with a naïf Madonna and child in an overhead niche. This tiny museum displays instruments, prescriptions, books, and other artifacts from 16th- and 17th-century pharmacies. Modern commerce is also integrated into Tárnok utca's historic homes; you'll encounter numerous folk souvenir shops and tiny boutiques lining the street. Tárnok utca funnels into **Szentháromság tér** ④ and the Trinity Column; this is also where you'll find the **Mátyás templom** ⑤ and, just behind it, the **Halászbástya** ⑥.

After exploring them, double back to Dísz tér and set out northward again on **Úri utca** ⑦, which runs parallel to Tárnok utca; this long street is lined with beautiful, genteel homes. The **Budavári Labirintus** ⑧, at No. 9, is worth a stop, as is the amusing little Telefónia Museum, at No. 49. At the end of Úri utca you'll reach **Kapisztrán tér** ⑨, where you'll find the **Hadtörténeti Múzeum** ⑩.

From here, you can walk south again on Országház utca (Parliament Street), the main thoroughfare of 18th-century Buda; it takes its name from the building at No. 28, which was the seat of Parliament from 1790 to 1807. You'll end up back at Szentháromság tér, with just two streets remaining to explore.

You can stroll up little Fortuna utca, named for the 18th-century Fortuna Inn, which now houses the **Magyar Kereskedelmi és Vendéglátóipari Múzeum** ⑪. At the end of Fortuna utca you'll reach **Bécsi kapu tér** ⑫, opening to Moszkva tér just below. Head back on Táncsics Mihály, where you will find both the **Középkori Zsidó Imaház** ⑬ and the **Zenetörténeti Múzeum** ⑭. Next door, at No. 9, is the baroque house (formerly the Royal Mint) where rebel writer Táncsics Mihály was imprisoned in the dungeons and freed by the people on the Day of Revolution, March 15, 1848. Continue down this street, and you'll find yourself in front of the Hilton hotel, back at Hess András tér, bordering Szentháromság tér.

Those whose feet haven't protested yet can finish off their tour of Castle Hill by strolling south back to Dísz tér on **Tóth Árpád sétány** ⑮, the romantic, tree-lined promenade along the Buda side of the hill.

TIMING

Castle Hill is small enough to cover in one day, but perusing its major museums and several tiny exhibits will require more time.

Sights to See

⑫ **Bécsi kapu tér** (Vienna Gate Square). Marking the northern entrance to Castle Hill, the stone gateway (rebuilt in 1936) called Vienna Gate opens toward Vienna—or, closer at hand, Moszkva tér a few short blocks below. The square named after it has some fine baroque and rococo houses but is dominated by the enormous neo-Romanesque (1913–17) headquarters of the **Országos Levéltár** (Hungarian National Archives), which resembles a cathedral-like shrine to paperwork. ⊠ *District I.*

❽ Budavári Labirintus (Labyrinth of Buda Castle). Used as a wine cellar during the 16th and 17th centuries and then as an air-raid shelter during World War II, the labyrinth—entered at Úri utca 9 below an early 18th-century house—can be explored with a tour or, if you dare, on your own. There are some English-language brochures available. ⊠ *District I, Úri u. 9, ☎ 1/375–6858.* 🎟 *800 Ft. ☉ Daily 9:30–7:30.*

❿ Hadtörténeti Múzeum (Museum of Military History). Fittingly, this museum is lodged in a former barracks, on the northwestern corner of Kapisztrán tér. The exhibits, which include collections of uniforms and military regalia, trace the military history of Hungary from the original Magyar conquest in the 9th century through the period of Ottoman rule to the mid-20th century. You can arrange an English-language tour in advance for around 1,000 Ft. ⊠ *District I, Tóth Árpád sétány 40,* ☎ *1/356–9522,* 🌐 *www.militaria.hu.* 🎟 *270 Ft. ☉ Apr.–Sept., Tues.– Sun. 10–6; Oct.–Mar., Tues.–Sun. 10–4.*

★ **❻ Halászbástya** (Fishermen's Bastion). The wondrous porch overlooking the Danube and Pest is the neo-Romanesque Fishermen's Bastion, a merry cluster of white stone towers, arches, and columns above a modern bronze statue of St. Stephen, Hungary's first king. Medieval fishwives once peddled their wares here, but now you see souvenirs and crafts merchants and musicians. ⊠ *District I, East of Szentháromság tér.*

❾ Kapisztrán tér (Capistrano Square). Castle Hill's northernmost square was named after St. John of Capistrano, an Italian friar who in 1456 recruited a crusading army to fight the Turks who were threatening Hungary. There's a statue of this honored Franciscan on the northwest corner; also here are the **Museum of Military History** and the remains of the 12th-century Gothic Mária Magdolna templom (Church of St. Mary Magdalene). Its *torony* (tower), completed in 1496, is the only part left standing; the rest of the church was destroyed by air raids during World War II.

★ **❶ Királyi Palota** (Royal Palace). A palace was built on this spot in the 13th century for the kings of Hungary and then reconstructed under the supervision of King Matthias during the 15th century. That in turn was demolished during the Turkish siege of Budapest in 1686. The Hapsburg empress Maria Theresa directed the building of a new palace in the 1700s. It was damaged during an unsuccessful attack by revolutionaries in 1849, but the Hapsburgs set about building again, completing work in 1905. Then, near the end of the Soviets' seven-week siege in February 1945, the entire Castle Hill district of palaces, mansions, and churches was reduced to rubble. Decades passed before reconstruction and whatever restoration was possible were completed. Archaeologists were able to recover both the original defensive walls and royal chambers, due in part to still surviving plans and texts from the reigns of Holy Roman Emperor Sisigimund and King Matthias.

Freed from mounds of rubble, the foundation walls and medieval castle walls were completed, and the ramparts surrounding the medieval royal residence were re-created as close to their original shape and size as possible. If you want an idea of the Hungarian home-life of Franz Josef and Sissi, however, you'll have to visit the baroque Gödöllő Palace. The Royal Palace today is used as a cultural center and museum complex.

The Royal Palace's baroque southern wing (Wing E) contains the **Budapesti Történeti Múzeum** (Budapest History Museum), displaying a fascinating permanent exhibit of modern Budapest history from Buda's liberation from the Turks in 1686 through the 1970s. Viewing the vintage 19th- and 20th-century photos and videos of the castle, the Széchenyi Lánchíd, and other Budapest monuments—and seeing them as the backdrop to the horrors of World War II and the 1956 Revolution—helps to put your later sightseeing in context; while you're browsing, peek out one of the windows overlooking the Danube and Pest and let it start seeping in.

Through historical documents, objects, and art, other permanent exhibits depict the medieval history of the Buda fortress and the capital as a whole. This is the best place to view remains of the medieval Royal Palace and other archaeological excavations. Some of the artifacts unearthed during excavations are in the vestibule in the basement; others are still among the remains of medieval structures. Down in the cellars are the original medieval vaults of the palace; portraits of King Matthias and his second wife, Beatrice of Aragon; and many late-14th-century statues that probably adorned the Renaissance palace. ⊠ *Királyi Palota (Wing E), District I, Szt. György tér 2,* ☎ *1/375–7533,* 🕸 *www.btm.hu.* 🎫 *400 Ft.* 🕐 *Mar.–mid-May and mid-Sept.–Oct., Wed.–Mon. 10–6; mid-May–mid-Sept., daily 10–6; Nov.–Feb., Wed.–Mon. 10–4.*

The collection at the **Ludwig Múzeum** includes more than 200 pieces of Hungarian and contemporary international art, including works by Picasso and Lichtenstein, and occupies the castle's northern wing. ⊠ *Királyi Palota (Wing A), District I, Dísz tér 17,* ☎ *1/375–7533,* 🕸 *www.ludwigmuseum.hu.* 🎫 *300 Ft.; free Tues.* 🕐 *Tues.–Sun. 10–6.*

The **Magyar Nemzeti Galéria** (Hungarian National Gallery), which is made up of the immense center block of the Royal Palace (Wings B, C, and D), exhibits Hungarian fine art, from medieval ecclesiastical paintings and statues through the Gothic, Renaissance, and baroque art, to a rich collection of 19th- and 20th-century works. Especially notable are the works of the romantic painter Mihály Munkácsy, the impressionist Pál Szinyei Merse, and the surrealist Mihály Tivadar Kosztka Csontváry, whom Picasso much admired. There is also a large collection of modern Hungarian sculpture. Labels and commentary for both permanent and temporary exhibits are in English. If you contact the museum in advance, you can book a tour for up to five people with an English-speaking guide. ⊠ *Királyi Palota (entrance in Wing C), District I, Dísz tér 17,* ☎ *1/375–7533,* 🕸 *www.mng.hu.* 🎫 *Gallery 600 Ft., tour 1,300 Ft.* 🕐 *Mid-Mar.–Oct., Tues.–Sun. 10–6; Nov.–mid-Jan., Tues.–Sun. 10–4; mid-Jan.–mid-Mar., Tues.–Fri. 10–4, weekends 10–6.*

The western wing (F) of the Royal Palace is the **Országos Széchenyi Könyvtár** (Széchenyi National Library), which houses more than 2 million volumes. Its archives include well-preserved medieval codices, manuscripts, and historic correspondence. This is not a lending library, but the reading rooms are open to the public (though you must show a passport), and even the most valuable materials can be viewed on microfilm. Small, temporary exhibits on rare books and documents are usually on display; the hours and admission fees for these are quite variable. Note that the entire library closes for one month every summer, usually in July or August. ⊠ *Királyi Palota (Wing F), District I, Dísz tér 17,* ☎ *1/224–3745 to arrange tour with English-speaking guide,* 🕸 *www.oszk.hu.* 🎫 *Tours 300 Ft.; exhibits vary.* 🕐 *Reading rooms Mon. 1–9, Tues.–Sat. 9–9; exhibits Mon. 1–6, Tues.–Sat. 10–6.*

⑬ Középkori Zsidó Imaház (Medieval Synagogue). The excavated one-room Medieval Synagogue is now used as a museum. On display are objects relating to the Jewish community, including religious inscriptions, frescoes, and tombstones dating to the 15th century. ⊠ *District I, Táncsics Mihály u. 26*, ☎ *1/375–7533 Ext. 243.* 🗐 *120 Ft.* ☉ *May–Oct., Tues.–Sun. 10–6.*

⑪ Magyar Kereskedelmi és Vendéglátóipari Múzeum (Hungarian Museum of Commerce and Catering). The 18th-century Fortuna Inn now serves visitors in a different way—as the Catering Museum. Displays in a permanent exhibit show the city as a tourist destination from 1870 to the 1930s; you can see, for example, what a room at the Gellért Hotel, still operating today, would have looked like in 1918. The Commerce Museum, just across the courtyard, chronicles the history of Hungarian commerce from the late 19th century to 1947, when the new, Communist regime "liberated" the economy into socialism. The four-room exhibit includes everything from an antique chocolate-and-caramel vending machine to early shoe-polish advertisements. You can rent an English-language recorded tour for 300 Ft. ⊠ *District I, Fortuna u. 4*, ☎ *1/212–1245.* 🗐 *200 Ft.* ☉ *Wed.–Fri. 10–5, weekends 10–6.*

★ ❺ Mátyás templom (Matthias Church). The ornate white steeple of the Matthias Church is the highest point on Castle Hill. It was added in the 15th century, above a 13th-century Gothic chapel. Officially the Buda Church of Our Lady, it has been known as the Matthias Church since the 15th century, in remembrance of the so-called "just king," who greatly added to and embellished it during his reign. Many of these changes were lost when the Turks converted it into a Mosque. The intricate white stonework, mosaic roof decorations, and some of its geometric patterned columns seem to suggest Byzantine, yet it was substantially rebuilt again in the neo-baroque style, 87 years after the Turkish defeat in 1686. One fortunate survivor of all the changes was perhaps the finest example of Gothic stone carving in Hungary, the Assumption of the Blessed Virgin Mary, visible above the door on the side of the church that faces the Danube.

The **Szentháromság Kápolna** (Trinity Chapel) holds an *encolpion,* an enameled casket containing a miniature copy of the Gospel to be worn on the chest; it belonged to the 12th-century king Béla III and his wife, Anne of Chatillon. Their burial crowns and a cross, scepter, and rings found in their excavated graves are also displayed here. The church's **treasury** contains Renaissance and baroque chalices, monstrances, and vestments. High Mass is celebrated every Sunday at 10 AM, sometimes with full orchestra and choir—and often with major soloists; get here early if you want a seat. During the summer there are usually organ recitals on Friday at 8 PM. Tourists are asked to remain at the back of the church during weddings and services (it's least intrusive to come after 9 AM weekdays and between 1 and 5 PM Sunday and holidays). ⊠ *District I, Szentháromság tér 2*, ☎ *1/355–5657.* 🗐 *300 Ft., treasury 300 Ft.* ☉ *Church daily 9–5; treasury Mon.–Sat. 9:30–5:30, Sun. 1–5:30.*

❷ Statue of Prince Eugene of Savoy. In front of the Royal Palace, facing the Danube by the entrance to Wing C, stands an equestrian statue of Prince Eugene of Savoy, a commander of the army that liberated Hungary from the Turks at the end of the 17th century. From here there is a superb view across the river to Pest. ⊠ *Királyi Palota (by Wing C entrance), District I, Dísz tér 17.*

❹ Szentháromság tér (Holy Trinity Square). This square is named for its baroque Trinity Column, erected in 1712–13 as a gesture of thanksgiving by survivors of a plague. The column stands in front of the famous Gothic Matthias Church, its large pedestal a perfect seat from which to watch the wedding spectacles that take over the church on spring and summer weekends: from morning till night, frilly engaged pairs flow in one after the other and, after a brief transformation inside, back out onto the square. ⊠ *District I.*

★ ⑮ **Tóth Árpád sétány** (Árpád Tóth Promenade). This romantic, tree-lined promenade along the Buda side of the hill is often mistakenly overlooked by sightseers. Beginning at the Museum of Military History, the promenade takes you "behind the scenes" along the back sides of the matte-pastel baroque houses that face Úri utca, with their regal arched windows and wrought-iron gates. On a late spring afternoon, the fragrance of the cherry trees and the sweeping view of the quiet Buda neighborhoods below may be enough to revive even the most weary. ⊠ *District I, from Kapisztrán tér to Szent György u.*

❼ **Úri utca** (Úri Street). Running parallel to Tárnok utca, Úri utca has been less commercialized by boutiques and other shops. The longest and oldest street in the castle district, it is lined with many stately houses, all worth special attention for their delicately carved details. Both gateways of the baroque palace at Nos. 48–50 are articulated by Gothic niches. The **Telefónia Múzeum** (Telephone Museum) is an endearing little museum entered through a central courtyard shared with the local district police station. Although vintage telephone systems are still in use all over the country, both the oldest and most recent products of telecommunication—from the 1882 wooden box with hose attachment to the latest digital marvels—can be observed and tested here. ⊠ *District I, Úri u. 49,* ☎ *1/201–8188.* 🎟 *100 Ft.* ☉ *Tues.–Sun. 10–4.*

....

NEED A   For a light snack, pastry, and coffee, **Café Miro** (⊠ District I, Úri u. 30,
BREAK?   ☎ 1/375–5458) is a fresh, hip alternative to the old-world Budapest
           cafés.

....

❸ **Várszínház** (Castle Theater). This former Franciscan church was transformed into a more secular royal venue in 1787 under the supervision of courtier Farkas Kempelen. The first theatrical performance in Hungarian was held here in 1790. Heavily damaged during World War II, the theater was rebuilt and reopened in 1978. While the building retains its original late-baroque-style facade, the interior was renovated with marble and concrete. It is now used as the studio theater of the National Theater and occasionally for classical recitals, and there is usually a historical exhibition in its foyer—usually theater-related, such as a display of costumes. ⊠ *District I, Színház u. 1–3,* ☎ *1/375-8649.*

⑭ **Zenetörténeti Múzeum** (Museum of Music History). This handsome gray-and-pearl-stone 18th-century palace is where Beethoven allegedly stayed in 1800 when he came to Buda to conduct his works. Now a museum, it displays rare manuscripts and old instruments downstairs in its permanent collection and temporary exhibits upstairs in a small, sunlit hall. The museum also often hosts intimate classical recitals. ⊠ *District I, Táncsics Mihály u. 7,* ☎ *1/214–6770 Ext. 250,* WEB *www.zti.hu/museum. htm.* 🎟 *400 Ft.; free Sun.* ☉ *Feb.–Nov., Tues.–Sun. 10–6.*

Tabán and Gellért-hegy (Tabán and Gellért Hill)

Spreading below Castle Hill is the old quarter called Tabán (from the Turkish word for "armory"). A onetime suburb of Buda, it was known at the end of the 17th century as Little Serbia (*Rác*) because so many Serbian refugees settled here after fleeing from the Turks. It later became a district of vineyards and small taverns. Though most of the small houses characteristic of this district have been demolished—mainly in the interest of easing traffic—a few traditional buildings remain.

Gellért-hegy (Gellért Hill), 761 ft high, is the most beautiful natural formation on the Buda bank. It takes its name from St. Gellért (Gerard) of Csanad, a Venetian bishop who came to Hungary in the 11th century and, legend has it, was rolled off the top of the hill in a cart by pagans. The walk up can be tough, but take solace from the cluster of hot springs at its foot; these soothe and cure bathers at the Rác, Rudas, and Gellért baths.

Numbers in the text correspond to numbers in the margin and on the Budapest map.

A Good Walk

From the **Semmelweis Orvostörténeti Múzeum** ⑯, walk around the corner to Szarvas tér, where you will find the **Szarvas-ház** ⑰ at No. 1, and a few yards toward the river to the **Tabán plébánia-templom** ⑱. Walking south on Attila út and crossing to the other side of Hegyalja út will take you to the foot of Gellért Hill. You are now close to two Turkish baths, the **Rác Fürdő** (Rác Baths) ⑲ and, on the other side of the **Erzsébet híd** ⑳, the **Rudas Fürdő** (Rudas Baths) ㉑. You might need to take a soak in one or the other after climbing the stairs to the top of the hill, a 30 minute walk. Here, overlooking Budapest, is the **Citadella** ㉒, with its panoramic views of Budapest and the nearby Liberation Monument. After exploring the area, you can descend the hill and treat yourself to a soak or a swim at one of the baths. Either return the way you came, or go down the southeastern side of the hill to the **Gellért Szálloda és Thermál Fürdő** ㉓ at its southeastern foot. If you don't feel like walking to the Gellért baths, you can also take Bus 27 down the back of the hill to Móricz Zsigmond körtér and walk back toward the Gellért on busy Bartók Béla út, or take Tram 47, 49, 18, or 19 a couple of stops to Szent Gellért tér.

TIMING

The Citadella and Szabadság szobor are lit in golden lights every night, but the entire Gellért-hegy is at its scenic best every year on August 20, when it forms the backdrop to the spectacular St. Stephen's Day fireworks display.

Sights to See

★ ㉒ **Citadella.** The sweeping views of Budapest from this fortress atop the hill were once valued by the Austrian army, which used it as a lookout after the 1848–49 War of Independence. Some 60 cannons were housed in the citadel, though never used on the city's resentful populace. In the 1960s the Citadel was converted into a tourist site. It has cafés, a beer garden, wine cellars, and a hostel. In its inner wall is a small graphic exhibition (with some relics) of Budapest's 2,000-year history.

Visible from many parts of the city, the 130-ft-high **Szabadság szobor** (Liberation Monument), which sits just below the southern edge of the Citadella, was originally planned as a memorial to a son of Hungary's then-ruler, Miklós Horthy, whose warplane had crashed in the Ukraine in 1942. However, by the time of its completion in 1947 (three years after Horthy was ousted), it had become a memorial to the Russian soldiers who fell in the 1944–45 siege of Budapest; and hence for decades it was associated chiefly with this. From afar it looks light, airy, and even liberating. A sturdy young girl, her hair and robe swirling in the wind, holds a palm branch high above her head. Until recently, she was further embellished with sculptures of giants slaying dragons, Red Army soldiers, and peasants rejoicing at the freedom that Soviet liberation promised (but failed) to bring to Hungary. Since 1992, her

100

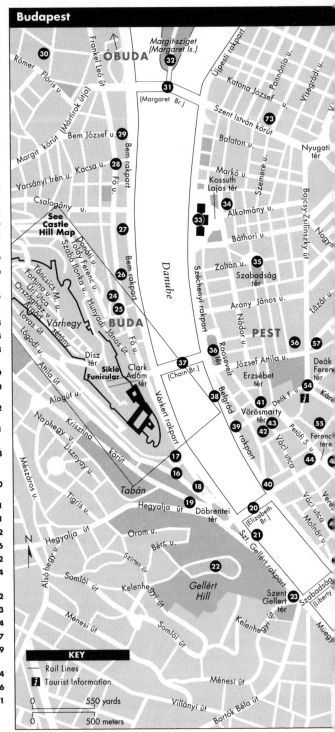

mood has lightened: in the Budapest city government's systematic purging of Communist symbols, the Red Combat infantrymen who had flanked the Liberation statue for decades were hacked off and carted away. A few are now on display among the other evicted statues in Szobor Park in the city's 22nd district. ⊠ *District XI, Citadella sétány,* ☎ *no phone.* ☝ *Free.* ☉ *Fortress daily.*

⑳ Erzsébet híd (Elizabeth Bridge). This bridge was named for Empress Elizabeth (1837–98), called Sissi, of whom the Hungarians were particularly fond. The beautiful but unhappy wife of Franz Joseph, she was stabbed to death in 1898 by an anarchist while boarding a boat on Lake Geneva. The bridge was built between 1897 and 1903; at the time, it was the longest single-span suspension bridge in Europe.

★ ㉓ Gellért Szálloda és Thermál Fürdő (Gellért Hotel and Thermal Baths). At the foot of Gellért Hill are these beautiful Art Nouveau establishments. The Danubius Hotel Gellért is the oldest spa hotel in Hungary, with hot springs that have supplied curative baths for nearly 2,000 years. It is the most popular among tourists, as you don't need reservations, and there's a wealth of treatments—including chamomile steam baths, salt-vapor inhalations, and hot mud packs. Many of these treatments require a doctor's prescription; they will accept prescriptions from foreign doctors. Because most staff speak English, it's quite easy to communicate. Men and women have separate steam and sauna rooms; both the indoor pool and the outdoor wave pool are coed. ⊠ *District XI, Gellért tér 1,* ☎ *1/466–5747 baths.* ☝ *Indoor bath, steam rooms, and swimming pool 1,800 Ft. per day, 2,200 Ft. with cabin; treatments extra.* ☉ *Baths weekdays 6 AM–6 PM, weekends 6 AM–4 PM.*

⑲ Rác Fürdő (Rác Baths). The Rác Baths take their name from the Serbians who settled in this area after fleeing the Turks, and it is said that King Matthias II used to visit these baths via secret tunnels from his palace on Castle Hill. Such antiquity will not be obvious from without: the canary-yellow building was rebuilt by Miklós Ybl in the mid-19th century. The Ottoman-era octagonal pool and cupola were retained during reconstruction. The waters are high in sodium and thought to be medicinal; you can also get a massage. Women can bathe on Monday, Wednesday, and Friday; men on Tuesday, Thursday, and Saturday. These baths are particularly popular with the gay community. ⊠ *District I, Hadnagy u. 8–10,* ☎ *1/356–1322.* ☝ *700 Ft.* ☉ *Mon.–Sat. 6:30–6.*

㉑ Rudas Fürdő (Rudas Baths). This bath is on the riverbank, the original Turkish pool making its interior possibly the most dramatically beautiful of Budapest's baths. A high, domed roof admits pinpricks of bluish-green light into the dark, circular stone hall with its austere columns and arches. Fed by eight springs with a year-round temperature of 44°C (111°F), the Rudas's highly fluoridated waters have been known for 1,000 years. The facility is open to men only and does not have a large gay following; a less interesting outer swimming pool is open to both sexes. Massages are available. ⊠ *District I, Döbrentei tér 9,* ☎ *1/201–1577.* ☝ *900 Ft.* ☉ *Weekdays 6 AM–6 PM, weekends 6 AM–noon.*

⑯ Semmelweis Orvostörténeti Múzeum (Semmelweis Museum of Medical History). This splendid baroque house was the birthplace of Ignác Semmelweis (1818–65), the Hungarian physician who proved the contagiousness of puerperal (childbed) fever. It's now a museum that traces the history of healing. Semmelweis's grave is in the garden. ⊠ *District I, Apród u. 1–3,* ☎ *1/375–3533.* ☝ *150 Ft.* ☉ *Tues.–Sun. 10:30–5:30.*

⑰ Szarvas-ház (Stag House). This Louis XVI–style building is named for the former Szarvas Café or, more accurately, for its extant trade sign, with an emblem of a stag not quite at bay, which can be seen above the arched entryway. The structure houses the Aranyszarvas restaurant, which preserves some of the mood of the old Tabán. ✉ *District I, Szarvas tér 1.*

OFF THE BEATEN PATH

SZOBOR PARK (STATUE PARK) – After the collapse of the Iron Curtain, Hungarians were understandably keen to rid Budapest of the symbols of Soviet domination. The Communist statues and memorials that once dotted Budapest's streets and squares have been moved to this open-air "Disneyland of Communism." As well as the huge figures of Lenin and Marx, there are statues of the Hungarian worker shaking hands with his Soviet army comrade, and Hungarian puppet prime minister János Kádár. Sometimes tacky but amusing souvenirs are for sale, and songs from the Hungarian and Russian workers' movements play on a tinny speaker system. To get there, take a red-numbered bus 7-173 to Etele tér, then the yellow Volán bus from platform 2. ✉ *District XXII, Balatoni út, corner of Szabadkai út,* ☎ *1/427–7500,* WEB *www.szoborpark.hu.* *300 Ft.* ⏲ *Daily 10–dusk.*

18 **Tabán plébánia-templom** (Tabán Parish Church). In 1736, this church was built on the site of a Turkish mosque and subsequently renovated and reconstructed several times. Its present form—mustard-colored stone with a rotund, green clock tower—could be described as restrained baroque. ✉ *District I, Attila u. 1.*

North Buda and Margaret Island

Most of these sights are along Fő utca (Main Street), a long, straight thoroughfare that starts at the Chain Bridge and runs parallel to the Danube. It is lined on both sides with multistory late-18th-century houses—many darkened by soot and showing their age more than those you see in sparklingly restored Castle Hill. This northbound exploration can be done with the help of Bus 86, which covers the waterfront, or on foot, although this is a fairly large area.

Numbers in the text correspond to numbers in the margin and on the Budapest map.

A Good Walk

The walk begins along Fő utca. Stop first to take in the arresting beauty of the **Corvin tér** |; just a block down Fő utca is the **Kapucinus Templom** ㉕, which was originally a Turkish mosque. Continue your walk up Fő utca, stopping at two other scenic squares, **Szilágyi Dezső tér** ㉖ and **Batthyány tér** ㉗, with its head-on view of Parliament across the Danube. From there, continue north on Fő utca, passing (or stopping to bathe at) the famous Turkish **Király-fürdő** ㉘. From **Bem József tér** ㉙, go one block north, turn left (away from the river) and walk up Fekete Sas utca, crossing busy Margit körút and turning right, one block past, up Mecset utca. This will take you up the hill to **Gül Baba türbéje** ㉚. From here, walk back to the river and cross the **Margit híd** ㉛ to explore **Margit-sziget** ㉜, an island park in the middle of the Dunda.

TIMING

The tour can fit easily into a few hours, including a good 1½-hour soak at the baths, unless you want to do a thorough exploration of Margaret Island; expect the walk from Bem József tér up the hill to Gül Baba türbéje to take about 25 minutes. Fő utca and Bem József tér can get congested during rush hours (from around 7:30 AM to 8:30 AM and 4:30 PM to 6 PM). A leisurely stroll from one end of Margaret Island to the other takes about 40 minutes, but it's nice to spend some extra time wandering. Remember that museums are closed Monday and that the

Király Baths are open to men and women on different days of the week.

Sights to See

27 **Batthyány tér.** There are tremendous views of Parliament from this square named after Count Lajos Batthyány, the prime minister shot dead in the 1848 revolution. The M2 subway, the HÉV electric railway from Szentendre, and various suburban and local buses converge on the square, and there's a covered market—as there has been since 1902. At No. 7 Batthyány tér is the beautiful, baroque twin-tower **Szent Anna-templom** (Church of St. Anne), dating from 1740–62, its oval cupola adorned with frescoes and statuary. ⊠ *District I, Fő u. at Batthyány u.*

NEED A
BREAK?

The **Angelika** café (⊠ District I, Batthyány tér 7, ☎ 1/212–3784), in the rectory of the Church of St. Anne, serves swirled meringues, chestnut-filled layer cakes, and delicious pastries, as well as a selection of salads and grilled meat dishes. You can sit inside on small velvet chairs at marble-top tables or at one of the umbrella-shaded tables outdoors. It's open daily 9 AM–midnight.

29 **Bem József tér.** This square near the river is not particularly picturesque and can get heavy with traffic, but it houses the statue of its important namesake, Polish general József Bem, who offered his services to the 1848 revolutionaries in Vienna and then Hungary. Reorganizing the rebel forces in Transylvania, he was the war's most successful general. It was at this statue on October 23, 1956, that a great student demonstration in sympathy with the Poles' striving for liberal reforms exploded into the brave and tragic Hungarian uprising suppressed by the Red Army. ⊠ *District II, Fő u. at Bem József u.*

24 **Corvin tér.** This small, shady square on Fő utca is the site of the turn-of-the-20th-century Folk Art Association administration building and the Budai Vigadó concert hall, at No. 8. ⊠ *District I, Fő u. at Ponty u.*

30 **Gül Baba türbéje** (Tomb of Gül Baba). Gül Baba, a 16th-century dervish and poet whose name means "father of roses" in Turkish, was buried in a tomb built of carved stone blocks with four oval windows. He fought in several wars waged by the Turks and fell during the siege of Buda in 1541. The tomb remains a place of pilgrimage; it is considered Europe's northernmost Muslim shrine and marks the spot where he was slain. Set at an elevation on Rózsadomb (Rose Hill), the tomb is near a good lookout for city views. ⊠ *District II, Mecset u. 14.* ☞ *300 Ft.* ☉ *May–Sept., Tues.–Sun. 10–6; Oct., Tues.–Sun. 10–4.*

OFF THE
BEATEN PATH

GYERMEK VASÚT – The 12-km (7-mi) Children's Railway—so called because it's operated primarily by children—runs from Széchenyi-hegy to Hűvösvölgy. The sweeping views make the trip well worthwhile for children and adults alike. Departures are from Széchenyi-hegy. To get to Széchenyi-hegy, take Tram 56 from Moszkva tér, and change to the cog railway (public transport tickets valid) at the Fogaskereku Vasút stop. Take the cog railway uphill to the last stop and then walk a few hundred yards down a short, partly forested road to the left, in the direction most others will be going. The railway terminates at Hűvösvölgy, where you can catch Tram 56 back to Moszkva tér. ⊠ *District XII, Szillágyi Erzsébet fasor and Pasaréti út,* 🌐 *www.gyermekvasut.com.* ☞ *One-way 150 Ft.* ☉ *Late Apr.–Oct., daily 8:45–5; Nov.–mid-Mar., Tues.–Fri. 10–4, weekends 10–5 (sometimes closed Tues.); mid-Mar.–late Apr., Tues.–Fri. 9:30–5, weekends 10–5.*

OFF THE
BEATEN PATH

JÁNOSHEGY – A *libegő* (chairlift) will take you to János Hill—at 1,729 ft, the highest point in Budapest—where you can climb a lookout tower for the best view of the city. To get there, take Bus 158 from Moszkva tér to the last stop, Zugligeti út. ⊠ *Chairlift: District XII, Zugligeti út 97,* ☎ *1/ 394-3764.* 🎫 *One-way 400 Ft., round-trip 500 Ft.* ☉ *Mid-May–Aug., daily 9–6; Sept.–mid-May (depending on weather), daily 9:30–4; closed every other Mon.*

㉕ Kapucinus templom (Capuchin Church). This church was converted from a Turkish mosque at the end of the 17th century. Damaged during the revolution in 1849, it acquired its current romantic-style exterior when it was rebuilt a few years later. ⊠ *District II, Fő u. 32.*

㉘ Király-fürdő (King Baths). In 1565 Sokoli Mustapha, the Turkish pasha of Buda, ordered the construction of Turkish baths within the old city walls, to ensure that the Turks could still bathe in the event of siege. A stone cupola, crowned by a golden moon and crescent, arches over the steamy, dark pools indoors. It is open to men on Monday, Wednesday, and Friday; to women on Tuesday, Thursday, and Saturday. These baths are very popular with the gay community. ⊠ *District II, Fő u. 84,* ☎ *1/202-3688.* 🎫 *500 Ft.* ☉ *Weekdays 6:30–6, Sat. 6:30–noon.*

㉛ Margit híd (Margaret Bridge). At the southern end of the island, the Margaret Bridge is the closer of the two entrances for those coming from downtown Buda or Pest. Just north of the Chain Bridge, the bridge walkway provides gorgeous mid-river views of Castle Hill and Parliament. The original bridge was built during the 1840s by French engineer Ernest Gouin in collaboration with Gustave Eiffel. Toward the end of 1944, the bridge was blown up by the retreating Nazis while it was still crowded with rush-hour traffic. It was rebuilt in the same unusual shape—forming an obtuse angle in midstream, with a short leg leading down to the island.

㉜ Margit-sziget (Margaret Island). More than 2½ km (1½ mi) long and covering nearly 200 acres, this island park is ideal for strolling, jogging, sunbathing, or just loafing. In good weather, it draws a multitudinous cross-section of the city's population out to its gardens and sporting facilities. The outdoor pool complex of the Palatinus Baths (toward the Buda side), built in 1921, can attract tens of thousands of people on a summer day. Nearby are a tennis stadium, a youth athletic center, boathouses, sports grounds, and, most impressive of all, the Nemzeti Sportuszoda (National Sports Swimming Pool), designed by the architect Alfred Hajós (while still in his teens, Hajós won two gold medals in swimming at the first modern Olympic Games, held in Athens in 1896). In addition, walkers, joggers, bicyclists, and rollerbladers do laps around the island's perimeter and up and down the main road, closed to traffic except for Bus 26 (and a few official vehicles), which travels up and down the island and across the Margaret Bridge to and from Pest.

The island's natural curative hot springs have given rise to the Danubius Grand and Thermal hotels on the northern end of the island and are piped into two spa hotels on the mainland, the Aquincum on the Buda bank and the Hélia on the Pest side.

To experience Margaret Island's role in Budapest life fully, go on a Saturday or Sunday afternoon to join and/or watch people whiling away the day. Sunday is a particularly good choice for strategic sightseers, who can utilize the rest of the week to cover those city sights and areas that are closed on Sunday. On weekdays, you'll share the island only with joggers and children playing hooky from school.

The island was first mentioned almost 2,000 years ago as the summer residence of the commander of the Roman garrison at nearby Aquincum. Later known as Rabbit Island (Insula Leporum), it was a royal hunting ground during the Árpád dynasty. King Imre, who reigned from 1196 to 1204, held court here, and several convents and monasteries were built here during the Middle Ages. (During a walk round the island, you'll see the ruins of a few of these buildings.) It takes its current name from St. Margaret, the pious daughter of King Béla IV, who at the ripe old age of 10 retired to a Dominican nunnery here.

Through the center of the island runs the **Művész sétány** (Artists' Promenade), lined with busts of Hungarian visual artists, writers, and musicians. Shaded by giant plane trees, it's a perfect place to stroll. The promenade passes close to the **rose garden** (in the center of the island), a large grassy lawn surrounded by blooming flower beds planted with hundreds of kinds of flowers. It's a great spot to picnic or to watch a game of soccer or Ultimate Frisbee, both of which are regularly played here on weekend afternoons. Just east of the rose garden is a small, free would-be petting zoo, the **Margit-sziget Vadaspark,** if the animals were allowed to be petted. A fenced-in compound houses a menagerie of goats, rabbits, donkeys, assorted fowl and ducks, and gargantuan peacocks that sit heavily on straining tree branches.

At the northern end of the island is a copy of the water-powered **Marosvásárhelyi zenélő kút** (Marosvásárhely Musical Fountain), which plays songs and chimes. The original was designed more than 150 years ago by a Transylvanian named Péter Bodor. It stands near a serene, artificial rock garden with Japanese dwarf trees and lily ponds. The stream coursing through it never freezes, for it comes from a natural hot spring causing it instead to give off thick steam in winter that enshrouds the garden in a mystical cloud.

㉖ Szilágyi Dezső tér. This is another of the charming little squares punctuating Fő utca; here you'll find the house where composer Béla Bartók lived, at No. 4. ⊠ *District I, Fő u. at Székely u.*

Downtown Pest and the Kis Körút (Little Ring Road)

Budapest's urban heart is full of bona fide sights plus innumerable tiny streets and grand avenues where you can wander for hours admiring the city's stately old buildings—some freshly sparkling after their first painting in decades, others silently but still gracefully crumbling.

Dominated by the Parliament building, the district surrounding Kossuth tér is the legislative, diplomatic, and administrative nexus of Budapest; most of the ministries are here, as are the National Bank and Courts of Justice. Downriver, the romantic Danube promenade, the Duna korzó, extends along the stretch of riverfront across from Castle Hill. With Vörösmarty tér and pedestrian shopping street Váci utca just inland, this area forms Pest's tourist core. Going south, the korzó ends at Március 15 tér. One block in from the river, Ferenciek tere marks the beginning of the university area, spreading south of Kossuth Lajos utca. Here, the streets are narrower and the sounds of your footsteps echo off the elegantly aging stone buildings.

Pest is laid out in broad circular *körúts* ("ring roads" or boulevards). Vámház körút is the first sector of the 2½-km (1½-mi) Kis körút (Little Ring Road), which traces the route of the Old Town wall from Szabadság híd (Liberty Bridge) to Deák tér. Construction of the inner körút began in 1872 and was completed in 1880. Changing names as it curves, after Kálvin tér it becomes Múzeum körút (passing by the National Museum) and then Károly körút for its final stretch ending at

Deák tér. Deák tér, the only place where all three subway lines converge, could be called the dead-center of downtown. East of Károly körút are the weathered streets of Budapest's former ghetto.

Numbers in the text correspond to numbers in the margin and on the Budapest map.

A Good Walk

After starting at Kossuth tér to see the **Országház** ㉝ and the **Néprajzi Múzeum** ㉞, it's worth walking a few blocks southeast to take in stately **Szabadság tér** ㉟ before heading back to the Danube and south to **Roosevelt tér** ㊱, which is at the foot of the **Széchenyi Lánchíd** ㊲. As this tour involves quite a bit of walking, you may want to take Tram 2 from Kossuth tér a few stops downriver to Roosevelt tér to save your energy. While time and/or energy may not allow it just now, at some point during your visit, a walk across the Chain Bridge is a must.

From Roosevelt tér go south, across the street, and join the **Korzó** ㊳ along the river, strolling past the **Vigadó** ㊴ at Vigadó tér, all the way to the **Belvárosi plébánia templom** ㊵ at Március 15 tér, just under the Elizabeth Bridge. Double back up the korzó to Vigadó tér and walk in from the river on Vigadó utca to **Vörösmarty tér** ㊶. Follow the crowds down pedestrian-only **Váci utca** ㊷, and when you reach Régiposta utca, take a detour to the right to see the **Görög Ortodox templom** ㊸. Return to Váci utca and continue south; at Ferenciek tere, look for the grand **Párisi Udvar** ㊹ arcade. Across busy Kossuth Lajos utca, you will find the **Ferenciek templom** ㊺. From here, stroll Petőfi Sándor utca, passing the Greek Orthodox temple, and **Egyetem tér** ㊻. Take a right on Szerb utca until you get to Veres Pálné utca, where you will find a 17th-century **Szerb Ortodox templom** ㊼. Continuing down Szerb utca, you'll find yourself at the southern end of Váci utca, facing **Vásárcsarnok** ㊽, the huge market hall. Across Vámház körút is the campus of the **Közgazdasági Egyetem** ㊾, the University of Economics, which was called Karl Marx University in the Communist days.

From here you can either walk or take Tram 47 or 49 to **Kálvin tér** ㊿. Just north of Kálvin tér on Múzeum körút is the **Magyar Nemzeti Múzeum** (51). The **Nagy Zsinagóga** (52) is about ¾ km (⅓ mi) farther north along the Kis körút (Small Ring Road)—a longish walk or one short stop by tram; around the corner from the synagogue is the **Zsidó Múzeum** (53). From here, more walking along the körút, or a tram ride to the last stop, brings you to Pest's main hub, Deák tér, where you'll find the **Evangélikus templom** (54). From here it's a short walk to the **Városház** (55), Budapest's old city hall building. The **Szent István Bazilika** (56) is an extra but rewarding 500-yard walk north on Bajcsy-Zsilinszky út.

TIMING

This is a particularly rich part of the city; the suggested walk will take the better part of a day, including time to visit the museums, stroll on the Korzó, and browse on Váci utca—not to mention time for lunch. Keep in mind that the museums are closed on Monday.

Sights to See

㊵ **Belvárosi plébánia templom** (Inner City Parish Church). Dating to the 12th century, this is the oldest ecclesiastical building in Pest. It's actually built on something even older—the remains of the Contra Aquincum, a 3rd-century Roman fortress and tower, parts of which are visible next to the church. There is hardly any architectural style that cannot be found in some part or another, starting with a single Romanesque arch in its south tower. The single nave still has its original Gothic chancel and some 15th-century Gothic frescoes. Two side chapels contain beautifully carved Renaissance altarpieces and tabernacles of red marble from the early 16th century. During Budapest's years of Turkish occupation, the church served as a mosque—a *mihrab*, a Muslim prayer niche, is a reminder of this. During the 18th century, the church was given two baroque towers and its present facade. In 1808 it was enriched with a rococo pulpit, and still later a superb winged triptych was added to the main altar. From 1867 to 1875, Franz Liszt lived only a few steps away from the church, in a town house where he held regular "musical Sundays" at which Richard and Cosima Wagner were frequent guests and participants. Liszt's own musical Sunday mornings often began in this church. An admirer of its acoustics and organ, he conducted many masses here, including the first Budapest performance of his *Missa Choralis*, in 1872. ⊠ *District V, Március 15 tér 2,* ☏ *1/318–3108.*

46 **Egyetem tér** (University Square). Budapest's University of Law sits here in the heart of the city's university neighborhood. On one corner is the cool gray-and-green marble **Egyetemi Templom** (University Church), one of Hungary's most beautiful baroque buildings. Built between 1725 and 1742, it has an especially splendid pulpit. ⊠ *District V.*

NEED A
BREAK?

Though billed as a café, **Centrál** (⊠ District V, Károlyi Mihály u. 9, ☏ 1/266–4572) is actually more a living museum. It enjoyed fame as an illustrious literary café during Budapest's late-19th- and early 20th-century golden age and, after years of neglect, was finally restored to its former glory a few years ago. Centrál's menu includes, with each main dish, a recommended wine by the glass—as well as a good selection of vegetarian dishes and desserts. Quite apart from anything else, it has some of the most spotless toilets in all of Budapest.

---

54 **Evangélikus Templom and Evangélikus Múzeum** (Lutheran Church and Lutheran Museum). The neoclassical Lutheran Church sits in the center of it all on busy Deák tér. Classical concerts are regularly held here. The church's interior designer, János Krausz, flouted then-traditional church architecture by placing a single large interior beneath the huge vaulted roof structure. The adjoining school is now the Lutheran Museum, which traces the role of Protestantism in Hungarian history and contains Martin Luther's original will. ⊠ *District V, Deák Ferenc tér 4,* ☏ *1/317–4173.* ▣ *Museum 300 Ft. (includes tour of church).* ☉ *Museum Mar.–Dec., Tues.–Sun. 10–6; Jan.–Feb., 10–5. Church only in conjunction with museum visit and during services (Sun. at 9, 11, and 6).*

45 **Ferenciek templom** (Franciscan Church). This pale yellow church was built in 1743. On the wall facing Kossuth Lajos utca is a bronze relief showing a scene from the devastating flood of 1838; the detail is so vivid that it almost makes you seasick. A faded arrow below the relief indicates the high-water mark of almost 4 ft. Next to it is the Nereids Fountain, a popular meeting place for students from the nearby Eötvös Loránd University. ⊠ *District V, Felszabadulás tér.*

43 **Görög Ortodox templom** (Greek Orthodox Church). Built at the end of the 18th century in late-baroque style, the Greek Orthodox Church was remodeled a century later by Miklós Ybl, who designed the Opera House and many other important Budapest landmarks. The church retains some fine wood carvings and a dazzling collection of icons by late-18th-century Serbian master Miklós Jankovich. ⊠ *District V, Petőfi tér 2/b.*

50 **Kálvin tér** (Calvin Square). Calvin Square takes its name from the neoclassical Protestant church that tries to dominate this busy traffic hub; more glaringly noticeable, however, is a Pepsi billboard as tall and wide as the bottom half of the church. The Kecskeméti Kapu, a main gate of Pest, once stood here, as well as a cattle market that was a notorious den of thieves. At the beginning of the 19th century, this was where Pest ended and the prairie began. ⊠ *District V.*

㊾ Közgazdasági Egyetem (University of Economics). Just below the Liberty Bridge on the waterfront, the monumental neo-Renaissance building was once the Customs House. Built in 1871–74 by Miklós Ybl, it is now also known as *közgáz* ("econ."), following a stint during the Communist era as Karl Marx University. ⊠ *District V, Fővám tér.*

★ **㊳ Korzó** (Promenade). The neighborhood to the south of Roosevelt tér has regained much of its past elegance—if not its architectural grandeur—with the erection of the Atrium Hyatt, Inter-Continental, and Budapest Marriott luxury hotels. Traversing all three and continuing well beyond them is the riverside *korzó*, a pedestrian promenade lined with park benches and appealing outdoor cafés from which one can enjoy postcard-perfect views of Gellért Hill and Castle Hill directly across the Danube. Try to take a stroll in the evening, when the views are lit up in shimmering gold. ⊠ *District V, from Eötvös tér to Március 15 tér.*

㊿ Magyar Nemzeti Múzeum (Hungarian National Museum). Built between 1837 and 1847, the museum is a fine example of 19th-century classicism—simple, well proportioned, and surrounded by a large garden. In front of this building on March 15, 1848, Sándor Petőfi recited his revolutionary poem, the "National Song" ("Nemzeti dal"), and the "12 Points," a list of political demands by young Hungarians calling on the people to rise up against the Hapsburgs. Celebrations of the national holiday commemorating the failed revolution are held on these steps every year on March 15.

What used to be the museum's biggest attraction, the **Szent Korona** (Holy Crown), was moved to the Parliament building in early 2000 to mark the millenary of the coronation of Hungary's first king, St. Stephen. The museum still has worthwhile rarities, however, including a completely furnished Turkish tent; masterworks of cabinetmaking and woodcarving, including pews from churches in Nyírbátor and Transylvania; a piano that belonged to both Beethoven and Liszt; and, in the treasury, masterpieces of goldsmithing, among them the 11th-century Constantions Monomachos crown from Byzantium and the richly pictorial 16th-century chalice of Miklós Pálffy. Looking at it is like reading the "Prince Valiant" comic strip in gold. The epic Hungarian history exhibit chronicles, among other things, the end of Communism and the much-celebrated exodus of the Russian troops. ⊠ *District IX, Múzeum krt. 14–16,* ☎ *1/338–2122.* 🎫 *600 Ft., free for families (2 adults, 2 children) on weekends.* ☉ *Mid-Mar.–mid-Oct., Tues.–Sun. 10–6; mid-Oct.–mid-Mar., Tues.–Sun. 10–5.*

★ **㊼ Nagy Zsinagóga** (Great Synagogue). Seating 3,000, Europe's largest synagogue was designed by Ludwig Förs and built between 1844 and 1859 in a Byzantine-Moorish style described as "consciously archaic Romantic-Eastern." Desecrated by German and Hungarian Nazis, it was painstakingly reconstructed with donations from all over the world; its doors reopened in the fall of 1996. While used for regular services during much of the year, it is generally not used in midwinter, as the space is too large to heat; between December and February, visiting hours are erratic. In the courtyard behind the synagogue, a weeping willow made of metal honors the victims of the Holocaust. Liszt and Saint-Saëns are among the great musicians who have played the synagogue's grand organ. ⊠ *District VII, Dohány u. 2–8,* ☎ *1/342–1335.* 🎫 *Free.* ☉ *Weekdays 10–3, Sun. 10–2.*

★ ㉞ **Néprajzi Múzeum** (Museum of Ethnography). The 1890s neoclassical temple formerly housed the Supreme Court. Now an impressive permanent exhibition, "The Folk Culture of the Hungarian People," explains all aspects of peasant life from the end of the 18th century until World War I; explanatory texts are provided in both English and Hungarian. Besides embroideries, pottery, and carvings—the authentic pieces you can't see at touristy folk shops—there are farming tools, furniture, and traditional costumes. The central room of the building alone is worth the entrance fee: a majestic hall with ornate marble staircases and pillars, and towering stained-glass windows. ⊠ *District V, Kossuth tér 12,* ☎ *1/332–6340,* WEB *www.neprajz.hu.* ☞ *500 Ft.* ☉ *Mar.–mid-Oct., Tues.–Sun. 10–5:30; mid-Oct.–Feb., Tues.–Sun. 10–4:30.*

★ ㉝ **Országház** (Parliament). The most visible symbol of Budapest's left bank is the huge neo-Gothic Parliament. Mirrored in the Danube much the way Britain's Parliament is reflected by the Thames, it lies midway between the Margaret and Chain bridges and can be reached by the M2 subway (Kossuth tér station) and waterfront Tram 2. A fine example of historicizing, eclectic fin-de-siècle architecture, it was designed by the Hungarian architect Ímre Steindl and built by a thousand workers between 1885 and 1902. The grace and dignity of its long facade and 24 slender towers, with spacious arcades and high windows balancing its vast central dome, lend this living landmark a refreshingly baroque spatial effect. The exterior is lined with 90 statues of great figures in Hungarian history; the corbels are ornamented by 242 allegorical statues. Inside are 691 rooms, 10 courtyards, and 29 staircases; some 88 pounds of gold were used for the staircases and halls. These halls are also a gallery of late-19th-century Hungarian art, with frescoes and canvases depicting Hungarian history, starting with Mihály Munkácsy's large painting of the Magyar Conquest of 896.

Since early 2000 Parliament's most sacred treasure has not been the Hungarian legislature but the newly exhibited **Szent Korona** (Holy Crown), which reposes with other royal relics under the cupola. The crown sits like a golden soufflé above a Byzantine band of holy scenes in enamel and pearls and other gems. It seems to date from the 12th century, so it could not be the crown that Pope Sylvester II presented to St. Stephen in the year 1000, when he was crowned the first king of Hungary. Nevertheless, it is known as the Crown of St. Stephen and has been regarded—even by Communist governments—as the legal symbol of Hungarian sovereignty and unbroken statehood. In 1945 the fleeing Hungarian army handed over the crown and its accompanying regalia to the Americans rather than have them fall into Soviet hands. They were restored to Hungary in 1978. The crown can be seen in the scope of daily tours of the Parliament building, which is the only way you can visit the Parliament, except during ceremonial events and when the legislature is in session (usually Monday and Tuesday from late summer to spring); its permanent home has yet to be decided at this writing. Lines may be long, so it's best to call in advance for reservations. The building can also be visited on group tours organized by IBUSZ Travel. ⊠ *District V, Kossuth tér,* ☎ *1/441–4904; 1/441–4415 tour reservations,* WEB *www.mkogy.hu.* ☞ *1,700 Ft.* ☉ *Weekdays 8–6, Sat. 8–4, Sun. 8–2; daily tours in English at 10 and 2, starting from Gate No. 10, just right of main stairs.*

㊹ **Párisi Udvar** (Paris Court). This glass-roof arcade was built in 1914 in richly ornamental neo-Gothic and eclectic styles. Nowadays it's filled with touristy boutiques. ⊠ *District VI, corner of Petőfi Sándor u. and Kossuth Lajos u.*

36 Roosevelt tér (Roosevelt Square). This square opening onto the Danube is less closely connected with the U.S. president than with the progressive Hungarian statesman Count István Széchenyi, dubbed "the greatest Hungarian" even by his adversary, Kossuth. The neo-Renaissance palace of the **Magyar Tudományos Akadémia** (Academy of Sciences) on the north side was built between 1862 and 1864, after Széchenyi's suicide. It is a fitting memorial, for in 1825, the statesman donated a year's income from all his estates to establish the academy. Another Széchenyi project, the Széchenyi Lánchíd, leads into the square; there stands a statue of Széchenyi near one of another statesman, Ferenc Deák, whose negotiations led to the establishment of the dual monarchy after Kossuth's 1848–49 revolution failed. Both men lived on this square. ⊠ *District V.*

★ **35 Szabadság tér** (Liberty Square). This sprawling square is dominated by the longtime headquarters of **Magyar Televizió** (Hungarian Television), a former stock exchange with what look like four temples and two castles on its roof. Across from it is a solemn-looking neoclassical shrine, the **Nemzeti Bank** (National Bank). The bank's Postal Savings Bank branch, adjacent to the main building but visible from behind Szabadság tér on Hold utca, is another exuberant Art Nouveau masterpiece of architect Ödön Lechner, built in 1901 with colorful majolica mosaics, characteristically curvaceous windows, and pointed towers ending in swirling gold flourishes. In the square's center remains a gold hammer and sickle atop a white stone obelisk, one of the few monuments to the Russian "liberation" of Budapest in 1945. There were mutterings that it, too, would be pulled down, which prompted a Russian diplomatic outcry; the monument, after all, marks a gravesite of fallen Soviet troops. With the Stars and Stripes flying out in front, and a high security presence, the **American Embassy** is at Szabadság tér 12. ⊠ *District V.*

37 Széchenyi Lánchíd (Chain Bridge). This is the oldest and most beautiful of the seven road bridges that span the Danube in Budapest. Before it was built, the river could be crossed only by ferry or by a pontoon bridge that had to be removed when ice blocks began floating downstream in winter. It was constructed at the initiative of the great Hungarian reformer and philanthropist Count István Széchenyi, using an 1839 design by the French civil engineer William Tierney Clark. This classical, almost poetically graceful and symmetrical suspension bridge was finished by his Scottish namesake, Adam Clark, who also built the 383-yard tunnel under Castle Hill, thus connecting the Danube quay with the rest of Buda. After it was destroyed by the Nazis, the bridge was rebuilt in its original form (though slightly widened for traffic) and was reopened in 1949, on the centenary of its inauguration. At the Buda end of the bridge is Clark Ádám tér (Adam Clark Square), where you can zip up to Castle Hill on the sometimes crowded **Sikló funicular.** ⊠ *District I, linking Clark Ádám tér with Roosevelt tér.* 🖾 *Funicular 400 Ft. uphill, 300 Ft. downhill.* ☉ *Funicular daily 7:30 AM–10 PM (closed every other Mon.).*

★ **56 Szent István Bazilika** (St. Stephen's Basilica). Handsome and massive, this is one of the chief landmarks of Pest and the city's largest church—it can hold 8,500 people. Its very Holy Roman front porch greets you with a tympanum bustling with statuary. The basilica's dome and the dome of Parliament are by far the most visible in the Pest skyline, and this is no accident: with the Magyar Millennium of 1896 in mind (the lavishly celebrated thousandth anniversary of the settling of the Carpathian Basin in 896), both domes were planned to be 315 ft high.

The millennium was not yet in sight when architect József Hild began building the basilica in neoclassical style in 1851, two years after the revolution was suppressed. After Hild's death, the project was taken over in 1867 by Miklós Ybl, the architect who did the most to transform modern Pest into a monumental metropolis. Wherever he could, Ybl shifted Hild's motifs toward the neo-Renaissance mode that Ybl favored. When the dome collapsed, partly damaging the walls, he made even more drastic changes. Ybl died in 1891, five years before the 1,000-year celebration, and the basilica was completed in neo-Renaissance style by József Kauser—but not until 1905.

Below the cupola is a rich collection of late-19th-century Hungarian art: mosaics, altarpieces, and statuary (what heady days the Magyar Millennium must have meant for local talents). There are 150 kinds of marble, all from Hungary except for the Carrara in the sanctuary's centerpiece: a white statue of King (St.) Stephen I, Hungary's first king and patron saint. Stephen's mummified right hand is preserved as a relic in the **Szent Jobb Kápolna** (Holy Right Chapel); press a button and it will be illuminated for two minutes. You can also climb the 364 stairs (or take the elevator) to the top of the cupola for a spectacular view of the city. Extensive restorations have been under way at the aging basilica for years and should wrap up by 2010. ⊠ *District V, Szt. István tér,* ☎ *1/311–0839.* 🖵 *Church free, Szt. Jobb chapel 150 Ft., cupola 500 Ft.* ☉ *Church Mon.–Sat. 9–7, Sun. 1–5. Szt. Jobb Chapel Apr.–Oct., Mon.–Sat. 9–5, Sun. 1–5; Nov.–Mar., Mon.–Sat. 10–4, Sun. 1–4. Cupola Apr. and Sept.–Oct., daily 10–5; May–Aug., daily 9–6.*

❹⓻ Szerb Ortodox templom (Serbian Orthodox Church). Built in 1688, this lovely burnt-orange church, one of Budapest's oldest buildings, sits in a shaded garden surrounded by thick stone walls decorated with a large tile mosaic of St. George defeating the dragon. Its opening hours are somewhat erratic, but if the wrought-iron gates are open, wander in for a look at the beautiful hand-carved wooden pews. ⊠ *District V, Szerb u.*

❹⓶ Váci utca. Immediately north of Elizabeth Bridge is Budapest's best-known shopping street and most unabashed tourist zone, Váci utca, a pedestrian precinct with electrified 19th-century lampposts and smart shops with credit-card emblems on ornate doorways. No bargain basement, Váci utca gets its special flavor from the mix of native furriers, tailors, designers, shoemakers, and folk artists, as well as an increasing number of internationally known boutiques. There are also bookstores and china and crystal shops, as well as food stores redolent of paprika. Váci utca's second half, south of Kossuth Lajos utca, was transformed into another pedestrian-only zone in the 1990s. This somewhat broader stretch of road, while coming to resemble the northern side, still retains a flavorful, more soothing ambience of its own. On both halves of Váci utca, watch your purses and wallets—against inflated prices *and* active pickpockets. ⊠ *District V, from Vörösmarty tér to Fővám tér.*

❺⓹ Városház (City Hall). The monumental former city council building, which used to be a hospital for wounded soldiers and then a resort for the elderly ("home" would be too cozy for so vast a hulk), is now Budapest's city hall. It's enormous enough to loom over the row of shops and businesses lining Károly körút in front of it but can only be entered through courtyards or side streets (it is most accessible from Gerlóczy utca). The Tuscan columns at the main entrance and the allegorical statuary of *Atlas, War,* and *Peace* are especially splendid. There was once a chapel in the center of the main facade, but now only its spire remains. ⊠ *District V, Városház u. 9–11,* ☎ *1/327–1000.* 🖵 *Free.* ☉ *Weekdays 9–5.*

48 **Vásárcsarnok** (Central Market Hall). The magnificent hall, a 19th-century iron-frame construction, was reopened in late 1994 after years of renovation (and disputes over who would foot the bill). Even during the leanest years of Communist shortages, the abundance of food came as a revelation to shoppers from East and West. Today, the cavernous, three-story market once again teems with people browsing among stalls packed with salamis and red-paprika chains. Upstairs you can buy folk embroideries and souvenirs. ⊠ *District IX, Vámház krt. 1–3,* ☏ *1/217–6067.* ⊙ *Mon. 6 AM–5 PM, Tues.–Fri. 6 AM–6 PM, Sat. 6 AM–2 PM.*

39 **Vigadó** (Concert Hall). Designed in a striking romantic style by Frigyes Feszl and inaugurated in 1865 with Franz Liszt conducting his own *St. Elizabeth Oratorio,* the concert hall is a curious mixture of Byzantine, Moorish, Romanesque, and Hungarian motifs, punctuated by dancing statues and sturdy pillars. Brahms, Debussy, and Casals are among the other phenomenal musicians who have graced its stage. Mahler's *Symphony No. 1* and many works by Bartók were first performed here. While you can go into the lobby on your own, the hall is open only for concerts. ⊠ *District V, Vigadó tér 2,* ☏ *1/318–9167 box office.*

NEED A BREAK? If you only visit one café in Budapest, stop on Vörösmarty Square at the **Gerbeaud** café and pastry shop (⊠ District V, Vörösmarty tér 7, ☏ 1/429–9000), founded in 1858 by Hungarian Henrik Kugler and a Swiss, Emil Gerbeaud. The decor (green-marble tables, Regency-style marble fireplaces) is as sumptuous as the tempting selection of cake and sweets. The Gerbeaud's piano was originally intended for the *Titanic* but was saved because it wasn't ready in time for the voyage.

★ **41** **Vörösmarty tér** (Vörösmarty Square). This large, handsome square at the northern end of Váci utca is the heart of Pest's tourist life. Street musicians and sidewalk cafés make it one of the liveliest places in Budapest and a good spot to sit and relax—if you can ward off the aggressive caricature sketchers. Grouped around a white-marble statue of the 19th-century poet and dramatist Mihály Vörösmarty are luxury shops, an airline office, and an elegant former pissoir. Now a lovely kiosk, it displays gold-painted historic scenes of the square's golden days. ⊠ *District V, at northern end of Váci u.*

53 **Zsidó Múzeum** (Jewish Museum). The four-room museum, around the corner from the Great Synagogue, has displays explaining the effect of the Holocaust on Hungarian and Transylvanian Jews. (There are labels in English.) In late 1993, burglars ransacked the museum and got away with approximately 80% of its priceless collection; several months later, the stolen objects were found in Romania and returned to their home. ⊠ *District VII, Dohány u. 2,* ☏ *1/342–8949.* ⊡ *600 Ft.* ⊙ *Mid-Mar.–mid-Oct., Mon.–Thurs. 10–5, Fri. and Sun. 10–2; mid-Oct.–mid-Mar., weekdays 10–3, Sun. 10–1.*

Andrássy Út

Behind St. Stephen's Basilica, at the crossroad along Bajcsy-Zsilinszky út, begins Budapest's grandest avenue, Andrássy út. For too many years, this broad boulevard bore the tongue-twisting name Népköztársaság útja (Avenue of the People's Republic) and, for a while before that, Stalin Avenue. In 1990, however, it reverted to its old name honoring Count Gyula Andrássy, a statesman who in 1867 became the first constitutional premier of Hungary. The boulevard that would eventually bear his name was begun in 1872, as Buda and Pest (and Óbuda) were about to be unified. Most of the mansions that line it were completed by 1884.

It took another dozen years before the first underground railway on the Continent was completed for—you guessed it—the Magyar Millennium in 1896. Though preceded by London's Underground (1863), Budapest's was the world's first electrified subway. Only slightly modernized but refurbished for the 1996 millecentenary, this "Little Metro" is still running a 4-km (2½-mi) stretch from Vörösmarty tér to the far end of City Park. Using tiny yellow trains with tanklike treads, and stopping at antique stations marked FÖLDALATTI (Underground) on their wrought-iron entranceways, Line 1 is a tourist attraction in itself. Six of its 10 stations are along Andrássy út.

Numbers in the text correspond to numbers in the margin and on the Budapest map.

A Good Walk

A walking tour of Andrássy út's sights is straightforward: begin at its downtown end, near Deák tér, and stroll its length (about 2 km [1 mi]) all the way to Hősök tere, at the entrance to Budapest's popular City Park. The first third of the avenue, from Bajcsy-Zsilinszky út to the eight-sided intersection called Oktogon, is framed by rows of eclectic city palaces with balconies held up by stone giants. First stop is the mansion of the **Postamúzeum** ⑤⑦. Continue until you reach the imposing **Magyar Állami Operaház** ⑤⑧ and across the street the **Drechsler Kastély** ⑤⑨. A block or two farther, on "Budapest's Broadway," Nagymező utca, where you'll find theaters, nightclubs, and cabarets, is the **Magyar Fotógráfusok Háza (Mai Manó Ház)** ⑥⓪ photographic museum. Continuing down Andrássy, turn right onto Liszt Ferenc tér, a pedestrian street dominated by the **Liszt Ferenc Zeneakadémia** ⑥①. Return to Andrássy, and continue until you come to Vörösmarty, where a short detour right will take you to **Liszt Ferenc Emlékmúzeum** ⑥②.

The Parisian-style boulevard of Andrássy alters when it crosses the Nagy körút (Outer Ring Road), at the Oktogon crossing. Four rows of trees and scores of flower beds make the thoroughfare look more like a garden promenade, but its cultural character lingers. Farther up, past **Kodály körönd** ⑥③, the rest of Andrássy út is dominated by widely spaced mansions surrounded by private gardens. At Kodály körönd take another detour, turning right onto Felső erdősor, then left onto Varosligeti fasor, where you will find the **Ráth György Múzeum** ⑥④ of Indian and Chinese art. Andrássy út ends at **Hősök tere** ⑥⑤. Finish your tour by browsing through the **Műcsarnok** ⑥⑥ and/or the **Szépművészeti Múzeum** ⑥⑦, and then perhaps take a stroll into the **Városliget** ⑥⑧. You can return to Deák tér on the Millenniumi Földalatti (Millennial Underground).

TIMING

As most museums are closed Monday, it's best to explore Andrássy út on other days, preferably weekdays or early Saturday, when stores are also open for browsing. During opera season, you can time your exploration to land you at the Operaház stairs just before 7 PM to watch the spectacle of opera goers flowing in for the evening's performance. City Park is best explored on a clear day.

Sights to See

⑤⑨ **Drechsler Kastély** (Drechsler Palace). Across the street from the Operaház is the French Renaissance–style Drechsler Palace. An early work by Ödön Lechner, Hungary's master of Art Nouveau, it is now the home of the National Ballet School and is generally not open to tourists. ⊠ *District VI, Andrássy út 25.*

★ **Hősök tere** (Heroes' Square). Andrássy út ends in grandeur at Heroes' Square, with Budapest's answer to Berlin's Brandenburg Gate. Cleaned and refurbished in 1996 for the millecentenary (1100th anniversary), the **Millenniumi Emlékmű** (Millennial Monument) is a semicircular twin colonnade with statues of Hungary's kings and leaders between its pillars. Set back in its open center, a 118-ft stone column is crowned by a dynamic statue of the archangel Gabriel, his outstretched arms bearing the ancient emblems of Hungary. At its base ride seven bronze horsemen: the Magyar chieftains, led by Árpád, whose tribes conquered the land in 896. Before the column lies a simple marble slab, the **Nemzeti Háborús Emlék Tábla** (National War Memorial), the nation's altar, at which every visiting foreign dignitary lays a ceremonial wreath. England's Queen Elizabeth upheld the tradition during her royal visit in May of 1992. In 1991 Pope John Paul II conducted a mass here. Just a few months earlier, half a million Hungarians had convened to recall the memory of Imre Nagy, the reform-minded Communist prime minister who partially inspired the 1956 revolution. Little would anyone have guessed then that in 1995, palm trees—and Madonna—would spring up on this very square in a scene from the film *Evita* (set in Argentina, not Hungary), nor that Michael Jackson would do his part to consecrate the square with a music video. ⊠ *District VI*.

㉓ **Kodály körönd.** A handsome traffic circle with imposing statues of three Hungarian warriors—leavened by a fourth one of a poet—Kodály körönd is surrounded by plane and chestnut trees. Look carefully at the towered mansions on the north side of the circle—behind the soot you'll see the fading colors of ornate frescoes peeking through. The circle takes its name from the composer Zoltán Kodály, who lived just beyond it at Andrássy út 89. ⊠ *District VI, Andrássy út at Szinyei Merse u.*

㉒ **Liszt Ferenc Emlékmúzeum** (Franz Liszt Memorial Museum). Andrássy út No. 67 was the original location of the old Academy of Music and Franz Liszt's last home; entered around the corner, it now houses a museum. Several rooms display the original furniture and instruments from Liszt's time there; another room shows temporary exhibits. The museum hosts excellent, free classical concerts year-round, except in August 1–20, when it is closed. ⊠ *District VI, Vörösmarty u. 35*, ☏ *1/300–9804*, WEB *www.lisztmuseum.hu.* ⊡ *300 Ft.* ☉ *Weekdays 10–6, Sat. 9–5. Classical concerts (free with admission) Sept.–July, Sat. at 11* AM.

㉑ **Liszt Ferenc Zeneakadémia** (Franz Liszt Academy of Music). This magnificent Art Nouveau building presides over the cafés and gardens of Liszt Ferenc tér. Along with **Vigadó**, this is one of the city's main concert halls. On summer days, the sound of daytime rehearsals adds to the sweetness in the air along this pedestrian oasis of café society, just off buzzing Andrássy út. The academy itself has two auditoriums: a green-and-gold 1,200-seat main hall and a smaller hall for chamber music and solo recitals. Further along the square is a dramatic statue of Liszt Ferenc (Franz Liszt) himself, hair blown back from his brow, seemingly in a flight of inspiration. Pianist Ernő (Ernst) Dohnányi and composers Béla Bartók and Zoltán Kodály were teachers here. ⊠ *District VI, Liszt Ferenc tér 8*, ☏ *1/342–0179*.

★ ㉛ **Magyar Állami Operaház** (Hungarian State Opera House). Miklós Ybl's crowning achievement is the neo-Renaissance Opera House, built between 1875 and 1884. Badly damaged during the siege of 1944–45, it was restored for its 1984 centenary. Two buxom marble sphinxes guard the driveway; the main entrance is flanked by Alajos Strobl's "romantic-realist" limestone statues of Liszt and of another 19th-century Hungarian composer, Ferenc Erkel, the father of Hungarian opera (his patriotic opera *Bánk bán* is still performed for national celebrations).

Inside, the spectacle begins even before the performance does. You glide up grand staircases and through wood-paneled corridors and gilt lime-green salons into a glittering jewel box of an auditorium. Its four tiers of boxes are held up by helmeted sphinxes beneath a frescoed ceiling by Károly Lotz. Lower down there are frescoes everywhere, with intertwined motifs of Apollo and Dionysus. In its early years, the Budapest Opera was conducted by Gustav Mahler (from 1888 to 1891) and, after World War II, by Otto Klemperer.

The best way to experience the Opera House's interior is to see a ballet or opera; and while performance quality varies, tickets are relatively cheap and easy to come by, at least by tourist standards. And descending from *La Bohème* into the Földalatti station beneath the Opera House was described by travel writer Stephen Brook in *The Double Eagle* as stepping "out of one period piece and into another." There are no performances in summer, except for the weeklong BudaFest international opera and ballet festival in mid-August. You cannot view the interior on your own, but 45-minute tours in English are usually conducted daily; buy tickets in the Opera Shop, by the sphinx at the Hajós utca entrance. (Large groups should call in advance.) ⊠ *District VI, Andrássy út 22,* ☎ *1/331–2550 (ext. 156 for tours).* 🎫 *Tours 1,200 Ft.* ☉ *Tours daily at 3 and 4.*

🔟 **Magyar Fotográfusok Háza (Mai Manó Ház)** (Hungarian Photographers' House [Manó Mai House]). This ornate turn-of-the-20th-century building was built as a photography studio, where the wealthy bourgeoisie would come to be photographed by imperial and royal court photographer Manó Mai. Inside, ironwork and frescoes ornament the curving staircase leading up to the exhibition space, the largest of Budapest's three photo galleries. ⊠ *District VI, Nagymező u. 20,* ☎ *1/302–4398.* 🎫 *200 Ft.* ☉ *Weekdays 2–6.*

🔟 **Műcsarnok** (Palace of Exhibitions). The city's largest hall for special exhibitions is a striking 1895 temple of culture with a colorful tympanum. Its program of events includes exhibitions of contemporary Hungarian and international art and a rich series of films, plays, and concerts. ⊠ *District XIV, Hősök tere,* ☎ *1/460–7000.* 🎫 *600 Ft.; free Tues.* ☉ *Tues.–Sun. 10–6.*

🔟 **Postamúzeum** (Postal Museum). The best of Andrássy út's many marvelous stone mansions can be visited now, for the Postal Museum occupies an apartment with frescoes by Károly Lotz (whose work adorns St. Stephen's Basilica and the Opera House). Among the displays is an exhibition on the history of Hungarian mail, radio, and telecommunications. English-language pamphlets are available. Even if the exhibits don't thrill you, the venue, which was restored in 2001, is worth the visit. ⊠ *District VI, Andrássy út 3,* ☎ *1/269–6838.* 🎫 *70 Ft.* ☉ *Apr.– Oct., Tues.–Sun. 10–6; Nov.–Mar., Tues.–Sun. 10–4.*

🔟 **Ráth György Múzeum** (György Ráth Museum). Just off Andrássy út, the museum houses a rich collection of exotica from the Indian subcontinent and Chinese ceramics. The **Hopp Ferenc Kelet-Ázsiai Művészeti Múzeum** (Ferenc Hopp Museum of Eastern Asiatic Arts; ⊠ District VI, Andrássy út 103, ☎ 1/322–8476), which is affiliated with the György Ráth, hosts changing exhibits. ⊠ *District VI, Városligeti fasor 12,* ☎ *1/342–3916.* 🎫 *160 Ft. (combined ticket for both museums).* ☉ *Oct.– mid-Apr., Tues.–Sun. 10–4; mid-Apr.–Sept., Tues.–Sun. 10–6.*

NEED A   The **Művész** café (⊠ District VI, Andrássy út 29, ☎ 1/352–1337) is
BREAK?   perhaps the only surviving "writer's café" where you will occasionally
           see a writer at work. The tarnished windows and wallpaper curling up
           at the edges give it a shabby chic appeal. Sit at a table outside during
           summer to watch the world passing by on Andrássy út.

★ ⑥⑦ **Szépművészeti Múzeum** (Museum of Fine Arts). Across Heroes' Square from the Palace of Exhibitions and built by the same team of Albert Schickedanz and Fülöp Herzog, the Museum of Fine Arts houses Hungary's best art collection, rich in Flemish and Dutch old masters. With seven fine El Grecos and five beautiful Goyas as well as paintings by Velázquez and Murillo, the collection of Spanish old masters is one of the best outside Spain. The Italian school is represented by Giorgione, Bellini, Correggio, Tintoretto, and Titian masterpieces and, above all, two superb Raphael paintings: *Eszterházy Madonna* and his immortal *Portrait of a Youth,* rescued after a world-famous art heist. Nineteenth-century French art includes works by Delacroix, Pissarro, Cézanne, Toulouse-Lautrec, Gauguin, Renoir, and Monet. There are also more than 100,000 drawings (including five by Rembrandt and three studies by Leonardo), Egyptian and Greco-Roman exhibitions, late-Gothic winged altars from northern Hungary and Transylvania, and works by all the leading figures of Hungarian art up to the present. A 20th-century collection was added to the museum's permanent exhibits in 1994, comprising an interesting series of statues, paintings, and drawings by Chagall, Le Corbusier, and others. Labels are in both Hungarian and English; there's also an English-language booklet for sale about the permanent collection. ⊠ *District XIV, Hősök tere,* ☎ *1/343–9759.* ▣ *500 Ft.* ⊙ *Tues.–Sun. 10–5:30.*

☾ ⑥⑧ **Városliget (City Park).** Heroes' Square is the gateway to a square kilometer (almost ½ square mi) of recreation, entertainment, beauty, and culture. A bridge behind the Millennial Monument leads across a boating basin that becomes an artificial ice-skating rink in winter; to the south of this lake stands a statue of George Washington, erected in 1906 with donations by Hungarian emigrants to the United States. You can soak or swim at the turn-of-the-20th-century Széchenyi Fürdő, jog along the park paths, or careen on Vidám Park's roller coaster. There's also the Petőfi Csarnok, a leisure-time youth center and major concert hall on the site of an old industrial exhibition. The restaurant Gundel is once again charming diners with its turn-of-the-20th-century ambience. Fair-weather weekends, when the children's attractions are teeming with youngsters and parents and the Széchenyi Fürdő brimming with bathers, are the best times for people-watchers to visit the park; if you go on a weekday, the main sights are rarely crowded.

The renovation that began in the once-depressing **Budapesti Állatkert** (Budapest Zoo) in the late 1990s is not expected to be finished until 2004, but the place is already cheerier, at least for humans—with petting opportunities aplenty and a new monkey house where endearing, seemingly clawless little simians climb all over you (beware of pickpockets). Don't miss the elephant pavilion, decorated with Zsolnay majolica and glazed ceramic animals. ⊠ *Városliget, District XIV, Állatkerti krt. 6–12,* ☎ *1/343–6075.* ▣ *650 Ft.* ⊙ *Mar. and Oct., daily 9–5; Apr. and Sept., daily 9–6; May, daily 9–6:30; June–Aug., daily 9–7; Nov.– Feb., daily 9–4 (last tickets sold 1 hr before closing).*

At the **Fővárosi Nagycirkusz** (Municipal Grand Circus), colorful performances by local acrobats, clowns, and animal trainers, as well as by international artists, are staged here in a small ring. ⊠ *Városliget, District XIV, Állatkerti krt. 7,* ☎ *1/343–9630.* ▣ *Weekdays 500 Ft.– 900 Ft., weekends 550 Ft.–950 Ft.* ⊙ *July–Aug., Wed.–Fri. at 3 and 7; Thurs. at 3, Sat. at 10, 3, and 7; Sun. at 10 and 3; Sept.–June, schedule varies.*

Széchenyi Fürdő (Széchenyi Baths), the largest medicinal bathing complex in Europe, is housed in a beautiful neo-baroque building in the middle of City Park. There are several thermal pools indoors as well as two outdoors, which remain open even in winter, when dense steam hangs thick over the hot water's surface—you can just barely make out the figures of elderly men, submerged shoulder deep, crowded around waterproof chessboards. Note that to use the baths, you pay a 1,500 Ft. deposit: the balance (minus the changing room or cabin fee) is returned when you leave. Facilities include medical and underwater massage treatments, carbonated bath treatments and mud wraps. ✉ *Városliget, District XIV, Állatkerti krt. 11,* ☎ *1/321–0310.* 🎟 *Changing room 400 Ft., cabin 700 Ft.* ☉ *Weekdays 6 AM–6 PM, weekends 6 AM–5 PM.*

Beside the City Park's lake stands **Vajdahunyad Vár** (Vajdahunyad Castle), a fantastic medley of Hungary's historic and architectural past, starting with the Romanesque gateway of the cloister of Jak in western Hungary. A Gothic castle, Transylvanian turrets, Renaissance loggia, baroque portico, and Byzantine decoration are all guarded by a spooky modern (1903) bronze statue of the anonymous medieval chronicler, who was the first recorder of Hungarian history. Designed for the millennial celebration in 1896, it was not completed until 1908. This hodgepodge houses the surprisingly interesting **Mezőgazdasági Múzeum** (Agricultural Museum), with intriguingly arranged sections on animal husbandry, forestry, horticulture, hunting, and fishing. ✉ *Városliget, District XIV, Széchenyi Island,* ☎ *1/343–3198.* 🎟 *200 Ft.* ☉ *Mid-Feb.–mid-Nov., Tues.–Fri. and Sun. 10–5, Sat. 10–6; mid-Nov.–mid-Feb., Tues.–Fri. 10–4, weekends 10–5.*

🦢 Budapest's somewhat weary amusement park, **Vidám Park,** is next to the zoo and is crawling with happy children with their parents or grandparents in tow. Rides are inexpensive (some are for preschoolers). There are also game rooms and a scenic railway. Next to the main park is a separate, smaller section for toddlers. In winter, only a few rides operate. ✉ *Városliget, XIV, Állatkerti krt. 14–16,* ☎ *1/343–0996.* 🎟 *400 Ft.* ☉ *Apr.–Oct., weekdays noon–7, weekends 10–7; Nov.–Mar., weekdays noon–6, weekends 10–7.*

Eastern Pest and the Nagy körút (Great Ring Road)

This section covers primarily Kossuth Lajos–Rákóczi út and the Nagykörút (Great Ring Road)—busy, less-touristy urban thoroughfares full of people, cars, shops, and Budapest's unique urban flavor.

Beginning a few blocks from the Elizabeth Bridge, Kossuth Lajos utca is Budapest's busiest shopping street. Try to look above and beyond the store windows to the architecture and activity along Kossuth Lajos utca and its continuation, Rákóczi út, which begins when it crosses the Kis körút (Little Ring Road) at the busy intersection called Astoria. Most of Rákóczi út is lined with hotels, shops, and department stores, and it ends at the grandiose Keleti (East) Railway Station, on Baross tér.

Pest's Great Ring Road, the Nagy körút, was laid out at the end of the 19th century in a wide semicircle anchored to the Danube at both ends; an arm of the river was covered over to create this 114-ft-wide thoroughfare. The large apartment buildings on both sides also date from this era. Along with theaters, stores, and cafés, they form a boulevard unique in Europe for its "unified eclecticism," which blends several different historic styles into a harmonious whole. Its entire length of almost 4½ km (2¾ mi) from Margaret Bridge to Petőfi Bridge is traversed by Trams 4 and 6, but strolling it in stretches is also a good way to experience the hustle and bustle of downtown Budapest.

Like its smaller counterpart, the Kis Körút (Small Ring Road), the Great Ring Road comprises sectors of various names. Beginning with Ferenc körút at the Petőfi Bridge, it changes to József körút at the intersection marked by the Museum of Applied Arts, then to Erzsébet körút at Blaha Lujza tér. Teréz körút begins at the busy Oktogon crossing with Andrássy út and ends at the Nyugati (West) Railway Station, where Szent István takes over for the final stretch to the Margaret Bridge.

Numbers in the text correspond to numbers in the margin and on the Budapest map.

A Good Walk

Beginning with a visit to the **Iparművészeti Múzeum** ⑥⑨, near the southern end of the boulevard, walk or take Tram 4 or 6 north (away from the Petőfi Bridge) to **Köztársaság tér** ⑦⓪. The neo-Renaissance **Keleti pályaudvar** ⑦① is a one-metro-stop detour away from Blaha Lujza tér. Continuing in the same direction on the körút, go several stops on the tram to **Nyugati pályaudvar** ⑦② and walk the remaining sector, Szent István körút, past the **Vígszínház** ⑦③ to Margaret Bridge. From the bridge, views of Margaret Island, to the north, and Parliament, Castle Hill, the Chain Bridge, and Gellért Hill, to the south, are gorgeous.

TIMING

As this area is packed with stores, it's best to explore during business hours—weekdays until around 5 PM and Saturday until 1 PM; Saturday will be most crowded. Keep in mind that the Iparművészeti Múzeum is closed Monday.

Sights to See

★ ⑥⑨ **Iparművészeti Múzeum** (Museum of Applied and Decorative Arts). The templelike structure housing this museum is indeed a shrine to Hungarian Art Nouveau, and in front of it, drawing pen in hand, sits a statue of its creator, Hungarian architect Ödön Lechner. Opened in the Magyar Millennial year of 1896, it was only the third museum of its kind in Europe. Its dome of tiles is crowned by a majolica lantern from the same source: the Zsolnay ceramic works in Pécs. Inside its central hall are playfully swirling whitewashed, double-decker, Moorish-style galleries and arcades. The museum, which collects and studies objects of interior decoration and use, has five departments: furniture, textiles, goldsmithing, ceramics, and everyday objects. ⊠ *District VIII, Üllői út 33–37,* ☎ *1/217–5222,* WEB *www.imm.hu.* 🖼 *300 Ft.* ☉ *Mid-Mar.– Oct., Tues.–Sun. 10–6; Nov.–mid-Mar., Tues.–Sun. 10–4.*

OFF THE
BEATEN PATH

GÖDÖLLŐI KIRÁLYI KASTÉLY The royal palace of Gödöllői, better known as the Grassalkovich Palace, has been referred to as the Hungarian Versailles, though this baroque mansion and former royal residence does suffer by comparison. This is because the palace was used as a barracks by Soviet troops after 1945, and much of the palace was still under restoration at this writing. Still, those interested in Emperor Franz Josef I and his legendarily beautiful and charismatic wife, Elizabeth (known as Sissi), will find this a rewarding half-day excursion. Sissi's violet-colored rooms contain secret doors, which allowed her to avoid tiresome guests. To get there, go to the Örs Vezér tere—last stop on the red metro line, and take the HÉV suburban train to the Szabadság tere stop. The palace sits across the street. ⊠ *Gödöllő,* ☎ *1/329–2340.* 🖼 *600 Ft.* ☉ *Tues.–Sun. 10–6.*

⑦① **Keleti pályaudvar** (East Railway Station). The grandiose, imperial-looking station was built in 1884 and considered Europe's most modern until well into the 20th century. Its neo-Renaissance facade, which resembles a gateway, is flanked by statues of two British inventors and railway pioneers, James Watt and George Stephenson. ⊠ *District VIII, Baross tér.*

70 **Köztársaság tér** (Square of the Republic). Surrounded by faceless concrete buildings, this square is not particularly alluring aesthetically but is significant because it was where the Communist Party of Budapest had its headquarters, and it was also the scene of heavy fighting in 1956. Here also is the city's second opera house, and Budapest's largest, the **Erkel Ferenc színház** (Ferenc Erkel Theater). ⊠ *District VIII, between Luther u. and Berzeriyi u.*

72 **Nyugati pályaudvar** (West Railway Station). The iron-laced glass hall of the West Railway Station is in complete contrast to—and much more modern than—the newer East Railway Station. Built in the 1870s, it was designed by a team of architects from Gustav Eiffel's office in Paris. ⊠ *District XIII, Teréz krt.*

★ **73** **Vígszínház** (Comedy Theater). This neo-baroque, late-19th-century, gemlike theater twinkles with just a tiny, playful anticipation of Art Nouveau and sparkles inside and out since its 1994 refurbishment. The theater hosts primarily musicals, such as Hungarian adaptations of *Cats,* as well as dance performances and classical concerts. ⊠ *District XIII, Pannónia u. 1,* ☎ *1/329–2340 box office,* WEB *www.vigszinhaz.hu.*

NEED A BREAK?	Hands down the best café in this part of town, the **Európa kávéház** (⊠ District XIII, Szent István krt. 7–9, ☎ 1/312–2362) has marble-top tables; top-notch elegance; and, yes, delectable sweets. While it seems (in the best sense) a century old, it's in fact only been around since the late 1990s. Here you can sample some Eszterházy torta (a rich, buttery cake with walnut batter and, here at least, a walnut on top) or a Tyrolean strudel with poppy-seed filling.

Óbuda

Until its unification with Buda and Pest in 1872 to form the city of Budapest, Óbuda (meaning Old Buda) was a separate town that used to be the main settlement; now it is usually thought of as a suburb. Although the vast new apartment blocks of Budapest's biggest housing project and busy roadways are what first strike the eye, the historic core of Óbuda has been preserved in its entirety.

Numbers in the text correspond to numbers in the margin and on the Budapest map.

A Good Walk

Óbuda is easily reached by car, bus, or streetcar via the Árpád Bridge from Pest or by the HÉV suburban railway from Batthyány tér to the Árpád Bridge. Once you're there, covering all the sights on foot involves large but manageable distances along major exhaust-permeated roadways. One way to tackle it is to take Tram 17 from its southern terminus at the Buda side of the Margaret Bridge to Kiscelli utca and walk uphill to the **Kiscelli Múzeum.** Then walk back down the same street all the way past **Flórián tér,** continuing toward the Danube and making a left onto Hídfő utca or Szentlélek tér to enter **Fő tér.** After exploring the square, walk a block or two southeast to the HÉV suburban railway stop and take the train just north to the museum complex at **Aquincum.**

TIMING

It's best to begin touring Óbuda during the cooler, early hours of the day, as the heat on the area's busy roads can get overbearing. Avoid Monday, when museums are closed.

Sights to See

Aquincum. This complex comprises the reconstructed remains of a Roman settlement dating from the 1st century AD and the capital of the Roman province of Pannonia. Careful excavations have unearthed a varied selection of artifacts and mosaics, giving a tantalizing inkling of what life was like in the provinces of the Roman Empire. A gymnasium and a central heating system have been unearthed, along with the ruins of two baths and a shrine to Mithras, the Persian god of light, truth, and the sun. The **Aquincum múzeum** (Aquincum Museum) displays the dig's most notable finds: ceramics; a red-marble sarcophagus showing a triton and flying Eros on one side and on the other, Telesphorus, the angel of death, depicted as a hooded dwarf; and jewelry from a Roman lady's tomb. ⊠ *District III, Szentendrei út 139,* ☎ *1/250–1650.* ⌑ *700 Ft.* ☉ *Apr. and Oct., Tues.–Sun. 10–5; May–Sept., Tues.–Sun. 10–6. Grounds open an hr earlier than museum.*

Flórián tér (Flórián Square). The center of today's Óbuda is Flórián tér, where Roman ruins were first discovered when the foundations of a house were dug in 1778. Two centuries later, careful excavations were carried out during the reconstruction of the square, and today the restored ancient ruins lie in the center of the square in mind-boggling contrast to the racing traffic and cement-block housing projects. ⊠ *District III, Vörösvári út at Pacsirtamező u.*

Fő tér (Main Square). Óbuda's old main square is its most picturesque part. The square has been spruced up in recent years, and there are now several good restaurants and interesting museums in and around the baroque **Zichy Kúria** (Zichy Mansion), which has become a neighborhood cultural center. Among the most popular offerings are the summer concerts in the courtyard and the evening jazz concerts. ⊠ *District III, Kórház u. at Hídfő u.*

Hercules Villa. A fine 3rd-century Roman dwelling, it takes its name from the myth depicted on its beautiful mosaic floor. The ruin was unearthed between 1958 and 1967 and is now only open by request (inquire at the Aquincum Museum). ⊠ *District III, Meggyfa u. 19–21.*

Kiscelli Múzeum (Kiscelli Museum). A strenuous climb up the steep, dilapidated sidewalks of Remetehegy (Hermit's Hill) will deposit you at this elegant, mustard-yellow baroque mansion. Built between 1744 and 1760 as a Trinitarian monastery, today it holds an eclectic mix of paintings, sculptures, engravings, and sundry items related to the history of Budapest. Included here is the printing press on which poet and revolutionary Sándor Petőfi printed his famous "Nemzeti Dal" ("National Song"), in 1848, inciting the Hungarian people to rise up against the Hapsburgs. ⊠ *District III, Kiscelli u. 108,* ☎ *1/388–7817.* ⌑ *300 Ft.* ☉ *Nov.–Mar., Tues.–Sun. 10–4; Apr.–Oct., Tues.–Sun. 10–6.*

Római amfiteátrum (Roman Amphitheater). Probably dating back to the 2nd century AD, Óbuda's Roman military amphitheater once held some 16,000 people and, at 144 yards in diameter, was one of Europe's largest. A block of dwellings called the Round House was later built by the Romans above the amphitheater; massive stone walls found in the Round House's cellar were actually parts of the amphitheater. Below the amphitheater are the cells where prisoners and lions were held while awaiting confrontation. ⊠ *District III, Pacsirtamező u. at Nagyszombat u.*

Zichy Kúria (Zichy Mansion). One wing of the Zichy Mansion is taken up by the **Óbudai Helytörténeti Gyüjtemény** (Óbuda Local History Collection). Permanent exhibitions here include traditional rooms from typical homes in the district of Békásmegyer and a popular exhibit covering the history of toys from 1860 to 1960. Another wing houses the **Kassák Múzeum,** which honors the literary and artistic works of a pioneer of the Hungarian avant-garde, Lajos Kassák. ⊠ *District III, Fő*

*tér 1, ☎ 1/250–1020 History Collection; 1/368–7021 Kassák Museum.
🎫 History Collection 120 Ft., Kassák Museum 100 Ft. ☺ History
Collection mid-Mar.–mid-Oct., Tues.–Fri. 2–6, weekends 10–6; mid-
Oct.–mid-Mar., Tues.–Fri. 2–5, weekends 10–5. Kassák Museum Mar.–
Sept., Tues.–Sun. 10–6; Oct.–Feb., Tues.–Sun. 10–4.*

DINING

A far cry from the smattering of options available in the socialist era,
Budapest's culinary scene now offers variety and quality both in sat-
isfyingly large portions. It's possible, for instance, to eat very good sushi
in Budapest, and the range of styles encompassed by the culinary clas-
sification "Hungarian" runs to more than just paprika and goulash served
up in faux Gypsy surroundings.

A few of the city's grander dining establishments overlook the Danube
and downtown from the imperious Buda Hill, while Pest has a busy restaurant scene, including bustling lunchtime bistros and late night cafés. To
be right up to the latest minute on the restaurant scene, you can always
rifle through local English-language press for fresh ideas on where to
dine. The *Budapest Sun* has fairly impartial restaurant reviews (in English) and is available in most centrally located newsstands.

For price range information, *see* Dining *in* Pleasures and Pastimes.

Downtown Pest and the Small Ring Road

$$–$$$$ ✕ **Café Kör** The wrought-iron tables, vaulted ceilings, and crisp white
★   tablecloths give this chic bistro a decidedly downtown feel. In the
             heart of the busy fifth district, Café Kör is ideal for lunch or dinner
             when touring nearby Andrássy út or St. Stephen's Basilica. The spe-
             cialty plate is a feast of rich goose liver paté, grilled meats, and cheeses,
             to be savored with a glass of Hungarian *pezsgő* (sparkling wine). True
             to its bistro aspirations, the daily specials are scribbled on the wall, in
             both Hungarian and English. ✉ *District V, Sas u. 17,* ☎ *1/311–0053.
             Reservations essential. No credit cards. Closed Sun.*

$$–$$$$ ✕ **Kárpátia.** As many a Hungarian will remind you, much of what is
             now Romanian Transylvania, including the Carpathian mountains, was
             once considered part of Hungary. The neo-Gothic interior and Gypsy
             musicians here conjure up that lost world, along with a menu that in-
             cludes "forgotten delicacies." There are in fact some 170 dishes, in-
             cluding the best *Hortobágyi* pancakes this side of the Puszta, and
             stuffed Transylvanian cabbage. You can dine outdoors, under a mar-
             quee, on summer nights. ✉ *District V, Ferenciek tere 7–8,* ☎ *1/317–
             3596. Reservations essential. AE, DC, MC, V.*

$$–$$$$ ✕ **Múzeum.** The gustatory anticipation sparked by this elegant, can-
             dlelit salon with mirrors, mosaics, and swift-moving waiters is matched
             by wholly satisfying, wonderful food. The salads are generous, the Hun-
             garian wines excellent, and the chef dares to be creative. Unusual for
             a restaurant of this standing, Múzeum does not take all major credit
             cards—there's an ATM on the premises, however. ✉ *District VIII,
             Múzeum krt. 11,* ☎ *1/338–4221. Jacket and tie. AE. Closed Sun.*

$$–$$$$ ✕ **Tom-George Restaurant & Bar.** Well-situated in the heart of down-
             town, Tom-George is Budapest's answer to urban chic. The spacious
             bar blends blond wood and wicker, giving the interior a relaxed yet
             sophisticated feel. Weekends find a young and stylish crowd choosing
             from the expansive cocktail menu. Minimalism at the table, though,
             belies exotic creativity in the kitchen. House specialties include nasi
             goreng with chicken breast and lamb with satay sauce. Sushi—perhaps
             Budapest's best—is glamorously prepared in a corner of the dining room.

District V, Oktober 6th utca 8, ☎ 1/266–3525. *Reservations essential. AE, V.*

$$–$$$ ✕ **Empire.** This is one eating and drinking establishment that anyone
★ nostalgic for Hapsburg-era magnificence shouldn't miss out on. After
sinking into one of the very comfortable leather chairs, you'll enjoy
the insulation from the traffic outside on Kossuth Lajos street—and
indeed the whole 21st century. Game dishes are the noted specialty. ⊠
District V, Kossuth Lajos u. 19, ☎ *1/317–3411. Reservations essential. AE, DC, MC, V.*

$–$$$ ✕ **Cyrano.** This smooth young bistro just off Vörösmarty tér has an
★ arty, contemporary bent, with wrought-iron chairs, green-marble
floors, and long-stem azure glasses. The creative kitchen sends out el-
egantly presented Hungarian and Continental dishes, from standards
such as goulash and chicken paprikás to more eclectic tastes such as
tender fried Camembert with blueberry jam. ⊠ *District V, Kristóf tér
7–8,* ☎ *1/266–3096. Reservations essential. AE, DC, MC, V.*

$–$$ ✕ **Baraka.** The deep velvet-red walls and airy balcony are offset by
★ the gleam of varnished floorboards in this elegant and refreshingly mod-
ern and hospitable restaurant tucked discreetly around the corner from
so much downtown action on quiet Magyar utca. The chicken in sweet
chili sauce is recommended, as is the New York cheesecake—so called
simply because the chef is from New York, but it's delicious all the same.
It's a welcome addition to the serious restaurant scene. ⊠ *District V,
Magyar u. 12–14,* ☎ *1/483–1355. Reservations essential. AE, DC, MC,
V. Closed Sun.*

$–$$ ✕ **Stex Ház.** In its own way, this three-level restaurant is every bit as
much of a classic as Gundel. Alfred Stex, a Hungarian, became a successful bootlegger in Prohibition America and then returned home to
open this restaurant. Faultlessly high-cholesterol working-class fodder
is paired with slightly sullen service. The food, when it arrives, makes
up for the waiters' sometimes frosty demeanor. If you like people-watching, there's a constant stream of customers in this gymnasium-size pro-
letarian palace. ⊠ *District XIII, Jószef krt. 55–57,* ☎ *1/318–5716. AE,
DC, MC, V.*

$–$$ ✕ **Vista Travel Café.** A favorite of lunching Hungarian businesspeo-
★ ple, backpackers, second-tier expatriates, and other assorted oddities,
Vista is a curious but successful hybrid of brassiere, café, cybercafé,
meeting place, and information center. The action in the kitchen can
creak at times, though it must be owed that dual-language menus
cheerfully warn you of that fact. You can fill in the paper place-mat
feedback forms while you wait for healthy, nutritious food to arrive.
Highlights include the Rarotonga sandwich, quiche Lorraine, pastas,
and all-day breakfast menu. ⊠ *District VII, Paulay Ede u. 7,* ☎ *1/268–
0888. AE, DC, MC, V.*

North Buda

$$–$$$$ ✕ **Fuji Japan.** If you need further convincing that Budapest now has
a truly international restaurant scene—or even if you just like excel-
lent Japanese food—then you'll make the trek to the Buda Hills and
this powerhouse of cuisine from the land of the rising sun. It's a spa-
cious place, with tables set a comfortable distance apart so that you
can watch the Japanese and Hungarian chefs at work and choose from
a menu of considerable depth, considering how far you are from the
sea. There's even a separate dining room where you can eat at low ta-
bles, in traditional Japanese style. ⊠ *District III, Csatárka u. 54/b,* ☎
1/325–7111. AE, DC, MC, V.

$–$$$ ✕ **Udvarház.** The views from this Buda hilltop restaurant are unsur-
passed. As you dine indoors at tables set with white linens or outdoors

124

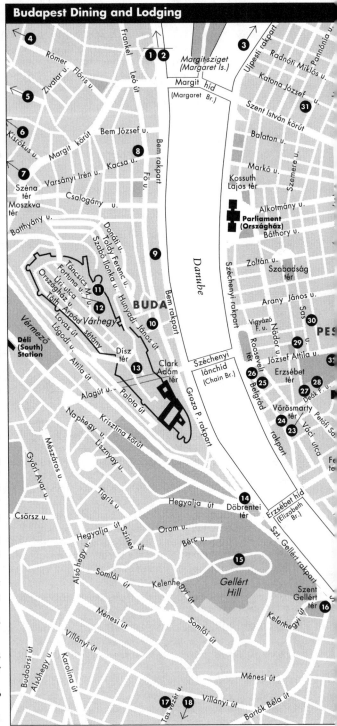

Budapest Dining and Lodging

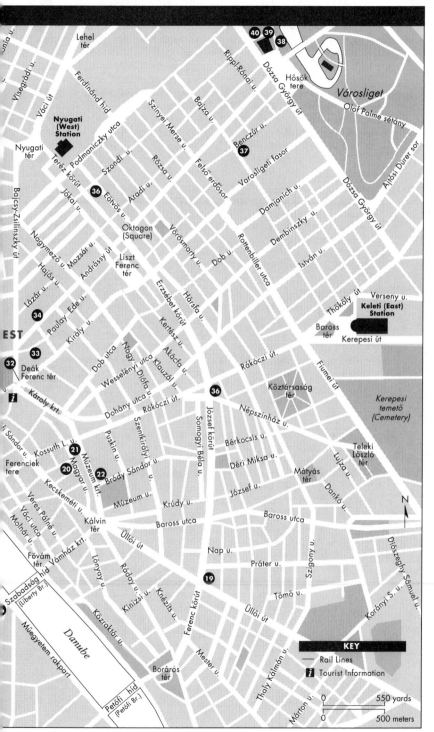

Lehel
tér

Visegrádi u.

Váci út

Ferdinánd híd

Rippl-Rónai u.

Dózsa György út

Hősök
tere

Városliget

Olof Palme sétány

Ajtósi Dürer sor

Nyugati
(West)
Station

Nyugati
tér

Podmaniczky utca

Szinyei Merse u.

Bajza u.

Benczúr u.

Dózsa György út

37

Bajcsy-Zsilinszky út

Teréz körút

Szondi u.

Aradi u.

Rózsa u.

Felső erdősor

Városligeti fasor

Jókai u.

Eötvös u.

36

Nagymező u.

Mozsár u.

Andrássy u.

Oktogon
(Square)

Vörösmarty u.

Dob u.

Rottenbiller utca

Damjanich u.

Dembinszky u.

István u.

Hajós u.

Lázár u.

Liszt
Ferenc
tér

Erzsébet körút

Hársfa u.

34

Paulay Ede u.

Király u.

Kertész u.

Akácfa u.

Thököly út

Verseny u.

**Keleti (East)
Station**

EST

33

Dob utca

Nagy Diófa u.

Klauzál u.

Rákóczi út

Baross
tér

Kerepesi út

32

Deák
Ferenc tér

Wesselényi utca

Dohány utca

Rákóczi út

Köztársaság
tér

Fiumei út

Kerepesi
temető
(Cemetery)

Károly krt.

Szentkirályi u.

József körút

Népszínház u.

Teleki
László
tér

rj Sándor u.

Kossuth L. u.

21

Puskin u.

Bérkocsis u.

Luza u.

Ferenciek
tere

20

Magyar u.

Bródy Sándor u.

Déri Miksa u.

Mátyás
tér

Dankó u.

Kecskeméti u.

Múzeum krt.

Somogyi Béla u.

József u.

Veres Pálné u.

Múzeum u.

Krúdy u.

Baross utca

Baross utca

N

Váci utca

Kálvin
tér

Üllői út

Nap u.

Szigony u.

Diószeghy Sámuel u.

Fővám
tér.

Vámház krt.

Lónyay u.

Ráday u.

Práter u.

Korányi S. u.

Szabadság híd
(Liberty Br.)

Kinizsi u.

Knézits u.

Ferenc körút

Üllői út

Tömő u.

19

Műegyetem rakpart

Köztárkár u.

Danube

KEY

— Rail Lines

i Tourist Information

Boráros
tér

Mester u.

Thaly Kálmán u.

Márton u.

Petőfi híd
(Petőfi Br.)

0   550 yards

0   500 meters

on the open terrace, your meals are accompanied by vistas of the
Danube bridges and Parliament far below. Excellent fresh fish is prepared tableside; you could also try veal and goose liver in paprika sauce,
served with salty cottage cheese dumplings. Catering to the predomi-
nantly tourist crowd, folklore shows and live Gypsy music frequently
enliven the scene. The buses up here are infrequent, so it's easier to
take a car or taxi. ⊠ *District III, Hármashatárhegyi út 2,* ☎ *1/388–
6921. AE, DC, MC, V. Closed Mon. Nov.–Mar. No lunch weekdays
Nov.–Mar.*

$–$$ ✕ **Náncsi Néni.** "Auntie Nancsi" has built a loyal following by serv-
★ ing up straightforward, home-style Hungarian cuisine in rustic surroundings. Chains of paprika and garlic dangle from the low wooden
ceiling above tables set with red-and-white gingham tablecloths and
fresh bread tucked into tiny baskets. Shelves along the walls are
crammed with jars of home-pickled vegetables, which you can purchase
to take home. The menu includes turkey breast fillets stuffed with ap-
ples, peaches, mushrooms, cheese, and sour cream. There is a garden
dining area open during warmer months, when reservations are essential.
⊠ *District III, Ördögárok út 80,* ☎ *1/397–2742. AE, DC, MC, V.*

$ ✕ **Marxim.** Relive the good old bad days of "goulash socialism" in this
tongue-in-cheek tribute to Hungary's socialist past, a pizza joint across
the street from a factory. Vintage propaganda covers the walls, and dining booths are even separated by barbed wire. The pizza here is per-
fectly serviceable, although the blaring techno and house music that
sometimes play in the background might be too revolutionary for
some. As well as many standard pizzas, the menu includes made-up
theme pizzas such as the Gulag Pizza, which is more nourishing than
it sounds. ⊠ *District II, Kisrókus u. 23,* ☎ *1/316–0231. AE, DC, MC,
V. Closed Sun.*

Óbuda

$$–$$$ ✕ **Kéhli.** This pricey but laid-back, sepia-toned neighborhood tavern
is on a hard-to-find street near the Óbuda end of the Árpád Bridge.
Practically all the food here arrives in huge servings, which was just
the way that Hungarian writer Gyula Krúdy (to whom the restaurant
is dedicated) liked it, when he was a regular customer. Dishes like their
hot pot with marrow bone and toast, or *lecsö* (a stew with a base of
onions, peppers, tomatoes, and paprika) make for great comfort food
on a cool day. ⊠ *District III, Mókus u. 22,* ☎ *1/250–4241 or 1/368–
0613. AE, DC, MC, V. No lunch weekdays.*

$–$$$ ✕ **Kisbuda Gyöngye.** Considered by many the finest restaurant in
★ Óbuda, this intimate place is filled with antique furniture, and its
walls are creatively decorated with an eclectic but elegant patchwork
of carved, wooden cupboard doors and panels. A violin-piano duo sets
a romantic mood, and in warm weather you can dine outdoors in the
cozy back garden. Try the tarragon ragoût of game, or their Flavors
of the Forest platter (with pheasant breast, wild duck and wild mush-
rooms, or stuffed plum wrapped in venison sirloin). ⊠ *District III, Keny-
eres u. 34,* ☎ *1/368–6402 or 1/368–9246. Reservations essential. AE,
DC, MC, V. Closed Sun.*

Tabán and Gellért Hill

$$$–$$$$ ✕ **Kacsa.** As its name ("The Duck") implies, the specialty in this up-
★ market Hungarian restaurant is duck. A special selection of duck dishes
includes duck stuffed with ox tongue and plums. Though the street-cor-
ner frontage is rather unprepossessing, inside you'll experience true sil-
ver-service dining in what could pass for the dining room of a
Hapsburg-era noble house. Yet the waiters and management are all rel-

atively young and energetic. You can ask to sit in the anteroom if the rather spirited piano and violin duet is too much for you. ⊠ *District I, Fő u. 75,* ☎ *1/209–9992. Reservations essential. AE, DC, MC, V.*

$$–$$$$ ✕ **Hemingway.** It takes some brio to pull off a restaurant with the style of Ernest Hemingway, but when that restaurant is housed in what looks like a 19th-century hunting lodge—complete with wooden balcony and lake views—the odds for success start to look better. The menu includes several kinds of seafood cooked on Mediterranean lava stone. Fans of heroic consumption will also appreciate a cocktail menu, with some 100 drinks, and a selection of after-dinner cigars. ⊠ *District XI, Kosztolányi Dezso tér 2 (on Feneketlen Lake),* ☎ *1/489–0236. Reservations essential. AE, DC, MC, V.*

$$–$$$$ ✕ **Rivalda.** On summer nights, you can choose to dine outside in an 18th-century courtyard or in the restaurant's rather rococo interior—with poplin stage curtains, theatrical masks, and peach-color walls. The food is a lighter take on Hungarian cuisine, with some excellent seafood dishes including cream of pumpkin bisque with smoked salmon, and fillet of pike perch. A terrific place for a celebration, whether intimate or with a group, Rivalda has a substantial vegetarian menu, still something of a rarity in Budapest. ⊠ *District I, Színház u. 5–9,* ☎ *1/489–0236. Reservations essential. AE, DC, MC, V.*

$–$$$ ✕ **Villa Doria.** A baroque villa near Castle Hill is the venue for this el-
★ egant yet friendly Italian restaurant. The interior is all high ceilings, chandeliers, and polished parquet floors, while a terrace looking onto a garden is perfect for summer dining. The menu runs the gamut from good old spaghetti Bolognese to a large selection of traditional Italian antipasta, pasta, fish, and meat dishes, as well as southern Italian specialties. ⊠ *District I, Döbrentei u. 9,* ☎ *1/225–3233. Reservations essential. AE, DC, MC, V. Closed Mon.*

City Park

$$$–$$$$ ✕ **Gundel.** This is the restaurant to boast about when you return
★ home. In a late-19th-century palazzo, Gundel has been open since 1894 and under the direction of Hungary's best-known restaurateur, George Lang, since 1992. Try some of his signature dishes, such as pan-roasted fillet of Balaton fogas Gundel-style, or the goose liver pâtés. The budget-conscious can still enjoy this famous restaurant by ordering one of the weekday business menus, a three-course meal for 3,000 Ft.–4000 Ft. A cheaper cellar restaurant, 1894, with a separate entrance opened in mid-2002. ⊠ *District XIV, Várisoliget, Állatkerti út 2,* ☎ *1/321–3550. Reservations essential. Jacket and tie. AE, DC, MC, V.*

$$–$$$$ ✕ **Robinson Restaurant.** Robinson can certainly lay claim to one of the more exotic locations in Budapest dining—on wooden platforms atop an artificial lake. Diners look out across the lake to the delightful architectural folly of Vajdahunyad Castle. You can sit outside on the terrace during summer, or enjoy the warm pastel interior in colder months. Service is doting and the menu creative, with dishes such as crisp roast suckling pig with champagne-drenched cabbage or fresh fogas stuffed with spinach. ⊠ *District XIV, Várisoliget, Városligeti-tó (City Park Lake),* ☎ *1/422–0222. Reservations essential. AE, DC, MC, V.*

$–$$$ ✕ **Bagolyvár.** George Lang opened this restaurant next door to his gastronomic palace, Gundel, in 1993. The informal yet polished dining room has a soaring wood-beam ceiling, and the kitchen produces first-rate daily menus of home-style Hungarian specialties. Soups, served in shiny silver tureens, are particularly good. Musicians entertain with *cimbalom* (hammered dulcimer) music nightly from 7 PM. In warm weather there is outdoor dining in a lovely back garden. ⊠ *District XIV, Várisoliget, Állatkerti út 2,* ☎ *1/468–3110. AE, DC, MC, V.*

LODGING

Budapest has seen a steady increase in the variety and overall quality of its tourist accommodations since 1989, including a number of up-scale, international-standard hotels that were due to open soon at this writing. Perhaps the most highly anticipated is the new Four Seasons Budapest in the palatial Gresham insurance building facing Erzebet Hid (Elizabeth Bridge).

All room rates given are based on double occupancy in high season. For luxury hotels, VAT of 12% and sometimes breakfast and a tourist tax of 3% will not be included in the room rate. Assume they are included unless there is a note to the contrary.

Advance reservations are strongly advised in the summer. In winter it's not anywhere near as difficult to find a hotel room, even at the last minute, and prices are usually reduced by 20%–30%. The best budget option is to book a private room or an entire apartment. Expect to pay between $20–$30 for a double room. The number of rooms available can be limited in high season, so if you're booking your accommodation on the spot, it may be best arrive in Budapest early in the morning.

Addresses below are preceded by the district number (in Roman numerals) and include the Hungarian postal code. Districts V, VI, and VII are in downtown Pest; District I includes Castle Hill, the main tourist district of Buda. For price ranges *see* Lodging *in* Pleasures and Pastimes.

Apartment Rentals

Apartments, available for short- and long-term rental, are often an economical alternative to staying in a hotel, with an increasing number of options available, as Hungarian entrepreneurs find uses for old family homes and inherited apartments. A short-term rental in Budapest will probably cost anywhere from $30 to $60 a day.

IBUSZ (⊠ District V, Petöfi tér, H-1051, ☎ 01/318–5707, 🄵🄰🄷 1/485–2769) is open 24 hours, renting out apartments in downtown Budapest, each consisting of two rooms plus a fully equipped kitchen and bathroom. Accommodation can also be arranged in private rooms—your host is usually a kindly elderly Hungarian lady. The two-person, high-season rate is approximately $40 a night. **To-Ma Tours** (⊠ District XI, Bartók Béla út 4, ☎ 1/353–0819, 🄵🄰🄷 1/269–5715) arranges private apartments and rooms. The apartments are remarkably spacious and resemble 1950s executive suites, without the telephone but with satellite TV and fully equipped kitchens. They're available for around $40 a night. **TRIBUS Hotel Service** (⊠ District V, Apáczai Csere János u. 1, ☎ 1/318–5776, 🄵🄰🄷 1/317–9099) has the advantage of being open 24 hours a day, booking private apartments and rooms in private homes; the company can also make hotel reservations.

Budapest Hotels

$$$$ ▥ **art'otel.** Boutique hotels may not be anything new in the West, but art'otel has the distinction of being Budapest's only boutique hotel, and it is a tribute to its class. From the multi-million-dollar art collection on the walls to the carpet and water fountains, the interior is all the work of one man, American artist Donald Sultan. Encompassing one new building and four 18th-century baroque houses on the Buda riverfront, the art'otel adroitly blends old and new. Some rooms also have splendid views of Fisherman's Bastion and the Matthias Church. ⊠ District I, Bem rakpart 16–19, H-1011, ☎ 1/487–9487, 🄵🄰🄷 1/487–9488, 🅆🄴🄱 *www.parkplazaww.com. 156 rooms, 9 suites. Restaurant, café, cable TV with movies, in-room data ports, in-room safes, minibars, hair salon, sauna, meeting rooms, parking (fee); no-smoking rooms. AE, DC, MC, V.*

$$$$ ▦ **Budapest Hilton.** You'll have to decide for yourself if this hotel, built in 1977 around the remains of a 17th-century Gothic chapel and adjacent to the Matthias Church, is a successful integration or not. The exterior certainly betrays the hotel's 1970s origins, but the modern and tasteful rooms and great views from Castle Hill will soothe the most delicate of aesthetic sensibilities. Rooms with the best Danube vistas cost more. Children, regardless of age, get free accommodation when sharing a room with their parents. VAT, tourist tax, and breakfast are not included in the rates. ✉ *District I, Hess András tér 1–3, H-1014,* ☎ *1/488–6600; 800/445–8667 in the U.S. and Canada;* FAX *1/488–6644,* WEB *www.hilton.com. 295 rooms, 26 suites. 3 restaurants, café, in-room data ports, gym, hair salon, sauna, 2 bars, dry cleaning, laundry service, business services, meeting rooms, travel services, parking (free and fee). AE, DC, MC, V.*

$$$$ ▦ **Budapest Marriott.** North American–style hospitality on the Pest side of the Danube begins with the buffet of glazed pastries served daily in the lobby and even the feather-light ring of the front-desk bell. Guest rooms have lushly patterned carpets, floral bedspreads, and etched glass. The hotel's prime Danube location makes for some breathtaking views. Gellért Hill, the Chain and Elizabeth bridges, and Castle Hill are visible from all guest rooms, as well as the lobby, ballroom, every guest room, and even the impressive hotel fitness center. ✉ *District V, Apáczai Csere János u. 4, H-1052,* ☎ *1/266–7000; 800/831–4004 in the U.S. and Canada;* FAX *1/266–5000,* WEB *www.marriott.com. 362 rooms, 11 suites. 3 restaurants, in-room data ports, health club, sauna, squash, bar, shops, baby-sitting, dry cleaning, laundry service, business services, meeting rooms, travel services, parking (fee); no-smoking rooms. AE, DC, MC, V.*

$$$$ ▦ **Hotel Inter-Continental Budapest.** Its days as the socialist-era Fórum Hotel now firmly consigned to the past, the Inter-Continental appeals to the modern business traveler. Every room has an executive-style work desk, and business rooms even contain a printer. The hotel is located right next to the Chain Bridge in Pest, and 60% of the rooms have views across the Danube to Castle Hill (these are more expensive). Rooms on higher floors ensure the least noise. All are decorated in pleasant pastels and furnished in the Biedermeier style typical of Central Europe. Rates do not include VAT, tourist tax, or breakfast. ✉ *District V, Apáczai Csere János u. 12–14 (Box 231, H-1368),* ☎ *1/327–6333,* FAX *1/327–6357,* WEB *www.budapest.intercontinental.com. 398 rooms, 16 suites. 2 restaurants, café, in-room data ports, pool, health club, bar, business services, meeting rooms, car rental, parking (fee); no-smoking floors. AE, DC, MC, V.*

$$$$ ▦ **Hyatt Regency Budapest.** The spectacular 10-story atrium—a mix
★ of glass-capsule elevators, cascading tropical greenery, an actual prop plane suspended over an open bar, and café—is surpassed only by the Hyatt's views across the Danube to Castle Hill. All rooms are decorated and furnished in muted blues and light woods, and many overlook the Danube or Roosevelt tér. These, of course, are more expensive than those with less commanding views. ✉ *District V, Roosevelt tér 2, H-1051,* ☎ *1/266–1234,* FAX *1/266–9101,* WEB *www.budapest.hyatt.com. 330 rooms, 23 suites. 3 restaurants, in-room data ports, indoor pool, gym, hair salon, sauna, 2 bars, casino, business services, meeting rooms, travel services, parking (fee); no-smoking rooms. AE, DC, MC, V.*

$$$$ ▦ **Kempinski Hotel Corvinus Budapest.** Madonna stayed here while
★ filming *Evita*, and so did Michael Jackson while shooting his "History" video on Heroes' Square. Rather cold and futuristic-looking on the outside, the hotel has rooms and suites that are spacious, with custom-made art deco fittings and furniture, as well as an emphasis on functional touches like three phones in every room. Large, sparkling bathrooms— most with tubs and separate shower stalls and stocked with every

toiletry—are the best in Budapest. Rates do not include VAT, tourist tax, or breakfast. ⊠ *District V, Erzsébet tér 7–8, H-1051,* ☎ *1/429–3777; 800/426–3135 in the U.S. and Canada;* FAX *1/429–4777,* WEB *www.kempinski-budapest.com. 342 rooms, 27 suites. 2 restaurants, in-room data ports, indoor pool, hair salon, health club, massage, bar, lobby lounge, pub, shops, dry cleaning, laundry service, business services, meeting rooms, travel services, parking (fee); no-smoking rooms. AE, DC, MC, V.*

$$$$ ⊞ **Le Méridien Budapest.** There could scarcely be more contrast between
★ the Le Méridien and its pointedly modern neighbor, the Kempinski. The rooms of this entirely renovated early 20th-century building are decorated in the French Empire style and are both comfortable and plush. Those on the higher floors are slightly smaller but come with an individual balcony. The elegant hotel restaurant is home to splendid afternoon teas prepared by pastry chef Alain Lagrange. Rates do not include VAT, tourist tax, or breakfast. ⊠ *District V, Erzsébet tér 9–10, H-1051,* ☎ *1/429–5500,* FAX *1/429–5555,* WEB *www.lemeridien-budapest.com. 218 rooms, 27 suites. Restaurant, café, cable TV, indoor pool, health club, bar, business services, meeting rooms. AE, DC, MC, V.*

$$$–$$$$ ⊞ **Danubius Hotel Gellért.** Budapest's most renowned hotel has a col-
★ orful past. Built between 1912 and 1918, the German Art Nouveau Jugendstil-style Gellért was favored by Otto von Hapsburg, son of the last emperor. The Gellért is undergoing an incremental overhaul, as bit by bit rooms are refurnished in the original Jugendstil style, with no end in sight. It is therefore a very good idea to inquire about completed rooms when you reserve. Weekend rates can be more friendly. All guests have free access to the monumental and ornate thermal baths. ⊠ *District XI, Gellért tér 1, H-1111,* ☎ *1/385–2200,* FAX *1/466–6631,* WEB *www.danubiusgroup.com/gellert. 220 rooms, 14 suites. 2 restaurants, café, room service, indoor pool, hair salon, spa, Turkish bath, bar, baby-sitting, dry-cleaning, laundry service, business services, meeting rooms, parking (fee); no-smoking rooms. AE, DC, MC, V. BP.*

$$$ ⊞ **Danubius Hotel Astoria.** Constructed as a hotel between 1912 and 1914, the Astoria has a fascinating and turbulent history. The first independent Hungarian government was formed here in 1918. On a darker note, Nazi high command used the Astoria more or less as its headquarters, as did the Soviet forces during the ill-fated revolution of 1956. For the present, rooms today at the Astoria are genteel, spacious, and comfortable, with renovations faithful to the original Empire-style decor. The Café Mirror, with its dripping chandeliers, is a wonderful place to relive the Mittel-European coffeehouse tradition. Rates do not include breakfast. ⊠ *District V, Kossuth Lajos u. 19–21, H-1053,* ☎ *1/317–3411,* FAX *1/318–6798,* WEB *www.danubiusgroup.com/astoria. 125 rooms, 5 suites. Restaurant, café, room service, in-room safes, minibars, cable TV, bar, nightclub, dry-cleaning, laundry service, baby-sitting, business services, meeting rooms, Internet, free parking; no-smoking rooms. AE, DC, MC, V.*

$$$ ⊞ **Danubius Thermal Hotel Helia.** A sleek Scandinavian design and less hectic location upriver from downtown make this spa hotel on the Danube a change of pace from its Pest peers. Rooms are reasonably spacious and also kitted out in the ubiquitous "Scandinavian" style popularized by IKEA. The spa facilities are the most spotlessly clean in Budapest, and an on-site medical clinic caters to English-speaking clients—including everything from electrotherapy to fitness tests. The staff is friendly and helpful, and most of the comfortable rooms have Danube views. All the room rates include use of the thermal bath and free parking. ⊠ *District XIII, Kárpát u. 62–64, H-1133,* ☎ *1/452–5800,* FAX *1/452–5801,* WEB *www.danubiusgroup.com/helia. 254 rooms, 8 suites. Restaurant, café, indoor pool, tennis court, hair salon, health* club, hot tub, massage, sauna, spa, steam room, Turkish bath, bar, business services, meeting rooms, free parking. AE, DC, MC, V. BP.

$$$ 🔝 **K+K Hotel Opera.** Location, location, location: the K+K Hotel Opera has it all, around the corner from Budapest's beautiful opera house and just far enough away from busy Andrássy utca to block out the noise of traffic. Sunflower-yellow walls and bamboo and wicker furniture give the rooms a cheerful aspect. A hearty breakfast buffet will set you up well for a day's sightseeing. ⊠ *District VI, Révay u. 24, H-1065,* ☎ *1/269—0222,* FAX *1/269—0230,* WEB *www.kkhotels.com. 90 rooms. Restaurant, cable TV, in-room data ports, in-room safes, minibars, gym, bar, laundry service, business services, concierge, meeting rooms, free parking. AE, DC, MC, V. BP.*

$$$ 🔝 **Park Hotel Flamenco.** This glass-and-concrete socialist-era leviathan looks out onto the supposedly bottomless Feneketlen Lake. Happily, once inside, you can almost forget the Stalinist architecture, due to the pleasant, contemporary furnishings. Service is thoroughly professional, and the terrace restaurant has nice views of the lake and park surrounding it. ⊠ *District XI, Tas Vezér u. 7, H-1113,* ☎ *1/372–2000,* FAX *1/365–8007,* WEB *www.danubiusgroup.com/flamenco. 350 rooms, 8 suites. 2 restaurants, indoor pool, hair salon, sauna, business services, laundry services, meeting rooms, travel services, parking (fee). AE, DC, MC, V.*

$$$ 🔝 **Radisson SAS Béke Hotel Budapest.** If you are arriving in Budapest's Nyugati Pal train station from Prague or Berlin, the Radisson could scarcely be better located, situated as it is on a bustling stretch of the Körút. Upon arrival at the Radisson, top-hat wearing bellmen will usher you through revolving doors into an impressive reception area, replete with sweeping marble staircase. The bland though comfortable and modern rooms are a faint disappointment after such grandeur, but snappy service and a great location compensate. Rates do not include VAT, tourist tax, or breakfast. ⊠ *District VI, Teréz krt. 43, H-1067,* ☎ *1/301–1600,* FAX *1/301–1615,* WEB *www.radisson.com. 238 rooms, 8 suites. 2 restaurants, café, in-room data ports, in-room safes, minibars, cable TV with movies, pool, hair salon, massage, sauna, 2 bars, baby-sitting, business services, meeting rooms, travel services, parking (fee); no-smoking rooms. AE, DC, MC, V.*

$$$ 🔝 **Sydney Apartment Hotel.** Most of the clientele here are business executives on longer-term stays in Budapest, but that shouldn't deter you from the home-away-from-home apartments and such amenities as self-catering kitchens and one of the nicest indoor pools in town. If it's room service you need, you might choose to give these 45- to 110-square-meter (484- to 1180-square ft) apartments a miss, though it should be noted that there is a very helpful 24-hour front-office service. Breakfast is an extra 2,700 Ft. ⊠ *District XIII, Hegedus Gyűla u. 52—54, H-1133,* ☎ *1/236–8888,* FAX *1/236–8899,* WEB *www.sydneyaparthotel.hu. 164 rooms, 10 suites. Kitchens, in-room data ports, indoor pool, gym, sauna, spa, meeting rooms, travel services, laundry facilities, free parking; no-smoking rooms. AE, DC, MC, V.*

$$ 🔝 **Carlton Hotel.** The Carlton is proof that you can stay in the Castle Hill district—even nestled at the foot of the hill itself—without paying a fortune. Rooms on the upper floors offer great Danube views. Both the reception area and the rooms are simply furnished and may even prove a little too stark for some tastes, but it's hard to do better for location and price. A large buffet breakfast is served every morning. ⊠ *District I, Apor Péter u. 3, H-1011,* ☎ *1/224–0999,* FAX *1/224–0990,* WEB *www.carltonhotel.hu. 95 rooms. Cable TV with movies, in-room data ports, in-room safes, minibars, bar, business services, meeting room, parking (fee); no-smoking rooms. AE, DC, MC, V. BP.*

$$ 🔝 **Mercure Hotel Budapest Nemzeti.** The egg-shell blue baroque facade of this turn-of-the-20th-century building is difficult to miss, even in this busy part of Pest. The high-ceiling lobby and public areas are festooned with pillars, arches, and wrought-iron railings. Rooms are comparatively plain but not unpleasant. Quadruple-glazed windows shield the front rooms from the noise of the busy intersection below. One should also be aware that this area can be a hangout for streetwalkers. ✉ *District XIII, József krt. 4, H-1088,* ☎ *1/303–9310,* FAX *1/314–0019,* ☎ FAX *1/303–9162,* WEB *www.mercure.com. 75 rooms, 1 suite. Restaurant, minibars, bar, meeting room, travel services. AE, DC, MC, V.*

$ 🏨 **Hotel Benczúr.** The leafy lanes of Budapest's embassy district are where you will find this quiet, simply furnished hotel. Majestic Heroes' Square is but a short walk away, and you can even travel back and forth to the center via the antique underground railway line, the Földalatti, by descending downstairs on Andrássy út to the well-signposted Hősök tere metro stop. Rooms come with modern phones and larger-than-usual bathrooms. The Benczúr shares the building with Hotel Pedagógus. ✉ *District VI, Benczúr u. 35, H-1068,* ☎ *1/342–7970,* FAX *1/342–1558,* WEB *www.hotelbenczur.hu. 93 rooms. Restaurant, minibars, massage, laundry service, meeting rooms, free parking; no-smoking rooms. MC, V. BP.*

$ 🏨 **Hotel Citadella.** The Citadella will appeal to the energetic, though its hilltop location can entail something of an upward hike after a day's sightseeing. This hotel and hostel combination is housed within a historical fort and does offer marvelous views from many of the room's small windows. None of the rooms has a bathtub, but half have showers. Continental breakfast is included in the rates. ✉ *District XI, Citadella sétány, Gellérthegy, H-1118,* ☎ *1/466–5794,* FAX *1/386–0505,* WEB *www.hotels.hu/hotelcitadella. 20 rooms, 10 with shared bath. Restaurant, shop, dance club, parking (fee). No credit cards. CP.*

$ 🏨 **Kulturinov.** This budget hotel can be found in rather noble quar-
★ ters, in this instance one wing of a magnificent 1902 neo-baroque castle. Rooms come with two or three beds and are clean and peaceful; they have showers but no tubs. The neighborhood—one of Budapest's most famous squares in the luxurious castle district—is magical. ✉ *District I, Szentháromság tér 6, H-1014,* ☎ *1/355–0122 or 1/375–1651,* FAX *1/375–1886. 16 rooms. Snack bar, refrigerators, library, meeting rooms. AE, DC, MC, V. BP.*

NIGHTLIFE AND THE ARTS

Nightlife

There is a mysterious quiet around the inner-city streets of Pest, even on some summer nights: mysterious because behind closed doors, on almost any night, you can indeed find hopping nightlife. For basic beer and wine drinking, *sörözős* and *borozós* (wine bars) abound, though it may help to master some basic Hungarian, as these places are unused to catering to tourists. The worst of them are little more than drunk tanks. For quiet conversation there are the so-called *drink-bárs* in most hotels and all over town, but some of these places tend to be a little seedy and will sometimes tack on a special foreigner surcharge.

Most nightspots and clubs have bars and dance floors, and some also have pool tables. Although some places do accept credit cards, it is still much more usual to pay in cash for your night on the town. As is the case in most other cities, the life of a club or disco in Budapest can be somewhat ephemeral. Those listed below are quite popular and seem to be here to stay. But for the very latest on the more transient "in" spots, consult the "Nightlife" section of the weekly *Budapest Sun* or *Budapest in Your Pocket,* published six times a year.

Budapest also has its share of seedy go-go clubs and "cabarets," some of which are known for scandalous billing and physical intimidation. Many a hapless single man has found himself having to pay an exorbitant drinks bill after accepting an invitation from a woman asking to join her for a drink. This scam is particularly prevalent on Váci utca. To avoid such rip-offs, at least make sure you don't order anything without first seeing the price.

Some of the most lively nightlife in Budapest hinges around the electronica scene; trance, techno, drum and bass, etc. Recreational drug use is fairly common, but travelers should be aware that penalties for possessing even small amounts of so-called soft drugs can be quite stiff.

A word of warning to the smoke-sensitive: although a 1999 law requiring smoke-free areas in many public establishments has already had a discernible impact in restaurants, the bar scene is a firm reminder that Budapest remains a city of smokers. No matter where you spend your night out, chances are you'll come home smelling of cigarette smoke.

Bars and Clubs

Angel Bar and Disco (⊠ District VII, Szövetség u. 33, ☏ 1/351–6490) is Budapest's busiest gay dance club, which attracts a mixed gay-straight crowd, who pack the floor to groove along to souped-up disco and happy house. It's closed Monday–Wednesday, and Saturday night is for men only. The biggest Irish pub in Central Europe, **Becketts** (⊠ District V, Bajcsy-Zsilinszky út 72, ☏ 1/311–1035) is a great place for a pub lunch, a quiet afternoon pint, or a rollicking good time in the evening as a band comes on and the place fills up. A gay-friendly crowd flocks to **Café Capella** (⊠ District V, Belgrád rakpart 23, ☏ 1/318–6231) for the frequent, glittery drag shows and club music until dawn. Of all the see-and-be-seen cafés in Budapest, **Cafe Vian** (⊠ District VI, Liszt Ferenc tér 9, ☏ 1/342–8991) is perhaps the most renowned, partly because of its unbeatable spot in "the tér"—Liszt Ferenc tér; it's a great place to while away the hours chatting and people-watching, either inside and surrounded by an ever-changing exhibit of modern art or outside in the summer under a canopy. Don't be put off by the surly bouncers; **Club Seven** (⊠ District VII, Akácfa 7, ☏ 1/478–9030) has more than one place to play, including an elegant cocktail bar separate from the main room, where an outgoing Hungarian crowd grooves to a mixture of live jazz, rock cover bands, and recorded dance music. Budapest has a truly glitzy international disco, **Dokk Backstage** (⊠ District III, Hajógyári sziget 122, ☏ 1/457–1023), which is great for people-watching, especially if you wish to observe the get-rich-quick set and their trophy girlfriends at play. Established Hungarian jazz headliners and young up-and-comers play Sunday–Tuesday in the popular though small stylishly brick-walled **Fat Mo's** (⊠ District V, Nyári Pál u. 11, ☏ 1/267–3199), which is open daily. Budapest finally has a cabaret that's just a little risqué without being overtly sleazy; it's **Moulin Rouge** (⊠ District VI, Nagymezö u. 17, ☏ 1/332–9000), where showgirls in sequins—and not much else—dance the can-can. **Oscar American Bar** (⊠ District I, Ostrom u. 14, ☏ 1/212–8017) attracts a mixed Hungarian and international crowd to venture over the Danube to perhaps Buda's most jumping neighborhood bar. Old-time Hollywood movie stills adorn its walls. One thing you can't fault **Old Man's Music Pub** (⊠ VII, Akácfa u. 13, ☏ 1/322–7645) for, and that's consistency; the place is packed even on a Monday, and in Hungary that means you'll be inhaling a fair bit of second-hand smoke. If that doesn't ruin your fun, enjoy the live bluesy rock, friendly chaos behind the bar, and a squeeze on the small dance floor. **Rigoletto** (⊠ District XIII, Visegrádi u. 9, ☏ 1/237–0666) packs them in weeknights as well as weekends, with a tempting two-for-the-price-of-one regular cocktail special. The music program is more varied—some nights live, mellow jazz; on weekends, commercial disco.

Casinos

Casinos all open daily 2 PM–4 or 5 AM. The centrally located and popular **Las Vegas Casino** (⊠ District V, Roosevelt tér 2, ☎ 1/317–6022) is in the Hyatt Regency hotel. In an 1879 building designed by prolific architect Miklós Ybl, who also designed the State Opera House, the **Várkert Casino** (⊠ District I, Miklós Ybl tér 9, ☎ 1/202–4244) is the most visually striking of the city's casinos.

The Arts

For the latest on arts events, consult the entertainment listings of the English-language press. Their entertainment calendars map out all that's happening in Budapest's arts and culture world—from thrash bands in wild clubs to performances at the Opera House. Hotels and tourist offices will provide you with a copy of the monthly publication *Programme,* which contains details of all cultural events.

Tickets

Tickets can be bought at the venues themselves, but many ticket offices sell them without an extra charge. Prices are still very low, so markups of even 30% shouldn't dent your wallet if you book through your hotel. Inquire at Tourinform if you're not sure where to go. Ticket availability depends on the performance and season—it's usually possible to get tickets a few days before a show, but performances by major international artists sell out early. Tickets to Budapest Festival Orchestra concerts and festival events also go particularly quickly.

Theater and opera tickets are sold at the **Central Theater Booking Office** (⊠ District VI, Andrássy út 18, ☎ 1/267–9737). For classical music concert, ballet, and opera tickets, as well as tickets for major pop and rock shows, go to the **National Philharmonic Ticket Office** (⊠ District V, Mérleg u. 10, ☎ 1/318–0281). You can also stop in at the office and browse through the scores of free programs and fliers and scan the walls coated with upcoming concert posters. **Music Mix Ticket Service** (⊠ District V, Váci utca 33, ☎ 1/317–7736) specializes in popular music but handles other genres as well.

Classical Music and Opera

The tiny recital room of the **Bartók Béla Emlékház** (Bartók Béla Memorial House; ⊠ District II, Csalán út 29, ☎ 1/394–4472) hosts intimate Friday-evening chamber music recitals by well-known ensembles from mid-March to June and September to mid-December. The **Budapest Kongresszusi Központ** (Budapest Convention Center; ⊠ District XII, Jagelló út 1–3, ☎ 1/209–1990) is the city's largest-capacity (but least atmospheric) classical concert venue and usually hosts the largest-selling events of the Spring Festival. The homely little sister of the Opera House, the **Erkel Színház** (Erkel Theater; ⊠ District VII, Köztársaság tér 30, ☎ 1/333–0540) is Budapest's other main opera and ballet venue. There are no regular performances in the summer, however. The **Liszt Ferenc Zeneakadémia** (Franz Liszt Academy of Music; ⊠ District VI, Liszt Ferenc tér 8, ☎ 1/342–0179), usually referred to as the Music Academy, is Budapest's premier classical concert venue, hosting orchestra and chamber music concerts in its splendid main hall. It's sometimes possible to grab a standing-room ticket just before a performance here. The glittering **Magyar Állami Operaház** (Hungarian State Opera House; ⊠ District VI, Andrássy út 22, ☎ 1/331–2550), Budapest's main venue for opera and classical ballet, presents an international repertoire of classical and modern works as well as such Hungarian favorites as Kodály's *Háry János*. Except during the one-week BudaFest international opera and ballet festival in mid-August, the Opera House is closed during the summer. Colorful operettas, such as those by Lehár and Kálmán, are staged at their main Budapest venue, the **Operetta Theater** (⊠ District VI, Nagymező u. 19, ☎ 1/353–2172). Classical concerts are held regularly at the **Pesti Vigadó** (Pest Concert Hall; ⊠ District V, Vigadó tér 2, ☎ 1/318–9167).

English-Language Movies
Many of the English-language movies that come to Budapest are subtitled in Hungarian rather than dubbed; this applies less so, however, to independent and art films, as well as—paradoxically—some of the major blockbusters and children's movies. Tickets are very inexpensive by Western standards (400 Ft.–700 Ft.). Consult the movie matrix in the *Budapest Sun* (WEB www.budapestsun.com) for a weekly list of what's showing. The centrally located multiplex **WestEnd Ster Century** (⊠ District VI, Váci út 1–3, ☎ 1/238–7222) usually has several mainstream movies playing.

Folk Dancing
Many of Budapest's district cultural centers regularly hold traditional regional folk-dancing evenings, or dance houses (*táncház*), often with general instruction at the beginning. These sessions provide a less touristy way to taste Hungarian culture.

Almássy téri Szabadidő központ (Almássy Square Recreation Center; ⊠ District VII, Almássy tér 6, ☎ 1/352–1572) holds numerous folk-dancing evenings, representing Hungarian as well as Greek and other ethnic cultures. Traditionally the wildest táncház is held Saturday night at the **Belvárosi Ifjúsági ház** (City Youth Center; ⊠ District V, Molnár u. 9, ☎ 1/317–5928), where the stomping and whirling go on way into the night; the center, like many such venues, closes from mid-July to mid-August. A well-known Transylvanian folk ensemble, Tatros, hosts a weekly dance house at the **Marczibányi téri Művelődési ház** (Marczibányi Square Cultural Center; ⊠ District II, Marczibányi tér 5/a, ☎ 1/212–5789), from 8 until midnight on Wednesday night.

Folklore Performances
The **Hungarian State Folk Ensemble** performs regularly at the **Budai Vigadó** (⊠ District I, Corvin tér 8, ☎ 1/201–3766); shows incorporate instrumental music, dancing, and singing. The **Folklór Centrum** (⊠ District XI, Fehérvári út 47, ☎ 1/203–3868) has been a major venue for folklore performances for more than 30 years. It hosts regular traditional folk concerts and dance performances from spring through fall. The **Várszinház** (National Dance Theater; ⊠ District I, Színház u. 19, ☎ 1/201–4407 or 1/356–4085) stages modern dance productions and is also a venue for performances by popular, local folk bands.

Theater
♻ The **Budapest Bábszínház** (Budapest Puppet Theater; ⊠ District VI, Andrássy út 69, ☎ 1/321–5200) produces colorful shows that both children and adults enjoy even if they don't understand Hungarian. Watch for showings of *Cinderella* (*Hamupipőke*) and *Snow White and the Seven Dwarfs* (*Hófehérke*), part of the theater's regular repertoire. The **Madách Theater** (⊠ District VII, Erzsébet krt. 31–33, ☎ 1/478–2041) produces colorful musicals in Hungarian, including a popular adaptation of *Cats*. For English-language dramas check out the **Merlin Theater** (⊠ District V, Gerlóczy u. 4, ☎ 1/317–9338). The **Thália Theater** (⊠ District VI, Nagymező u. 22–24, ☎ 1/331–0500) specializes in musicals. The sparkling **Vígszínház** (Comedy Theater; ⊠ District XIII,

Pannónia u. 1, ☎ 1/329–2340) hosts classical concerts and dance performances but is primarily a venue for musicals, such as the Hungarian adaptation of *West Side Story.*

OUTDOOR ACTIVITIES AND SPORTS

Bicycling

Because of constant thefts, bicycle rentals are difficult to find in Hungary. For more information on bicycle rental, try Tourinform. **Bringóhintó** (⊠ District VIII, Hajós Alfréd sétány 1, across from Thermal Hotel, ☎ 1/329–2072), a rental outfit on Margaret Island, offers popular four-wheel pedaled contraptions called *Bringóhintók,* as well as traditional two-wheelers; standard bikes cost about 800 Ft. per hour or 1,500 Ft. until 8 AM the next day, with a 10,000 Ft. deposit. For brochures and general information on bicycling conditions and suggested routes, contact the **Magyar Kerékpáros Túrázók Szövetsége** (Bicycle Touring Association of Hungary; ⊠ District V, Bajcsy-Zsilinszky út 31, 2nd floor, Apt. 3, ☎ 1/332–7177).

Golf

Golf is still a new sport in Hungary but one that is attracting a growing number of players. The golf course closest to Budapest is 35 km (22 mi) north of the city at the **Budapest Golfpark** (⊠ Kisoroszi, ☎ 1/317–6025, 1/317–2749, or 26/392–463). The park has an 18-hole, 72-par course and a driving range, with carts and equipment for rent; it is closed from mid-November to mid-March. Transport to the Budapest Golfpark and back can be arranged through the **Golf Country Service** (⊠ District V, Váci u. 19–21 [Millennium Center Passage], ☎ 1/318–8030).

Health and Fitness Clubs

Gold's Gym (⊠ District VIII, Szentkirályi u. 26, ☎ 1/267–4334) has good weight-training and cardiovascular equipment and hourly aerobics classes in larger-than-usual spaces. **Michelle's Health & Fitness** (⊠ District II, Rózsakert Shopping Center, Gábor Áron u. 74, ☎ 1/391–5808) is a popular and well-equipped fitness center in the Buda hills. The **World Class Fitness Centre** (⊠ District V, Marriott hotel, Apáczai Csere János u. 4, ☎ 1/266–4290) really does live up to its name, with a well-equipped gymnasium, regular aerobics classes, plus sauna and squash court.

Horseback Riding

Note that English saddle, not Western, is the standard in Hungary. Experienced riders can ride at the **Budapesti Lovas Klub** (Budapest Equestrian Club; ⊠ District VIII, Kerepesi út 7, ☎ FAX 1/313–5210) for about 1,500 Ft. per hour. Call about two weeks ahead to assure yourself a horse. In the verdant outskirts of Buda, the **Petneházy Lovas Centrum** (Petneházy Equestrian Center; ⊠ District II, Feketefej út 2, Adyliget, ☎ 1/397–5048) offers horseback-riding lessons and trail rides for 1,800 Ft.–2,500 Ft. per hour.

Jogging

The path around the perimeter of **Margaret Island,** as well as the numerous pathways in the center, is level and inviting for a good run. **Városliget** (City Park) in flat Pest has paths good for jogging.

Spas and Thermal Baths

Newer, modern baths are open to the public at hotels, such as the **Danubius Grand Hotel Margitsziget** and the **Danubius Thermal Hotel Helia.** They lack the charm of their older peers but provide the latest treatments.

Gellért Thermal Baths (⊠ District XI, Gellért tér 1, ☎ 1/466–5747) are the most famous in Budapest. The baths are open weekdays 6 AM–6 PM, weekends 6 AM–4 PM. Admission is 1,800 Ft. per day, 2,200 Ft. with a cabin. **Király Baths** (⊠ District II, Fő u. 84, ☏ 1/202–3688) are open weekdays 6:30 AM–6 PM, Saturday 6:30–noon. The baths are open to men on Monday, Wednesday, and Friday; to women on Tuesday, Thursday, and Saturday. These baths are very popular with the gay community. Admission is 500 Ft. The **Lukács Baths** (⊠ District II, Frankel Leó u. 25–29, ☏ 1/326–1695) were built in the 19th century but modeled on the Turkish originals and fed with waters from a source dating from the Bronze Age and Roman times. The complex is open Monday–Saturday 6 AM–7 PM, Sunday 6 AM–5 PM; the facilities are coed. Admission to the baths is 450 Ft. The **Rác Baths** (⊠ District I, Hadnagy u. 8–10, ☏ 1/356–1322) are among the oldest in Budapest. Admission is 700 Ft. They are open Monday–Saturday 6:30 AM–6 PM. Women can bathe on Monday, Wednesday, and Friday; men on Tuesday, Thursday, and Saturday. These baths are particularly popular with the gay community. The **Rudas Baths** (⊠ District I, Döbrentei tér 9, ☏ 1/201–1577) are open to men only and do not have a large gay following; a less interesting outer swimming pool is open to both sexes. Massages are available. Admission is 900 Ft. The baths are open weekdays 6 AM–6 PM, weekends 6–noon. **Széchenyi Baths** (⊠ Városliget, District XIV, Állatkerti krt. 11, ☏ 1/321–0310) are the largest medicinal bathing facility in Europe. Admission is 400 Ft., 700 Ft. for a cabin. The baths are open weekdays 6 AM–6 PM, weekends 6 AM–5 PM.

Tennis and Squash

There are some 30 tennis clubs in Budapest, and some hotels also hire courts out to nonguests. The **Hungarian Tennis Association** (⊠ District XIV, Dózsa György út 1–3, ☏ 1/252–6687) produces a yearbook with a complete list of the country clubs with courts. **On-line Squash Club** (⊠ Forrás u. 8, Budaörs, ☏ 23/501–2620), on the near outskirts of town, is a trendy full-facility fitness club with five squash courts. Hourly rates run 2,000 Ft.–2,800 Ft., depending on when you play. The club rents equipment and stays open until 11 PM on weekdays, 9 PM on weekends. **Városmajor Tennis Academy** (⊠ District VII, Városmajor u. 63–69, ☏ 1/202–5337) has five outdoor courts (clay and hexapet) available daily 7 AM–10 PM. They are lit for night play and covered by a tent in winter. Court fees run around 1,400 Ft. per hour in summer, 1,800 Ft.–3,000 Ft. in winter. Racket rentals and lessons are also offered. The **World Class Fitness Center** (⊠ District V, Marriott hotel, Apáczai Csere János u. 4, ☏ 1/266–4290) has one excellent squash court available for 2,500 Ft.–4,500 Ft. an hour, depending on when you play; be sure to reserve it a day or two in advance.

SHOPPING

Shopping Districts

You'll find plenty of expensive boutiques, folk-art and souvenir shops, foreign-language bookstores, and classical-record shops on or around touristy **Váci utca,** Budapest's famous, upscale pedestrian-only promenade in District V. While a stroll along Váci utca is integral to a Budapest visit, browsing among some of the smaller, less touristy, more typically Hungarian shops in Pest—on the **Kis körút** (Small Ring Road) and **Nagy körút** (Great Ring Road)—may prove more interesting and less pricey. Lots of arty boutiques are springing up in the section of District V **south of Ferenciek tere** and **toward the Danube,** and around **Kálvin tér. Falk Miksa utca,** also in District V, running south from Szent István körút, is one of the city's best antiques districts, lined on both sides with atmospheric little shops and galleries.

Department Stores and Malls

Proof perhaps of this region's emerging consumer class, Budapest in the last few years has seen a swag of new department stores opening and a shopping-mall building boom. **Duna Plaza** (⊠ District XIII, Váci út 178, ☏ 1/465–1666) has 170 shops, a bowling alley, a Greek taverna, and an ice-skating rink. A special shoppers' bus leaves every half hour from Keleti train station to the **Polus Centre** (⊠ District XV, Szentmihályi út 131, ☏ 1/415–2114). There's a huge Tesco, some Hungarian department stores, fast food restaurants, and a bowling alley. **Skála Metro** (⊠ District VI, Nyugati tér 1–2, ☏ 1/353–2222) is definitely not the newest, but it is centrally located above the Nyugati underground rail station. Central Europe's biggest mall, the **Westend City Center** (⊠ District VI, Váci út 1–3, ☏ 1/238–7777), sits behind the Nyugati (West) Railway Station and teems with activity day and night, staying open weekdays until 9.

Markets

For true bargains and possibly an adventure, make an early morning trip to the vast **Ecseri Piac** (⊠ District IX, Nagykőrösi út 156 [Bus 54 from Boráros tér], ☏ 1/282–9563), on the outskirts of the city. A colorful, chaotic market that shoppers have flocked to for decades, it is an arsenal of secondhand goods, where you can find everything from frayed Russian army fatigues to Herend and Zsolnay porcelain vases to antique silver chalices. Goods are sold at permanent tables set up in rows, from trunks of cars parked on the perimeter, and by lone, shady characters clutching just one or two items. As a foreigner, you may be overcharged, so prepare to haggle—it's part of the flea-market experience. Also, watch out for pickpockets. Ecseri is open weekdays 6 AM–1 PM, Saturday 8–3, but the best selection is on Saturday morning. A colorful outdoor flea market is held weekend mornings from 7 to 2 at **Petőfi Csarnok** (⊠ District XIV, Városliget, Zichy Mihály út 14, ☏ 1/251–7266). The quantity and selection are smaller than at Ecseri Piac, but it's a fun flea-market experience closer to the city center. Red-star medals, Russian military watches, and other memorabilia from Communist days are popular buys here. Although it's mostly a food market, you can get souvenirs and other trinkets upstairs at the **Vásárcsarnok** (⊠ District IX, Vámház krt. 1–3, ☏ 1/217–6067), which is open Monday 6 AM–5 PM, Tuesday–Friday 6 AM–6 PM, and Saturday 6 AM–2 PM.

Specialty Stores

Antiques

Falk Miksa utca, lined with antiques stores, is a delightful street for multiple-shop browsing. The shelves and tables at tiny **Anna Antikvitás** (⊠ District V, Falk Miksa u. 18–20, ☏ 1/302–5461) are stacked with exquisite antique textiles—from heavily embroidered wall hangings to dainty lace gloves. The store also carries assorted antique objets d'art. **BÁV Műtárgy** (⊠ District V, Ferenciek tere 12, ☏ 1/318–3381; District V, Kossuth Lajos u. 1–3, ☏ 1/318–6934; District V, Szent István krt. 3, ☏ 1/331–4534), the State Commission Trading House, has antiques of all shapes, sizes, kinds, and prices at its several branches around the city. Porcelain is the specialty at the branch on Kossuth Lajos utca, and paintings at the Szent István körút store.**Darius Antiques** (⊠ District V, Falk Miksa u. 24–26, ☏ 1/311–2603) specializes in Biedermeier furniture and the Viennese baroque style. If antique weapons are your interest, then **Móró Régiség** (⊠ District V, Szent István krt. 1, ☏ 1/312–7877), with its range of militaria and firearms, is definitely worth a stop. **Polgár Galéria és Aukciósház** (⊠ District V, Kossuth Lajos u. 3, ☎ 1/318–6954) sells everything from jewelry to furniture and also holds several auctions a year.**Style Antique** (⊠ District V, Király u. 25, ☎ 1/321–3473) deals in expertly restored antique pinewood furniture.

Art Galleries

Budapest has dozens of art galleries showing and selling old works as well as the very latest. **Budapest Galéria Kiállítóterme** (Budapest Exhibition Hall; ⊠ District III, Lajos u. 158, ☎ 1/388–6771) specializes in Hungarian contemporary paintings. In a Bauhaus-era building is the **Fészek Galéria** (⊠ District VII, Kertész u. 36, ☎ 1/342–6548), which displays works by up-and-coming Hungarian artists and hosts concerts and theater performances in its often smoke-filled club room. New York celebrity Yoko Ono opened **Gallery 56** (⊠ District V, Falk Miksa u. 7, ☎ 1/269–2529) to show art by internationally known artists, such as Keith Haring, as well as works by up-and-coming Hungarian artists.

Books

You'll encounter book-selling stands throughout the streets and metro stations of the city, many of which sell English-language souvenir picture books at discount prices. **Váci utca** is lined with bookstores that sell glossy coffee-table books about Budapest and Hungary. Whet your appetite for further travels at **Bamako** (⊠ District VI, Andrássy út 1), Budapest's best source for English-language travel guides. **Bestsellers** (⊠ District V, Október 6 u. 11, ☎ 1/312–1295) sells almost entirely English-language books and publications, including Hungarian classics translated into English, popular British and American best-sellers, and newspapers and magazines. The **Central European University Bookshop** (⊠ District V, Nádor u. 9, ☎ 1/327–3096), in the Central European University, should be your first stop for books concerned with Central European politics and history. **Király Books** ⊠ District I, Fö u. 79, ☎ 1/214–0972) has two floors of books in English and French. **Párisi Udvar Könyvesbolt** (⊠ District V, Petőfi Sándor u. 2, ☎ 1/235–0380) specializes in foreign-language books, especially travel-related. You will find the store inside the arcade.

China, Crystal, and Porcelain

Hungary is famous for its age-old Herend porcelain, which is hand-painted in the village of Herend near Lake Balaton. High-quality Hungarian and Czech crystal is considerably less expensive here than in the United States. Crystal and porcelain dealers also sell their wares at the Ecseri Piac flea market, often at discount prices, but those looking for authentic Herend and Zsolnay should beware of imitations.

Goda Kristály (⊠ District V, Váci u. 9, ☎ 1/318–4630) has beautiful colored and clear pieces. **Haas & Czjzek** (⊠ District VI, Bajcsy-Zsilinszky út 23, ☎ 1/311–4094) has been in the business for more than 100 years, selling porcelain, glass, and ceramic pieces in traditional and contemporary styles. The brand's largest Budapest store, **Herendi Porcelain Shop** (⊠ District V, József Nádor tér 11, ☎ 1/317–2622), sells the delicate (and pricey) pieces, from figurines to dinner sets. For the Herend name and quality without the steep price tag, visit **Herend Village Pottery** (⊠ District II, Bem rakpart 37, ☎ 1/356–7899), where you can choose from Herend's practical line of durable ceramic cups, dishes, and table settings. Crystal, porcelain, and jewelry are all available at **Monarch Porcelain** (⊠ District V, Váci u. 42, ☎ 1/318–1117), in a large exhibition area. Shipping or free hotel delivery can be arranged. Hungary's exquisite Zsolnay porcelain, created and hand-painted in Pécs, is sold at the **Zsolnay Porcelain Shop** (⊠ District V, Kígyó u. 4, ☎ 1/318–3712) and a few other locations.

Clothing

Budapest is not Milan, though many of the big European and American brand names are represented in shopping centers like the Westend City Center. **Manier** (⊠ District V, Váci u. 48 [entrance at Nyári Pál u. 4], ☎ 1/318–1812) is a popular haute couture salon run by talented Hungarian designer Anikó Németh offering women's pieces ranging from quirky to totally outrageous. The store's second branch is across the street at Váci utca 53. Hungarian haute couture is represented by **Monarchia** (⊠ District V, Szabad sajtó út 6, ☎ 1/318–3146), even on Saturday mornings. **Orlando** (⊠ District VI, Rózsa u. 55, ☎ 341–4795), showcases fashions by four young Hungarian designers, both off-the-rack and tailor-made. A reputable men's bespoke suit service resides at **Taylor & Schneider** (⊠ District VI, Nagymezö u. 31, ☎ 312–0842), but you had best bring a translator to specify what you want.

Folk Art

Handmade articles, such as embroidered tablecloths and painted plates, are sold all over the city by Transylvanian women wearing traditional scarves and colorful skirts. You can usually find them standing at **Moszkva tér, Jászai Mari tér,** outside the **Kossuth tér** metro, around **Váci utca,** and in the larger metro stations. **Holló Műhely** (⊠ District V, Vitkovics Mihály u. 12, ☎ 1/317–8103) sells the work of László Holló, a master wood craftsman who has resurrected traditional motifs and styles of earlier centuries. There are lovely hope chests, chairs, jewelry boxes, candlesticks, and more, all hand-carved and hand-painted with cheery folk motifs—a predominance of birds and flowers in reds, blues, and greens.

Home Decor and Gifts

Impresszió (⊠ District V, Károly krt. 10, ☎ 1/337–2772) is a little boutique packed with home furnishings, baskets, picture frames, and decorative packaging, all made of natural materials and reasonably priced. The courtyard it calls home includes similar shops and a pleasant café. A few blocks away, just down the street from the Holló Műhely, lies the **Interieur Stúdió** (⊠ District V, Vitkovics Mihály u. 6, ☎ 1/266–1666), offering wooden brushes, bookmarks, and even a birdcage; candles of all shapes and sizes; and sundry other objects for the home.

Music

Recordings of Hungarian folk music or of pieces played by Hungarian artists are widely available on compact discs, though cassettes and records are much cheaper and are sold throughout the city. CDs are normally quite expensive—about 4,000 Ft.

FOTEX Records (⊠ District V, Szervita tér 2, ☎ 1/318–3395; District V, Váci u. 13, ☎ 1/318–3128; District VI, Teréz krt. 27, ☎ 1/332–7175; District XII, Alkotás út 11, ☎ 1/355–6886) is a flashy, western-style music store with a cross section of musical types but focused on contemporary pop. **MCD Amadeus** (⊠ District V, Szende Pál u. 1, ☎ 1/318–6691), just off the Duna korzó, has an extensive selection of classical CDs. **MCD Zeneszalon** (⊠ District V, Vörösmarty tér 1, ☎ no phone) has a large selection of all types of music and is centrally located. Its separate, extensive section on Hungarian artists is great for gift- or souvenir-browsing. The **Rózsavölgyi Zenebolt** (⊠ District V, Szervita tér 5, ☎ 1/318–3500) is an old, established music store crowded with sheet music and largely classical recordings but with other selections as well.

Toys

For a step back into the world before Pokémon cards and action figures, stop in at the tiny **Játékszerek Anno** (Toys Anno; ⊠ District VI, Teréz krt. 54, ☎ 1/302–6234) store, where fabulous repros of antique

European toys are sold. From simple paper puzzles to lovely stone building blocks to the 1940s wind-up metal monkeys on bicycles, these "nostalgia toys" are beautifully simple and exceptionally clever. Even if you're not a collector, it's worth a stop just to browse.

Wine

The burgeoning awareness of Hungary's wine culture has seen a number of upmarket wine stores specializing in Hungarian wines. A good place to start looking for Hungarian wines is **Budapest Bortársaság** (Budapest Wine Society; ⊠ District I, Batthyány u. 59, ☎ 1/212–2569 or 1/212–0262, ℻ 1/212–5285); the cellar shop at the base of Castle Hill always has an excellent selection of Hungarian wines. In Pest, **In Vino Veritas** (⊠ District VII, Dohány u. 58–62, ☎ 1/341–3174 or 1/341–0646, ℻ 1/321–1953) is a well-stocked store. **Monarchia Wine Shop** (⊠ District IX, Kinizsi u. 30–36, ☎ 1/456–9898) stocks well-presented selections of Hungarian and international wines and is open until 6 PM on Saturday.

SIDE TRIP TO LAKE BALATON

Lake Balaton, the largest lake in Central Europe, stretches 80 km (50 mi) across Hungary. Its vast surface area contrasts dramatically with its modest depths: only 9¾ ft at the center and just 52½ ft at its deepest point, at the Tihany Félsziget (Tihany Peninsula). The Balaton—the most popular playground of this landlocked nation—lies just 90 km (56 mi) to the southwest of Budapest, so it's within easy reach of the capital by car, train, bus, and even bicycle. On a hot day in July or August, it seems the entire country and half of Germany are packed towel to towel on the lake's grassy public beaches, paddling about in the warm water and consuming fried meats and beer at the omnipresent snack bars.

On the lake's hilly northern shore, ideal for growing grapes, is Balatonfüred, Hungary's oldest spa town, famed for natural springs that bubble out curative waters. The national park on the Tihany Peninsula lies just to the south, and regular boat service links Tihany and Balatonfüred with Siófok on the southern shore. Flatter and more crowded with resorts, cottages, and trade-union rest houses, the southern shore (beginning with Balatonszentgyörgy) has fewer sights and is not as attractive as the northern one: north-shore locals say the only redeeming quality of the southern shore is its views back across the lake to the north. Families with small children prefer the southern shore for its shallower, warmer waters—you can walk for almost 2 km (1 mi) before it deepens. The water warms up to 25°C (77°F) in summer.

Every town along both shores has at least one *strand* (beach). The typical Balaton strand is a complex of blocky wooden changing cabanas and snack bars, fronted by a grassy flat stretch along the water for sitting and sunbathing. Most have paddleboat and other simple boat rentals. A small entrance fee is usually charged.

If you're interested in exploring beyond the beach you can set out by car, bicycle, or foot, on beautiful village-to-village tours—stopping to view lovely old baroque churches, photograph a stork family perched high in its chimney-top nest, or climb a vineyard-covered hill for sweeping vistas. Since most vacationers keep close to the shore, a small amount of exploring into the roads and countryside heading away from the lake will reward you with a break from the summer crowds.

Numbers in the margin correspond to numbers on the Lake Balaton map.

Veszprém

❶ *116 km (72 mi) southwest of Budapest.*

Hilly Veszprém is the center of cultural life in the Balaton region.
★ **Várhegy** (Castle Hill) is the most picturesque part of town, north of
Szabadság tér. **Hősök kapuja** (Heroes' Gate), at the entrance to the castle, houses a small exhibit on Hungary's history. Just past the gate and
down a little alley to the left is the **Tűztorony** (Fire Tower); note that
the lower level is medieval, while the upper stories are baroque. There
is a good view of the town and surrounding area from the balcony.
Tower: ☎ *88/425–204.* ◙ *150 Ft.* ☉ *Apr.–mid-Oct., daily 10–6.*

Vár utca, the only street in the castle area, leads to a small square in
front of the **Bishop's Palace** and the **cathedral**; outdoor concerts are
held here in the summer. Vár utca continues past the square up to a
terrace erected on the north staircase of the castle. Stand beside the modern statues of St. Stephen and his queen, Gizella, for a far-reaching view
of the old quarter of town.

OFF THE   **HEREND** – This is the home of Hungary's renowned hand-painted porce-
BEATEN PATH   lain. The factory here, founded in 1839, displays many valuable pieces
in its **Herend Porcelán Művészeti Múzeum** (Herend Museum of Porcelain
Arts). You can also tour the factory itself. In the adjoining Apicius Restaurant, you can even dine off their collection of porcelain, worth several
million forint. Herend lies 16 km (10 mi) northwest of Veszprém on Road
8. ✉ *Kossuth Lajos u. 144,* ☎ *88/261–518,* ⅦⒺⒷ *www.herend.com.* ◙
Factory and museum 1,000 Ft., museum only, 300 Ft. ☉ *Apr.–Oct.,
daily 9–5:30; Nov.–Mar., Mon.–Sat. 9–4:30.*

Dining and Lodging

$ ✕ **Szürkebarát Borozó.** The plain off-white walls of the Gray Monk
Tavern may be less than inspiring, but the hearty Hungarian fare at
this cellar restaurant in the city center more than compensates. For an
unusual (but very Hungarian) appetizer, try the paprika-spiced *velős
pirítós* (marrow on toast; missing from the English menu and sometimes unavailable); or for a main course, gnaw away at "Ms. Baker's
pork hoofs." ✉ *Szabadság tér 12,* ☎ *88/327–684. No credit cards.*

$$ ☷ **Éllő Panzió.** In this 18-room pension just southwest of the town cen-
ter, you'll find ubiquitous golden lamp shades coupled with no lack of
red—on the carpeting, the velvety chairs, and the curtains. Rooms in
the newer annex building are more spacious than those in the chalet-
like main house. Service is friendly. ✉ *József Attila u. 25, H-8200,* ☎
88/420–097 or 88/424–118, ⒻⒶⓍ *88/329–711,* ⅦⒺⒷ *www.hotels.hu/ello.
18 rooms. Breakfast room. DC, MC, V.*

Balatonfüred

❷ *18 km (11 mi) south of Veszprém, 115 km (71 mi) southwest of Buda-
pest.*

Fed by 11 medicinal springs, Balatonfüred first gained popularity as
a health resort (the lake's oldest) where ailing people with heart con-
ditions and fatigue would come to take or, more accurately, to drink
a cure. The waters, said to have stimulating and beneficial effects on
the heart and nerves, are still an integral part of the town's identity
and consumed voraciously, but only the internationally renowned car-
diac hospital has actual bathing facilities. Today Balatonfüred, also
known simply as Füred, is probably the Balaton's most popular des-
tination, with every amenity to match. Above its busy boat landing,
beaches, and promenade lined with great plane and poplar trees, the

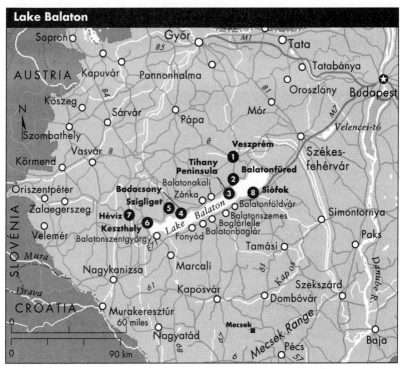

Lake Balaton

twisting streets of the Old Town climb hillsides thickly planted with vines. The climate and landscape also make this one of the best wine-growing districts in Hungary. Every year in July, the most elaborate of Lake Balaton's debutante cotillions, the Anna Ball, is held here.

The center of town is **Gyógy tér** (Spa Square), where the bubbling waters from five volcanic springs rise beneath a slim, colonnaded pavilion. In the square's centerpiece, the neoclassical **Well House** of the Kossuth Spring, you can sample the water, which has a pleasant, surprisingly refreshing taste despite the sulfurous aroma; for those who can't get enough, a 30-liter-per-person limit is posted. All the buildings on the square are pillared like Greek temples. At No. 3 is the **Horváth Ház** (Horváth House), where the Szentgyörgyi-Horváth family arranged the first of what was to become the Anna Ball in 1825 in honor of their daughter Anna.

The Anna Ball now takes place every July in another colonnaded building on the square, the **former Trade Unions' Sanatorium** (1802). Under its arcades is the **Balatoni Pantheon** (Balaton Pantheon): aesthetically interesting tablets and reliefs honoring Hungarian and foreign notables who either worked for Lake Balaton or spread the word about it. Among them is Jaroslav Hašek, the Czech author of the *Good Soldier Schweik,* who also wrote tales about Balaton.

On the eastern side of the square is the **Állami Kórház** (State Hospital), where hundreds of patients from all over the world are treated. Here, too, Rabindranath Tagore, the Indian author and Nobel Prize winner, recovered from a heart attack in 1926. The tree that he planted to commemorate his stay stands in a little grove at the western end of the paths leading from the square down to the lakeside. Tagore also wrote a poem for the planting, which is memorialized beneath the tree on a strikingly animated bust of Tagore: WHEN I AM NO LONGER ON EARTH, MY TREE,/LET THE EVER-RENEWED LEAVES OF THY SPRING/MURMUR TO THE

WAYFARER:/THE POET DID LOVE WHILE HE LIVED. In the same grove are trees honoring visits by another Nobel laureate, the Italian poet Salvatore Quasimodo, in 1961, and Indian prime minister Indira Gandhi, in 1972. An adjoining grove honors Soviet cosmonauts and their Hungarian partner-in-space, Bertalan Farkas.

Trees, restaurants, and shops line the **Tagore sétány** (Tagore Promenade), which begins near the boat landing and runs for nearly a kilometer (almost ½ mi).

A stroll up **Blaha Lujza utca** from Gyógy tér will take you past several landmarks, such as the **Blaha Lujza Ház** (Lujza Blaha House), a neoclassical villa built in 1867 and, later, the summer home of this famous turn-of-the-20th-century actress, humanist, and singer (today it's a hotel). The sweet little **Kerek templom** (Round Church), consecrated in 1846, was built in a classical style and has a truly rounded interior.

NEED A BREAK?
The plush **Kedves Café** (⊠ Blaha Lujza u. 7, ☎ 87/343–229), built in 1795, was once the favorite summer haunt of well-known Hungarian writers and artists. Now more touristy than literary, it is still one of Lake Balaton's most popular and famous pastry shops.

Dining and Lodging

$$–$$$ ✕ **Baricska Csárda.** This rambling reed-thatched inn has wood-beamed
★ rooms, vaulted cellars, terraces, and views of both vineyards and the lake. The food is hearty yet ambitious: roasted trout, fish paprikás with gnocchi to soak up the creamy sauce, and delicious desserts mixing pumpkin and poppy seeds. In summer, Gypsy wedding shows are held nightly under the grape arbors. ⊠ *Baricska dülő off Rte. 71 (Széchenyi út) behind Shell station,* ☎ *87/343–105. Reservations essential. AE, DC, MC, V. Closed Nov.–mid-Mar.*

$$–$$$ ✕ **Tölgyfa Csárda.** Perched high on a hilltop, the Oak Tree Tavern has breathtaking views over the steeples and rooftops of Balatonfüred and the Tihany Peninsula. The dining room and menu are worthy of a first-class Budapest restaurant, and nightly live Gypsy music keeps things festive. ⊠ *Meleghegy (up the hill at the end of Csárda u.),* ☎ *87/343–036. No credit cards. Closed late Nov.–Apr.*

$$$$ 🕮 **Annabella.** The cool, spacious guest quarters in this large, Miami-
★ style high-rise are especially pleasant in summer heat. The resort overlooks the lake and Tagore Promenade and has access to excellent swimming and water-sports facilities. All rooms have balconies; for the best views, request a room on a high floor with a view of the Tihany Peninsula. ⊠ *Deák Ferenc u. 25, H-8231,* ☎ *87/342–222,* 𝐅𝐀𝐗 *87/483–029,* 𝐖𝐄𝐁 *www.danubiusgroup.com. 383 rooms, 5 suites. Restaurant, café, indoor pool, pool, hair salon, massage, sauna, bicycles, bar, nightclub, baby-sitting, laundry service, travel services. AE, DC, MC, V. Closed late Oct.–mid-Apr.*

$$$$ 🕮 **Marina.** A central beachfront location is the Marina's main draw. Rooms in the homey 12-story building range from snug to small; suites have balconies but suffer from tiny bathrooms and dark bedrooms. Your safest bet is to get a high-floor "Superior" room with a lake view. Or better yet, stay in the "Lido" wing, which opens directly onto the water and where rooms (suites only) get plenty of sun. ⊠ *Széchenyi út 26, H-8230,* ☎ *87/343–460,* 𝐅𝐀𝐗 *87/343–052,* 𝐖𝐄𝐁 *www.danubiusgroup.com. 349 rooms, 34 suites, 34 apartments. Restaurant, indoor pool, hair salon, massage, sauna, beach, boating, bowling, bar, pub, nightclub, laundry service, travel services. AE, DC, MC, V. Closed Oct.–late Apr.*

$$ 🕮 **Park.** Hidden on a side street in town but close to the lakeshore, the Park is noticeably calmer than Füred's bustling main hotels. Rooms are large and bright, with high ceilings and tall windows. Suites have

large, breezy balconies but small bathrooms. ✉ *Jókai u. 24, H-8230,* ☎ ᶠᴬˣ *87/343–203 or 87/342–005. 27 rooms, 5 suites. Restaurant, gym, sauna, bar, meeting room, free parking. No credit cards.*

$ 🔢 **Blaha Lujza Ház.** Hungary's fin-de-siècle songbird and actress Lujza Blaha spent her summers at this neoclassical villa, which has been converted into a hotel. The rooms are a bit cramped—there's not much room to negotiate your way around the bed sometimes. But the front-desk staff is helpful, and the breakfast room, which functions as a restaurant on summer evenings, is a pleasant place to begin the day with a buffet or cooked breakfast. ✉ *Blaha u. 4, H-8230,* ☎ *87/581–210,* ᶠᴬˣ *87/581–219. 22 rooms. Restaurant, gym, bar, free parking; no-smoking rooms. No credit cards.*

Outdoor Activities and Sports

BEACHES

Most hotels have their own private beaches, with water-sports facilities and equipment or special access to these nearby. Besides these, Balatonfüred has three public beaches, where you can rent sailboards, paddleboats, and other water toys; these are also available at Hungary's largest campground, **Füred Camping** (✉ Széchenyi u. 24, next to the Marina hotel, ☎ 87/343–823). Although motorboats are banned from the lake, if you're desperate to water-ski you can try the campground's electric water-ski machine, which tows enthusiasts around a 1-km (½-mi) circle. A two-tow ticket runs around 900 Ft.

BICYCLING

In season you can rent bicycles from temporary, private outfits set up in central locations around town and near the beaches; one is usually working at the entrance to Füred Camping (✉ Széchenyi u. 24, next to the Marina hotel). Inquire at the tourist office for other current locations. Average prices for mountain-bike rentals are 1,000 Ft. per hour or 3,500 Ft. per day. You can also usually rent mopeds in front of the Halászkert restaurant (✉ Széchenyi út 2) for around 1,300 Ft. per hour and 5,000 Ft. per day.

HORSEBACK RIDING

Trail rides and horseback-riding lessons are available from mid-May to the end of September for about 2,500 Ft. an hour at the **Diana Lovasudvar** (Diana Riding Center; ✉ Rte. 71 just southwest of the town center; turn right at the sign about 100 yards beyond the giant campground on the lake, ☎ 87/481–894).

Tihany and the Tihany Félsziget (Tihany Peninsula)

❸ *11 km (7 mi) southwest of Balatonfüred.*

The famed town of Tihany, with its twisting, narrow cobblestone streets and hilltop abbey, is on the Tihany Félsziget (Tihany Peninsula), joined to the mainland by a narrow neck and jutting 5 km (3 mi) into the lake. Only 12 square km (less than 5 square mi), the peninsula is not only a major tourist resort but perhaps the most historic part of the Balaton area. In 1952 the entire peninsula was declared a national park, and because of its geological rarities, it became Hungary's first nature-conservation zone. On it are more than 110 geyser craters, remains of former hot springs, reminiscent of those found in Iceland, Siberia, and Wyoming's Yellowstone Park.

The smooth Belső Tó (Inner Lake), 82 ft higher than Lake Balaton, is one of the peninsula's own two lakes; around it are barren yellowish-white rocks and volcanic cones rising against the sky. Though the hills surrounding the lake are known for their white wines, this area produces a notable Hungarian red, Tihany cabernet.

★ On a hilltop overlooking the old town is the **Bencés Apátság** (Benedictine Abbey), with foundations laid by King András I in 1055. Parts of the abbey were rebuilt in baroque style between 1719 and 1784. The abbey's charter—containing some 100 Hungarian words in its Latin text, making it the oldest written source of the Hungarian language—is kept in Pannonhalma, but a replica is on display in the abbey's 11th-century crypt. The contrast between the simple crypt, where a small black crucifix hangs over the tomb of King András, and the abbey's lavish baroque interior—all gold, gilted silver, and salmon—could scarcely be more marked. The altar, abbot's throne, choir parapet, organ case, and pulpit were all the work of Sebestyén Stuhloff. Local tradition says he immortalized the features of his doomed sweetheart in the face of the angel kneeling on the right-hand side of the altar to the Virgin Mary. A magnificent baroque organ, adorned by stucco cherubs, can be heard during evening concerts in summer.

In a baroque house adjoining and entered through the abbey is the **Bencés Apátsági Múzeum** (Benedictine Abbey Museum). The best exhibits are in the basement lapidarium: relics from Roman colonization, including mosaic floors; a relief of David from the 2nd or 3rd century; and 1,200-year-old carved stones—all labeled in English as well as Hungarian. Three of the upstairs rooms were lived in for five days in 1921 by the last emperor of the dissolved Austro-Hungarian monarchy, Karl IV, in a futile foray to regain the throne of Hungary. Banished to Madeira, he died of pneumonia there a year later. The rooms are preserved with nostalgic relish for Emperor Franz Joseph's doomed successor. ⊠ *Első András tér 1,* ☎ *87/448–405 abbey; 87/448–650 museum.* ▣ *250 Ft.* ☉ *May–Sept., Mon.–Sat. 9–5:30, Sun. 11–5:30; Apr. and Oct., Mon.–Sat. 10–4:30, Sun. 11–4:30; Nov.–Mar. (church and lapidarium only), Mon.–Sat. 11–4.*

The **Szabadtéri Múzeum** (Open-air Museum), Tihany's outdoor museum of ethnography, assembles a group of old structures, including a potter's shed, complete with a local artist-in-residence. Also here is the former house of the Fishermen's Guild, with an ancient boat—used until 1934—parked inside. ⊠ *Along Batthyány u. and neighboring streets,* ☎ *no phone.* ☉ *May–Sept., Tues.–Sun. 10–6.*

It's said that from **Visszhang domb** (Echo Hill), just a brief stroll from the Benedictine Abbey, as many as 16 syllables can be bounced off the abbey wall. With noise from builders and traffic, these days you may have to settle for a two-second echo. The hill is at the end of Piski István sétány.

NEED A BREAK?   You can practice projecting from the terraces of the **Echo Restaurant** (⊠ Visszhang út 23, ☎ 87/448–460), an inn atop Echo Hill. While you're at it, try some fogas, carp, and catfish specialties.

Dining and Lodging

$–$$ ✕ **Halásztanya.** Views of the inner lake and local fish specialties—such as fogas fillets with garlic—contribute to this restaurant's popularity. ⊠ *Visszhang u. 11,* ☎ *87/448–771. Reservations not accepted. AE, MC, V. Closed Nov.–Easter.*

$–$$ ✕ **Pál Csárda.** Two thatch cottages house this simple restaurant, where cold fruit soup and fish stew are the specialties. You can eat in the garden, which is decorated with gourds and strands of dried peppers. ⊠ *Visszhang u. 19,* ☎ *87/448–605. Reservations not accepted. AE, MC, V. Closed Oct.–Apr.*

$$$$ ▥ **Club Tihany.** Picture Club Med transposed to late-1980s Central Europe, and you'll have some idea of what to expect at Club Tihany. This

32-acre lakeside holiday village stays busy year-round. Accommodations include standard hotel rooms and 160 bungalows, all with kitchen facilities. The list of activities is impressive—from fishing to thermal bathing at the spa. In summer, when the hotel is filled to capacity, the scramble for the breakfast buffet can be a little unnerving. ⊠ *Rév u. 3, H-8237,* ☎ *87/448–088 or 87/538–500,* 𝐅𝐀𝐗 *87/448–083,* 𝐖𝐄𝐁 *www. clubtihany.hu. 330 rooms, 161 bungalows. 3 restaurants, kitchens, tennis court, pool, gym, hair salon, spa, tennis, beach, fishing, 2 bars, wine bar, meeting rooms. AE, DC, MC, V.*

$$$–$$$$
★
🏨 **Kastély Hotel.** Lush landscaped lawns surround this stately neo-baroque mansion on the water's edge, built in the 1920s for Archduke József Hapsburg and taken over by the Communist state in the '40s (it is still owned by the government). Inside, it's all understated elegance; rooms have soaring ceilings and crisp sheets. Rooms with lake-facing windows and/or balconies (slightly more expensive) are the best. Next door, a newer, uninviting concrete building houses the Kastély's sister, the Park Hotel, with 44 less expensive, though dated, rooms. ⊠ *Fürdő telepi út 1, H-8237,* ☎ *87/448–611,* 𝐅𝐀𝐗 *87/448–409,* 𝐖𝐄𝐁 *www.hotelfured.hu. 25 rooms, 1 suite. Restaurant, café, miniature golf, 2 tennis courts, sauna, beach, bar. AE, DC, MC, V. Closed mid-Oct.–mid-Apr.*

Nightlife and the Arts

Well-known musicians perform on the Benedictine Abbey's magnificent organ during the popular summer **organ-concert series,** which runs from July to August 20. Concerts are generally held weekends at 8:30 PM. Contact the abbey (☎ 87/448–405) for information and tickets.

Outdoor Activities and Sports

FISHING

Belső-tó (Inner Lake) is a popular angling spot in which you can try your luck at hooking ponty, catfish, and other local fish. Fishing permits can be bought on site at the fishing warden's office (☎ 87/448–082), on the premises of the Horgásztanya restaurant, on the southwest side of the lake.

HIKING

Footpaths crisscross the entire peninsula, allowing you to climb the small hills on its west side for splendid views of the area or hike down Belső-tó (Inner Lake). If in midsummer you climb the area's highest hill, the **Csúcshegy** (761 ft—approximately a two-hour hike), you'll find the land below carpeted with purple lavender. Introduced from France into Hungary, lavender thrives on the lime-rich soil and strong sunshine of Tihany. The State Lavender and Medicinal Herb Farm here supplies the Hungarian pharmaceutical and cosmetics industries.

En Route
The miniature town of Örvényes, about 7 km (4½ mi) west of Tihany, has the only working *vízi malom* (water mill) in the Balaton region. Built in the 18th century, it still grinds grain into flour while also serving as a tiny museum. In the miller's room is a collection of folk art, wood carvings, pottery, furniture, and pipes. On a nearby hill stand the ruins of a **Romanesque church**; only its chancel has survived. On Templom utca, a few steps from the bridge, is the baroque **St. Imre templom** (St. Imre Church), built in the late 18th century. *Water mill:* ⊠ *Szent Imre u. 1,* ☎ *87/449–360.* 🎫 *100 Ft.* ☉ *May–Sept., Tues.–Sun. 9–4.*

Balatonudvari, another kilometer (½ mi) west of Örvényes, is a pleasant beach resort famous for its cemetery, which was declared a national shrine because of its beautiful, unique heart-shape tombstones carved from white limestone at the turn of the 18th century. The cemetery is essentially on the highway, at the eastern end of town; it is easily visible from the road. Balatonudvari's beach itself is at **Kiliántelep,** 2 km (1 mi) to the west.

Badacsony

★ ❹ *41 km (25 mi) southwest of Tihany.*

One of the northern shore's most treasured images is the slopes of Mt. Badacsony (1,437 ft high), simply called the Badacsony, rising from the lake. The mysterious, coffinlike basalt peak of the Balaton Highlands is actually an extinct volcano flanked by smaller cone-shape hills. The masses of lava that coagulated here created bizarre and beautiful rock formations. At the upper edge, salt columns tower 180 to 200 ft like organ pipes in a huge semicircle. In 1965 Hungarian conservationists won a major victory that ended the quarrying of basalt from Mt. Badacsony, which is now a protected nature-preservation area.

The land below has been tilled painfully and lovingly for centuries. There are vineyards everywhere and splendid wine in every inn and tavern. In descending order of dryness, the best-loved Badacsony white wines are Rizlingszilváni, Kéknyelű, and Szürkebarát. Their proud producers claim that "no vine will produce good wine unless it can see its own reflection in the Balaton." They believe it is not enough for the sun simply to shine on a vine; the undersides of the leaves also need light, which is reflected from the lake's mirrorlike surface. Others claim the wine draws its strength from the fire of old volcanoes.

Many restaurants and inns have their own wine tastings, as do the numerous smaller, private cellars dotting the hill. Look for signs saying *bor* or *Wein* (wine, in Hungarian and German, respectively) to point the way. Most places are open mid-May to mid-September daily from around noon until 9 or 10.

Badacsony is really an administrative name for the entire area and includes not just the mountain but also five settlements at its foot. A good starting point for Badacsony sightseeing is the **Egry József Múzeum** (József Egry Museum), formerly the home and studio of a famous painter of Balaton landscapes. His evocative paintings depict the lake's constantly changing hues, from its angry bright green during storms to its tranquil deep blues. ⊠ *Egry sétány 12,* ☎ *87/431–044.* ▭ *200 Ft.* ☉ *May–Sept., Tues.–Sun. 10–6.*

Szegedy Róza út, the steep main street climbing the mountain, is flanked by vineyards and villas. This is the place to get acquainted with the writer Sándor Kisfaludy and his beloved bride from Badacsony, Róza Szegedy, to whom he dedicated his love poems. At the summit of her street is **Szegedy Róza Ház** (Róza Szegedy House), a baroque winepress house built in 1790 on a grand scale—with thatched roof, gabled wall, six semicircular arcades, and an arched and pillared balcony running the length of the four raftered upstairs rooms. It was here that the hometown girl met the visiting bard from Budapest. The house now serves as a memorial museum to both of them, furnished much the way it was when Kisfaludy was doing his best work immortalizing his two true loves, the Badacsony and his wife. ⊠ *Szegedy Róza út 87,* ☎ *87/ 430–906.* ▭ *200 Ft.* ☉ *May–Sept., Tues.–Sun. 10–6.*

The steep climb to the **Kisfaludy kilátó** (Kisfaludy Lookout Tower) on Mt. Badacsony's summit is an integral part of the Badacsony experience and a rewarding bit of exercise. Serious summitry begins behind the Kisfaludy House at the **Rózsakő** (Rose Stone), a flat, smooth basalt slab with many carved inscriptions. Local legend has it that if a boy and a girl sit on it with their backs to Lake Balaton, they will marry within a year. From here, a trail marked in yellow leads up to the foot of the columns that stretch to the top. Steep flights of stone steps take you through a narrow gap between rocks and basalt walls until you reach a tree-lined plateau. You are now at the 1,391-ft level. Follow the blue triangular markings along a path to the lookout tower. Even with time out for rests and views, the ascent from Rózsakő should take less than an hour.

Just outside of town, **Rizapuszta** (✉ Káptalantóti út, Badacsonytomaj, Rizapuszta, ☎ 87/471–243) is a cellar and restaurant with regular tastings.

Dining and Lodging

$$–$$$$ ✕ **Halászkert.** The festive Fish Garden has won numerous international awards for its fine Hungarian cuisine. Inside are wooden rafters and tables draped with cheerful traditional blue-and-white *kékfestő* tablecloths; outside is a large terrace with umbrella-shaded tables. The extensive menu has such fresh-from-the-lake dishes as the house halászlé, and *párolt* (steamed) harcsa drenched with a paprika-caper sauce. ✉ *Park u. 5,* ☎ *87/431–054 or 87/431–113. AE, DC, MC, V. Closed Nov.–Apr.*

$–$$$ ✕ **Kisfaludy-ház.** Perched above the Szegedy Róza House is this Badacsony institution, once a winepress house owned by the poet Sándor Kisfaludy's family. Its wine cellar lies directly over a spring, but the main draw is a vast two-tier terrace that affords a breathtaking view of virtually the entire lake. Naturally, the wines are excellent and are incorporated into some of the cooking, such as creamy wine soup. ✉ *Szegedy Róza u. 87,* ☎ *87/431–016. AE, DC, MC, V. Closed Nov.–Apr.*

$–$$ ✕ **Szent Orbán Borház.** Part of the illustrious Szent Orbán winery, this restaurant overlooks some of the vineyard's 30 acres. On summer days golden light bathes the 19th-century former farmhouse, which has heavy wooden heirloom furniture and an antique porcelain stove. There are written menus, but charming servers also recite the dishes (in English and other languages), and they'll steer you toward sampling two unique house wines, Budai zöld and Kéknyelű—both based on legendary varietals from Roman times. Smoked goose liver paté is frequently available as an appetizer; changing seasonal specialties often feature fresh fish from Lake Balaton, including fogas. ✉ *Szegedy Róza u. 22,* ☎ *87/431–382. AE, DC, MC, V.*

$$$–$$$$ 🏨 **Club Hotel Badacsony.** A private beach is just a step away from this hotel right on the shore of Lake Balaton. The Club Hotel, in the Badacsonytomaj neighborhood, is the largest in the area. Rooms are bright and clean. ✉ *Balatoni út 14, H-8258 Badacsonytomaj,* ☎ *87/471–040,* FAX *87/471–059,* WEB *www.hotels.hu/club_hotel_badacsony. 52 rooms, 4 suites. Restaurant, café, tennis court, hair salon, massage, sauna, beach, bowling, meeting rooms. AE, DC, MC, V. Closed Nov.–Apr.*

$$ 🏨 **Hotel Volán.** This bright yellow, restored 19th-century mansion is a cheerful, family-oriented inn with a manicured yard for sunning and relaxing. Well-kept rooms are in the main house and in four modern additions behind it. ✉ *Római út 168, H-8261 Badacsony,* ☎ FAX *87/431–013,* WEB *www.hotels.hu/volan_badacsony. 23 rooms. Restaurant, bar, pool. No credit cards. Closed Nov.–mid-Feb.*

Outdoor Activities and Sports

The upper paths and roads along the slopes of Mt. Badacsony are excellent for scenic walking. Well-marked trails lead to the summit of Mt. Badacsony.

For beach activities, you can go to one of Badacsony's several beaches or head 6 km (4 mi) northeast, to those at Balatonrendes and Ábrahámhegy, combined communities forming quiet resorts.

Szigliget

★ **❺** *11 km (7 mi) west of Badacsony.*

The village of Szigliget is a tranquil, picturesque town with fine thatch-roof winepress houses and a small beach. Towering over the town is the ruin of the 13th-century **Óvár** (Old Castle), a fortress so well protected that it was never taken by the Turks; it was demolished in the early 18th century by Hapsburgs fearful of rebellions. A steep path starting from Kisfaludy utca brings you to the top of the hill, where you can explore the ruins, under ongoing archaeological restoration (a sign maps out the restoration plan), and take in the breathtaking views.

Down in the village on Iharos út, at the intersection with the road to Badacsony, the Romanesque remains of the **Avas templom** (Avas Church), from the Árpád dynasty, still contain a 12th-century basalt tower with a stone spire. The **Eszterházy summer mansion** in the main square, Fő tér, was built in the 18th century and rebuilt in neoclassical style in the 19th. In recent decades a retreat for writers, it is closed to the public—but just as well, for the bland inside has little to do with its former self. The mansion has a 25-acre park with yews, willows, walnuts, pines, and more than 500 kinds of ornamental trees and shrubs.

Keszthely

❻ *18 km (10 mi) west of Szigliget.*

With a beautifully preserved pedestrian avenue (Kossuth Lajos utca) in the historic center of town, the spectacular baroque Festetics Kastély, and a relative absence of honky-tonk, Keszthely is far more classically attractive and sophisticated than other large Balaton towns. Continuing the cultural and arts tradition begun by Count György Festetics two centuries ago, Keszthely hosts numerous cultural events, including an annual summer arts festival. Just south of town is the vast swamp called Kis-Balaton (Little Balaton), formerly part of Lake Balaton and now a nature preserve filled with birds. Water flowing into Lake Balaton from its little sibling frequently churns up sediment, making the water around Keszthely's beaches disconcertingly cloudy.

The **Pethő Ház** (Pethő House), a striking town house of medieval origin, was rebuilt in baroque style with a handsome arcaded gallery above its courtyard. Hidden deep inside its courtyard is the restored 18th-century **synagogue**, in front of which stands a small memorial honoring the 829 Jewish people from the neighborhood, turned into a ghetto in 1944, who were killed during the Holocaust. ⊠ *Kossuth Lajos u. 22.*

★ Keszthely's magnificent **Festetics Kastély** (Festetics Palace) is one of the finest baroque complexes in Hungary. Begun around 1745, it was the seat of the enlightened and philanthropic Festetics dynasty, which had acquired Keszthely six years earlier. The palace's distinctive church-like tower and more than 100 rooms were added between 1883 and 1887; the interior is lush. The **Helikon Könyvtár** (Helikon Library) in the south wing contains some 52,000 volumes, with precious codices and documents of Festetics family history. Chamber and orchestral concerts are held in the **Mirror Gallery** ballroom or, in summer, in the courtyard. The palace opens onto a splendid park lined with rare plants and fine sculptures. ⊠ *Kastély u. 1,* ☎ *83/312–191.* ⌨ *1,500 Ft. (1,200 Ft. extra for videotaping, 500 Ft. for no-flash photos).* ☉ *June, Tues.– Sun. 9–5; July–Aug., daily 9–6; Sept.–May, Tues.–Sun. 10–5.*

Supposedly the largest of its kind in Central Europe, Keszthely's **Babamúzeum** (Doll Museum) exhibits some 450 porcelain figurines dressed in 240 types of colorful folk dress. The building has a pastoral look, created not only by the figurines—which convey the multifarious beauty of village garb—but also by the ceiling's huge, handcrafted wooden beams. On the two upper floors are wooden models of typical homes, churches, and ornate wooden gates representative of all regions in and near present-day Hungary that Magyars have inhabited since conquering the Carpathian basin in 896. The museum's pièce de résistance is the lifework of an elderly peasant woman from northern Hungary: a 9-yard-long model of Budapest's Parliament building, patched together over 14 years from almost 4 million snail shells (which are 28 million years old, no less) originating from the Pannon Sea, which once covered much of Hungary. ✉ *Kossuth u. 11,* ☎ *83/318–855.* 🖭 *Doll Museum 250 Ft., model of Parliament 200 Ft.* ☉ *May–Sept., daily 10–5; Oct.–Apr., daily 9–5.*

Dining and Lodging

$–$$ ✕ **Hungária Gösser Söröző.** This beer garden keeps long hours and plenty of beer on tap. The food is better than you might guess judging just from the touristy atmosphere. Aside from barroom snacks, the huge menu includes *ropogós libacomb hagymás törtburgonyával* (crunchy goose drumstick with mashed potatoes and onions) and *töltött paprika* (stuffed peppers). ✉ *Kossuth Lajos u. 35, north of Fő tér,* ☎ *83/312–265. AE, DC, MC, V.*

$$$$ 🏨 **Danubius Hotel Helikon.** There are plenty of sports facilities at this large lakeside hotel: an indoor swimming pool, indoor tennis courts, sailing, surfing, rowing, fishing, and, in winter, skating. The comfortable modern rooms are on the small side, but they have soothing cream-and-blue bedspreads and curtains. ✉ *Balaton part 5, H-8360,* ☎ *83/311–330,* 🖷 *83/315–403,* 🌐 *www.danubiusgroup.com. 224 rooms, 8 suites. Restaurant, 2 tennis courts, indoor pool, hair salon, health club, sauna, beach, boating, fishing, bowling, ice-skating, bar. AE, DC, MC, V.*

$$$ 🏨 **Béta Hotel Hullám.** This turn-of-the-20th-century mansion with an elegant twin tower sits right on the Balaton shore. Rooms are clean and simply furnished with functional brown furniture. You can use the pool and the numerous recreational facilities at the nearby Danubius Hotel Helikon. ✉ *Balatonpart 1, H-8360,* ☎ *83/312–644,* 🖷 *83/315–338,* 🌐 *www.betahotels.hu. 28 rooms, 6 suites. Restaurant, minibars, beach, bar; no room phones. AE, DC, MC, V. Closed Nov.–Apr.*

Nightlife and the Arts

The **Balaton Festival,** held annually in May, includes high-caliber classical concerts and other festivities in venues around town and outdoors on Kossuth Lajos utca. In summer, classical concerts and master classes take place almost daily in the Festetics Palace's Mirror Hall.

Outdoor Activities and Sports

BALLOONING

Hot-air balloon rides in the Keszthely region have become popular, despite the high price (28,000 Ft. per person). Dr. Bóka György (a practicing M.D. and balloon pilot) and his friendly team will take you up in his blue-and-yellow balloon for an hour-long tour—the trip includes a post-landing champagne ritual. Flights depend strongly on wind and air-pressure conditions; in summer, they can usually fly only in early morning and early evening. Transportation to and from the site is included. Contact **Med-Aer** (✉ *Móricz Zsigmond u. 7,* ☎ *83/312–421* or *06/309–576–321*) at least one week in advance to reserve your spot.

HORSEBACK RIDING

János Lovarda (János Stable; ✉ Sömögyedüllő, ☎ 83/314–855) offers lessons, rides in the ring, and carriage rides.

WATER SPORTS

You can rent paddleboats and other water toys at the public beach next to the Béta Hotel Hullám or from the Danubius Hotel Helikon.

Hévíz

❼ *6 km (4 mi) northwest of Keszthely.*

Hévíz is one of Hungary's biggest and most famous spa resorts, with the largest natural curative thermal lake in Europe. Lake Hévíz covers nearly 60,000 square yards, with warm water that never grows cooler than 33°C–35°C (91.4°F–95°F) in summer and 30°C–32°C (86°F–89.6°F) in winter, thus allowing year-round bathing, particularly where the lake is covered by a roof and looks like a racetrack grandstand. Richly endowed with sulfur, alkali, calcium salts, and other curative components, the Hévíz water is recommended for spinal, rheumatic, gynecological, and articular disorders and is drunk to help digestive problems and receding gums. Fed by a spring producing 86 million liters (22.7 million gallons) of water a day, the lake cycles through a complete water change every 28 hours. Squeamish bathers, however, should be forewarned that along with its photogenic lily pads, the lake naturally contains assorted sludgy mud and plant material. It's all supposed to be good for you, though—even the mud, which is full of iodine and estrogen.

The vast spa park has hospitals, sanatoriums, expensive hotels, and a casino. The public bath facilities are in the **Szent András Kórház** (St. Andrew Hospital), a large, turreted medicinal bathing complex on the lakeshore with a large staff on hand to treat rheumatological complaints. Bathing for more than three hours at a time is not recommended. ⊠ *Dr. Schulhof Vilmos sétány 1,* ☎ *83/340–587.* 🎫 *500 Ft. (valid for 3 hrs).* ☉ *May–Sept., daily 8:30–5:30; Oct.–Apr., daily 9–4:30.*

The beautifully furnished **Talpasház** (House on Soles) takes its name from an interesting architectural detail: its upright beams are encased in thick foundation boards. Exquisite antique peasant furniture, textiles, and pottery fill the house along with the work of contemporary local folk artists. Some of their work is for sale on the premises, and you can also create your own works on a pottery wheel. Contact the caretaker, Csaba Rezes, who lives next door at No. 15, if the door happens to be closed. ⊠ *Dózsa György u. 17,* ☎ *85/377–364 caretaker.* 🎫 *100 Ft.* ☉ *Late May–Sept., Tues.–Sun. variable hrs (call the caretaker to let you in).*

OFF THE
BEATEN PATH

CSILLAGVÁR (STAR CASTLE) – It's worth stopping in Balatonszentgyörgy to see this castle, hidden away at the end of a dirt road past a gaping quarry. The house was built in the 1820s as a hunting lodge for László, the Festetics family's eccentric. Though it's not star-shape inside, wedge-shape projections on the ground floor give the outside this effect. Today the castle houses a museum of 16th- and 17th-century life in the border fortresses of the Balaton. ⊠ *Irtási dűlő,* ☎ *85/377–532.* 🎫 *100 Ft.* ☉ *May–Aug., daily 9–6.*

Lodging

$$$$ 🏨 **Danubius Thermal Hotel Aqua.** This large, luxurious spa-hotel in the city center has its own thermal baths and physiotherapy unit (plus a full dental service!). The rooms are smaller than average and therefore not suited to families who intend to share a single room. Numerous cure packages are available. ⊠ *Kossuth Lajos u. 13–15, H-8380,* ☎ *83/341–090,* 𝖥𝖠𝖷 *83/340–970,* 𝖶𝖤𝖡 *www.danubiusgroup.com. 227 rooms. Restaurant, pool, hair salon, massage, sauna, spa, bar. AE, DC, MC, V.*

$$$$ 🏨 **Hotel Palace Hévíz.** There's a suggestion of Hercule Poirot about the art-deco exterior and atrium of the Hevis, as though the Belgium detective might wander in wagging his finger at you at any moment. All those gleaming white surfaces turn out to be new, however, as the hotel is a recent construction. The hotel has thermal baths, various treatments, and its own dental center. ✉ *Rákóczi u. 1–3, H-8380,* ☎ *83/ 545–900,* 🆋 *83/545–901,* 🌐 *www.palace-heviz.hu. 160 rooms. Restaurant, café, indoor pool, hair salon, massage, sauna, bar, some pets allowed. AE, DC, MC, V.*

$$$$ 🏨 **Rogner Hévíz Hotel Lotus Therme.** No expense has been spared at this spa and "wellness" hotel promoting relaxation and invigoration. In addition to enjoying thermal baths, a fitness center, and various purification and detoxification therapies, you can join in golf and tennis excursions. There are even in-house dieticians. The hotel itself is a large, crescent-shape building just off the E71. ✉ *Lótuszvirág u. 80, H-8380,* ☎ *83/500–501,* 🆋 *83/500–513,* 🌐 *www.lotustherme.com. 231 rooms. Restaurant, café, cable TV, indoor pool, hair salon, health club, massage, sauna, bar, shops; no-smoking rooms. AE, DC, MC, V.*

Siófok

❽ *110 km (68 mi) southeast of Hévíz, 105 km (65 mi) southwest of Budapest.*

Siófok is the largest city on the southern shore and one of Hungary's major tourist and holiday centers. It is also arguably the least beautiful. In 1863 a railway station was built for the city, paving the way for its "golden age" at the turn of the 20th century. In the closing stages of World War II the city sustained heavy damage; to boost tourism during the 1960s, the Pannonia Hotel Company built four of what many consider to be the ugliest hotels in the area. If, however, these were Siófok's *only* ugly buildings, there would still be hope for a ray of aesthetic redemption. With the exception of the twin-tower train station and the adjacent business district stretching a few blocks to the *Víztorony* (water tower), dating from 1912, the city is overrun by drab modern structures. Its shoreline is now a long, honky-tonk strip crammed with concrete-bunker hotels, discos, go-go bars, and tacky restaurants. So while Siófok is not for those seeking a peaceful lakeside getaway, it is exactly what hordes of action-seeking young people want—an all-in-one playground.

One worthwhile attraction is the **Kálmán Imre Múzeum** (Imre Kálmán Museum), housed in the birthplace of composer Kálmán (1882–1953), known internationally as the Prince of Operetta. Inside this small house-cum-museum are his first piano, original scores, his smoking jacket, and lots of old pictures. ✉ *Kálmán Imre sétány 5,* ☎ *84/311–287.* 🖅 *200 Ft.* ☉ *Tues.–Sun. 9–5.*

Dining and Lodging

$$–$$$ ✕ **Millennium Étterem.** Imre Makovecz, one of Hungary's preeminent architects, oversaw renovation of this elegant restaurant, once an old villa, in the early '90s. The menu lists several Hungarian specialties as well as fresh, local fish, including whole trout and pike perch. ✉ *Fő u. 93–95,* ☎ *84/312–546. AE, DC, MC, V.*

$–$$ ✕ **Csárdás Étterem.** The oldest and one of the best restaurants in Siófok, the Csárdás Étterem consistently wins awards for its hearty, never-bland Hungarian cuisine. House specialties include a breaded and fried pork fillet stuffed with cheese, ham, and smoked bacon. ✉ *Fő u. 105,* ☎ *84/310–642. AE, MC, V.*

$$$$ 🏨 **Hotel Atrium Janus Siófok.** Every room in this bright luxury hotel is clean and comfortably contemporary. The "relaxation center" down-

stairs has a swimming pool, sauna, and whirlpool. ⊠ *Fő u. 93–95, H-8600,* ☎ *84/312–546,* ℻ *84/312–432,* ⦿ *www.janushotel.hu. 22 rooms, 7 suites. Restaurant, café, in-room safes, minibars, indoor pool, gym, sauna, bar, meeting rooms. AE, DC, MC, V.*

$$$ 🏨 **Hotel Fortuna.** This three-story, bright-yellow rectangular block has the advantage of being somewhat removed from the multilane traffic of the city's main street and about 100 yards from the lakeshore. The rooms are modern and, like the building's facade, awash in a soothing yellow; all have balconies. ⊠ *Erkel Ferenc u. 51, H-8600,* ☎ ℻ *84/311–087 or 84/313–476. 41 rooms, 5 suites. Restaurant, bar, playground, meeting rooms. AE, DC, MC, V.*

Nightlife and the Arts

The town remains loyal to Siófok-born operetta composer Imre Kálmán and hosts popular operetta concerts regularly in the summer at the **Kulturális Központ** (Cultural Center; ⊠ Fő tér 2, ☎ 84/311–855).

Outdoor Activities and Sports

GO-CARTS

Speed demons can whiz around the **Go-Cart Track** (⊠ Rte. 70, by railroad crossing, ☎ 84/311–917 or 06/209–512–510), which is open from mid-May through September; a 10-minute drive costs about 1,800 Ft.

TENNIS

The **Sport Centrum** (⊠ Küszhegyi út, ☎ 84/314–523) has eight tennis courts as well as a handball court, sauna, and, lest things get too athletic, a bar.

WATER SPORTS

Boating and other water-sports equipment is available for hire at the **MOL Water Sports Center** (☎ 84/311–161), on the waterfront on Vitorlás utca 10. Kayaks and canoes cost 500 Ft.–600 Ft. per hour, sailboats around 6,000 Ft. per hour.

Lake Balaton Essentials

BUS TRAVEL

Buses headed for the Lake Balaton region depart from Budapest's Erzsébét tér station daily; contact Volánbusz for current schedules.

Buses frequently link Lake Balaton's major resorts. Arrive at the bus station early. Tickets with seat reservations can be bought in the stations up to 20 minutes prior to departure, otherwise from the driver; reservations cannot be made by phone. Contact the tourist offices or Volánbusz for schedule and fare information.

➤ BUS SCHEDULES: **Volánbusz** (☎ 1/485–2162 in Budapest).

CAR TRAVEL

Driving is the most convenient way to explore the area, but keep in mind that traffic can be heavy during summer weekends.

Expressway E71/M7 is the main artery between Budapest and Lake Balaton. At press time still under construction, it had gotten as far as the lake's northeastern point and will eventually reach southwestern Hungary. From here Route 7 from Budapest joins the E71 and continues along the lake's southern shore to Siófok and towns farther west. Route 71 goes along the northern shore to Balatonfüred and lakeside towns southwest. The drive from Budapest to Siófok takes about 1½ hours, except on weekends, when traffic can be severe. From Budapest to Balatonfüred is about the same.

FERRY TRAVEL

The slowest but most scenic way to travel among Lake Balaton's major resorts is by ferry. Schedules for MAHART Tours, the national ferry company, are available from most of the tourist offices in the region.

➤ FERRY INFORMATION: **MAHART Tours** (☎ 1/318–1704 in Budapest).

TOURS

You can arrange tours directly with the hotels in the Balaton area and with the help of Tourinform offices; these can include boat trips to vineyards, folk-music evenings, and overnight trips to local inns.

FROM BUDAPEST

Cityrama takes groups twice a week from April to October from Budapest to Balatonfüred for a walk along the promenade and then over to Tihany for a tour of the abbey. After lunch, you'll take a ferry across the Balaton and then head back to Budapest, with a wine-tasting stop on the way.

IBUSZ Travel has several tours to Balaton from Budapest; inquire at the office in Budapest.

➤ CONTACT: **Cityrama** (☎ 1/302–4382 in Budapest). **IBUSZ Travel** (✉ District V, Ferenciek tere 10, ☎ 1/485–2762 or 1/317–7767, WEB www.ibusz.hu).

BOAT TOURS

MAHART arranges several sailing excursions on Lake Balaton. From Balatonfüred, the *Csongor* sets out several times daily in July and August for an hour-long jaunt around the Tihany Peninsula. Most other tours depart from Siófok also in the same period, including the "Tihany Tour," on Saturday at 10 AM, with stops for guided sightseeing in Balatonfüred and Tihany; and the "Sunset Tour," a 1½-hour cruise at 7:30 PM daily during which you can sip a glass of champagne while watching the sun sink. The "Badacsony Tour" departs from Keszthely and goes to Badacsony at 10:30 AM Thursday.

➤ CONTACT: **MAHART** (☎ 84/312–308).

TRAIN TRAVEL

Daily express trains run from Budapest's Déli (South) Station to Siófok and Balatonfüred. The roughly two-hour trip costs about 900 Ft. each way.

Trains from Budapest serve the resorts on the northern shore; a separate line links resorts on the southern shore. There is no train service to Tihany. While most towns are on a rail line, it's inconvenient to decipher the train schedules; trains don't run very frequently, so planning connections can be tricky. Since many towns are just a few miles apart, getting stuck on a local train can feel like an endless stop-start cycle. Also bear in mind that, apart from some trains between Budapest and Veszprém, you cannot reserve seats on the Balaton trains—it's first come, first seated.

➤ TRAIN STATIONS: **Balatonfüred train station** (✉ Castricum tér, ☎ 87/343–652). **Siófok train station** (✉ Millenium tér, ☎ 84/310–061). **Veszprém train station** (✉ Jutasi út 34, 2 km [1 mi] outside of town, ☎ 88/329–999).

VISITOR INFORMATION

The Balaton Communication and Information Hotline is an excellent source of travel information for the region (in Hungarian only), with a comprehensive Web site (with some English information).

➤ TOURIST INFORMATION: **Badacsony Tourinform** (✉ Park u. 6, ☎ FAX 87/431–046). **Balaton Communication and Information Hotline** (☎ 88/406–963, WEB www.balaton.hu). **Balatonfüred Tourinform**

(✉ Széchenyi u. 47, ☎ 87/580–480). **Balatontourist** (✉ Tagore sétány 1, ☎ 87/342–822 or 87/343–471). **Hévíz Tourist** (✉ Rákóczi u. 4, ☎ 83/341–348). **Keszthely Tourinform** (✉ Kossuth u. 28, ☎ FAX 83/314–144). **Siófok IBUSZ** (✉ Fő u. 174, ☎ 84/315–213). **Siófok Tourinform** (✉ Víztorony, ☎ 84/315–355). **Tihany Tourinform** (✉ Kossuth u. 20, ☎ FAX 87/448–804). **Veszprém Tourinform** (✉ Vár u. 4, ☎ FAX 88/404–548).

BUDAPEST A TO Z

AIR TRAVEL

The most convenient way to fly between Hungary and the United States is with Malév Hungarian Airlines' nonstop direct service between JFK International Airport in New York and Budapest's Ferihegy Airport—still the only such flight that exists. Several other airlines offer connecting service from North America, including Austrian Airlines (through Vienna), British Airways (through London), Czech Airlines (through Prague), and Lufthansa (through Frankfurt or Munich).

➤ CARRIERS: **Austrian Airlines** (☎ 1/296–0660). **British Airways** (☎ 1/411–5555). **ČSA** (Czech Airlines; ☎ 1/318–3175). **Lufthansa** (☎ 1/429–8011). **Malév** (☎ 1/235–3535 ticketing; 1/235–3888 flight information). **Swiss** (☎ 1/328–5000).

AIRPORTS AND TRANSFERS

Ferihegy Repülőtér, Hungary's only commercial airport with regularly scheduled service, is 24 km (15 mi) southeast of downtown Budapest. All non-Hungarian airlines operate from Terminal 2B; those of Malév, from Terminal 2A. (The older part of the airport, Terminal 1, no longer serves commercial flights, so the main airport is now often referred to as Ferihegy 2 and the terminals simply as A and B.)

➤ AIRPORT INFORMATION: **Ferihegy Repülőtér** (☎ 1/296–9696; 1/296–8000 same-day arrival information; 1/296–7000 same-day departure information).

TRANSFERS

Many hotels offer their guests car or minibus transportation to and from Ferihegy, but all of them charge for the service. You should arrange for a pickup in advance. If you're taking a taxi, allow anywhere between just 25 minutes during nonpeak hours and at least an hour during rush hours (7 AM–9 AM from the airport, 4 PM–6 PM from the city).

Official airport taxis are queued at the exit and overseen by a taxi monitor; their rates are fixed according to the zone of your final destination. A taxi ride to the center of Budapest will cost around 4,500 Ft. Trips to the airport are about 3,500 Ft. from Pest, 4,000 Ft. from Buda. Avoid taxi drivers who approach you before you are out of the arrivals lounge.

Minibuses run every half hour from 5:30 AM to 9:30 PM from the Hotel Kempinski on Erzsébet tér (near the main bus station and the Deák tér metro hub) in downtown Budapest. It takes almost the same time as taxis but costs only 800 Ft.

The LRI Airport Shuttle provides convenient door-to-door service between the airport and any address in the city. To get to the airport, call to arrange a pickup; to get to the city, make arrangements at LRI's airport desk. Service to or from either terminal costs 1,800 Ft. per person; since it normally shuttles several people at once, remember to allow time for a few other pickups or drop-offs.

➤ CONTACTS: **Airport Minibus** (☎ 1/296–8555). **Airport Taxis** (☎ 1/341–0000). **LRI Airport Shuttle** (☎ 1/296–8555).

BOAT TRAVEL

From late July through early September, two swift hydrofoils leave Vienna daily at 8 AM and 1 PM (once-a-day trips are scheduled mid-April–late July and September–late October). After a 5½-hour journey downriver, with a stop in the Slovak capital, Bratislava, and views of Hungary's largest church, the cathedral in Esztergom, the boats head into Budapest via its main artery, the Danube. The upriver journey takes about an hour longer.

➤ BOAT AND FERRY LINES: **MAHART Tours** (in Budapest: ⊠ International Mooring Point, V, Belgrád rakpart, ☎ 1/318–1743; in Vienna: Handelskai 265, Vienna, ☎ 1/729–2161 or 1/729–2162, WEB www.maharttours.com).

BUS AND TRAM TRAVEL WITHIN BUDAPEST

Trams (*villamos*) and buses (*autóbusz*) are abundant and convenient. A one-fare ticket (106 Ft.; valid on all forms of public transportation) is valid for only one ride in one direction. Tickets are widely available in metro stations and newsstands and must be validated on board by inserting them downward facing you into the little devices provided for that purpose, then pulling the knob. Alternatively, you can purchase a *napijegy* (day ticket, 850 Ft.; a three-day "tourist ticket" costs 1,500 Ft.), which allows unlimited travel on all services within the city limits. Hold on to whatever ticket you have; spot checks by aggressive undercover checkers (look for the red armbands) are numerous and often targeted at tourists. Trolley-bus stops are marked with red, rectangular signs that list the route stops; regular bus stops are marked with similar light blue signs. (The trolley buses and regular buses themselves are red and blue, respectively.) Tram stops are marked by light blue or yellow signs. Most lines run from 5 AM and stop operating at 11 PM, but there is all-night service on certain key routes. Consult the separate night-bus map posted in most metro stations for all-night service.

CAR RENTALS

Rates are high. Daily rates for automatics begin around $55–$60 plus 60¢ per kilometer (½ mi); personal, theft, and accident insurance (not required but recommended) runs an additional $25–$30 per day. Rates tend to be significantly lower if you arrange your rental *from home* through the American offices. Locally based companies usually offer lower rates. Americana Rent-a-Car, for example, has unlimited-mileage weekend specials, and rates include free delivery and pickup of the car anywhere in Budapest. SPQR rents limousines.

Foreign driver's licenses are generally accepted by car rental agencies but are technically not legally valid.

➤ MAJOR AGENCIES: **Avis** (⊠ District V, Szervita tér 8, ☎ 1/318–4240; Ferihegy Repülőtér, Terminal 2A, ☎ 1/296–7265; Ferihegy Repülőtér, Terminal 2B, ☎ 1/296–6421). **Budget** (⊠ Hotel Mercure Buda, District I, Krisztina krt. 41–43, ☎ 1/214–0420; Ferihegy Repülőtér, Terminal 2A, ☎ 1/296–8481; Ferihegy Repülőtér, Terminal 2B, ☎ 1/296–8197). **Europcar** (⊠ District VIII, Ulloi út 60–62, ☎ 1/477–1080; Ferihegy Repülőtér, Terminal 2A, ☎ 1/296–6688; Ferihegy Repülőtér, Terminal 2B, ☎ 1/296–6610). **Hertz** (also known in Hungary as Mercure Rent-a-Car; ⊠ Marriott hotel, District V, Apáczai Csere János u. 4, ☎ 1/266–4361; Ferihegy Repülőtér, Terminal 2A, ☎ 1/296–6988; Ferihegy Repülőtér, Terminal 2B, ☎ 1/296–7171).

➤ LOCAL AGENCIES: **Americana Rent-a-Car** (⊠ Ibis Hotel Volga, District XIII, Dózsa György út 65, ☎ 1/350–2542 or 1/320–8287). **EUrent** ⊠ District XXIII, Szentlőrinc út, ☎ 1/421–8333 or 1/421–8300). **Fox Autorent** ⊠ District XI, Vegész u. 17–25, ☎ 1/382–9000). **SPQR** (⊠ District XIII, Váci út 175, ☎ 1/237–7334 or 1/237–7300).

CAR TRAVEL

The main routes into Budapest are the M1 from Vienna (via Győr), the M3 from near Gyöngyös, the M5 from Kecskemét, and the M7 from the Balaton; the M3 and M5 are being upgraded and extended to Hungary's borders with Slovakia and Yugoslavia, respectively. Budapest, like any Western city, is plagued by traffic jams during the day, but motorists should have no problem later in the evening. Motorists not accustomed to sharing the city streets with trams should pay extra attention. You should be prepared to be flagged down numerous times by police conducting routine checks for drunk driving and stolen cars. Be sure all of your papers are in order and readily accessible; unfortunately, the police have been known to give foreigners a hard time.

To drive in Hungary, Americans and Canadians are supposed to have an International Driver's License—although domestic licenses are usually accepted anyway. It can, however, get messy and expensive if you are stopped by a police officer who insists you need an International Driver's License (which, legally, you do), so it's best to obtain the international license. If you're from the United Kingdom you may use your domestic license.

PARKING

Gone are the "anything goes" days of parking in Budapest, when cars parked for free practically anywhere in the city, straddling curbs or angled in the middle of sidewalks. Now most streets in Budapest's main districts have restricted, fee-based parking; there are either parking meters that accept coins (usually for a maximum of two hours) or attendants who approach your car as you park and charge you according to how many hours you intend to stay. Hourly rates average 200 Ft. In most cases; overnight parking (generally after 6 PM and before 8 AM) in these areas is free. Budapest also has a number of parking lots and a few garages; two central-Pest garages in District V are at Szervita tér and Aranykéz utca 4–6.

CUSTOMS AND DUTIES

ON ARRIVAL

Objects for personal use may be imported freely. If you are over 16, you may bring in 250 cigarettes or 50 cigars or 250 grams of tobacco, plus 2 liters of wine, 1 liter of spirits, and 100 milliliters of perfume. (You also may leave Hungary with this much, plus 5 liters of beer). If you bring in more than $400 in cash and think you may be taking that much out, technically speaking you should declare it on arrival. A customs charge is made on gifts valued in Hungary at more than 30,500 Ft.

ON DEPARTURE

Take care when you leave Hungary that you have the right documentation for exporting goods. Keep receipts of any major purchases. A special permit is needed for works of art, antiques, or objects of museum value. Upon leaving, you are entitled to a value-added tax (VAT) refund on new goods (i.e., not works of art, antiques, or objects of museum value) valued at 50,000 Ft. or more (VAT inclusive). But applying for the refund may rack up more frustration than money: cash refunds are given only in forints, and you may find yourself in the airport minutes before boarding with a handful of soft currency; while you can take out up to 350,000 Ft., converting it back home will difficult. If you otherwise don't have much hard currency on you, you can convert up to about 100,000 of the forints into dollars to come up with the $400-in-cash export limit. If you made your purchases by credit card you can file for a credit to your card or to your bank account (again in forints), but don't expect it to come through in a hurry. If you intend to apply for the credit, make sure you get customs to stamp the original purchase invoice before you leave the country. For more information, pick up a tax refund brochure from any tourist office or hotel, or contact Intel Trade Rt. in Budapest. For further Hungarian customs information, inquire at the National Customs and Revenue Office. If you have trouble communicating, ask Tourinform (1/438–8080) for help.

➤ INFORMATION: **Intel Trade Rt.** (⌧ District I, Csalogány u. 6-10, Budapest, ☎ 1/201–8120 or 1/356–9800). **National Customs and Revenue Office** (⌧ Regional Directorate for Central Hungary, District XIV, Hungária krt. 112–114, Budapest, ☎ 1/470–4121 or 470–4122). **Tourinform** (☎ 1/438–8080).

EMBASSIES AND CONSULATES

All embassies and consulates are in Budapest.

➤ CONTACTS: **Australian Consulate** (⌧ District VII, Királyhágó tér 8–9, Budapest, ☎ 1/457–9777). **British Embassy** (⌧ District V, Harmincad u. 6, Budapest, ☎ 1/266–2888, FAX 1/266–0907). **Canadian Consulate** (⌧ District XII, Budakeszi út 32, Budapest, ☎ 1/392–3360). **New Zealand Consulate** (⌧ District VI, Teréz krt. 38, Budapest, ☎ 1/331–4908). **U.S. Embassy** (⌧ District V, Szabadság tér 12, Budapest, ☎ 1/475–4400).

EMERGENCIES

You call for a general ambulance or call Falck-SOS, a 24-hour private ambulance service with English-speaking personnel. If you need a doctor, ask your hotel or embassy for a recommendation, or visit R-Clinic, a private clinic staffed by English-speaking doctors offering 24-hour medical and ambulance service. The clinic accepts major credit cards and prepares full reports for your insurance company. Profident Dental Services is a private, English-speaking dental practice consisting of Western-trained dentists and hygienists, with service available 24 hours a day. Most pharmacies close between 6 PM and 8 PM, but several stay open at night and on the weekend, offering 24-hour service, with a small surcharge for items that aren't officially stamped as urgent by a physician. You must ring the buzzer next to the night window and someone will respond over the intercom. Staff is unlikely to speak English. Late-night pharmacies are usually located across from the train stations.

➤ EMERGENCY SERVICES: **Ambulance** (☎ 104). **Falck–SOS** (☎ 1/200–0100). **Hungarian Automobile Club's breakdown service** (☎ 1/345–1744 or 188). **Police** (☎ 107).

➤ DOCTORS AND DENTISTS: **R-Clinic** (⌧ District II, Felsőzöldmáli út 13, ☎ 1/325–9999). **Profident Dental Services** (⌧ District VII, Karoly Körót u. 1, ☎ 1/342–6972).

➤ LATE-NIGHT PHARMACIES: **Eighth District** (⌧ District VIII, Rákóczi út 39, near the Keleti train station, ☎ 1/314–3695). **Sixth District** (⌧ District VI, Teréz körút 41, near the Nyugati train station, ☎ 1/311–4439). **Twelfth District** (⌧ District XII, Alkotás utca 1/b, across from the Déli train station, ☎ 1/355–4691).

ENGLISH-LANGUAGE MEDIA

Several English-language weeklies have sprouted up to placate Budapest's large expatriate community. The *Budapest Sun* and the *Budapest Business Journal* are sold at major newsstands, hotels, and tourist points. The mini-guidebook *Budapest in Your Pocket* appears six times a year and is also widely available. *Where Budapest,* a free monthly magazine, is available only at major hotels.

HOLIDAYS AND LANGUAGE

HOLIDAYS

January 1, March 15 (Anniversary of 1848 Revolution); Easter Sunday and Easter Monday (in March, April, or May); May 1 (Labor Day);

August 20 (St. Stephen's and Constitution Day); October 23 (1956 Revolution Day); December 24–26.

LANGUAGE
Hungarian (*Magyar*) tends to look and sound intimidating at first because it is not an Indo-European language. Generally, older people speak some German, and many younger people speak at least rudimentary English, which has become the most popular language to learn. It's a safe bet that anyone in the tourist trade will speak at least one of the two languages. Also note that when giving names, Hungarians put the family name before the given name, thus Janos Szabo (John Taylor) becomes Szabo Janos.

MAIL AND SHIPPING
Airmail letters and postcards generally take seven days to travel between Hungary and the United States, sometimes more than twice as long, however, during the Christmas season. Postage for an airmail letter to the United States costs about 160 Ft.; an airmail letter to the United Kingdom and elsewhere in Western Europe costs about 150 Ft. Airmail postcards to the United States cost about 110 Ft. and to the United Kingdom and the rest of Western Europe about 100 Ft.

Budapest's main post office branch is downtown. The post offices near Budapest's Keleti (East) and Nyugati (West) train stations stay open until 9 PM on weekdays, the former just as long on weekends while the latter shuts its doors at 8 PM. The American Express office in Budapest has poste restante services.
➤ POST OFFICE: **American Express** (⊠ District V, Deák Ferenc u. 10 H-1052 Budapest, ☎ 1/235–4330). **Downtown Budapest post office branch** (⊠ District V, Magyar Posta 4. sz., Viroshiz u. 18, H-1052 Budapest). **Keleti post office** (⊠ District VIII, Baross tér 11/C, Budapest). **Nyugati post office** (⊠ District VI, Teréz krt. 51, Budapest).

MONEY MATTERS
Even with inflation and the 25% value-added tax (VAT) in the service industry, enjoyable vacations with all the trimmings still remain less expensive in Hungary than in nearby Western European cities such as Vienna.

Eurocheque holders can cash personal checks in all banks and in most hotels. Many banks also cash American Express and Visa traveler's checks. American Express has a full-service office in Budapest, which also dispenses cash to its cardholders; a smaller branch on Castle Hill, at the Sisi Restaurant, has a currency exchange that operates daily from March to mid-January. Budapest also has a Citibank offering full services to account holders, including a 24-hour cash machine.
➤ CONTACTS: **American Express** (⊠ District V, Deák Ferenc u. 10, Budapest, ☎ 1/235–4330, FAX 1/267–2028; ⊠ Sisi Restaurant, District 1, Castle Hill, ☎ 1/264–0118). **Citibank** (⊠ District V, Vörösmarty tér 4).

CURRENCY
Hungary's unit of currency is the forint (Ft.). There are bills of 200, 500, 1,000, 2,000, 5,000, 10,000 and 20,000 forints and coins of 1, 2, 5, 10, 20, 50, and 100 forints.

CURRENCY EXCHANGE
At this writing, the exchange rate was approximately 249 Ft. to the U.S. dollar, 158 Ft. to the Canadian dollar, 386 Ft. to the pound sterling, and 243 Ft. to the euro. It is probably still wise to bring traveler's checks, which can be cashed all over the country in banks and hotels. There is still a black market in hard currency, but changing money on the street is risky and illegal, and the bank rate almost always comes

close. Stick with banks and official exchange offices. There are also many cash-exchange machines in Budapest, into which you feed paper currency for forints. Most bank automats and cash-exchange machines are clustered around their respective bank branches throughout downtown Pest.

CREDIT CARDS

All major credit cards are accepted in Hungary, but don't rely on them in smaller towns or less expensive accommodations and restaurants. Twenty-four-hour cash machines have sprung up throughout Budapest and in major towns around the country. Some accept Plus-network bank cards and Visa credit cards, others Cirrus and MasterCard. You can withdraw forints only (automatically converted at the bank's official exchange rate) directly from your account. Some levy a 1% or $3 service charge. Instructions are in English.

➤ LOST CREDIT CARDS: **American Express** (☎ 336/393–111 collect to the U.S.). **Diners Club** (☎ 640–248–424). **Mastercard** (☎ 680–012–517). **Visa** (☎ 680–011–272).

PASSPORTS AND VISAS

Only a valid passport is required of U.S., British, Canadian, and New Zealand citizens; Australian citizens must obtain a visa.

➤ HUNGARIAN EMBASSIES: **Australia** (✉ 17 Beale Crescent Deakin Act., Canberra 2600, ☎ 6126/282–3226). **Canada** (✉ 299 Waverley St., Ottawa, Ontario K2P 0V9, ☎ 613/230–9614). **New Zealand** (Consulate General: ✉ 151 Orangi Kaupapa Rd., Wellington 6005, ☎ 4/938–0427). **United States** (✉ 3910 Shoemaker St. NW, Washington, DC 20008, ☎ 202/362–6730). **United Kingdom** (✉ 35b Eaton Pl., London SW1X 8BY, ☎ 0171/235–5218).

SUBWAY TRAVEL

Service on Budapest's subways is cheap, fast, and frequent; stations are easily located on maps and streets by the big letter "M" (for metro). Tickets—106 Ft.; valid on all forms of mass transportation—can be bought at hotels, metro stations, newsstands, and kiosks. They are valid for one ride only; you can't change lines or direction. Tickets must be validated in the time-clock machines in station entrances and should be kept until the end of the journey, as there are frequent checks by undercover inspectors; a fine for traveling without a ticket is 2,500 Ft. Other options include a one-day ticket (850 Ft.), a three-day "tourist ticket" (1,700 Ft.), and a seven-day ticket (2,100 Ft., passport photo required); all allow unlimited subway travel within city limits.

Line 1 (marked FÖLDALATTI), which starts downtown at Vörösmarty tér and follows Andrássy út out past Gundel restaurant and City Park, is an antique tourist attraction in itself, built in the 1890s for the Magyar Millennium; its yellow trains with tank treads still work. Lines 2 and 3 were built 90 years later. Line 2 (red) runs from the eastern suburbs, past the Keleti (East) Railway Station, through the city center, and under the Danube to the Déli (South) station. One of the stations, Moszkva tér, is where the Várbusz (Castle Bus) can be boarded. Line 3 (blue) runs from the southeastern suburbs to Deák tér, through the city center, and northward to the Nyugati (West) station and the northern suburbs. On all three lines, fare tickets are canceled in machines at the station entrance. All three metro lines meet at the Deák tér station and run from 4:30 AM to shortly after 11 PM.

TAXIS

There are plenty of honest taxi drivers in Budapest and a few too many dishonest ones. Fortunately, the reliable ones are easy to spot: they will have a company logo and phone number, and a working meter. If one is hailed on the street, the base fare is generally 200 Ft. and then 200 Ft. each kilometer thereafter. When ordering a taxi by phone (and all the companies here have English-speaking operators), the rate falls to around 200 Ft. base fare, then 150 Ft.–180 Ft. per kilometer.

➤ CONTACTS: **BudaTaxi** (☎ 1/233–3333). **Citytaxi** (☎ 1/211–1111). **Est Taxi** (☎ 1/244–4444). **Fő taxi** (☎ 1/222–2222). **Radio Taxi** (☎ 1/377–7777). **6x6 Taxi** (☎ 1/266–6666).

TELEPHONES

Within Hungary, most towns can be dialed directly: dial "06" and wait for the buzzing tone; then dial the local number. Cellular phone numbers are treated like long-distance domestic calls: dial "06" before the number (when giving their cellular phone numbers, most people include the 06 anyway). It is unnecessary to use the city code, 1, when dialing within Budapest

DIRECTORY AND OPERATOR ASSISTANCE

Dial "198" for directory assistance for all of Hungary. There is usually someone on-hand who can speak English. You can also consult *The Phone Book,* an English-language telephone directory full of important Budapest numbers as well as cultural and tourist information; it's provided in guest rooms of most major hotels, as well as at many restaurants and English-language bookstores. The slim but information-packed city guide *Budapest in Your Pocket* lists important phone numbers; it appears six times a year and can be found at newsstands and hotels.

INTERNATIONAL CALLS

Direct calls to foreign countries can be made from Budapest and all major provincial towns by dialing "00" and waiting for the international dialing tone; on pay phones the initial charge is 60 Ft.

The country code for Hungary is 36. When dialing from outside the country, drop the initial 06 prefix for area codes outside of Budapest.
➤ ACCESS CODES: **AT&T** (☎ 06/800–01111). **MCI** (☎ 06/800–01411). **Sprint** (☎ 06/800–01877).

PUBLIC PHONES

Coin-operated pay phones accept 10-Ft., 20-Ft., 50-Ft., and 100-Ft. coins; the minimum initial amount is 20 Ft. Given that these phones often swallow up change without allowing a call in exchange, however, it's best when possible to use gray card–operated telephones, which outnumber coin-operated phones in Budapest and the Balaton region. The cards—available at post offices and most newsstands and kiosks—come in units of 60 (800 Ft.) and 90 (1,800 Ft.) calls.

TIPPING

Taxi drivers and hairdressers expect 10%–15% tips, while porters should get 200 Ft.–400 Ft. Coatroom attendants receive 100 Ft.–200 Ft., as do gas-pump attendants if they wash your windows or check your tires; dressing-room attendants at thermal baths receive 50 Ft.–100 Ft. for opening and closing your locker. Gratuities are not included automatically on bills at most restaurants; when the waiter arrives with the bill, you should immediately add a 10%–15% tip to the amount, as it is not customary to leave the tip on the table. If a Gypsy band plays exclusively for your table, you should leave at least 200 Ft. in a plate discreetly provided for that purpose.

TOURS

ORIENTATION TOURS

IBUSZ Travel conducts three-hour bus tours of the city that operate all year and cost about 5,500 Ft. Starting from Erzsébet tér, they take in

parts of both Buda and Pest. They can also provide English-speaking personal guides on request. Cityrama also offers a three-hour city bus tour (about 5,500 Ft. per person). Both have commentary in English.
➤ CONTACTS: **Cityrama** (✉ District V, Báthori u. 22, ☎ 1/302–4382, WEB www.cityrama.hu). **IBUSZ Travel** (✉ District V, Petőfi tér 3, ☎ 1/318–5707, WEB www.ibusz.hu).

BOAT TOURS:
Hour-long evening sightseeing cruises on the *Danube Legend* depart nightly at 8:15 in April and October and three times nightly (at 8:15, 9, and 10) from May through September. Guests receive headphones with recorded explanations of the sights (available in some 24 languages). Boats depart from Pier 6–7 at Vigadó tér.

The *Duna-Bella* takes six two-hour Danube cruises a day—daylight hours only, but tours do include a one-hour walk on Margaret Island. Recorded commentary is provided through earphones. The tour is offered July through August six times a day; May through June and in September three times a day; and April and October once a day. Boats depart from Pier 6–7 at Vigadó tér.

From March until October at noon every day boats leave from the dock at Vigadó tér on 1½-hour cruises between the railroad bridges north and south of the Árpád and Petőfi bridges, respectively. The trip, organized by MAHART Tours, runs only on weekends and holidays (once a day, at noon) in March and April; then there are regular daytime services until October 31. Evening cruises are at 7:30, except between mid-June and the end of August, when boats leave at 8:15 PM. The cost is 1,200 Ft., 1,500 Ft. on summer evening cruises, with a band and disco on board.
➤ CONTACTS: *Danube Legend* (District V, Vigadó tér, Pier 6–7, ☎ 1/317–2203 reservations and information). *Duna-Bella* (District V, Vigadó tér, Pier 6–7, ☎ 1/317–2203 reservations and information). **MAHART Tours** (District V, Vigadó tér, ☎ 1/484–4000, 1/484–4013, WEB www.maharttours.com).

SPECIAL-INTEREST TOURS
Absolute Walking Tours has broken the mold for guided walking tours in Central Europe. The company offers historical and general interest tours but also creatively executed theme tours, such as the "Hammer & Sickle Tour" and a "Budapest Dark Side" night tour. The 3½-hour Budapest walk costs 3,500 Ft., 3,000 Ft. for students, with no reservations necessary; just show up at 10:30 AM on Deák tér in front of the Evangélikus Templon, a pale yellow Lutheran church.

Chosen Tours offers a three-hour combination bus and walking tour (2,600 Ft.) called "Budapest Through Jewish Eyes," highlighting the sights and cultural life of the city's Jewish history. Tours run daily except Saturday and include free pickup and drop-off at central locations. Arrangements can also be made for off-season tours, as well as custom-designed tours.
➤ CONTACTS: **Absolute Walking Tours** (✉ District XV, Bocskai u. 143a, ☎ 1/266–1729, WEB www.budapestours.com). **Chosen Tours** (✉ District XII, Pagony u. 40, ☎ FAX 1/355–2202).

TRAIN TRAVEL
There are three main *pályaudvar* (train stations) in Budapest: trains to and from Vienna usually operate from the Keleti station, while those to the Lake Balaton region depart from the Déli. You can get information, regardless of the station, 24 hours a day through a central train information number.
➤ TRAIN STATIONS: **Keleti** *Pályaudvar* (East Railway Station; ✉ District VIII, Baross tér). **Nyugati** *Pályaudvar* (West Railway Station;

⊠ District V, Nyugati tér). **Déli** *Pályaudvar* (South Railway Station; ⊠ District XII, Alkotás u.). **Train Information** (☏ 1/461–5500 international train information; 1/461–5400 domestic train information).

TRAVEL AGENCIES
➤ CONTACTS: **American Express** (⊠ District V, Deák Ferenc u. 10, ☏ 1/235–4330, FAX 1/267–2028). **Getz International** (⊠ District V, Falk Miksa u. 5, ☏ 1/312–0645 or 1/312–0649, FAX 1/312–1014). **Vista Travel Center** (⊠ District VI, Andrássy út 1, ☏ 1/269–6032 or 1/269–6033, FAX 1/269–6031).

VISITOR INFORMATION
Tourinform has continued to expand and smarten up its act. Its main office is now open 24 hours, and it has several other help desks around town. The Tourism Office of Budapest has developed the Budapest Card, which entitles holders to unlimited travel on public transportation; free admission to many museums and sights; and discounts on various services from participating businesses. The cost at this writing was 3,700 Ft. for two days, 4,500 Ft. for three days; one card is valid for an adult plus one child under 14.
➤ CONTACTS: **Tourinform** (⊠ District V, Vörösmarty tér, ☏ 1/438–8080, FAX 1/356–1964; ⊠ District V, Sütő u. 2, ☏ 1/317–9800; ⊠ District VI, Liszt Ferenc tér 11, ☏ 1/342–9390). **Tourism Office of Budapest** (⊠ District V, Március 15 tér 7, ☏ 1/266–0479; ⊠ District VI, Nyugati pályaudvar, ☏ 1/302–8580).

4 BACKGROUND AND ESSENTIALS

Further Reading

Vocabulary

FURTHER READING

SINCE THE REVOLUTIONS of 1989–1990, a number of leading journalists have produced highly acclaimed books detailing the tumultuous changes experienced by Eastern and Central Europeans and the dramatic effects these changes have had on individual lives. Timothy Garten Ash's eyewitness account, *The Magic Lantern: The Revolution of '89 Witnessed in Warsaw, Budapest, Berlin, and Prague,* begins with Václav Havel's ringing words from his 1990 New Year's Address: "People, your government has returned to you!" Winner of both a National Book Award and a Pulitzer Prize, *The Haunted Land* is Tina Rosenberg's wide-ranging, incisive look at how Poland, the Czech Republic, and Slovakia (as well as Germany) are dealing with the memories of 40 years of communism.

In *Exit into History: A Journey Through the New Eastern Europe,* Eva Hoffman returns to her Polish homeland and five other countries—Hungary, Romania, Bulgaria, the Czech Republic, and Slovakia—and captures the texture of everyday life of a world in the midst of change. Isabel Fonseca's *Bury Me Standing: The Gypsies and Their Journey* is an unprecedented and revelatory look at the Gypsies—or Roma—of Eastern and Central Europe, the large and landless minority whose history and culture have long been obscure.

Travelogues worth reading, though less recent, include Claudio Magris's widely regarded *Danube,* which follows the river as it flows from its source in Germany to its mouth in the Black Sea; Brian Hall's *Stealing from a Deep Place,* a lively account of a solo bicycle trip through Romania and Bulgaria in 1982, followed by a stay in Budapest; Patrick Leigh Fermor's *Between the Woods and the Water,* which relates his 1934 walk through Hungary and Romania and captures life in these lands before their transformation during World War II and under the Soviets.

Forty-three writers from 16 nations of the former Soviet bloc are included in *Description of a Struggle: The Vintage Book of Contemporary Eastern European Writing,* edited by Michael March. Focusing on novels, poetry, and travel writing, the *Traveller's Literary Companion to Eastern and Central Europe* is a thorough guide to the vast array of literature from this region available in English translation. It includes country-by-country overviews, dozens of excerpts, reading lists, biographical discussions of key writers that highlight their most important works, and guides to literary landmarks. A recent novel about the lure of Eastern Europe for young expatriate Americans is *Prague* by Arthur Phillips.

Czech Republic

English readers have an excellent range of both fiction and nonfiction about the Czech Republic at their disposal. The most widely read Czech author of fiction in English is probably Milan Kundera, whose well-crafted tales illuminate both the foibles of human nature and the unique tribulations of life in Communist Czechoslovakia. *The Unbearable Lightness of Being* takes a look at the 1968 invasion and its aftermath through the eyes of a strained young couple. *The Book of Laughter and Forgetting* deals in part with the importance of memory and the cruel irony of how it fades over time; Kundera was no doubt coming to terms with his own forgetting as he wrote the book from his Paris exile. *The Joke,* Kundera's earliest work available in English, takes a serious look at the dire consequences of humorlessness among Communists.

Born and raised in the German-Jewish enclave of Prague, Franz Kafka scarcely left the city his entire life. *The Trial* and *The Castle* strongly convey the dread and mystery he detected beneath the 1,000 golden spires of Prague. Kafka worked as a bureaucrat for 14 years, in a job he detested; his books are, at least in part, an indictment of the bizarre bureaucracy of the Austro-Hungarian Empire, though they now seem eerily prophetic of the even crueler and more arbitrary Communist system that was to come.

The most popular Czech authors at the close of the 20th century were those banned by the Communists after the Soviet invasion of 1968. Václav Havel and members of the Charter 77 illegally distributed self-published manuscripts, or *samizdat* as they were called, of these banned authors—among them, Bohumil Hrabel, Josef Škvorecký, and Ivan Klíma. Hrabel, perhaps the most beloved of all Czech writers, never left his homeland; many claim to have shared a table with him at his favorite pub in Prague, U Zlatéyho tygra. His books include *I Served the King of England* and the lyrical *Too Loud a Solitude,* narrated by a lonely man who spends his days in the basement compacting the world's greatest works of literature along with bloodied butcher paper into neat bundles before they get carted off for recycling and disposal. Škvorecký sought refuge and literary freedom in Toronto in the early 1970s. His book *The Engineer of Human Souls* reveals the double censorship of the writer in exile—censored in the country of his birth and unread in his adopted home. Still, Škvorecký did gain a following thanks to his translator, Paul Wilson—who lived in Prague in the 1960s and '70s until he was ousted for his assistance in dissident activities. Wilson also set up 68 Publishers, which is responsible for the bulk of Czech literature translated into English. Novelist, short story writer, and playwright Ivan Klíma is now one of the most widely read Czech writers in English; his books include the novels *Judge on Trial* and *Love and Garbage,* and *The Spirit of Prague,* a collection of essays about life in the post-Communist Czech Republic.

Václav Havel, onetime dissident playwright turned president of the Czech Republic, is essential nonfiction reading. The best place to start is probably *Living in Truth,* which provides an absorbing overview of his own political philosophy and of Czechoslovak politics and history over the last 30 years. Other recommended books by Havel include *Disturbing the Peace* (a collection of interviews with him) and *Letters to Olga.* Havel's plays explore the absurdities and pressures of life under the former Communist regime; the best example of his absurdist dramas is *The Memorandum,* which depicts a Communist bureaucracy more twisted than the streets of Prague's Old Town.

Among the most prominent of the younger Czech writers is Jáchym Topol, whose *A Visit to the Train Station* documents the creation of a new Prague with a sharp wit that cuts through the false pretenses of American youth occupying the city.

Hungary

Hungarians have played a central role in the intellectual life of the 20th century, although their literary masters are less well known to the West than those who have excelled in other arts, such as Béla Bartok in music and Andre Kertesz and Robert and Cornell Capa in photography.

Novelist and poet Daző Kosztolányi was prominent in European intellectual circles after World War I and was greatly admired by Thomas Mann. His novels, including *Anna Édes* and *Skylark,* are known for their keen psychological insight and social commentary. Also worth discovering is novelist and essayist György Konrád, one of Hungary's leading 20th-century dissidents, whose *The Loser* is a disturbing reflection on intellectual life in a totalitarian state. The English writer Tibor Fischer's novels *Under the Frog* and *The Thought Gang* deal with life in contemporary Hungary. John Lukacs's *Budapest 1900: A Historical Portrait of a City and Its Culture* is an oversize, illustrated study of Hungary's premier city at a particularly important moment in its history. For a more in-depth look at the city, András Török's *Budapest: A Critical Guide* offers detailed historical and architectural information and is illustrated with excellent drawings.

Although not widely known in the west, Imre Kertész received the 2002 Nobel Prize in Literature for his searching exploration of his own past as a Holocaust survivor from Auschwitz. The Nobel committee awarded him the prize in part because of his exploration of "the possibility of continuing to live and think as an individual in an era in which the subjection of human beings to social forces has become increasingly complete." At this writing, only two of his works were available in English: *Fateless,* his first novel about a survivor of Auschwitz based on his own experiences in the camp, and *Kaddish for a Child Not Yet Born,* a novel about a middle-aged Holocaust survivor who tries to explain to a friend why he feels he can't bring a child into the world after living the horror of the Holocaust.

CZECH VOCABULARY

English	Czech	Pronunciation

Basics

English	Czech	Pronunciation
Yes/no	Ano/ne	**ah**-no/neh
Please	Prosím	**pro**-seem
Thank you	Děkuji	**dyek**-oo-yee
Pardon me	Pardon	**par**-don
Hello.	Dobrý den	**dob**-ree den
Do you speak English?	Mluvíte anglicky?	**mloo**-vit-eh ahng-**glit**-ski?
I don't speak Czech.	Nemluvím česky.	nem-**luv**-eem ches-ky
I don't understand.	Nerozumím.	neh-rohz-**oom**-eem
Please speak slowly.	Prosím, mluvte pomalu.	**pro**-seem, **mloov**-teh poh-**mah**-lo
Please write it down.	Prosím napište.	**pro**-seem nah-**peesh**
Show me.	Ukažte mně.	oo-**kazh**-te mnye
I am American (m/f)	Jsem američan/ američanka	sem ah-**mer**-i-chan/ ah-mer-i-**chan**-ka
English (m/f)	Angličan/angličanka	**ahn**-gli-chan/Ahn-gli-**chan**-ka
My name is . . .	Jmenuji se . . .	**ymen** weh-seh
On the right/left	Napravo/nalevo	na-**pra**-vo/na-**leh**-vo
Arrivals	Přílety	**pshee**-leh-tee
Where is . . . ?	Kde je . . . ?	g'deh yeh
. . . the station?	. . . Nádraží?	nah-**drah**-zee
. . . the train?	. . . Vlak?	vlahk
. . . the bus/tram?	. . . Autobus/tramvaj?	**out**-oh-boos/**tram**-vie
. . . the airport?	. . . Letiště?	**leh**-tish-tyeh
. . . the post office?	. . . Pošta?	**po**-shta
. . . the bank?	. . . Banka?	**bahn**-ka
Stop here	Zastavte tady	**zah**-stahv-teh **tah**-dee
I would like (m/f) . . .	Chtěl (chtěla) bych . . .	kh'tyel (**kh'tyel**-ah) bihk
How much does it cost?	Kolik to stoji?	ko-**lik** toh **stoy**-ee
Letter/postcard	Dopis/pohlednice	doh-**pis**-ee/poh-**hled**-nit-seh
By airmail	Letecky	**leh**-tet-skee
Help!	Pomoc!	**po**-motz

Numbers

English	Czech	Pronunciation
One	Jeden	ye-**den**
Two	Dva	dvah
Three	Tři	tshree
Four	Čtyři	ch'**ti**-zhee
Five	Pět	pyet
Six	Šest	shest
Seven	Sedm	**sed**-oom
Eight	Osm	**oh**-soom
Nine	Devět	**deh**-vyet
Ten	Deset	**deh**-set
One hundred	Sto	stoh
One thousand	Tisíc	**tee**-seets

Days of the Week

English	Hungarian	Pronunciation
Sunday	Neděle	**neh**-dyeh-leh
Monday	Pondělí	**pon**-dye-lee
Tuesday	Žterý	**oo**-teh-ree
Wednesday	Středa	**stshreh**-da
Thursday	Čtvrtek	ch't'v'**r**-tek
Friday	Pátek	**pah**-tek
Saturday	Sobota	**so**-boh-ta

Where to Sleep

English	Hungarian	Pronunciation
A room	Pokoj	**poh**-koy
The key	Klíč	kleech
With bath/shower	S koupelnou/sprcha	s'**ko**-pel-noh/ **sp'r**-kho

Food

English	Hungarian	Pronunciation
The menu	Jídelní lístek	**yee**-dell-nee **lis**-tek
The check, please.	Učet, prosím.	**oo**-chet **pro**-seem
Breakfast	Snídaně	**snyee**-dan-ye
Lunch	Oběd	**ob**-yed
Dinner	Večeře	**ve**-cher-zhe
Bread	Chléb	khleb
Butter	Máslo	**mah**-slo
Salt/pepper	Sůl/pepř	sool/pepsh
Bottle	Láhev	**lah**-hev
Red/white wine	Červené/bílé víno	**cher**-ven-eh/**bee**-leh **vee**-no
Beer	Pivo	**piv**-oh
Mineral water	Minerálka voda	min-eh-**rahl**-ka **vo**-da
Milk	Mléko	**mleh**-koh
Coffee	Káva	**kah**-va
Tea (with lemon)	Čaj (s citrónem)	tchai (se tsi-**tro**-nem)

HUNGARIAN VOCABULARY

English	Hungarian	Pronunciation

Basics

English	Hungarian	Pronunciation
Yes/no	Igen/nem	**ee**-gen/nem
Please	Kérem	**kay**-rem
Thank you (very much)	Köszönöm (szépen)	**kuh**-suh-num (**seh**-pen)
Excuse me	Bocsánat	**boh**-chah-not
I'm sorry.	Sajnálom.	**shahee**-nah-lome
Hello/how do you do	Szervusz	**sair**-voose
Do you speak English?	Beszél angolul?	**bess**-el **on**-goal-ool
I don't speak Hungarian.	Nem tudok magyarul.	nem **too**-dock **muh**-jor-ool
I don't understand.	Nem értem.	nem **air**-tem
Please speak slowly.	Kérem, beszéljen lassan.	**kay**-rem, **bess**-el-yen lush-shun
Please write it down.	Kérem, írja fel.	**kay**-rem, **eer**-yuh fell

Please show me.	Megmutatná nekem.	meg-**moo**-taht-nah **neh**-kem
I am American.	Amerikai vagyok.	uh-**meh**-rick-ka-ee **vud**-yoke
I am English.	Angol vagyok.	**un**-goal **vud**-yoke
My name is . . .	Vagyok . . .	**vud**-yoke
Right/left	Bal/jobb	buhl/yobe
Open/closed	nyitva/zárva	**nit**-va/**zahr**-voh
Arrival/departure	Érkezés/ indulás	**er**-keh-zesh/ **in**-dool-ahsh
Where is . . . ?	Hol van . . . ?	hole vun
. . . the train station?	. . . a pályaudvar?	uh pah-yo-**oot**-var
. . . the bus station?	. . . a buszállomás?	uh **boose**-ahlo-mahsh
. . . the bus stop?	. . . a megálló?	uh **meg**-all-oh
. . . the airport?	. . . A repülőtér?	uh rep-ewluh-**tair**
. . . the post office?	. . . a pósta?	uh **pohsh**-tuh
. . . the bank?	. . . a bank?	uh bonhk
Stop here	Tlljon meg itt	**all**-yon meg it
I would like . . .	Szeretnék . . .	**sair**-et-neck
How much does it cost?	Mennyibe kerül?	**men**-yibe kair-**ule**
Letter/postcard	levél/képeslap	**lev**-ehl/**kay**-pesh-lup
By airmail	Légi póstaval	**lay**-gee **pohsh**-tuh-vol
Help!	Segítség!	**shay**-geet-shaig

Numbers

One	Egy	edge
Two	Kettő	**ket**-tuh
Three	Három	**hah**-rome
Four	Négy	**nay**-ge
Five	Öt	ut
Six	Hat	huht
Seven	Hét	hate
Eight	Nyolc	nyolts
Nine	Kilenc	**kee**-lents
Ten	Tíz	teez
One hundred	Száz	sahz
One thousand	Ezer	**eh**-zer

Days of the Week

Sunday	Vasárnap	**vuh**-shar-nup
Monday	Hétfő	**hate**-fuh
Tuesday	Kedd	ked
Wednesday	Szerda	**ser**-duh
Thursday	Csütörtök	**chew**-tur-tuk
Friday	Péntek	**pain**-tek
Saturday	Szombat	**som**-but

Where to Sleep

A room	Egy szobá	edge **soh**-bah
The key	A kulcsot	uh **koolch**-oat
With bath/a shower	Fúrdőszo-bával/ egy zuhany	**fure**-duh-soh-bah-vul/ edge **zoo**-hon

Food

A restaurant	A vendéglő/ az étterem	uh **ven**-deh-gluh/ uz **eht**-teh-rem
The menu	A étlap	uh **ate**-lop
The check, please.	A számlát kérem.	uh **sahm**-lot **kay**-rem
I'd like to order this.	Kéem ezt.	**kay**-rem etz
Breakfast	Reggeli	**reg**-gell-ee
Lunch	Ebéd	**eb**-ehd
Dinner	Vacsora	**votch**-oh-rah
Bread	Kenyér	**ken**-yair
Butter	Vaj	voy
Salt/pepper	Só/bors	show/borsh
Bottle	Üveg	**ew**-veg
Red/white wine	Vörös/fehér bor	**vuh**-ruhsh/**feh**-hehr **bor**
Beer	Sör	shur
Water/mineral water	Víz/kristályvíz	veez/**krish**-tah-**ee**-veez
Milk	Tej	tay
Coffee (with milk)	Kávé/tejeskávé	**kah**-vay/**tey**-esh-**kah**-vay
Tea (with lemon)	Tea (citrommal)	**tay**-oh **tsit**-rome-mol
Chocolate	Csokoládé	chaw-kaw-**law**-day

INDEX

Index

Fodor's Key to the Guides

America's guidebook leader publishes guides for every kind of traveler. Check out our many series and find your perfect match.

Fodor's Gold Guides

America's favorite travel-guide series offers the most detailed insider reviews of hotels, restaurants, and attractions in all price ranges, plus great background information, smart tips, and useful maps.

Fodor's Road Guide USA

Big guides for a big country—the most comprehensive guides to America's roads, packed with places to stay, eat, and play across the U.S.A. Just right for road warriors, family vacationers, and cross-country trekkers.

COMPASS AMERICAN GUIDES

Stunning guides from top local writers and photographers, with gorgeous photos, literary excerpts, and colorful anecdotes. A must-have for culture mavens, history buffs, and new residents.

Fodor's CITYPACKS

Concise city coverage with a foldout map. The right choice for urban travelers who want everything under one cover.

Fodor's EXPLORING GUIDES

Hundreds of color photos bring your destination to life. Lively stories lend insight into the culture, history, and people.

Fodor's POCKET GUIDES

For travelers who need only the essentials. The best of Fodor's in pocket-size packages for just $9.95.

Fodor's To Go

Credit-card–size, magnetized color microguides that fit in the palm of your hand—perfect for "stealth" travelers or as gifts.

Fodor's FLASHMAPS

Every resident's map guide. 60 easy-to-follow maps of public transit, parks, museums, zip codes, and more.

Fodor's CITYGUIDES

Sourcebooks for living in the city: Thousands of in-the-know listings for restaurants, shops, sports, nightlife, and other city resources.

Fodor's AROUND THE CITY WITH KIDS

68 great ideas for family days, recommended by resident parents. Perfect for exploring in your own backyard or on the road.

Fodor's ESCAPES

Fill your trip with once-in-a-lifetime experiences, from ballooning in Chianti to overnighting in the Moroccan desert. These full-color dream books point the way.

Fodor's FYI

Get tips from the pros on planning the perfect trip. Learn how to pack, fly hassle-free, plan a honeymoon or cruise, stay healthy on the road, and travel with your baby.

Fodor's Languages for Travelers

Practice the local language before hitting the road. Available in phrase books, cassette sets, and CD sets.

Karen Brown's Guides

Engaging guides to the most charming inns and B&Bs in the U.S.A. and Europe, with easy-to-follow inn-to-inn itineraries.

Baedeker's Guides

Comprehensive guides, trusted since 1829, packed with A–Z reviews and star ratings.

At bookstores everywhere.   www.fodors.com/books